AIR CAMPAIGN

SINK THE *TIRPITZ* 1942–44

The RAF and Fleet Air Arm duel with Germany's mighty battleship

Angus Konstam

OSPREY PUBLISHING
Bloomsbury Publishing Plc
PO Box 883, Oxford, OX1 9PL, UK
1385 Broadway, 5th Floor, New York, NY 10018, USA
E-mail: info@ospreypublishing.com
www.ospreypublishing.com

OSPREY is a trademark of Osprey Publishing Ltd

First published in Great Britain in 2018

© Osprey Publishing Ltd, 2018

All rights reserved. No part of this publication may be reproduced or transmitted in any form or by any means, electronic or mechanical, including photocopying, recording, or any information storage or retrieval system, without prior permission in writing from the publishers.

A catalogue record for this book is available from the British Library.

ISBN: PB 9781472831590; eBook 9781472831583; ePDF 9781472831576; XML 9781472831606

18 19 20 21 22   10 9 8 7 6 5 4 3 2 1

Maps by bounford.com
3D BEVs by The Black Spot
Index by Fionbar Lyons
Typeset by PDQ Digital Media Solutions, Bungay, UK
Printed in China through World Print Ltd.

Front Cover: Art by Jim Laurier, © Osprey Publishing
Back Cover: Photo courtesy of the Stratford Archive, art © Osprey Publishing

Osprey Publishing supports the Woodland Trust, the UK's leading woodland conservation charity. Between 2014 and 2018 our donations are being spent on their Centenary Woods project in the UK.

To find out more about our authors and books visit www.ospreypublishing.com. Here you will find extracts, author interviews, details of forthcoming events and the option to sign up for our newsletter.

A Question of Time
During World War II, the United Kingdom used Greenwich Mean Time (GMT) in winter, and Double British Summer Time (DBST) in summer. The latter replaced British Summer time (BST) from 1941 until 1945. In winter, GMT was also advanced an hour during the war, so that it was effectively GMT+1, the same as BST. DBST was two hours ahead of peacetime GMT, making it GMT+2. These changes were introduced so that that the United Kingdom was on a similar time zone to the mainland of Continental Europe. However, DBST was not implemented on a regular basis. Rather its use varied due to what the government termed 'strategic necessity'. During the period covered in this book, DBST was in effect from; 5 April to 9 August 1942, 4 May to 15 August 1943, and 8 August to 17 September 1944. So, for the sake of convenience, all timings given in this book are given using the UK system, with DBST used during the date ranges just mentioned, and GMT (or rather peacetime GMT+1, or BST) for all other periods. In the rare instances where German or Norwegian timings are at variance, they are described as being in local time, while the equivalent time in GMT is also listed.
Confusingly though, during the Fleet Air Arm attacks on *Tirpitz* during the spring and summer of 1944, DBST was used throughout these operations, to bring air operations into line with Norwegian time, which had been altered by the Germans to correspond with the time zones being used in parts of Eastern Europe. So, for these operations DBST is used.

Photographs
All photographs and line maps are courtesy of the Stratford Archive.

Title page photograph:
Aboard the escort carrier *Empress* on 3 April 1944, the Fleet Air Arm Hellcat pilots of 800 and 804 Squadrons study a relief map of the Kaafjord, in a last-minute briefing before the start of Operation *Tungsten*. Two hours later the first of their attack waves would be strafing the decks of the *Tirpitz*.

AIR CAMPAIGN

CONTENTS

INTRODUCTION	4
CHRONOLOGY	6
ATTACKERS' CAPABILITIES	8
DEFENDERS' CAPABILITIES	17
CAMPAIGN OBJECTIVES	25
THE CAMPAIGN	30
AFTERMATH AND ANALYSIS	88
FURTHER READING	94
INDEX	95

INTRODUCTION

The *Tirpitz*, photographed during her brief stay in the Bodenfjord near Narvik, during the late summer of 1942. This picturesque fjord was used as a rendezvous and repair area by the Kriegsmarine, as it lay beyond easy reach of British bombers.

In May 1941 the world's attention focused on the German battleship *Bismarck*, and her brief but deadly sortie into the Atlantic Ocean. She was the most modern battleship afloat, and while the Nazi propaganda machine dubbed her 'unsinkable', she was eventually hunted down and destroyed by the Royal Navy. This victory, though, came at a terrible cost – the loss of the battlecruiser *Hood*, and all but three of her crew. By then, the British Admiralty were uncomfortably aware that this formidable battleship had a sister ship – the *Tirpitz*, which was undergoing sea trials in the Baltic. She was so powerful she was capable of sinking any capital ship in the British Home Fleet, and if she joined forces with other major German warships she could alter the course of the war at sea.

Air attacks against her had begun when she was still under construction, but these were both half-hearted and unsuccessful. Then, the threat she posed became more than just theoretical. This was a direct result of the German invasion of Russia in June 1941. Two months later the first Arctic Convoy arrived in Archangel. This maritime lifeline was as much a diplomatic enterprise as a military one, carrying military hardware and supplies from Britain, Canada and the United States to the Soviet Union, to help it stave off the German onslaught. When in January 1942 the *Tirpitz* sailed to Norway, she represented a major threat to this vital convoy route. So, Churchill ordered that she should be destroyed. The Royal Navy could only bring her to battle if she put to sea, so this meant she had to be attacked from the air, in her lair at the end of a remote Norwegian fjord.

The British Home Fleet was forced to retain battleships and aircraft carriers in the area to protect the Arctic Convoys from attack by *Tirpitz*, the German battleship rarely put to sea. So, this would primarily be an air campaign, where the performance of the various types of aircraft used against her would be critical to the success of the operation. Even more important was the ordnance they could use against her, and the skill of the air crews who would direct it against the battleship.

The intermittent air campaign against *Tirpitz* lasted for more than two and a half years. These desperate attacks involved hundreds of aircraft from both Bomber Command and the Fleet Air Arm, and a range of aircraft and ordnance. Attacking the *Tirpitz* in her various Norwegian lairs was never going to be easy. Planners had to contend with a number of problems, including the range to the target, the defensive capabilities of the defences surrounding *Tirpitz*, and the geography of her berth. Then there were the problems caused by the highly changeable weather over Norway, combined with huge seasonal variations in the amount of daylight. Even if all these challenges were overcome, any attacking force still had to deal with the ship herself, one of the best-protected warships in existence, and one which mounted a formidable array of anti-aircraft guns. Of all these factors, the biggest constraint was range. While *Tirpitz*'s first base in the Faettenfjord near Trondheim was within range of British heavy bombers flying from airfields in the north-east of Scotland, her second lair in the Kaafjord, a spur of the larger Altenfjord at the northernmost tip of Norway, was out of range. So, innovative solutions had to be found to overcome these problems.

It was arguably the most sustained air operation of the war, but the mighty German battleship proved remarkably resilient. So, for much of the war she remained a 'fleet in being', forcing the Allies to tie down warships which were vitally needed in other theatres. *Tirpitz* finally succumbed in November 1944, sunk by mammoth bombs dropped by 617 'Dambusters' Squadron. While her career was not as spectacular as that of her famous sister ship, it was much longer, and her impact on the course of the war was considerably greater.

This photograph, taken from the highest crane in the naval yard, shows *Tirpitz* during the early stages of her fitting out in the Kriegsmarinewerft Wilhelmshaven. Her superstructure is being erected, on top of her thick armoured deck, which was located two decks below her upper deck. The barbettes of her main and secondary gun turrets are already in place.

CHRONOLOGY

1936
2 November *Tirpitz* laid down in Wilhelmshaven.

1939
1 April *Tirpitz* launched.

3 September Britain declares war on Germany.

1940
8/9 October RAF bombers attack Wilhelmshaven. No hits on *Tirpitz*.

1941
8/9 January RAF bombers attack Wilhelmshaven. No hits on *Tirpitz*.

29/30 January RAF bombers attack Wilhelmshaven. No hits on *Tirpitz*.

25 February *Tirpitz* commissioned.

28 February/1 March RAF bombers attack Wilhelmshaven. No hits on *Tirpitz*.

6 March *Tirpitz* transits the Kaiser Wilhelm Canal to Kiel, to begin sea trials in the Baltic.

27 May *Bismarck* sunk by warships of the British Home Fleet.

28/29 May RAF bombers attack Kiel. No hits on *Tirpitz*.

20/21 June RAF bombers attack Kiel. No hits on *Tirpitz*.

22 June Operation *Barbarossa* – German invasion of the Soviet Union begins.

21–31 August Operation *Dervish* – first Arctic Convoy sails to northern Russia.

1942
15 January *Tirpitz* arrives in the Faettenfjord.

30/31 January Operation *Oiled* – RAF attack on *Tirpitz* in the Faettenfjord. No hits.

6–9 March Operation *Sportpalast* – *Tirpitz* sorties in attempt to attack Convoy PQ-12.

9 March Torpedo attack on *Tirpitz* off Lofoten Islands by aircraft from HMS *Victorious*.

30/31 March RAF attack on *Tirpitz* in the Faettenfjord. No hits.

27/28 April RAF attack on *Tirpitz* in the Faettenfjord. No hits.

28/29 April RAF attack on *Tirpitz* in the Faettenfjord. No hits.

2 July *Tirpitz* sails from Faettenfjord to the Altenfjord, during Operation *Rösselsprung*, the German operation to destroy Convoy PQ-17.

5–6 July *Tirpitz* sorties from the Altenfjord, in attempt to intercept Convoy PQ-17.

9 July *Tirpitz* arrives in the Bogenfjord, near Narvik.

24 October *Tirpitz* returns to the Faettenfjord.

30/31 October Operation *Title* – underwater attack on *Tirpitz* in the Faettenfjord using human torpedoes; aborted due to bad weather.

1943
11–13 March *Tirpitz* moves north to the Bogenfjord, to join *Scharnhorst*.

22–24 March *Tirpitz* proceeds from the Bogenfjord to the Kaafjord, at the end of the Altenfjord. This will become her new 'lair'.

22 September Operation *Source* – underwater attack on *Tirpitz* in the Kaafjord using midget submarines (X-Craft). *Tirpitz* badly damaged.

29 September *Tirpitz* commences a lengthy period of self-repair, to render her operational again.

1944
10/11 February Soviet Air Force attack on *Tirpitz* in Kaafjord. No hits.

3 April Operation *Tungsten* – naval air strike on *Tirpitz* in the Kaafjord. Battleship damaged.

24 April Operation *Planet* – naval air strike cancelled due to bad weather.

15 May Operation *Brawn* – naval air strike cancelled due to bad weather.

28 May Operation *Tiger Claw* – naval air strike cancelled due to bad weather.

17 July Operation *Mascot* – naval air strike on *Tirpitz* in the Kaafjord. No hits.

22 August Operation *Goodwood I* – naval air strike on *Tirpitz* in the Kaafjord. No hits. Followed by Operation *Goodwood II* – naval air strike on *Tirpitz* in the Kaafjord. No hits.

24 August Operation *Goodwood III* – naval air strike on *Tirpitz* in the Kaafjord. Battleship slightly damaged.

29 August Operation *Goodwood IV* – naval air strike on *Tirpitz* in the Kaafjord. No hits.

15 September Operation *Paravane* – RAF attack on *Tirpitz* in the Kaafjord. Battleship badly damaged.

15–16 October *Tirpitz* moves from Kaafjord to new moorings off Haakøy Island, near Tromsø.

29 October Operation *Obviate* – RAF attack on *Tirpitz* off Haakøy Island. Battleship slightly damaged.

12 November Operation *Catechism* – *Tirpitz* sunk off Haakøy Island near Tromsø. Up to 1,000 of her crew are killed in the attack or its aftermath.

The funnel of *Tirpitz* being lifted into place during her fitting out in the Kriegsmarinewerft (Naval Shipyard) Wilhelmshaven. The battleship's forward superstructure is already in place, while the foreground is dominated by the heavily armoured barbette ring of 'Dora' turret.

ATTACKERS' CAPABILITIES
To sink a battleship

Aircraft of Bomber Command

From the outset Bomber Command decided to attack *Tirpitz* using four-engined heavy bombers. Smaller twin-engined bombers lacked the range. In 1942 that meant the Short Stirling, the Handley Page Halifax or the brand-new Avro Lancaster. Of these the Stirling and the Halifax were broadly similar in terms of performance. However, the Stirling had a ceiling of just 16,500ft, while the other two heavy bombers could fly at least 5,000ft higher. This made the Stirling more susceptible to enemy flak. Both the Stirling and the Halifax carried a similar-sized payload (14,000lb and 13,000lb respectively). However, to reach Trondheim from the airfield at Lossiemouth in the north-east of Scotland, the Stirling would have to reduce its payload to 12,000lb. On the same mission the Halifax could carry its full payload. So, after the initial small bombing raid on 30/31 January 1942, when a combination of Stirlings and Halifaxes were used, the Stirling squadrons were returned to other bombing duties, and the task of dealing with the *Tirpitz* fell to the crews of the Halifaxes, augmented in April by Lancasters.

The Lancaster was one of the outstanding heavy bombers of the war. Although its general performance was similar to that of the Halifax, the Lancaster enjoyed a big advantage in terms of range. Also, while both bombers had a broadly similar payload (13,000lb for the Halifax, and 14,000lb for the Lancaster), the configuration of the Lancaster's bomb bays proved far more versatile. That meant that while the Halifax could be converted to carry large bombs such as the 4,000lb 'cookie', or 'blockbuster' bomb, which was used during the spring raids on the *Tirpitz* in 1942, it was incapable of carrying larger bombs. As a result, only the Lancaster could carry the 12,000lb 'Tallboy', which was used against the *Tirpitz* with devastating effect in late 1944. Even then, to attain the range needed to reach their target, these bombers had to be lightened by removing their upper turret. That, of course, made them extremely vulnerable to German fighters.

The Short Stirling was one of the three British four-engined bombers produced according to the Air Ministry's specifications. The Stirling was used in the first RAF bombing raid on the *Tirpitz* in January 1942, while she was moored in the Faettenfjord. The Stirling's major disadvantage when compared to the Halifax and the Lancaster was its low ceiling.

Short Stirling heavy bomber	
Entered service:	May 1940
Length:	87ft 3in (26.6m)
Wingspan:	99ft 1in (30.2m)
Weight when laden:	59,400lb (26,944kg)
Powerplant:	4× Bristol Hercules engines
Max. speed:	282mph (454kph) at 12,500ft (3,800m)
Range:	2,330 miles (3,750km) with bomb payload
Ceiling:	16,500ft (5,030m)
Armament:	2× machine guns (MG) in nose turret, 2× MG in upper turret, 4× MG in tail turret
Bomb payload:	14,000lb (6,350kg)
Crew:	7

Handley Page Halifax heavy bomber	
Entered service:	November 1940
Length:	71ft 7in (21.82m)
Wingspan:	104ft 2in (31.75m)
Weight when laden:	54,400lb (24,675kg)
Powerplant:	4× Bristol Hercules engines
Max. speed:	282mph (454kph) at 13,500ft (4,115m)
Range:	1,860 miles (3,000km) with bomb payload
Ceiling:	24,000ft (7,315m)
Armament:	1× MG in nose cupola, 4× MG in upper turret, 4× MG in rear turret
Bomb payload:	13,000lb (5,897kg)
Crew:	7

Avro Lancaster heavy bomber	
Entered service:	February 1942
Length:	69ft 4in (21.11m)
Wingspan:	102ft (31.09m)
Weight when laden:	55,000lb (24,948kg)
Powerplant:	4× Rolls Royce Merlin engines
Max. speed:	282mph (454kph) at 13,000ft (4,000m)
Range:	2,530 miles (4,073km) with bomb payload
Ceiling:	21,400ft (6,500m)
Armament:	2× MG in nose turret, 2× MG in upper turret, 4× MG in rear turret
Bomb payload:	14,000lb (6,400kg), although this could be modified to 22,000lb (10,000kg) for single heavy ordnance such as Tallboy or Grand Slam, at the expense of range and performance
Crew:	7

Aircraft of the Fleet Air Arm

Tirpitz's sister ship *Bismarck* was crippled by a single 18in torpedo hit on her vulnerable rudder. The aircraft which released it was a Fairey Swordfish, a lumbering biplane which looked obsolete, but which actually proved a highly effective aircraft. The Swordfish was designated a Torpedo/Bomber/Reconnaissance aircraft (TBR) by the Fleet Air Arm, and so had to perform three roles. This merely added to its versatility, and explained why it remained in active service throughout the war. However, the Swordfish never saw action against the *Tirpitz*. That task fell to the Fairey Albacore, another biplane that was billed as the replacement for

ATTACKERS' CAPABILITIES

the elderly Swordfish, but which was actually taken out of service before its predecessor. The Albacore (nicknamed the 'Applecore' by the Navy) proved less manoeuvrable than the Swordfish, even though it was both faster and more comfortable, having an enclosed cockpit. However, in May 1942 it was the only aircraft embarked in the carrier *Victorious* which could damage the *Tirpitz*.

During the Fleet Air Arm's attacks on the *Tirpitz* in the Kaafjord in the summer of 1944, the fleet's main strike aircraft was the Fairey Barracuda. It was designed as a replacement for the Swordfish and the Albacore, although with the exception of its speed and manoeuvrability, it was not significantly better than either of its predecessors. The Barracuda was slightly easier to fly, and its improved visibility made it better suited to carrier landings. The largest ordnance it could carry, apart from an 18in aerial torpedo, was a 1,600lb armour-piercing (AP) bomb, and it was this, together with the 500lb semi-armour-piercing (SAP) bomb and the 600lb anti-submarine bomb, that it used against the *Tirpitz*. For all this, though, it was still too slow to attack the German battleship effectively before word of its approach reached the ship and her protective smoke screen was deployed. Ultimately, it was this lack of speed which condemned the Fleet Air Arm to failure in their efforts to put *Tirpitz* out of action.

A Fairey Albacore taking off from the deck of an Illustrious-class fleet carrier – probably *Victorious* – while behind her a Seafire is preparing to begin her take-off run. This Albacore is unarmed, so is probably flying on a reconnaissance patrol.

Fairey Albacore TBR	
Entered service:	March 1940
Length:	39ft 10in (12.14m)
Wingspan:	50ft (15.24m) – wings could be folded for storage
Weight when laden:	10,460lb (4,755kg)
Powerplant:	1× Bristol Taurus II engine
Max. speed:	161mph (225kph) at 1,625ft (500m)
Range:	817 miles (1,497km) with torpedo or bomb payload
Ceiling:	20,700ft (6,310m)
Armament:	1× forward-facing MG on starboard wing, 1–2× MG in rear cockpit
Bomb/torpedo payload:	2,000lb (907kg) of bombs, or 1× 18in torpedo
Crew:	3

Fairey Barracuda TBR	
Entered service:	January 1943
Length:	39ft 9in (12.12m)
Wingspan:	49ft 2in (14.99m) – wings could be folded for storage
Weight when laden:	13,200lb (6,000kg)
Powerplant:	1× Rolls Royce Merlin engine
Max. speed:	228mph (367kph) at 1,750ft (533m)
Range:	686 miles (1,104km) with torpedo or bomb payload
Ceiling:	16,600ft (5,080m)
Armament:	2× MG in rear cockpit
Bomb/torpedo payload:	1,800lb (820kg) of bombs, or 1× 18in torpedo
Crew:	3

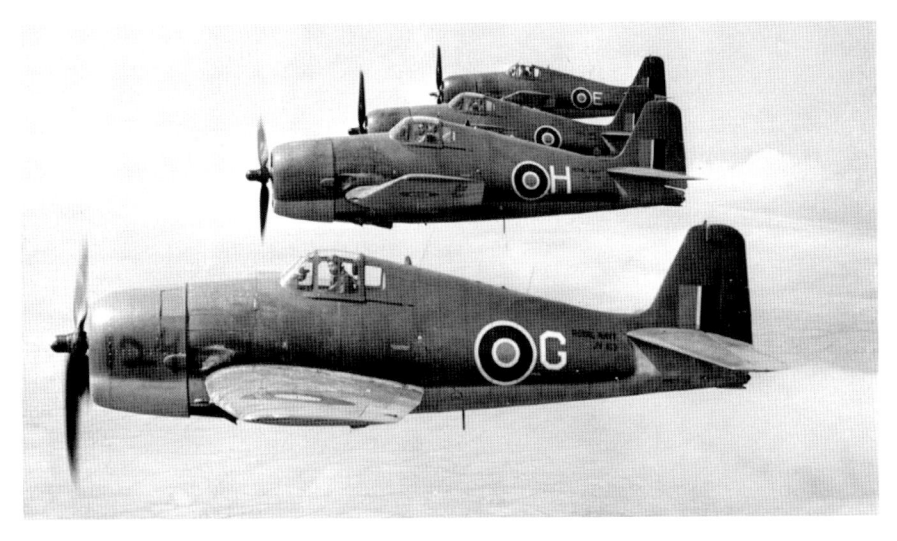

The American-built Grumman F6F Hellcat entered service with the Fleet Air Arm in late 1942, where for a time it was known as the Grumman Gannet, to conform with British nomenclature. During Operation Tungsten, *Hellcats operating from the escort carrier* Empress *successfully strafed and bombed the* Tirpitz *in the Kaafjord.*

In addition to these bombers, the Fleet Air Arm used a number of fighters in their air strikes against the battleship. Of these, the American-built Grumman Hellcats and Vought Corsairs were capable of carrying small 500lb bombs, and therefore inflicting some minor damage to the battleship, if they were able to target her. Other naval fighters of British design – the Supermarine Seafire and the two-seater Fairey Firefly – were purely used as fighters, although in theory both could also carry a small bomb payload. Incidentally the Firefly also functioned as an anti-submarine aircraft, and as a reconnaissance plane. The advantage of these naval fighters over the Barracuda was their speed. The Hellcat had a top speed of 391mph, while the Corsair could manage an even more impressive 446mph. During Operation *Goodwood* this proved invaluable, as they were able to reach the *Tirpitz* before she could deploy her protective smoke screen.

Photographic reconnaissance

Before any operation could be planned, the attackers needed to know as much as they could about the battleship, her anchorage, and the defences around her. This information was supplied in part by Norwegian agents, but mostly it came from photographs, supplied by the Photographic Reconnaissance Unit (PRU). These flights, usually carried out by specially adapted Spitfires and later by Mosquitos, would continue for as long as the *Tirpitz* remained at large. When the battleship moved to the Kaafjord in northern Norway, the British planners had to rely on information gathered by Soviet reconnaissance planes, which lacked the specialist photographic equipment used by the PRU. However, by the summer of 1944 the PRU was able to operate from bases in northern Russia, and after an initial evaluation the photographs were flown to Britain by flying boats, where they were fully analyzed.

Between 1942 and 1944 these would provide operational planners with the basic information they needed. Not only did this

The Vought F4U Corsair was another American-built fighter, which entered service with the Fleet Air Arm in November 1943. After some minor modifications it proved a robust and highly effective aircraft. During the spring and summer of 1944 Corsairs operating from the carriers Formidable *and* Victorious *provided fighter cover for the Fleet Air Arm strikes on the* Tirpitz.

reveal exactly where the *Tirpitz* was moored, and which direction she faced; it also showed her degree of operational readiness. In addition, regular PRU sorties gathered information on shore defences, torpedo nets, patrolling guard boats, the location of escort warships and supply ships, and weather conditions. Without this information the air operations against the *Tirpitz* would have had almost no chance of success.

Ordnance

While *Tirpitz* was being built, the bombers attacking Wilhelmshaven and Kiel used 250lb and 500lb general purpose bombs, designated as medium-capacity (MC) ordnance by the RAF. These were dropped at night, from a high altitude, and so the chances of hitting the battleship were slim. Even if they did strike her they would do little damage due to her well-protected armoured deck. The best that could be hoped for was the reduction of her fighting potential through damage to sensors, fire-control equipment and flak guns. During 1944 these smaller bombs were used by the Fleet Air Arm during their attacks on *Tirpitz*. By then, semi-armour-piercing (SAP) and armour-piercing (AP) bombs were being used, but while these could pierce unarmoured decks, they were still incapable of inflicting a mortal wound.

A more powerful bomb was needed to inflict any real damage. In the port raids of 1940–41, a number of experimental 2,000lb high-capacity (HC) bombs were dropped. These were the first specialized British heavy bombs of the war. Their cast-steel cylinders were packed with Amatol explosive, and when released a drogue would deploy to stabilize the bomb as it fell. Although this type of ordnance proved ineffective in these port raids, by late 1941 a smaller but theoretically armour-piercing version was available. This was carried during the abortive January 1942 raid on *Tirpitz* in the Faettenfjord.

A larger 4,000lb HC version was developed, which had a similar cylindrical appearance, but due to its weight a drogue was omitted. The poor aerodynamic qualities of this bomb meant that its path was unpredictable once released, but by 1943 this problem was overcome by the addition of a nose cone and a circular drum fin. This allowed them to be optimistically designated AP bombs. These 4,000lb HC bombs were termed 'blockbuster' bombs by the press, as they were primarily designed to demolish urban areas. The airmen, though, nicknamed them 'cookies'. Each contained over 3,000lb of Amatol, and if an AP version hit the *Tirpitz* it was hoped that it would pierce her armoured deck and explode deep inside the ship. In practice, however, these large, thin-skinned bombs proved little more effective than conventional bombs.

The Fleet Air Arm used an American-designed 1,600lb AP bomb. Specifically designed to penetrate the deck armour of an enemy warship, it had a hardened, pointed nose and a box fin. Although theoretically capable of piercing *Tirpitz*'s armoured deck if released at a high enough point during the dive, it proved another disappointment. The effectiveness of those bombs that hit *Tirpitz* was limited, as they had been filled with only half the requisite amount of explosive thanks to defects during production. They were also plagued by a faulty detonator.

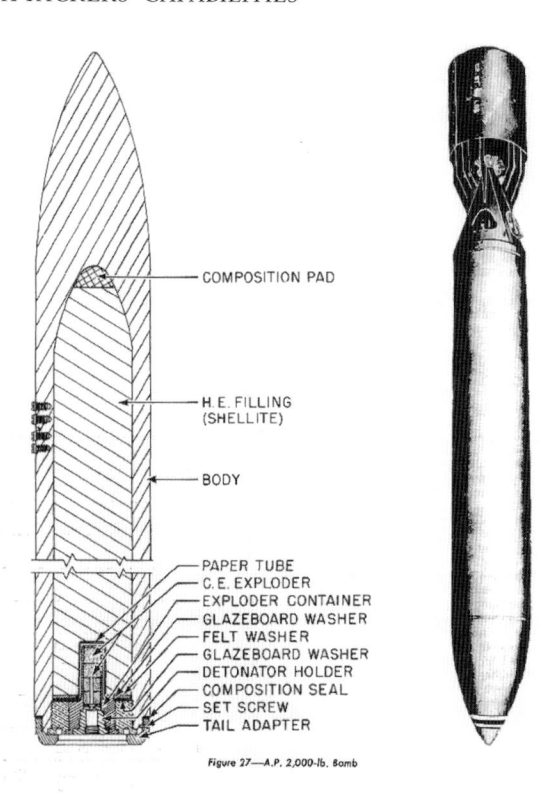

The 2,000lb armour-piercing (AP) bomb was specifically designed to be used, as its manual claimed, 'for attacks against heavily armoured targets, such as capital ships'. It was strongly built so that it didn't break up on impact, and its sleek lines and hardened nose cone encouraged it to penetrate a ship's armoured deck before exploding.

250lb MC (medium capacity) bomb

User:	Royal Air Force, Fleet Air Arm. Introduced October 1941
Weight:	225lb (102kg). Explosive charge 63lb (28.58kg) Amatol
Fusing:	Instantaneous (contact)
Structure:	Cylindrical, with nose cone, thin casing and banded stabilizer at tail
Effect:	Conventional bomb, incapable of penetrating armoured plate
Note:	This superseded the 250lb GP (general purpose) bomb first introduced in 1926

500lb MC bomb

User:	Royal Air Force, Fleet Air Arm. Introduced October 1941
Weight:	499lb (226kg). Explosive charge varies depending on explosive, but usually 232lb (105kg) Torpex
Fusing:	Instantaneous (contact)
Structure:	Streamlined, with thin casing and banded stabilizer at tail
Effect:	Conventional bomb, incapable of penetrating armoured plate
Note:	This superseded the 250lb GP (general purpose) bomb first introduced in 1926

500lb SAP (semi-armour-piercing) or AP (armour-piercing) bomb

User:	Royal Air Force, Fleet Air Arm. Introduced February 1942 (SAP), March 1942 (AP)
Weight:	490lb (222kg) for SAP, 450lb (204kg) for AP. Explosive charge 90lb (41kg) TNT for SAP, 83lb (38kg) Shellite for AP
Fusing:	Delay (6 seconds) for SAP, delay (12 seconds) for AP
Structure:	Streamlined, with thickened casing (up to 1.3in/3.3cm), hardened nose cone and drum stabilizer at tail
Effect:	SAP capable of penetrating 2in (5cm) of deck armour from 2,500ft (762m). AP capable of penetrating 3.5in (8.9cm) of deck armour at 3,100ft (945m)

2,000lb HC (high capacity) Mark II bomb

User:	Royal Air Force. Introduced December 1941
Weight:	1,723lb (782kg). Explosive charge varies depending on explosive, but usually 1,230lb (558kg) Amatol
Fusing:	Delay (12 seconds)
Structure:	Cylindrical, tapering to rear, with thin casing and rear cylinder stabilizer, although some were adapted to use conventional MC banded stabilizer at tail
Effect:	Conventional bomb, capable of wreaking considerable damage to unarmoured structures
Note:	This was essentially a precursor of the larger Blast Bombs, designed to destroy non-armoured targets. Although available from late 1941, these bombs were still being developed, and only entered service officially in June 1943

2,000lb AP Mark I bomb

User:	Royal Air Force. Introduced October 1941
Weight:	1,934lb (877kg). Explosive charge 166lb (75.3kg) Shellite
Fusing:	Delay (11 seconds)
Structure:	Streamlined, thick-walled, with hardened nose cone and banded stabilizer at tail
Effect:	Developed specifically to use against 'heavily armoured targets' such as warships

4,000lb HC blast bomb Mark II 'cookie'

User:	Royal Air Force. Introduced March 1941
Weight:	3,930lb (1,783kg). Explosive charge 2,882lb (1,307kg) Amatol
Fusing:	Delayed contact (12 seconds)
Structure:	Cylindrical, with thin casing and rear cylinder stabilizer in tail
Effect:	Blast bomb
Note:	These bombs were fitted with a light-gauge metal plate nose attachment to improve aerodynamic performance

14 ATTACKERS' CAPABILITIES

On board HMS *Furious*, London-born naval armourer Bob Cotcher chalks a message on the side of a 1,600lb AP bomb slung beneath a Barracuda of 830 Squadron, shortly before the commencement of Operation *Tungsten*. The addition of graffiti to ordnance was not unknown in the Fleet Air Arm, although it was generally frowned upon in Bomber Command.

1,600lb AP Mark I bomb	
User:	Fleet Air Arm. Introduced February 1943
Weight:	1,590lb (721kg). Explosive charge 209lb (95kg) Explosive D (Dunnite)
Fusing:	Delayed contact (12 seconds)
Structure:	Conical, hardened nose cone, with stabilizing fins at tail
Effect:	Armour-piercing, designed to penetrate 5in (13.7cm) of deck armour from 4,500ft (1,370m)
Note:	Of US manufacture, first introduced in US Navy in May 1942

The Fleet Air Arm also employed the 18in Mark XII torpedo, introduced before the war, which had a range of 1,500 yards at 40 knots, and carried a warhead of 388lb of Torpex explosive. This was the torpedo which crippled the *Bismarck*, so in March 1942 it could have done the same to the *Tirpitz*. However, torpedoes were only useable if *Tirpitz* put to sea. Once the battleship took refuge in its Norwegian lairs, torpedo attacks were pointless, as the battleship was always protected by multiple barriers of anti-torpedo netting and moored in narrow fjords which lacked the space for a torpedo run to take place.

18in Mark XII torpedo	
User:	Fleet Air Arm. Introduced 1937
Weight:	1,548lb (702kg). Explosive charge 388lb (176kg) Torpex
Fusing:	Impact fuse
Power:	Burner-cycle engine
Effect:	Underwater detonation against target hull, with standard depth setting of 25ft (7.5m)
Range:	1,500 yards (1,370m) at 40 knots, 3,500 yards (3,200m) at 27 knots
Note:	Air-launched torpedo

Various types of mines were dropped during these attacks, including the Mark XIX spherical contact mine, adapted for use by the RAF. The casings of these mines were strengthened to allow them to be dropped from the air, and their horns removed. They contained 770lb of Amatol, and in theory they should have been effective. Instead they proved another disappointment, and they were only used during the spring raids of 1942. The Fleet Air Arm tried using 600lb anti-submarine (AS) Mark VIII bombs, which effectively were air-dropped depth charges. The idea was that if they hit the *Tirpitz*, they would inflict the same damage as a 500lb AP bomb. If they missed, they would explode in the water and inflict underwater damage. They proved another disappointment. So too did the bizarre 500lb 'Johnny Walker' (JW) mine-bomb. Once dropped this 'oscillating mine' would sink to the seabed, then repeatedly rise and fall while moving laterally, until it came into contact with the underside of a ship, when it would explode. When used during Operation *Paravane* they failed to inflict any damage.

600lb AS (anti-submarine) bomb	
User:	Fleet Air Arm. Introduced March 1944
Weight:	550lb (249.48kg). Explosive charge 439lb (199.13kg) Torpex
Fusing:	Hydrostatic, with depth settings up to 260ft (79.3m), or delayed contact (8 seconds)
Structure:	Cylindrical, thin casing, with detachable nose cone and stabilizing fins at tail
Effect:	Anti-submarine bomb, operating like a depth charge, but also capable of being used as a conventional GP bomb of similar capabilities to a 500lb SAP
Note:	Nose cone designed to detach on entering water

JW ('Johnny Walker') mine Mark I	
User:	Royal Air Force. Introduced July 1944
Weight:	400lb (181.44kg). Explosive charge 90lb (40.8kg) Torpex
Fusing:	Contact fuse, and self-destruct mechanism when all compressed gas was expended
Power:	Compressed CO_2 gas system
Structure:	Cylindrical, with buoyancy chamber and parachute housing in tail
Effect:	Oscillating mine. On landing in water the mine would sink to the seabed, and a hydrostatic/timer switch would trigger the injection of compressed gas into the buoyancy chamber at 60ft (18.29m), raising the mine to the surface. The air would then be expelled, and the process would be repeated until the gas was expended
Note:	Designated 'JW' as an abbreviation for 'Johnny Walker', a reference both to the popular brand of whisky and to the appearance the mine had of 'walking' across the seabed towards its target. A parachute was attached to the tail, which was deployed when the mine was released from the aircraft. It was designed to fall away when the mine entered the water. Lateral 'walking' range was estimated at approximately 30ft (9.14m)

Spherical contact mine Mark XIX (mod)	
User:	Royal Air Force. Introduced March 1942
Weight :	1,000lb (453.6kg). Explosive charge 700lb (280kg) Amatol
Fusing:	Hydrostatic delay pistol, mechanical delay (12 seconds)
Structure:	Specially thickened spherical steel casing
Effect:	Delayed detonation on surface, or hydrostatic detonation under water at 12–18ft (3.6–5.4m)
Note:	Originally a small naval mine, introduced in 1938. Modified for RAF use by the removal of strengthening of the casing, and the removal of the mooring fittings and the eight external switch horns

ATTACKERS' CAPABILITIES

Officially designated the 12,000lb Deep Penetration (DP) Bomb, Mark I, the Tallboy was so large that it could only be carried by Lancasters which had their bomb bay doors modified to accommodate them. It was filled with 5,200lb of Torpex. When released from 18,000ft from a bomber travelling at 200mph, the bomb had a strike velocity of 1,097fps.

Finally, there was the Tallboy. Designed by Barnes Wallis, the inventor of the 'bouncing bomb', this huge 12,000lb MC bomb was specifically designed to attack hardened targets. It was designated an 'earthquake bomb', as it was designed to burrow into the earth on impact, where its explosive blast would shake the earth enough to cause fortified structures to collapse. These pointed, aerodynamically shaped bombs had a thick, hardened-steel casing, were fin-stabilized and when dropped from high altitude would reach supersonic speeds on impact. They could penetrate or undermine thick concrete structures – and could do the same to the armoured deck of a battleship. Each Tallboy was filled with 5,200lb of Torpex, and it was felt that a near miss would cause almost as much damage to the *Tirpitz* as a direct hit. This was certainly the case during Operation *Catechism*, when the hits may have caused intensive internal damage to the battleship, but it was the near misses that not only caused her to capsize, but effectively dug a grave in the seabed for her.

12,000lb Tallboy (M)	
User:	Royal Air Force. Introduced June 1944
Weight:	12,000lb (5.400kg). Explosive charge 5,200lb (2,400kg) Torpex
Fusing:	Impact detonation or delayed detonation (12 seconds)
Structure:	Streamlined casing, with hardened pointed nose cone, and four stabilizing fins at tail
Effect:	Deep penetration or 'earthquake' bomb, designed to burrow beneath surface before exploding
Note:	This bomb could only be dropped from a specially converted Lancaster bomber. Its official designation was 'Bomb, HE, Aircraft, MC, 12,000lb', but Tallboy (M) was far more commonly used.

DEFENDERS' CAPABILITIES
Fortress in the fjords

The *Tirpitz* has often been portrayed as a lonely ship, stranded for most of the war in remote Norwegian fjords, far from the support network of shipyards, supply centres and support ships which usually attend the needs of capital ships. While this may have been true in terms of geography, she was far from lonely. For most of her time in Norway she formed part of a battle group of Kriegsmarine warships, which were in turn supported by ancillary vessels such as tankers, maintenance ships, flak vessels and numerous fishing boats, commandeered as tenders, torpedo net boats and patrol craft. She was protected by a ring of anti-aircraft defences and smoke screen equipment, while at least in the Trondheimsfjord a powerful coastal battery kept enemy warships at bay. She also benefited from a string of coastal radar stations, lookout posts and Luftwaffe airfields. Then of course, there was *Tirpitz* herself, a floating leviathan of steel and weaponry which had her own potent array of flak guns, and a highly trained crew capable of repairing almost any damage their ship might suffer.

The Faettenfjord, where the *Tirpitz* was based from January 1942 until March 1943, was just 2,560 yards long, with the narrow Vududalen valley at its eastern end, and the island of Saltøya to the west, where the fjord entered the Åsenfjord, which itself was the eastern arm of the Trondheimsfjord. *Tirpitz* was moored on its northern side, beneath the wooded hill shown here. At that point the fjord was only 300 yards wide.

The battleship

In April 1939, Frau von Hassel, the daughter of Grand Admiral Alfred von Tirpitz, broke a bottle of Riesling over the bow of Germany's latest battleship *Tirpitz*, and as Reichsführer Adolf Hitler and a huge crowd watched, *Tirpitz*'s flag-draped hull slid into the waters of Wilhelmshaven harbour. Her sister ship *Bismarck* had been launched in Hamburg two months before, and was already fitting out. When they entered service these two battleships were the most modern capital ships afloat, equipped with a powerful main armament and sophisticated fire-control equipment which made them considerably more effective than the ageing battleships of the Royal Navy. Although *Bismarck* was famously sunk on her first operational voyage in May 1941, *Tirpitz* would spend her active life in Norwegian waters. While she rarely made operational sorties, she remained a latent threat to the Allies, due to her considerable ability to wreak devastation if she ever did fall upon an Arctic Convoy.

In terms of firepower her armament was conventional. Her eight 38cm guns had a range of 36,520m metres (38,280 yards) at their maximum elevation of 30 degrees – the equivalent of 19 nautical miles. They were mounted in four twin turrets – two forward and two aft – named 'Anton', 'Bruno', 'Caesar' and 'Dora', and guided by highly effective optical rangefinders. While *Tirpitz* carried a FuMo radar, she never attained the radar fire-control capability of her British counterparts. These guns were augmented by a secondary armament of 15cm guns, mounted in six twin turrets, three on each beam. In theory, by 1944 both her main and secondary guns could be used as heavy flak guns, firing high explosive (HE) rounds with timed fuses. However, her real anti-aircraft (AA) strength lay in her formidable array of flak guns.

Her 10.5cm guns, carried in eight twin mounts, had a rate of fire of around 16–18 rounds per minute, and a range of 17,700m (19,357 yards), with a ceiling of 12,500m (41,010ft). Their job was to lay down a box barrage of heavy flak, to deter enemy bombers from flying through it. Supporting them were a similar number of 3.7cm medium flak guns, with a rate of fire of 30 rounds per minute, a range of 8,500m (9,300 yards) and a ceiling of 4,800m (15,750ft) when firing tracer. Finally her 20mm light flak guns provided 'point defence' at ranges of 4,900m (5,360 yards) or less, with a rate of fire in excess of 120 rounds per minute. By early 1944 her 20mm armament had been dramatically increased by the addition of 18 quadruple 20mm flak mounts. This gave the flak batteries of *Tirpitz* a formidable level of firepower.

The battleship had an armoured belt 320mm thick which protected her hull, but which tapered below the waterline to a thinner 170mm-thick belt, designed to protect her from torpedo attack. More importantly in terms of air attack, this belt formed the sides of an armoured citadel, covered by an armoured deck designed to protect her vitals (her magazines and engine spaces) from aerial attack. It was humpbacked in shape, so it sloped towards the

The battleship *Tirpitz* was launched in Wilhelmshaven on 1 April 1939. The ceremony was watched by the Führer und Reichskanzler Adolf Hitler, although the launching itself was performed by Ilse von Hassel, a daughter of Grand Admiral Alfred von Tirpitz (1849–1930), the founder of the modern German Navy.

OPPOSITE *TIRPITZ'S* ANTI-AIRCRAFT ARMAMENT AND FIRE CONTROL

KMS *Tirpitz* had a conventional layout, similar to the German 'super-dreadnoughts' which entered service during the last years of World War I. The eight 38cm guns of her main battery were mounted in four twin turrets, labelled (from bow to stern) 'Anton', 'Bruno', 'Caesar' and 'Dora'. Their fire was directed by two 10.5m rangefinders, mounted on rotating domes sited in her foretop and atop her after superstructure. Secondary rangefinders, to permit the turrets to fire under local control, were also mounted in each turret.

Her secondary battery of 12 15cm guns was carried in six twin turrets, three on each beam. These were designated as either 'P' or 'S' (for port or starboard), and numbered (from bow to stern) 'I', 'II' or 'III'. They were directed by a 7m rangefinder mounted on top of the bridge. This could also serve the main gun battery if required. Similarly, a 6.5m rangefinder was mounted in each secondary turret, for firing under local control.

Her anti-aircraft defences consisted of 16 10.5cm guns, mounted in eight twin turrets, two on each beam of her forward and after superstructure. They were augmented by 16 3.7cm medium flak guns, in eight twin mounts, also grouped in a similar way, with four mounts on each beam, split between the forward and after superstructure. *Tirpitz* had four fire control stations for these heavy and medium flak guns, two on either side of the mainmast, one behind the mainmast and one behind 'Caesar' turret. Each of these contained a 4m SL-8 rangefinder. The 3.7cm flak guns were also equipped with manual sights, in case the anti-aircraft fire control system was not operational.

A large number of 20mm light flak guns were mounted around the ship, as shown in the diagram. The numbers of these increased markedly while *Tirpitz* was in Norwegian waters. These were fired using manual sights, although the quadruple mounts added in 1942–43 were linked to the SL-8 fire control system. Finally, *Tirpitz* carried a pair of quadruple torpedo mountings, fitted amidships, one on each beam.

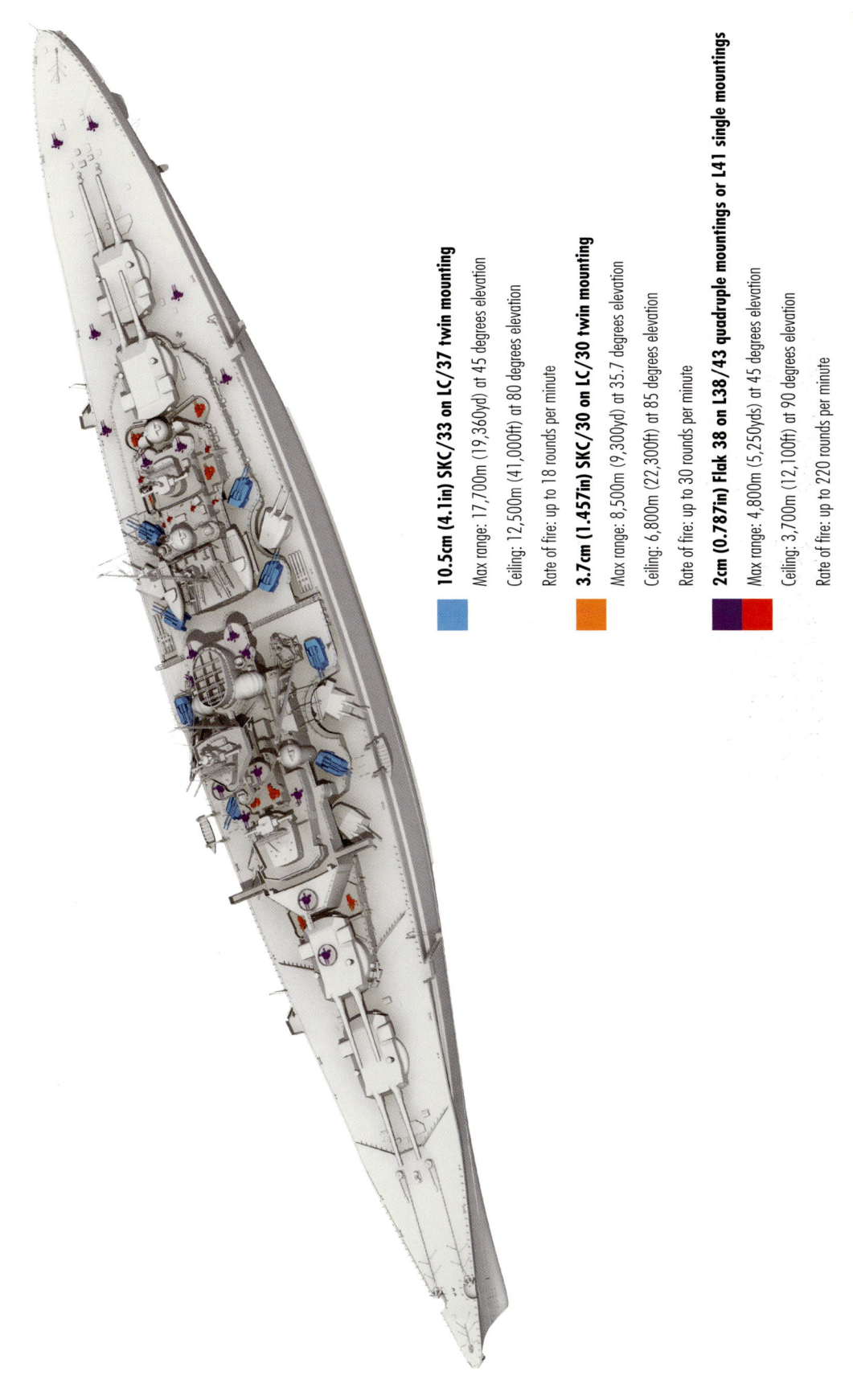

10.5cm (4.1in) SKC/33 on LC/37 twin mounting
Max range: 17,700m (19,360yd) at 45 degrees elevation
Ceiling: 12,500m (41,000ft) at 80 degrees elevation
Rate of fire: up to 18 rounds per minute

3.7cm (1.457in) SKC/30 on LC/30 twin mounting
Max range: 8,500m (9,300yd) at 35.7 degrees elevation
Ceiling: 6,800m (22,300ft) at 85 degrees elevation
Rate of fire: up to 30 rounds per minute

2cm (0.787in) Flak 38 on L38/43 quadruple mountings or L41 single mountings
Max range: 4,800m (5,250yds) at 45 degrees elevation
Ceiling: 3,700m (12,100ft) at 90 degrees elevation
Rate of fire: up to 220 rounds per minute

sides of the ship, where it eventually joined the armoured belt. These sloped sides increased the protective capabilities of the deck. This armoured deck lay two deck levels below the actual upper deck, a steel deck clad in teak which was more lightly protected, but was still thick enough to shield the compartments beneath it from splinter damage or smaller bomb hits. The citadel did not protect the bow and the stern of the ship, which were primarily covered by her upper deck plates, although her propeller shafts were screened by a 110mm-thick armoured layer.

Taken together, the anti-aircraft batteries and her protective armour made *Tirpitz* a difficult target for Allied bombers. She had weaknesses, though. Although the armoured deck might protect her vitals, many of the ship's living spaces were situated above it, and so were vulnerable. While her main and secondary turrets were well protected, her smaller flak guns were not, and the smaller weapons lacked gun-shields to protect their crews from bomb splinters or strafing attacks. This would prove particularly problematic during Operation *Tungsten*. Her other weakness was to underwater damage, from torpedoes, mines, or the explosive power of earthquake bombs. In several attacks she suffered flooding damage, and ultimately it was this weakness which would prove her undoing.

KMS *Tirpitz*	Bismarck class battleship
Built:	Kriegsmarinewerft, Wilhelmshaven
Laid down:	2 November 1936
Launched:	1 April 1939
Commissioned:	25 February 1941
Length:	823ft 6in (251m) overall
Beam:	118ft 1in (36m)
Draught:	30ft 6in (9.3m) standard lading
Displacement:	45,474 tonnes (50,425 tonnes fully laden, rising to 53,500 tonnes in 1944)
Propulsion:	3× Brown-Boveri geared turbines, 12× Wagner high-pressure boilers, powering three propellers, and generating 160,796 steam horsepower (shp)
Max. speed:	30 knots
Range:	8,870 nautical miles at 19 knots
Armament (1942):	8× 38cm (15in) SK/C-34 main guns in four twin turrets 12× 15cm (6in) SK/L-55 secondary guns in six twin turrets 16× 10.5cm (4.1in) SK/C-33 heavy flak guns in eight twin mounts 16× 3.7cm (1.5in) SK/C-30 medium flak guns in eight twin mounts 12× 2cm (0.8in) Flak 30 light flak guns in 12 single mounts* 8× 53.3cm (21in) torpedoes, in two quadruple mounts * *During the winter of 1943–44, this was augmented by the addition of another 78 2cm (0.8in) Flak 30 light flak guns in 18 quadruple mounts*
Aircraft:	4× Arado 196 A-3 reconnaissance float planes, 1× catapult
Sensors:	FuMo23 'radar', Gruppenhorchgerät (GHG) hydrophone system
Protection:	Belt: 320mm (13in) Turrets: 360mm (14in) Armoured deck: 100–120mm (3.9–4.7in) Upper deck: 50mm (2in)
Complement:	2,608 officers and men (1943)

The Norwegian lairs

During her time in Norway, *Tirpitz* used four anchorages. One of these in the Bogenfjord near Narvik was only a temporary sanctuary, a mustering place for Kriegsmarine naval forces, and a base used for summer training exercises or temporary repairs. It was protected by flak positions and torpedo nets, and by the booms and patrol boats which guarded the entrance to the main Ostfjord. However, this was not really *Tirpitz*'s true home. She had two of those. From January 1942 until March 1943 it was the Faettenfjord near Trondheim, and after that it became the Kaafjord, near Alten, and the northernmost tip of Norway. Then, from October 1944 until her sinking in November, *Tirpitz* was moored off the island of Haakøy, near Tromsø. This last berth proved the exception to the rule – all the others were carefully chosen so that the landscape played a major part in the battleship's defence.

The Faettenfjord was a small spur of the Åsenfjord, 16 miles north-west of the town of Trondheim. The Åsenfjord was at the eastern end of the Trondheimsfjord, while the town itself, on its southern shore, lay another 65 miles from the open sea. The Trondheimsfjord was protected from naval incursions by coastal batteries at Hysnes and Brettingen, but the real defensive value of the Faettenfjord was that it was only 300 yards wide, and flanked to north and south by steep hills. While its western end opened out onto the Åsenfjord, the entrance was split in two by the small hilly island of Saltøya, where the *Tirpitz*'s crew established shore facilities, including sports fields and a rest camp. To the east the Faettenfjord opened into the narrow valley of Vadudalen, but the wooded slopes and steep mountains to the south made it an unattractive avenue for aviators. *Tirpitz* was moored close to the northern slope of the fjord, with her stern facing west. This facing, the narrowness of the fjord and the torpedo nets surrounding the ship rendered *Tirpitz* immune from torpedo attack. So, any attacking aircraft had to use bombs, and attack from the west. This lack of options helped the Germans immensely as they planned the local defences.

The Kaafjord was similar to the Faettenfjord, in that it was a narrow fjord, about 1,000 yards wide in the part where *Tirpitz* had her moorings. Here she lay end-on to a point of land, nestling in the curve of a small bay called Barbrudalen. In the spring of 1944, after Operation *Tungsten*, *Tirpitz* was moved to the other side of the fjord, with her stern moored to a spit of land called Straumsneset. The Kaafjord was 3½ miles long, and lay at the southern end of the larger Altenfjord. The ship herself lay 5 miles from the small town of Alta, while the open sea lay 75 miles away from the ship, at the north-western end of the winding fjord. Like the Faettenfjord, the Kaafjord was flanked by high ground, with a high ridge on the south-eastern shore of the fjord, high hills to the south, and even higher ground leading to a mountainous plateau on the north-western side. So, once again a torpedo attack was impossible, leaving attackers with the option of coming in up the fjord, or over the mountains.

Tirpitz's final lair was her least favourable. It lay next to the small island of Haakøy, and the neighbouring smaller island of Grindøy. It was 3½ miles to the west of the town of Tromsø, which lay on the far side of another island, Tromsøya. To the east and south of the anchorage was an even larger island, Kvaløya. The small stretch of water between the southern side of Haakøy and Kvaløya was known as the Sørbotn Channel. It formed part of the network of small fjords which separated Tromsø from the open sea, 32 miles away. As the largest town in northern Norway Tromsø was an important strategic asset, and *Tirpitz* was sent there to defend the port from Allied attack. However, compared with her other smaller anchorages the Haakøy one was exposed, with an open body of water on one side, and no towering mountains to shelter beneath.

Tirpitz moored in the Faettenfjord, with her stern pointing towards Saltøya Island, which can be glimpsed in the background. She was usually surrounded by ship's boats, tugs, lighters and supply vessels, as well as rafts carrying camouflage nets. Further out, the line of buoys delineates the position of her anti-torpedo nets.

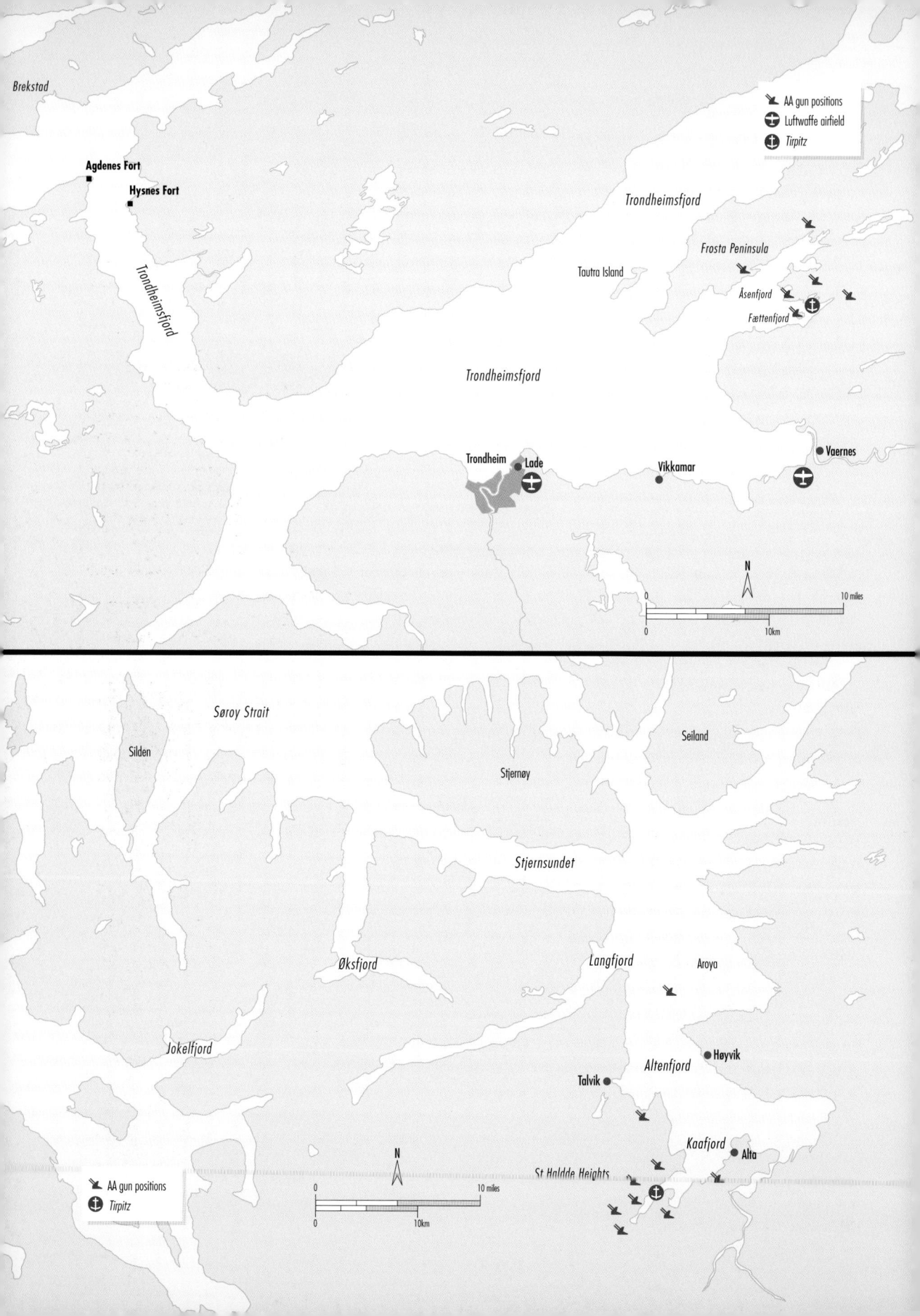

OPPOSITE THE FAETTENFJORD AND KAAFJORD ANCHORAGES

In all these cases, the real bonus of these lairs was their distance from British air bases. The Faettenfjord lay 632 miles from the forward airfields in north-east Scotland used by the Royal Air Force (RAF) in the spring raids of 1942. That was within range of British heavy bombers. The Bodenfjord was nearly 963 miles away, which theoretically was just within range of Lancasters. So too was the Haakøy anchorage near Tromsø, which was 1,049 miles away from Lossiemouth and neighbouring airfields, and so was reachable only if extra fuel tanks could be carried. At 1,146 miles, the Kaafjord lay well beyond the range of British bombers flying from Scottish airfields. That was why, in September 1944, the RAF used an airfield near Archangel in the Soviet Union for Operation *Paravane*, a mere 600 miles from the Kaafjord. These distances, though, are direct. The need to choose an approach avoiding enemy radar or airfields, and a route which gave the attackers some degree of surprise, often meant opting for a much longer flight path. So geography combined with the performance of British bombers conspired to make an attack on the *Tirpitz* a tough proposition.

The local defences

In the Faettenfjord, *Tirpitz* lay at the centre of a ring of flak defences which were there purely to protect her and other nearby warships from attack. A total of 16 flak batteries of various types and sizes were scattered over the immediate area of the fjord, and the nearby anchorage of Lofjord, used by German cruisers such as the *Admiral Hipper* and *Prinz Eugen*. These included 24 heavy flak guns of 8.8cm calibre, while six more protected Trondheim. A total of 16 lighter flak guns, of 3.7cm and 20mm calibres, made up the rest of these anti-aircraft defences, which were placed to cover both naval anchorages. Another 15 light flak guns protected Vaernes airfield, 7 miles south of the Faettenfjord.

In addition, two flak ships were moored nearby, one in the Åsenfjord and the other in the Lofjord. These were obsolete Norwegian warships captured by the Germans, and provided with an assortment of flak guns of various calibres. They would subsequently be moved to the Bodenfjord, to the Altenfjord and finally to the waters off Haakøy. Anti-aircraft fire would also come from the numerous warships in the area. This usually included a number of destroyers, but could include larger vessels, such as the battlecruiser *Scharnhorst*, the armoured cruisers *Admiral Scheer* or *Lützow*, or the heavy cruisers *Admiral Hipper* or *Prinz Eugen*.

Searchlight positions were mounted at two points on the southern shore of the Faettenfjord, while others protected Vaernes airfield and Trondheim. *Tirpitz* herself was surrounded by anti-torpedo nets, as she

The defences of the Faettenfjord, 1942–43
This shows the location of flak batteries surrounding the Faettenfjord and the nearby Lofjord, the searchlight battery facing the *Tirpitz* on the far shore of the Faettenfjord, and the various moored trawlers serving as smoke screen vessels. They were augmented by more smoke generators mounted around the shore of both anchorages. The numbers refer to the semi-permanent mooring assigned to various major Kriegsmarine warships:
1. *Tirpitz*, battleship
2. *Admiral Scheer*, armoured cruiser (or pocket battleship)
3. *Admiral Hipper*, heavy cruiser
4. *Prinz Eugen*, heavy cruiser
(Map by Nick Buxey)

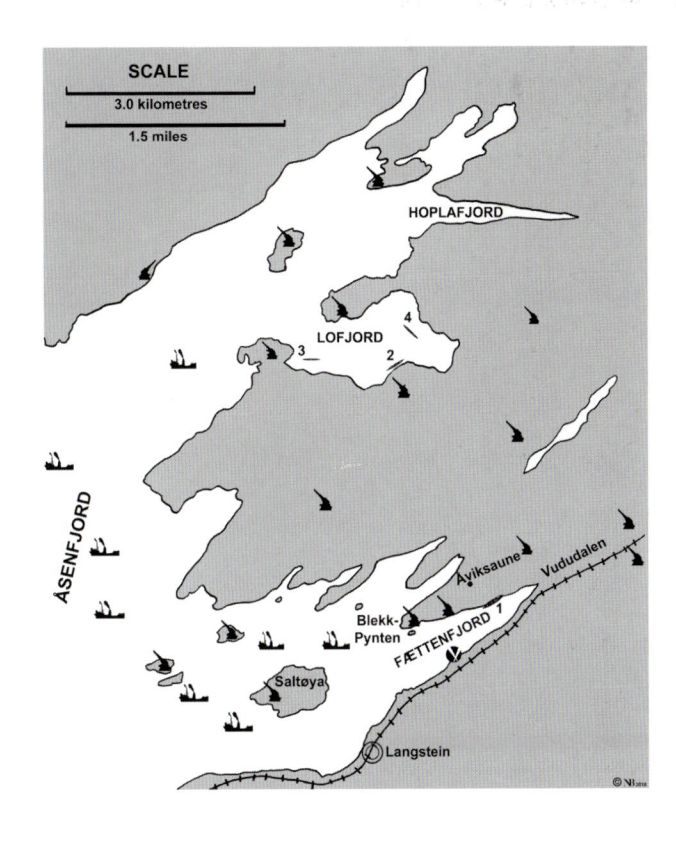

was in all her anchorages, operated by boom defence trawlers. Further naval patrols combed the waters of the Trondheimsfjord, and a boom spanned its western end, near Brettingen battery.

However, of all the defences put in place to protect *Tirpitz*, the most effective was her smoke screen. This was provided by chemical smoke generators, which were mounted around the shore of the Faettenfjord and in parts of the Lofjord. In addition, yet more smoke generators were mounted in smoke boats – converted trawlers, eight of which were permanently stationed on the seaward side of both anchorages. In the event of an air attack these would be set off electronically, and it was reckoned that within ten minutes an impenetrable barrier of white smoke would shroud not only the *Tirpitz*, but the whole of the Faettenfjord as well.

Tirpitz in the Altenfjord, being guided through the channel by tugs in March 1943, on her way to her new 'lair' in the Kaafjord. The photograph was taken by Torstein Raby, a member of the Norwegian resistance movement, using a camera hidden in his suitcase.

In the Kaafjord a similar arrangement was put in place. In fact, most of the flak guns and smoke generators were simply transported up there in coastal convoys, along with their crews, stores and equipment. In the spring of 1944 there were 38 heavy flak guns in place around the fjord, supported by 22 light flak mounts, some of which were quadruple flak pieces.

Air warnings tended to come from one of the chain of radio direction finding (RDF, or 'radar') stations which covered the Norwegian coast. They could detect approaching aircraft at a range of about 50 miles, but it was only in the winter of 1943–44 that improved radar sets and a more thorough coverage made this early warning system truly effective. Similarly, the network was never fully extended so it could detect aircraft approaching from the east, where the mountainous spine of Norway and Sweden made accurate detection difficult. However, in Lapland the Germans maintained coastal radar stations which were able to provide some coverage over the flat landscape to the south. These RDF stations were augmented by lookout posts, and by observers standing watch in other key locations, such as on airfields, in towns or at military barracks. Despite a somewhat convoluted command chain, the system worked, and in most cases the captain of the *Tirpitz* was able to sound 'Action Stations' and deploy his protective smoke screen before the enemy bombers appeared.

The weak link in the German defensive screen was air cover. Luftwaffe airfields near the battleship's lairs – Vaernes near the Faettenfjord, Banak near Kaafjord and Bardufloss near Haakøy – should in theory have provided fighter cover for *Tirpitz* in the event of an air attack. These airfields were also linked in to the radar network, so intercepting an approaching bomber formation or naval air strike should have been a reasonably simple undertaking. However, intense rivalry between the Luftwaffe and the Kriegsmarine, a complicated command structure and a general reluctance to risk precious air assets meant that in virtually every case, the attacking aircraft were never intercepted. So, for instance, in the spring of 1940 there were 30 Bf 109 fighters at Vaernes and 30 Bf 110s. None of them intercepted the spring bombing raids that year. The biggest failure came in November 1944, where despite a direct phone link between *Tirpitz* and the airfield at Bardufloss, no fighters took to the air to protect the *Tirpitz* on the day of her loss.

CAMPAIGN OBJECTIVES
The battle for Arctic waters

A fleet in being

The *Tirpitz* was sent to Norway to join the Kriegsmarine forces there, and to form the core of a battle group which could disrupt the Allied convoys sailing to northern Russia. Norway was the ideal base for this mission, as it lay close to this convoy route, particularly in the north, where from sheltered anchorages such as the Altenfjord this battle group could easily venture deep into the Arctic Sea. The same coastline also provided a haven for U-boats, which took only two days to form a patrol line astride these convoy routes. Norway contained several air bases, and the Luftwaffe had built up their bomber strength there. So, while the Arctic Convoys could be harried from the air and from below the surface, warships such as *Tirpitz* would bide their time and choose the right moment to strike.

This, however, was only the theory. While U-boats and land-based aircraft played havoc with these convoys, surface forays were rare. The principal reason for this was the Reichsführer, who, after the loss of the *Bismarck*, was wary of committing surface ships to an action where the odds might not be completely in their favour. So, for all her immense fighting potential, *Tirpitz* spent much of the war at her moorings in the Norwegian fjords, screened by camouflage netting and torpedo nets, with her crew growing increasingly frustrated as the war was being waged elsewhere. In the two instances where *Tirpitz* did make a sortie, she failed to make contact with the enemy, except when she was attacked by British naval aircraft. This strike, carried out by Albacore torpedo bombers from HMS *Victorious*, led to two directives from Hitler. The first was that in future she would only sortie if there were no British aircraft carriers operating in the area. The second was that no offensive operation would be undertaken without Hitler's consent.

The result was the atrophy of the battleship's fighting potential. So, instead of forming a key part of a surface battle group which could sever the strategically vital convoy route between the Western Allies and the Soviet Union, she was relegated to becoming the centrepiece of the naval doctrine of a 'fleet in being'. This concept, famously proposed by the American naval strategist

In early July 1942, the German naval battle group in Norway sailed north from the Bogenfjord near Narvik to the Altenfjord, which they planned to use as a base from which to attack Convoy PQ-17. This photograph, taken from the stern of a German destroyer, shows two of these warships – the armoured cruiser *Lützow*, followed by her sister the *Admiral Scheer*. During this voyage, the *Lützow* struck an uncharted rock, and had to return to Narvik for repairs.

ARCTIC OCEAN

Bear Island

Scattering of PQ-17 1942 ✕

Battle of the Barents Sea 1942 ✕

Barents Sea

Battle of North Cape 1943 ✕

North Cape

Hammerfest
Kaafjord · Banak
⚓ ✈
Haakoy · Alta
Tromsø
Kirkenes · Petsamo
Bodenfjord ⚓ Bardufoss ✈
Lofoten Islands
Narvik
Trondheim
Kola Inlet
Murmansk

Bodo

Norwegian Sea

Fættenfjord ⚓
Vaernes ✈

NORWAY

FINLAND

Bergen
Oslo
SWEDEN

Shetland

Orkney
Scapa Flow

Stavanger

SOVIET UNION

North Sea

DENMARK

UK

N

0 — 200 miles
0 — 200 km

Legend:
- Winter limits of pack ice
- ····· Front line 1942–44
- ✕ Battle
- ⚓ Tirpitz anchorage
- ←--- Arctic Convoys' winter route

OPPOSITE THE STRATEGIC SITUATION 1942–44

Alfred Thayer Mahan (1840–1914), explained how a naval force could influence a naval war, even without leaving port. If it did so, it might lose the battle, and hence the war. However, by remaining in port it served as a 'fleet in being', forcing the enemy to continually deploy a bigger force, just in case it ever did sortie. Thus, even though she remained in the Faettenfjord or the Kaafjord, the *Tirpitz* would force the British Home Fleet to deploy precious battleships and aircraft carriers in support of the Arctic Convoys. This would then prevent these capital ships from being deployed in more active theatres, such as the Mediterranean or the Far East.

So, for Captain Topp of the *Tirpitz* and his successors, their objective was to survive, and to maintain their fighting potential. This stratagem, endorsed by Grand Admiral Raeder and then his successor Admiral Karl Dönitz, meant doing whatever was required to protect the battleship from attack, which could only come from submersibles or from aircraft. Naval defences were therefore put in place – an outer ring of search aircraft, then destroyers, followed by booms and guard vessels screening the seaward entrances to the fjords where the *Tirpitz* lay. Finally, coastal sentries, torpedo nets and lookouts would play their part. The defences against air attacks have already been described, but the problem of cooperation with the Luftwaffe was never overcome.

The naval command structure was also particularly complex. A Commanding Admiral Norway controlled all Kriegsmarine resources in Norway. The country was divided into North, South, West and Polar Coast areas, and at various times *Tirpitz* came under the control of the North and Polar commands. The commanding admiral, though, was answerable to the Chief of Naval Command in Germany, and through him to the Commander-in-Chief of the Navy, and to the Reichsführer. The Luftwaffe had its own command structure, with Luftflotte 5 based in Oslo controlling all air units in Norway, Finland and northern Russia. Under it, Fliegerführer Nord had operational control in Norway, and it in turn was divided into three regional commands. A separate structure dealt with Luftwaffe administration. What this meant for *Tirpitz* was that any request for air support had to surmount several administrative hurdles. This, combined with inter-service rivalry, meant that the *Tirpitz* and her crew were badly let down by the Luftwaffe.

Grand Admiral Erich Raeder (1876–1960) had to juggle the two strategic demands of his warships in Norway – attacking the Arctic Convoys and maintaining a 'fleet in being'. He resigned in early 1943, following Hitler's criticism of the Kriegsmarine after the battle of the Barents Sea. Here he is inspecting *Tirpitz* in the Faettenfjord anchorage, accompanied by two of his senior staff, and followed by Captain Topp.

The British goal

The British goal was simply the reverse of the German one. It needed to sink the 'fleet in being' in order to send its much-needed capital ships to other hard-pressed theatres of war. Prime Minister Winston Churchill was particularly aware of this – he understood the concept of 'a fleet in being' with much greater clarity than Hitler ever did. So, from January 1942 on, he pressed both Bomber Command and the Admiralty to deal with the *Tirpitz*. For the Admiralty, this meant maintaining the capital ship strength of the Home Fleet, so that if *Tirpitz* ever did sortie to attack a convoy, a distant covering force of two battleships was on hand to intercept it. Where possible this distant covering force was supported by an aircraft carrier, as was the case with *Victorious* in March 1942. Effectively, all the Navy could do during 1942 and 1943 was to contest control of the sea, and so help the vital convoys reach Murmansk and Archangel.

OPPOSITE BOMBER ROUTES AND CARRIER LAUNCH LOCATIONS

By 1944, though, new fleet carriers had entered service, and a new breed of small escort carriers were available, to protect convoys and augment the fleet carriers for special operations. Even then, the Home Fleet had to gather all its available carrier strength in order to carry out the air offensive against the *Tirpitz* that ran intermittently throughout the spring and summer of 1944. This was a risky undertaking, as the torpedoing of HMS *Nabob* demonstrated (see page 65). Still, while the Admiralty might not agree, Churchill argued that the loss of one or two fleet carriers in exchange for the *Tirpitz* might be a price worth paying.

The situation was different for Bomber Command. While the bomber crews who took part in the spring raids of 1942 might not have experienced that kind of highly specialist attack before, they were at least well-versed in the business of flying bombing missions over long distances, and knew what was expected. The use of heavy bombs such as the 'cookie' gave these air crews a reasonable chance of inflicting damage on the *Tirpitz* if they could hit her, and the attacks themselves were pressed home with a grim determination. However, the lack of any serious damage inflicted during these costly raids meant that Bomber Command became reluctant to commit more of their precious bomber force on such a problematic target. Logistically, though, these missions paved the way for the RAF raids of late 1944. They demonstrated that a large bomber force could reach Norway from forward airfields in north-east Scotland, and that with the right ordnance much better results could be achieved.

The move of the *Tirpitz* to the Kaafjord placed her beyond the range of another strike of this kind, but by 1944 the ordnance to do the job had become available. The 12,000lb Tallboy bomb was almost custom-built for the task, and by 1944 Bomber Command's 5 Group had two squadrons which had already used these mammoth bombs, and their aircraft were equipped to carry them. Operation *Paravane* in September 1944 was the result of extensive planning by the staff of 5 Group, who not only oversaw the modification of the Lancasters to reach a forward base in northern Russia, and planned this epic flight across northern Europe, but also masterminded the raid which followed. The real stars of the operation, though, were the men of 9 and 617 Squadrons, led by Wing Commander 'Willy' Tait. They demonstrated the effectiveness of the Tallboy, causing the damage which would bring the battleship within range of the same bombers, this time flying from British airfields.

The planning of all these air operations, from the spring of 1942 on, had been meticulous. Large relief models of the target areas had been produced by both the RAF and the Royal Navy, and these helped the pilots understand the target area. This was important, as the geography of the Faettenfjord and Kaafjord played a major part in the operation. This was less true of the final attacks on the *Tirpitz* as she lay off Tromsø. What was needed there was the ability to fly further than a British bomber force had flown before on a mission of this kind, and clear skies when it reached the target. The first hurdle was overcome by good planning and ingenuity. The second relied on luck.

The first mission, Operation *Obviate*, was thwarted by a sudden change of weather which no meteorologist could have predicted. The second, Operation *Catechism*, took place in near-perfect flying conditions, and as a result, *Tirpitz* was destroyed. The Allies had finally achieved their objective, after what was one of the longest air campaigns of the war. By then, however, the *Tirpitz* had ceased to be a viable 'fleet in being'. This dénouement, then, was more about 'payback' than strategy.

In March 1943 Admiral Otto Schniewind (1887–1964) became the commander of the Marinegruppenkommandos Nord (Marine Group Command North), responsible for all Kriegsmarine warships in Norwegian waters, as well as in the Baltic and the North Sea. His attempts to use *Tirpitz* more aggressively were thwarted by Hitler.

THE CAMPAIGN
Targeting *Tirpitz*

Background

On 9 April 1940, German troops began landing in Norway. In the Trondheimfjord, the heavy cruiser *Admiral Hipper* shelled the coastal defences, and by the end of the day Trondheim was in German hands. The same was true of Narvik, Bergen, Stavanger and Oslo. Although the fighting would continue until early June, the outcome was never really in doubt. Norway fell and became an occupied country. However, the cost had been high. The Kriegsmarine had played its part in the operation, but of the 22 destroyers, cruisers and battlecruisers involved, three cruisers and ten destroyers had been lost, and two battlecruisers damaged. Grand Admiral Raeder said that having Norway was worth the loss of half of his battle fleet, as it gave his fleet a base outside the confined waters of the North Sea.

This would become of crucial importance following the German invasion of the Soviet Union in June 1941. For the moment though Norway remained relatively unimportant, as German naval efforts were concentrated on the development of naval bases on the French Atlantic coast and the launching of commerce raids into the North Atlantic. During this phase of the war the *Tirpitz* was still being fitted out in Wilhelmshaven. After that she was undergoing her sea trials. So, she missed out on Operation *Berlin*, the first of the Kriegsmarine's surface operations in the North Atlantic, which took place in early 1941. This successful sortie by the battlecruisers *Scharnhorst* and *Gneisenau* was followed in May 1941 by Operation *Rheinübung*, an operation involving *Tirpitz*'s sister ship *Bismarck* and the heavy cruiser *Prinz Eugen*.

On 27 May *Bismarck* was cornered and sunk by warships of the British Home Fleet. For the crew of *Tirpitz*, the only consolation was that the armoured citadel of their sister ship was proof against the British shells, although her superstructure and turrets were comprehensively damaged and she became little more than a floating wreck. The German crew had actually begun to scuttle their own ship to prevent her falling into enemy hands, when she was struck by torpedoes launched from a British cruiser. One or more of them hastened the end of the

The Tirpitz, pictured in Kiel by a British PRU flight in September 1941 as she lies alongside the quay, at the entrance to the naval shipyard's inner basin. She was based there intermittently during her sea trials and 'working up' exercises, where she attracted the attention of RAF bombers.

battleship by demolishing her stern. The sinking of her sister ship meant that *Tirpitz* was now the Kriegsmarine's only fully fledged battleship.

The bombing raids against her began in the summer of 1940, just after the Fall of France, while she was still being fitted out in Wilhelmshaven. Most of these raids, though, were aimed at the port itself rather than the ship, and she emerged unscathed. In early March 1941 she passed through the Kaiser Wilhelm Canal to Kiel, which would serve as her base while she conducted sea trials. PRU flights monitored her progress, and a small raid using twin-engine Whitley bombers was launched against her, but this was thwarted by bad weather. She also emerged unscathed from a larger raid in June. Any further chance to damage *Tirpitz* in Kiel evaporated when the battleship finally set off to war.

The invasion of the Soviet Union in June 1941 changed the whole strategic picture in Europe. The Western Allies were put under intense diplomatic pressure to help the Soviet Union. So, in August, as German tanks drove on Moscow, a small convoy was despatched. The Dervish Convoy consisted of six merchant ships, which assembled in Iceland before heading east to Archangel in northern Russia, which it reached on 31 August. Dervish was the ad hoc forerunner of the Arctic Convoys, a maritime lifeline between Britain and the Soviet Union which was of the utmost strategic importance. A total of 78 Arctic Convoys would make the dangerous journey to northern Russia and back, battling the elements as much as the Germans. By necessity, this convoy route ran close to the Norwegian coast. From August on, therefore, Norway was once more an area of considerable strategic importance.

By the start of January 1942 *Tirpitz* had completed her crew training, and was ready for active service. On 13 January the ship transited the Kiel Canal and emerged from its western end that evening. Signals claiming she was returning to Wilhelmshaven were merely a ruse. Instead she took on fuel, stores and replacement equipment, and headed north. The British were unaware of this activity until the morning of 17 January, and so they lost track of the German battleship. By then the *Tirpitz* had arrived at her new berth near Trondheim. It was not until 23 January that she was spotted by a PRU flight. *Tirpitz* was 16 miles northwest of Trondheim, moored in the Faettenfjord. It was a near-perfect spot. The small finger-shaped fjord was just 300 yards wide where the *Tirpitz* was moored, with high ground on two sides. Attacking her there was going to be extremely difficult.

Captain Karl Topp (1895–1981) commanded the *Tirpitz* for two years, from her commissioning in February 1941 until February 1943, when he was promoted, and given an administrative command in Berlin. Known affectionately as 'Charlie' by his crew, he was regarded as one of the finest seamen in the Kriegsmarine, and one of its most competent captains.

Operation *Oiled*

Prime Minister Winston Churchill considered the bombing of the *Tirpitz* of major importance, writing that 'No other target is comparable to it.' The Fleet Air Arm quickly ruled out the feasibility of an attack using torpedoes, while its dive bombers were too small to carry a decent payload. So it was up to Bomber Command. It was decided to carry out a night attack at the end of the month, when there was sufficient moonlight to see the target. This mission would be codenamed Operation *Oiled*. On 28 January, 27 heavy bombers set off for RAF Lossiemouth,

On the morning of 9 March, *Tirpitz* and an accompanying destroyer were spotted off the Lofoten Islands by search aircraft operating from the fleet carrier *Victorious*. Here the wing of the reconnaissance Albacore can be seen, as the pilot dips the wings to allow the observer to take a clear photograph of the enemy battleship.

was Admiral Tovey. He now knew *Tirpitz* was at sea, and with a force of two battleships, a battlecruiser and the aircraft carrier *Victorious* he had the power to sink her if she could be brought to battle. However, he had to find her first. By 1600hrs on 7 March, *Tirpitz* was roughly between PQ-12 and the Home Fleet, with the convoy 60 miles to the east of her, and the Home Fleet 80 miles to the west.

It was a frustrating time for both commanders. At 1600hrs that afternoon, the German destroyer *Friedrich Ihn* came upon the Russian freighter *Izhora*, a straggler from QP-8. She was sunk by gunfire. That, though, told Ciliax that he had missed the homebound convoy. So at 1045hrs on 8 March he decided to spend the day cruising towards the west, in an attempt to catch up with QP-8. *Tirpitz* cruised on her own, as the previous evening Ciliax had ordered his destroyers to put into Narvik to refuel. Finally, at 2025hrs that evening he turned southwards and headed home towards Trondheim. Tovey learned of this through Ultra signal intercepts, and he realized that his only chance of intercepting *Tirpitz* now was by crippling her in an air strike. That would allow the Home Fleet to overhaul her. Interestingly, it was a similar situation to that which had faced him the previous year, when he was pursuing *Bismarck*. It was now up to the air crews of HMS *Victorious*.

Throughout that night (8/9 March), Ciliax and Tovey headed south and south-west respectively, with the British hoping to be in a position to launch an air strike against *Tirpitz* shortly after dawn. By that time she would be to the west of the Lofoten Islands, where Ciliax planned to rendezvous with his destroyers. Also, if necessary *Tirpitz* could put in to Narvik. *Victorious* had 18 Albacores embarked, from 817 and 832 Squadrons. The intention was to fly off six of these at dawn to search for the German battleship, while the remaining 12 would form the strike force, led by Lieutenant Commander Lucas, commander of 832 Squadron. The weather had improved slightly during the night, and the fog lifted. Visibility was now good, and the cloud base was 4,000ft.

At 0640hrs on 9 March, the search aircraft were flown off, fanning out to the south-east, flying at just below the level of the clouds. Just over 50 minutes later, at 0732hrs, the strike force was flown off too. This was a gamble – if the *Tirpitz* remained undetected, then all the aircraft would eventually have to return and refuel, which meant it would be almost noon before another strike could be launched. However, at 0803hrs, *Tirpitz* was spotted west of the Lofoten Islands, heading south, escorted by the newly refuelled *Friedrich Ihn*. Soon three of the search aircraft were shadowing the battleship. They were spotted by the Germans at 0810hrs, and just over 20 minutes later *Tirpitz* flew off one of her Arado spotter planes, to act as her own scout. The Arado attacked one of the shadowing Albacores, but was hit itself. Leaking fuel, the Arado made off towards Bødo airfield, 75 miles to the south-east, as the *Tirpitz* wasn't prepared to stop to recover the aircraft.

At 0805hrs the sighting report was passed to Lucas, and he adjusted his course to intercept. Meanwhile Ciliax realized that a carrier was close by, and that a naval air strike was likely. So, he altered course towards the east, heading for the Moskenes Strait, between the Lofoten Islands and the Norwegian mainland. This was the entrance to the Vestfjorden, which led to Narvik. He also notified the Luftwaffe airfield at Bødo, requesting air cover. While records show that this message was received, cooperation between the Luftwaffe and the Kriegsmarine was poor, and the request was bogged down in official channels. Even though a squadron of modern Fw 190 fighters was just ten minutes' flying time away, *Tirpitz* and her attendant destroyer were left to fend for themselves.

Then, at 0842hrs, Lucas spotted the *Tirpitz*. She was 20 miles to the south-west, steaming east at high speed. At the time the strike aircraft had been flying at 500ft, below the level of German coastal radar, but on spotting the *Tirpitz* Lucas ordered his aircraft to climb into the clouds, so they could approach without being seen. However, a fully laden Albacore had a top speed of just 130 knots, and Lucas' planes were flying into the face of a 35-knot wind, blowing from the east, so it would be at least 30 minutes before the aircraft would be in a position to begin their attack. The 12 Albacores were divided into four sub-flights, each of three aircraft. Effectively Lucas led the strike, as its commander overall as well as of the two sub-flights of his own 832 Squadron. Lieutenant Commander Sugden commanding 817 Squadron officially commanded the planes of his own squadron, and one from 832 Squadron. However, during the attack the four sub-flights became intermingled, and Lucas directly commanded a sub-flight from each squadron (1/832 Squadron and 2/817 Squadron), while Sugden led the remaining two sub-flights. (1/817 Squadron and 2/832 Squadron)

Operation *Sportpalast*, 9 March 1942

On 6 March 1942, *Tirpitz* sailed from the Trondheimsfjord in an attempt to intercept and destroy Convoy PQ-12. Codenamed Operation *Sportpalast*, this sortie was well planned, but it was dogged by bad weather, and the convoy eluded the battleship. Eventually Vice Admiral Ciliax ordered her to return to port. Then, early on the morning of 9 March, search aircraft from the British carrier *Victorious* spotted the battleship and an escorting destroyer to the west of the Lofoten Islands. A naval air strike was launched, made up of 12 Albacore torpedo bombers. They sighted *Tirpitz* at 0842hrs, and their strike leader divided his force into two groups, so it could attack the battleship from two sides at once.

The first wave attacked from port at 0920hrs, but all six torpedoes missed. It was now up to the six Albacores who were manoeuvring to attack the battleship from her starboard side. They began their approach, but were hampered by the slow speed of their biplanes and a strong headwind. Eventually, however, they reached their attack positions about 2,000 yards off the starboard beam of the battleship, and dropped to 100ft to begin their torpedo run. The German flak was intense, coming both from the *Tirpitz* and the destroyer *Friedrich Ihn*. The Albacores dropped their torpedoes at 0925hrs, then began banking away to the south. However, two were hit before they released their torpedoes. This captures the moment when Lieutenant Commander Sugden's sub-flight of 817 Squadron launched its attack. Albacores 5B and 5L have launched their 18in torpedoes, but in the foreground 5C has been hit, and is about to crash into the sea. All the torpedoes missed, largely because the battleship began turning as the airmen made their attack. Six naval airmen were lost in the abortive strike.

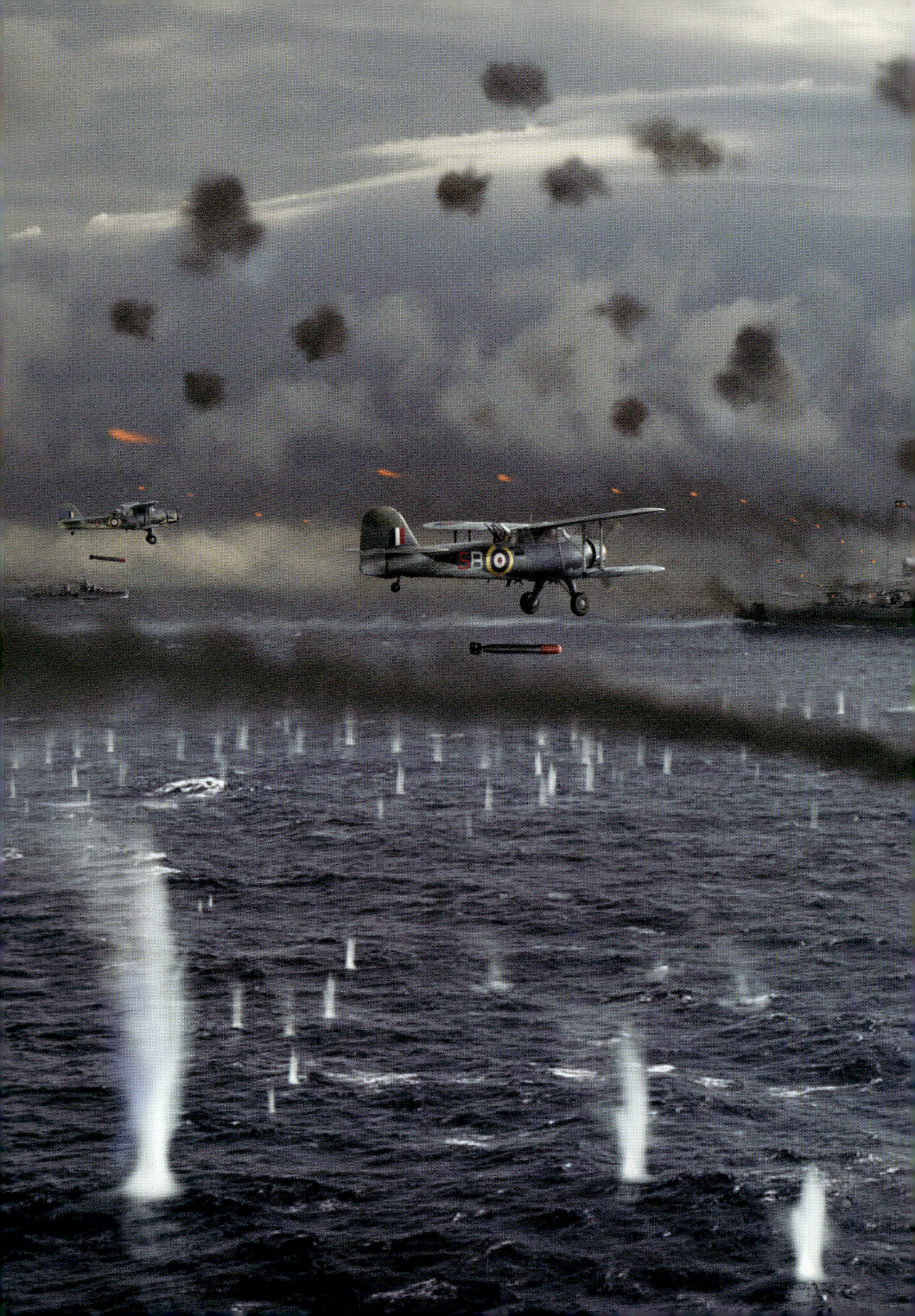

Jim Laurier

Lucas then gave the order that all sub-flights would make individual attacks, rather than attacking together. This reflected contemporary Fleet Air Arm tactics. According to the textbook, the ideal attack involved getting about a mile-and-a-half ahead of the ship, then peeling off to port or starboard before beginning the attack run. The idea was for half of the strike to attack the target from port, and the rest to starboard. The torpedo planes would drop down to 200ft while they manoeuvred, but during the attack run they would descend to between 50 and 100ft before releasing their torpedoes. Each Albacore carried a single 18in torpedo. This could run at 40 knots for 1,500 yards, and its warhead of 388lb of explosives detonated on impact. From 1,500 yards this would therefore take about 68 seconds to reach its target. As it was moving too, then the Albacore had to 'lead' the target, so that both it and the torpedo reached the same spot at the same time. In the case of *Tirpitz*, steaming at 28 knots, this meant launching a torpedo at a point 1,400 yards ahead of the ship.

The textbook called for the launch of torpedoes at a range of 1,000 yards from the target. However, the compilers of the textbook weren't being shot at while making their frustratingly slow approach, and while the air crews of *Victorious* were fairly experienced, it took more than training to press home a perfect torpedo attack in a lumbering biplane. The further a torpedo dropped from its target, the longer it took to reach it, and the further the aiming point had to be from the ship. A longer run made it more likely that the crew of the target ship could react by turning away from the oncoming torpedoes, thus 'combing' their tracks.

At 0917hrs, the strike aircraft broke through the cloud cover and began their attack. At that point *Tirpitz* was ahead of them, steaming at full speed in the same direction. As the strike force split into its four sub-flights, two edged forward towards the port beam of the battleship, and two to starboard. It was Lucas who launched the attack. By 0920hrs his 1st sub-flight of 832 Squadron aircraft (4A, 4B and 4C) were a mile away from the battleship, on her port beam. The flak was heavy, but it could have been worse, as the gunners divided their fire among the four groups of aircraft. On Lucas' order his sub-flight turned to starboard, and at 30 seconds past 0920hrs they launched their torpedoes. The range was a little under 1,500 yards. On the bridge of *Tirpitz*, Captain Topp saw the launch and immediately ordered his ship to turn hard to port. While that meant heading towards the three oncoming torpedoes, it also meant that it turned the ship away from the six Albacores gathering off his starboard beam.

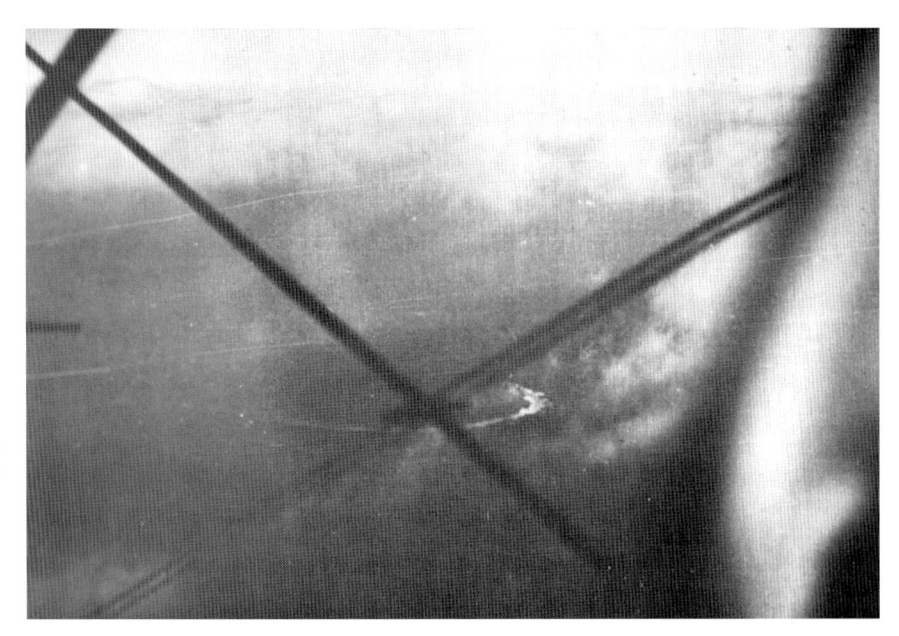

In this photograph, taken from an Albacore of the second wave, which is still manoeuvring into position, the *Tirpitz* can be seen turning hard to port, to avoid the torpedoes launched at her from the low-flying aircraft of the first wave.

The three torpedoes passed astern of the battleship. Meanwhile, Lucas' second strike – aircraft 5M, 5H and 4G of 817 Squadron – found themselves to starboard of the battleship's track, so they crossed her wake, and made their approach off her port quarter. When *Tirpitz* turned to port it put them in a better position. The sub-flight dropped its torpedoes 30 seconds after 0921hrs, then turned away. However, the torpedo run was excessive – almost 2,000 yards – and again the torpedoes missed their target. Lucas reported that the closest only came within 150 yards of their target.

That left the two sub-flights led by Lieutenant Commander Sugden (1/817 Squadron and 2/832 Squadron), who ordered them to keep on the starboard side of the battleship and to try to get ahead of her. The six aircraft now attracted all the German flak, from both *Tirpitz* and the *Friedrich Ihn*. The two sub-flights were flying almost directly into the 35-knot wind, so progress was agonizingly slow. Then, at 0925hrs, *Tirpitz* began turning to port, as Topp resumed his easterly course. This also put Sugden's aircraft in a better attacking position.

They were now about 2,500 yards off the battleship's starboard bow, with one sub-flight ahead of the other. On Sugden's command they both turned and began their torpedo runs. To the south 4M of 832 Squadron dropped its torpedo 30 seconds after *Tirpitz* began her turn, while 1,000 yards to the north two aircraft from Sugden's sub-flight of 817 Squadron (5L and 5B) released their torpedoes at virtually the same moment. The sixth aircraft, 4R of 832 Squadron, was on Sugden's starboard quarter, and it dropped its torpedo with the others. However, as they began their run two of the aircraft – 4P from 832 Squadron and 5C from 817 Squadron – took direct hits and both aircraft crashed into the sea. Somehow the other aircraft managed to avoid the storm of flak, and released their torpedoes.

Four torpedoes were now heading towards the *Tirpitz*, which had completed her turn, and was settling onto her new easterly course. All of them had dropped their torpedoes early, though – post-engagement reports estimate that the distance was 1,600 yards. Once again, *Tirpitz* was able to comb the oncoming torpedo tracks. All of the torpedoes passed in front of her, although one was within 20 yards of the battleship. On board *Tirpitz*, Lieutenant

A pair of Albacores – 5L and 5B from 817 Squadron – try to bank and climb after releasing their torpedoes at the *Tirpitz*. The photograph was taken from Albacore 4R of 832 Squadron, which was 500 yards to starboard of the pair when they launched their torpedoes. All three aircraft made it back to *Victorious*.

Räder recalled seeing a British airman, sitting on the top wing of his biplane as it wallowed in the swell. As the surviving aircraft flew out of range, the battleship continued on towards the Vestfjorden, and shortly before 2000hrs she dropped anchor in the Bogenfjord, a small arm of the larger Ofotfjorden, facing Narvik.

The surviving Albacores all made it back to *Victorious* by 1100hrs that morning, but no further strikes were attempted. In his report, Captain Bovell of *Victorious* criticized the inexperienced Lucas for attacking from a disadvantageous position. However, while the Fleet Air Arm officially deemed the strike 'disappointing', Vice Admiral Ciliax praised the courageous nature of the attack. The fact remained, however that the Fleet Air Arm had missed a rare opportunity to attack the *Tirpitz* at sea. Few knew it at the time, but it would also be the Home Fleet's last chance to strike her on the open sea.

Tirpitz remained in the Bogenfjord for three more days. Then, just before midnight on 12 March, the battleship and five destroyers slipped out of the fjord, hidden by darkness and poor visibility. The British were unaware that the *Tirpitz* had sailed south until the evening of 13 March, when Norwegian agents reported her arrival back in the Faettenfjord. While Operation *Sportpalast* might have been a failure for both sides, it had one lasting consequence. When he learned of the air strike Hitler ordered that in future the battleship would only sortie if British aircraft carriers were neutralized first. Meanwhile, *Tirpitz* would remain in the Faettenfjord.

Bomber Command tries again: March–April 1942
The March raid

Once again, Bomber Command was ordered to deal with the battleship. Daytime attacks were ruled out, as the greater risks outweighed any improvement in bombing accuracy. Any attack would be carried out at night, preferably when moonlight illuminated the target. Given the range, this necessitated starting the raid from north-eastern Scotland. This time, two new types of ordnance were available. The first of these was the 4,000lb HC 'blockbuster' bomb (nicknamed the 'cookie'), which had to be dropped from at least 4,000ft to avoid

Built to specifications issued by the Air Ministry in 1936, the Handley Page Halifax proved a reliable four-engined heavy bomber, although it was less versatile than the Avro Lancaster, as its bomb bay was incapable of being modified to fit extremely large bombs such as the Tallboy.

damaging the aircraft. A spherical contact mine was also available, having been modified so it could be dropped from a heavy bomber.

On 27 March, 44 and 97 Squadrons from 5 Group sent 12 Lancasters to Lossiemouth, six from each squadron. 10 Squadron of 4 Group also arrived with ten Halifaxes, while the 12 Halifaxes of 35 Squadron and ten from 76 Squadron from the same group went to nearby airfields at Tain and Kinloss. All of these planes were modified to take extra fuel. The idea was to arm the Lancasters and 76 Squadron with 4,000lb 'cookies', as well as 500lb bombs. The Halifaxes of 10 and 39 Squadrons would each carry four mines.

The ten Halifaxes carrying the 'cookies' would fly up the fjord and precision-drop their bombs on *Tirpitz* from a height of 4,000–5,000ft. After releasing the 'cookies', they were to circle around and use their 500lb bombs to target nearby flak positions. Meanwhile the 12 Lancasters would drop their 'cookies' on nearby Vaernes airfield. It was expected that this phase would take place on 30 March between 2145hrs and 2230hrs.

This second phase involved the 22 mine-carrying Halifaxes approaching *Tirpitz* from the west, then releasing the mines from 600ft. The aim was to target the stern, or just behind it, or to drop the mines between the battleship and the shore. The hope was that the damage caused would force *Tirpitz* to return to Germany for repairs. Both weapons, though, were untested on capital ships.

At the last moment the Lancaster part of the operation was cancelled. So, at 1800hrs on 30 March, the 32 Halifaxes took off and headed out over the North Sea. Destroyers were stationed along the route in case aircraft had to crash-land in the sea. The flying time to the target was three-and-a-half hours, and the return leg, which passed close to Orkney and Shetland, was 30 minutes longer. When the bombers got within 100 miles of the Norwegian coast they dropped to 500ft, to reduce the risk of detection by German radar. In fact, they were detected and the defenders were ready for them.

The flight to the target was uneventful, but when the first wave of Halifaxes from 76 Squadron reached the fjord they found that cloud formed a dense band from 1,000 to 6,000ft. *Tirpitz* was completely obscured. At 2200hrs the flak batteries opened up as the bombers approached the unseen battleship, their crews hoping for a break in the clouds. On board *Tirpitz* they heard rather than saw the aircraft, but Captain Topp ordered the ship's anti-aircraft guns to hold their fire for the moment, to avoid revealing their position.

Still, the flak from the shore batteries was heavy, and four bombers were shot down over the fjord. Some 25 bombs were dropped on flak positions but *Tirpitz* remained untouched. The aircraft circled around until fuel began running low, and then they headed home. Two more damaged bombers were forced down in the North Sea , which brought the total losses to six aircraft – two from 10 Squadron, three from 35 Squadron and one from 76 Squadron. The official report on the mission concluded that 'Thick cloud over the target and mist in valleys and fjords made identification of the battleship impossible'. In fact they never even got close to spotting it.

The first April raid

For the moment the bombers were returned to their regular schedule of raids over Germany. Meanwhile, PRU flights revealed a strengthening of the anti-aircraft defences in the area, and the reinforcement of the air base at Vaernes. *Tirpitz* remained in the Faettenfjord, covered by her camouflage screen and protected by torpedo nets. Churchill and the War Cabinet insisted that another attempt be made as soon as possible, so the planners at Bomber Command set about organizing a further strike. The basic plan would remain the same, but the attack would take place later – around midnight – as it was thought the defenders would be less alert.

Experience had shown that releasing a 'cookie' at anything below 6,000ft risked damage to the aircraft, so the height of the bombing run was altered accordingly. Similarly, trial and error during practice flights had shown that the optimum height for dropping the mines was 150ft, so this release height was changed too. The bombers would now fly closer to Orkney and Shetland on both legs, to improve the chances of rescue if forced to ditch in the sea. Also, a model of the Faettenfjord had been produced, and this greatly helped the crews understand the geography of the target area.

The planners were aware that on the last occasion the Germans had been ready for them, and they put this down to the efficiency of the German radar chain. So, both before and during the raid, secondary attacks would take place elsewhere to distract the radar operators. A squadron of Hudsons would raid shipping off Ålesund, 150 miles south of Trondheim, while pairs of Beauforts would carry out hit-and-run raids on Lade and Vaernes airfields near Trondheim, as well as Herdla airfield near Bergen.

In the final briefing, the bomber crews were ordered to fly up the Trondheimsfjord, then begin their bombing runs over Saltøya Island, 1½ miles west of the *Tirpitz*. After the attack they were to turn to port, passing over the Lofjord before heading back along the northern shore of the Trondheimsfjord. For those planes carrying mines, it was stressed that if they couldn't see the target they should drop their mines over the high ground beside the battleship. That way the mines might roll down the slope and explode between the ship and the shore. At 150ft, though, that meant having to avoid her mainmast, the tip of which was 165ft above the battleship's waterline.

The mission was due to begin on the evening of 25 April, but for the next two days the airfields were fogged in. Finally, at 2000hrs on 27 April, the bombers took off. Two Lancasters were forced back due to mechanical trouble, but a reserve Lancaster was sent up to take their place. A total of 42 bombers were now en route to the target, 31 Halifaxes and 11 Lancasters, all flying at 5,000ft.

The route took them north past Shetland, and then north-east to a point 70 miles from the Norwegian coast at Ålesund. They would then fly north, before turning west-north-west for their final approach to the fjord. The first wave was due over the Trondheimsfjord shortly before midnight. Two hours into the mission one more Halifax was forced back due to engine failure. The rest finally crossed the Norwegian coast above Kristiansund, climbed to 12,000ft and began their final approach.

Despite all the diversions the Germans spotted the bombers on radar, and were ready for them. One airman recalled, 'As we neared the coast we could see flak inland, and as

500lb general purpose (GP) bombs being loaded into the bomb bay of a Halifax heavy bomber. During the Bomber Command raids on *Tirpitz* in early 1942, this bomb type was among the assortment of ordnance used against the battleship, or carried to deal with flak batteries around the Faettenfjord.

we crossed it our worst fears were confirmed.' This was due to the diversionary raid on Trondheim by Beaufighters. All it really achieved was to keep the anti-aircraft gunners alert. So, as soon as the bombers appeared over the Trondheimsfjord they encountered heavy flak.

The first wave consisted of the Lancasters carrying the 4,000lb 'cookies'. The Halifaxes of 76 Squadron followed behind them. As the bombers made their final approach they found that some flak batteries on the high ground flanking the fjord were actually firing down at them. Searchlights, flares and lines of tracer lit up the sky. This time, with the clouds above the bombers, and the area illuminated, the battleship was clearly visible.

As the bombers passed Saltøya Island they encountered a box barrage of flak. One of the Lancasters from 97 Squadron was hit and spiralled downwards to crash in the mountains to the east. None of its seven-man crew survived. Somehow the other bombers made it through and at 0006hrs the leading Lancaster of 44 Squadron dropped its 'cookie' over the target from 7,500ft. The rest of the wave did the same. Some of the crews thought they saw their bombs hit the ship, but in fact none of the bombs struck their target.

At this stage *Tirpitz* was still visible, as her smoke screen still hadn't been deployed. The smoke was finally released at 0012hrs, and was fully in place when the mine-dropping Halifaxes arrived. Many of the crews didn't get a clear view of *Tirpitz* during their attack, and dropped their bombs or mines on where they thought the battleship was through the smoke. Still, the bombers in the wave completed their run, and banked away to the north. Some even circled round for a second pass before dropping their bombs and banking away. One Halifax of 76 Squadron left it too late and dropped its 'cookie' on the *Admiral Scheer* instead.

In the Faettenfjord the crew of the *Tirpitz* had to become adept at camouflage. Sharp surfaces were draped with tarpaulins and any other material that came to hand, while fir trees were used to break up the lines of the deck. Eventually a series of camouflage nets attached to the shore and to rafts moored at the bow of the ship would shroud the ship even more effectively.

14,000ft

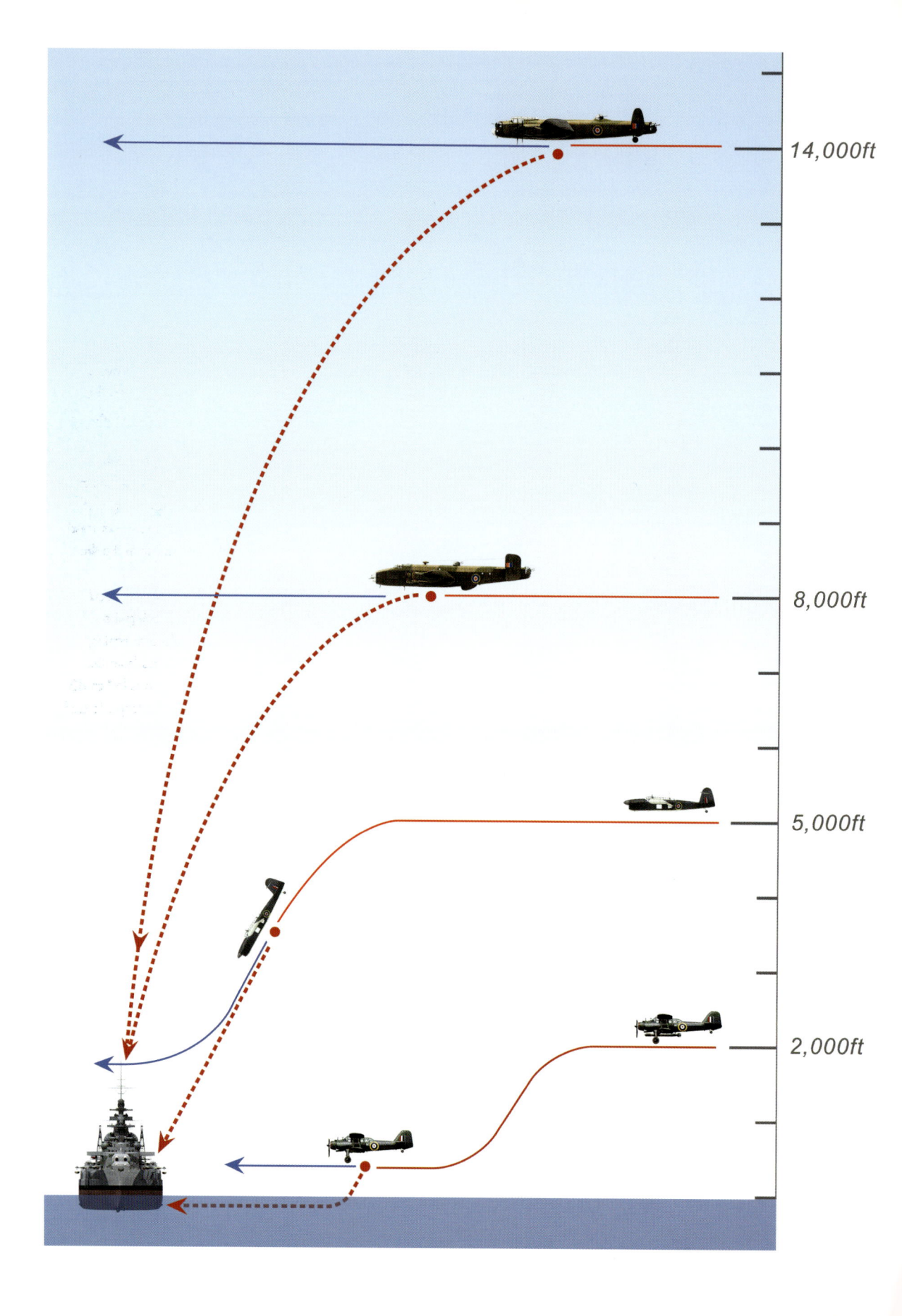

8,000ft

5,000ft

2,000ft

OPPOSITE BOMBING TECHNIQUES EMPLOYED AGAINST *TIRPITZ*, 1942–44

This diagram illustrates the four bombing techniques used against *Tirpitz* during her time in Norwegian waters. At the top is an Avro Lancaster heavy bomber, carrying a single 12,000lb deep penetration bomb, or Tallboy. The optimum height for the bomb's release was 13,500–14,000ft, with the aircraft flying level at approximately 200mph. In fact, release heights during the three Tallboy attacks on *Tirpitz* varied from 12,000 to 17,400ft. The release point was calculated by means of a specially developed SABS Mark IIA bomb sight, and the bomb rotated rapidly as it fell, which increased accuracy considerably. Its strong construction and high terminal velocity ensured that it would penetrate the armour of the battleship, while even a near miss would rely on the 'earthquake' effects of the bomb's blast to cause severe underwater damage to the target.

During the RAF's raids on the Faettenfjord in 1942 it was intended that the Handley Page Halifax heavy bombers who took part in the missions would fly over the target at an altitude of around 6,000–8,000ft, maintaining a steady airspeed of around 220mph. However, after the first attack in January, it was felt that accuracy would be improved by reducing the bombing height to around 6,000ft. Any lower and those bombers using the 4,000lb HC bombs that some of these bombers carried on the spring raids risked being damaged by the explosion of their own ordnance. Those Halifaxes carrying spherical mines dropped them from 200–250ft.

When the Fleet Air Arm used the Fairey Barracuda dive/torpedo bomber to attack *Tirpitz* in the Kaafjord during the late spring and summer of 1944, the aircraft approached the target at a height of around 5,000ft; they would then dive at an angle of around 45 degrees or more, before releasing their bombs at a recommended height of 3,500ft. A dive angle of 65 degrees or more would place a dangerous strain on the airframe of the bomber. The heaviest piece of ordnance carried in these strikes was the 1,600lb AP bomb, which was aerodynamically designed to spin quickly as it fell, and to strike the ship at a high velocity, which increased its ability to penetrate the deck armour of the target.

Finally the Fairey Albacore was also capable of carrying bombs, but the diagram here shows how the aircraft was used during a torpedo attack of the kind conducted by the Fleet Air Arm against *Tirpitz* in early 1942. On approaching the target the biplane would fly at an altitude of around 2,000ft, then drop down to within 100ft of the sea before releasing its 18in torpedo. At this point its airspeed would be around 100 knots. The ideal range was about 1,000 yards from the target, but in practice the ordnance was often released sooner, at ranges of up to 1,500 yards. The torpedo travelled at 40 knots. Ideally the torpedo would be aimed ahead of the battleship, to compensate for the movement of both the torpedo and the target, until ideally both converged at the aiming point.

The job of the first wave wasn't done. They still had to release their 500lb bombs on flak positions, and then circle, drawing flak away from the second wave. The second wave, the mine-carrying Halifaxes of 10 and 35 Squadrons, flew past Trondheim at around 0025hrs. However, by the time they reached Saltøya Island the Faettenfjord was filled with smoke. By then the bombers had dropped down to 250ft, and with 35 Squadron leading, they began their attack at 0040hrs.

Although the German flak batteries were fully alert, they had been firing at high-flying bombers, so at first these low-flying newcomers took them by surprise. Most of the bomber crews never saw the battleship through the smoke, but their study of the model of the fjord paid off. Of the 11 aircraft in 35 Squadron, seven dropped their mines in the area of the target. Of the others, one bombed a patrol boat, and another Halifax was shot down over the Åsenfjord before it reached its target.

As soon as the bombers released their mines they banked to port, and skimmed over the Lofjord before making their escape up the Trondheimsfjord. The last group to make its attack was the Halifaxes of 10 Squadron. They approached the target at about 0105hrs, and dropped their mines from heights of 200ft or more, in the vain hope of seeing the battleship's masts above the smoke. One airman, Flying Officer Watts, recalled the experience as he entered the Faettenfjord: 'At that very moment we flew into a smoke screen so dense it seemed to be solid. It was like flying in cotton wool. There was no sense of motion, no spatial relativity. We knew we were thundering alongside a solid rocky cliff wall … speeding towards an equally solid cliff wall not far ahead – all sight unseen.' He released his bomber's mines when he thought the *Tirpitz* was roughly beneath them, and the pilot banked away, hoping to clear the cliff ahead of them. As Watts put it dryly, 'No one would have wished to end their life like a fly squashed on the wall.'

By 0120hrs, the last of the bombers was heading homeward. One of the 10 Squadron bombers had to ditch in the Trondheimsfjord, while another damaged plane crash-landed further inland, on the frozen surface of Lake Hoklingen. Both crews survived, and apart from one injured airman they even escaped captivity by making it over the Swedish frontier. In total five aircraft were lost – four Halifaxes and one Lancaster. However, for all this effort and these losses, the *Tirpitz* was completely undamaged. All of the 'cookies' missed, while the smoke screen protected her from the mines. At dawn the crew of the *Tirpitz* found the surface of the Faettenfjord covered by dead fish, killed by the exploding mines. So, as the exhausted bomber crews returned to their rooms and slept, the decision was made to repeat the attack the following night.

The second April raid

The only major change was in the timing. By the time the mine-dropping aircraft reached the Faettenfjord the *Tirpitz* had been hidden by smoke. So, this time a tighter schedule was planned, with very little gap between two waves. This time, the first wave consisted of nine Halifaxes from 76 Squadron and six Lancasters each from 44 and 97 Squadrons. All but one of these bombers would carry a 4,000lb 'cookie' and 250lb or 500lb GP bombs, while one Lancaster attached to 76 Squadron only carried a mixture of the smaller bombs. Once again, the 15 remaining Halifaxes from 10 and 35 Squadrons were armed with five spherical mines apiece.

On the evening of 28 April the bombers took off from 2030hrs, with the 76 Squadron Halifaxes joining up with the Lancasters to form the first wave. One of the mine-laden Halifaxes failed to take off due to mechanical trouble, which reduced the strength of the second wave to 14 aircraft. This time there was a scaled-back version of the diversions intended to confuse the German radar operators. Also, they would take place just before the bombers arrived, to avoid alerting the defenders. Ahead of the bombers a diversionary force of four Beaufighters crossed the coast, and kept a lookout for enemy fighters. In fact although several 'nightfighters' were reported over Trondheimsfjord, no German aircraft were in the vicinity. The likelihood is that these were actually the Beaufighters, which were circling over Trondheim as the first wave flew past. Only one German fighter was in the area, and it was ordered to keep out of the way of the flak barrage.

The British plan called for the first wave to release their 4,000lb bombs between 0030hrs and 0040hrs. The second wave, flying in low, were expected to drop their mines between 0041hrs and 0050hrs. After bombing the main target, the bombers would bank away to the north, releasing their smaller bombs over flak batteries or other targets before heading home. By now the force had been reduced further, as two Halifaxes from 35 Squadron had been forced back due to engine failure. Visibility was good, but the crew of the *Tirpitz* were forewarned, and this time the smoke screen was deployed before the first wave even reached the target.

The 'cookie'-armed bombers dropped their ordnance into the smoke from 6,000–8,000ft. Some of the Lancasters held on to 'cookies' and instead they released them over the *Admiral Scheer* and *Prinz Eugen*, in the Lofjord, which for some reason was free of smoke. It was significant that while some of these crews later asserted that the flak was heavier than the night before, some of the crew of the second wave claimed the opposite. This suggests that the flak guns were targeting the higher-flying bombers. It was only after the second-wave bombers climbed out of the smoke that they faced the full brunt of enemy flak. The bombers dropped their smaller bombs at targets between the Faettenfjord and the Lofjord, but one plane, forced off course by flak, released its 'cookie' over Vaernes airfield, a few miles away to the south.

The British 500lb semi-armour piercing bomb was used against the *Tirpitz* in all three of the RAF raids on her in the Faettenfjord during the spring of 1942, and the Fleet Air Arm attacks on the battleship in the Kaafjord during the summer of 1944.

Then it was the turn of the mine-laden Halifaxes. This time the majority of them released their ordnance from around 150–250ft, and strangely, while the smoke screen obscured the target, a gap in it appeared during the bombing run, so some of the aircraft had a good clear view of the *Tirpitz*. Until then the battleship's anti-aircraft gunners had held their fire to avoid revealing their position. Now they blazed away. Several of the bombers were damaged, but somehow all of them made it out of the fjord. In one Halifax from 35 Squadron the pilot recalled that 'We were so low on the treetops that the mid-upper gunner reported that we had disturbed a bird from her nest, to which the rear gunner added that there were four eggs in it!'

Again, the bombers released their smaller 500lb bombs over flak installations to the north of the Faettenfjord. Then the planes turned west over the Lofjord. A few bombers found that their mines were jammed in their bomb bays, and had to be prised out during the flight home. Two Halifaxes from 35 Squadron were shot down in the raid. One limped up the Åsen valley, flying west until it crashed on the shores of Movatnet (Lake Movaten), just 3 miles beyond the spot on Lake Hoklingen where another Halifax from the same squadron had crashed the night before. The second caught fire and spun down into the Åsenfjord. In both cases the majority of the crew survived the crash, but became prisoners of war.

In all, 18 'cookies' and 48 mines were dropped that night, but none of them hit the *Tirpitz*, or at least caused her any damage. Many of the mines lodged in the steep wooded slope on the north side of the fjord. Others landed in the fjord, and the battleship's crew could feel the pressure waves from their explosions transmitted through the water. Once again, though, the only significant casualty was the fish of the Faettenfjord. The smoke screen had done its job.

Despite plans for more operations, it was decided that this would be the last raid by Bomber Command for some time. These had been night raids, carried out by night bombers, and with spring turning to summer the days were getting longer. So, further attacks were suspended until the autumn. The air crews needed a break too. They had suffered significant losses: 10 Squadron had lost four Halifaxes, 76 Squadron had lost one and 35 Squadron seven bombers. One Lancaster of 97 Squadron had also been shot down. A total of 60 airmen had been killed during the three missions, and 18 taken prisoner. That amounted to approximately 12 per cent of the men who had participated in the attacks. All this sacrifice had been in vain. *Tirpitz* remained undamaged, and the threat she posed to the Arctic Convoys was as great as ever.

| RAF Bomber Command losses during *Tirpitz* attacks, spring 1942 ||||||||
| | Mission ||| Total aircraft losses | Crew losses |||
	30/31 March	27/28 April	28/29 April		Killed	POWs	Rescued/escaped
10 Sqn	2	2	-	4× Halifaxes	16	8	-/4
35 Sqn	3	2	2	7× Halifaxes	30	10	-/4
76 Sqn	1	-		1× Halifax	7	-	7/-
97 Sqn	-	1	-	1× Lancaster	7	-	-

Notes:
In addition, a Beaufighter (248 Squadron) was lost on 27/28 April (2 crew killed), while throughout March and April 3 PRU Spitfires were shot down in the area (2 crew killed, 1 POW).
Incidentally, in 2008, Halifax 'S-Sugar' (W1048) of 35 Squadron, which crash-landed in Lake Hoklingen on the night of 27/28 April, was recovered by divers in 1973. The aircraft was subsequently transported to Britain, where it was restored. It is now displayed in the RAF Museum.

Hiatus: May 1942–April 1944

This failure by Bomber Command was to have grave consequences. It was now late spring in the Arctic, and the days were getting longer. The long winter nights had helped screen the convoys from Luftwaffe search planes and U-boats, but now the season of near-perpetual sun was approaching. During the winter the Luftwaffe had reinforced its air bases in Norway, and now Luftflotte 5 had the capacity to search far out into the Arctic Sea, and carry out large-scale attacks using torpedo- and bomb-armed aircraft. While the Admiralty would have liked to suspend convoy operations until the autumn, Churchill was under pressure from both Roosevelt and Stalin, so he ordered that they continue, regardless of the risk. What followed would show just how much an influence the *Tirpitz* exerted on this naval campaign.

In mid-May 1942, the Admiralty learned that the Germans were planning a strike against the next Arctic Convoy. Codenamed Operation *Rösselsprung* (the knight's move in chess), this would involve a task force commanded by Admiral Otto Schniewind, whose flagship was *Tirpitz*. On 27 June, Arctic Convoy PQ-17 sailed from Hvalfjörður in Iceland, bound for Archangel. It consisted of 35 merchant ships and 14 escorts, while a 'Covering Force' of four heavy cruisers shadowed it. Admiral Tovey commanded the 'Distant Covering Force' of two battleships and the carrier *Victorious*. In theory this should have been a powerful enough force to thwart any move made by Admiral Schniewind.

On 1 July, PQ-17 was spotted by a U-boat, and at 2000hrs the next day *Tirpitz* put to sea, accompanied by the armoured cruiser *Admiral Scheer*, the heavy cruiser *Admiral Hipper* and four destroyers. A second armoured cruiser, *Lützow*, was damaged by grounding while attempting to accompany Schniewind's force, so she returned to Narvik for repairs. By the morning of 4 July the German task force was anchored in the Altenfjord, near the northernmost tip of Norway. There, Schniewind waited for the order to strike.

Tirpitz in the Bodenfjord near Narvik, photographed in July 1942 by a high-flying PRU plane. The battleship is protected by a double line of torpedo nets, while supply and support vessels cluster around her. While this base was beyond the effective range of bombers flying from Britain, she was still at risk from attacks launched by British carriers.

Tirpitz in the Altenfjord in July, waiting to play her part in Operation *Rösselsprung* – the attack on Convoy PQ-17. As the sun is setting, her anti-aircraft guns are elevated, ready to counter any sudden air attack from either the Fleet Air Arm or the Soviet Air Force.

The *Tirpitz*, photographed in the Faettenfjord by a low-flying PRU aircraft during the winter of 1942–43. She lies at her regular berth on the north side of the small fjord, surrounded by a cluster of smaller vessels, with pontoons carrying camouflage netting sitting off her bow and stern.

Meanwhile PQ-17 continued its voyage, the escorts successfully fending off attacks by German torpedo bombers. However, that afternoon the British Admiralty learned that *Tirpitz* was in the Altenfjord, just a few hours away from the convoy. Neither the cruiser covering force nor the escort could protect the convoy from *Tirpitz*, and Tovey's capital ships were 350 nautical miles to the west – too far away to intervene. PQ-17 was on its own.

The First Sea Lord, Admiral of the Fleet Sir Dudley Pound, then made one of the most controversial decisions of the naval war. At 2100hrs that evening he ordered the convoy to scatter, and the cruisers to withdraw to the west. For the next few days, the merchant ships tried to reach the safety of Soviet ports. Most never made it, being picked off by U-boats and Luftwaffe bombers. Of the 35 merchant ships which sailed from Iceland, only 11 made it to safety.

Ironically, the First Sea Lord gave his 'scatter' order when he thought that *Tirpitz* was about to fall upon the convoy. In fact, she remained in Altenfjord until 1120hrs on 5 July. Even then, after a brief sortie (5–6 July), Hitler was alarmed that a British carrier was at sea, and that evening he cancelled the operation and ordered Schniewind to return to the fjord. Ironically, *Victorious* was too far away to intervene. By 9 July, *Tirpitz* was back in the Bogenfjord, near Narvik. The whole operation revealed just how much Hitler feared British naval air power, and just as significantly, how much *Tirpitz* was viewed as a 'bogey man' by the British Admiralty.

The extent to which *Tirpitz* dominated naval

In this high-altitude photograph taken by a Soviet reconnaissance plane in May 1943, and subsequently marked by Admiralty intelligence analysts, *Tirpitz* can be seen moored close to the north-western side of the Kaafjord, while support vessels are anchored further north, and in the small bay off Kvenvik, to the south-east.

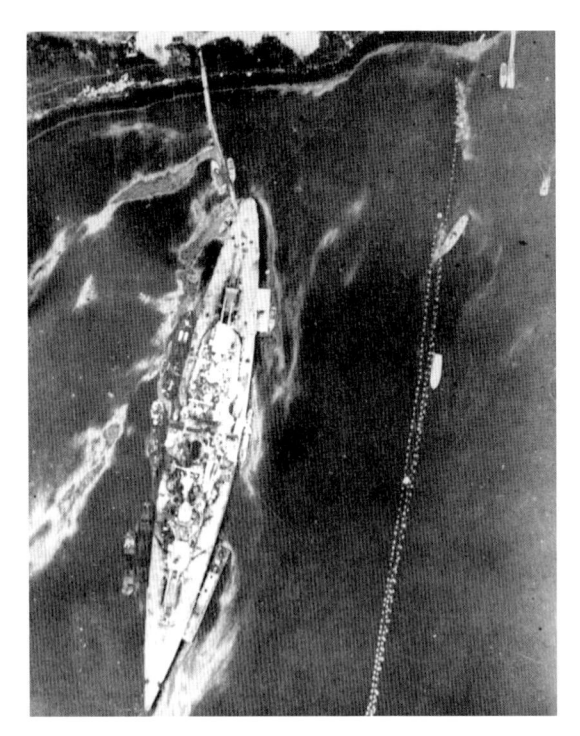

Tirpitz in the Kaafjord in late September 1943, pictured by a PRU aircraft in the immediate aftermath of Operation *Source*, the attack on her by British midget submarines. Oil can be seen leaking from her fuel tanks, while various small support vessels cluster around her, inside her torpedo nets. Astern of her is a walkway linking her to the shore, and the small boat landing stage is on the spit behind her.

planning was displayed again later in July, when Convoy PQ-18 was postponed. The reason was that PRU flights over the Faettenfjord had revealed that the battleship's moorings were empty. This led to Stalin accusing the Royal Navy of shirking a fight at a time when Russian servicemen were fighting for their very survival. Actually *Tirpitz* was still in the Bogenfjord taking part in gunnery exercises. By 24 October she was back in the Faettenfjord. It was there that the British carried out another attack on her. Operation *Title* involved the ferrying of human torpedoes (known as 'chariots') across the North Sea from Shetland, towed beneath Norwegian fishing boats. Once in the Trondheimsfjord they and their two-man crews would be sent off to attack the battleship. The operation was due to be carried out during the night of 30/31 October. However, unexpected rough weather led to the attack being abandoned. At the time the chariots were in the Åsenfjord, just 5 miles from their target.

During all this, the idea of carrying out another bomb attack on the *Tirpitz* never really went away. In June a plan for a Lancaster raid was drawn up, flying from Lossiemouth. This time the bombers would carry either 4,000lb 'cookies' or smaller AP bombs. This scheme was put on hold when the *Tirpitz* spent the summer in the Bogenfjord, as it was beyond effective range. The return of *Tirpitz* to the Faettenfjord led to the scheme being revived. This developed into a daylight attack using 81 Lancasters, but by November the notion was shelved again, largely due to the onset of the long winter nights. Another scheme using US Air Force B-17s was mooted, flying from a base near Murmansk, but this was never fully pursued. So, as 1942 drew to a close *Tirpitz* remained a latent threat.

What almost ended this threat without a bomber being risked was the battle of the Barents Sea. On New Year's Eve 1942 *Lützow*, *Admiral Hipper* and seven destroyers attacked the Arctic Convoy JW-51B. The Germans were driven off by British light cruisers and destroyers, and *Hipper* was damaged. Hitler was so outraged by this failure that he threatened to disarm the Kriegsmarine's larger surface ships and use their guns as coastal defence pieces. He had never grasped the notion of 'a fleet in being', whereby the presence of *Tirpitz*, for example, tied down a larger number of enemy warships. This led to the resignation of Grand Admiral Raeder, and his replacement by the U-boat chief, Admiral Dönitz. For a while the fate of *Tirpitz* looked bleak, but in February Hitler relented, and the battleship was spared. In fact, under Vice Admiral Oskar Kummetz she became the flagship of a battle group that also included *Scharnhorst* and *Lützow*. Meanwhile, in late February, Captain Topp was promoted, and Captain Hans Meyer became the new commander of *Tirpitz*.

By the start of 1943 Bomber Command began exploring other options, including the use of a 'bouncing bomb' of the kind used by Lancasters of 617 Squadron during their attacks on German dams that May. However, despite extensive testing, it never proved suitable for attacks on a battleship. By the spring the daylight heavy bomber raid planned the previous year might have been resurrected but in mid-March a PRU flight revealed that the Faettenfjord was empty again. This caused concern in the Admiralty, who feared that *Tirpitz* might be attempting a break-out into the North Atlantic. Then, on 24 March, she reappeared in the Kaafjord, at the end of the Altenfjord, her base during Operation *Rösselsprung* the previous summer. This would be the battleship's new lair for the next 16 months.

The Kaafjord was well beyond the range of most aircraft flying from Britain. The exception was the US Army Air Force's new B-17F, but while the Americans proved amenable to the

The ship's band of the *Tirpitz* play to celebrate the birthday of the battleship's commander, Captain Topp. The band also gave regular concerts on board, to help boost morale, as well as performing ceremonial duties. In action, the bandsmen served as medical orderlies.

idea of using it for a long-range strike, the RAF opposed the plan, as by this stage of the war their priority was the bombing of Germany by both day and night. So, while plans to use Soviet airfields continued to be unfeasible due to diplomatic bureaucracy, *Tirpitz* was left to her own devices, save for flights by the PRU. In September *Tirpitz*, and *Scharnhorst* sortied to bombard Spitzbergen, in an operation designed as much as a training exercise as a demonstration of naval potential. However, German naval power in the Arctic was about to be dramatically undermined.

At 0812hrs on 22 September *Tirpitz* was rocked by two massive explosions. The cause was large mines, placed there by two British midget submarines, or 'X-Craft'. This attack, codenamed Operation *Source*, had been months in the planning, and involved the towing of six of these X-Craft to the mouth of the Altenfjord by British submarines. Once released, three were to attack *Tirpitz*, two *Scharnhorst* and one *Lützow*. In the end the only two X-Craft to reach their target were *X-6* and *X-7* which laid their charges beneath the *Tirpitz* before they were detected, forced to the surface and their three-man crews captured. The first charge exploded level with the battleship's forward turrets, and jammed the mounting. The second buckled the ship's bottom, causing extensive flooding. The result was that *Tirpitz* was put out of action, and would now need extensive repairs before she was operational again. But instead of returning to a German shipyard, the work would be done *in situ* in the Altenfjord. A steamer carrying 750 civilian workmen was sent north, and through that winter these artisans did what they could to repair the damage.

The second blow to German naval power in the region came on 26 December 1943, at the battle of North Cape. In a scheme dubbed Operation *Ostfront*, *Scharnhorst* sortied from the Altenfjord to intercept the Arctic Convoy JW-55A. The convoy was successfully screened by British cruisers, and the German battlecruiser turned away. Before she could reach the Norwegian coast she was cornered and sunk by the Home Fleet, led by its new commander, Admiral Fraser, whose flagship was the battleship *Duke of York*. Her 14in guns made short work of *Scharnhorst*, which sank, taking all but 22 of her crew down with her.

In a few months, what had once been a powerful German battle group had now been neutralized. That winter, PRU Spitfires as well as Soviet reconnaissance flights reported that the steamer *Monte Rosa* housing the civilian workers was berthed alongside *Tirpitz*, as was a 20-ton floating crane and the repair ship *Neumark*. A flak ship and five destroyers guarded her from a distance, while the fjord was now ringed by anti-aircraft defences and smoke generators, mounted either on the shore or on board moored fishing boats. By late January 1944 the PRU reported that her gun turrets were now able to rotate again, but signal intercepts revealed that she still had engine problems. So, although work on *Tirpitz* was progressing, it would be some while before she was operational.

On the night of 10/11 February a force of 15 Soviet Pe-2 twin-engined bombers took off from Vaenga airfield near Murmansk, each carrying a single 2,000lb bomb. Although the operation began in good visibility thanks to a full moon, by the time the bombers reached the Altenfjord the target area was obscured by squalls of snow. The *Tirpitz* was taken unawares, and there wasn't time to deploy her smoke screen before the bombers arrived. However, owing to the poor visibility only four of the planes spotted the target and were able to release their bombs from 4,000ft. All of them missed the battleship, although the Soviets later claimed that one had been a near miss. Two days later, the Soviets agreed to allow a PRU detachment to be based at Vaenga, and by the end of the month these planes were operational. However, a spate of bad weather and the short days meant that it would be April before these were able to achieve worthwhile results. The images were flown back to Britain by Catalina seaplanes.

This was important, as by the middle of March *Tirpitz* was operational again, although she still had problems with her engines and gun turrets. Only a spell in a German dry dock could fully restore her to her former condition. However, she could steam at 27 knots, despite the vibrations caused by her engine defects. With her guns largely repaired, she could also fight. Consequently the Admiralty still considered her a major threat to convoy operations. Fortunately for them, the Home Fleet now had the strength not only to fully screen these convoys, but also to take offensive action against the *Tirpitz* using naval air power.

Before Operation *Tungsten* commenced, the air crews were briefed on their mission using a detailed scale model of the south-eastern end of the Altenfjord and the Kaafjord. Here, Commander Selwyn Harrison of HMS *Furious* is describing the area's flak defences to the crews of a sub-flight of 830 Squadron's Barracudas.

The Fleet Air Arm offensive 1944

In late January 1944, the Admiralty ordered Admiral Forbes commanding the Home Fleet to draw up plans to attack the *Tirpitz* in the Altenfjord. They added that the ideal time for this would be 7–16 March – the same time as the battleship was carrying out her post-repair trials. The hope was to catch her manoeuvring in the fjord, beyond the range of her shore-based flak batteries and smoke screens. In fact Forbes was one step ahead of the Admiralty. The previous December he had ordered his deputy, Vice Admiral Sir Henry Moore, to draft plans for a naval air strike on *Tirpitz*, while the battleship was still in the Kaafjord. Moore certainly had enough air power at his disposal, and the operation he came up with would involve no fewer than five aircraft carriers and over 100 aircraft. Still, the operation had to wait until late March, when the fleet carrier *Victorious* would rejoin the fleet after a refit. This attack – the largest air strike yet staged by the Fleet Air Arm – was codenamed Operation *Tungsten*.

Operation *Tungsten*

While *Victorious* completed her refit the air crews practised the attack in Loch Eriboll, on the west coast of Scotland. The refit in Liverpool was speeded up, so that by the time a dress rehearsal was staged over the loch on 28 March, *Victorious* was able to take part. Two days later, on 30 March, *Victorious* accompanied Forbes' two battleships as they left Scapa Flow and headed towards the Arctic Sea. Ostensibly Forbes put to sea to cover the sailing of an Arctic Convoy, JW-58. His main aim, though, was to link up with another task force, which had departed in secret

Hellcats of 800 Squadron ranged on the deck of the escort carrier *Empress* on the morning of 3 April 1944, before the start of Operation *Tungsten*. The fleet carrier *Furious* is astern of *Empress*, followed by the escort carriers *Searcher* and *Pursuer*, and an escorting light cruiser.

and was already at sea. This consisted of the carrier *Furious* and the escort carriers *Emperor*, *Fencer*, *Pursuer* and *Searcher*, plus escorts. Once the task forces combined, they would then move into position to the west of North Cape.

The operation was scheduled for 4 April, but the report of good weather over northern Norway encouraged Forbes to bring the attack forward by 24 hours, to 3 April. The two forces rendezvoused in the afternoon of 2 April, and after detaching *Victorious* to join the carrier group, Forbes with his battleships and their escorts left the rest of the force, and moved away to the north-east, where he could cover both the carrier group and the convoy. By dawn on 3 April, the carriers and their escorts, now redesignated as Force 7, were in position. This was 77 nautical miles from the coast and 124 nautical miles north-west of the *Tirpitz*, which the PRU reported was still moored in the Kaafjord. Best of all for the British, it appears that their presence was completely undetected, despite the clear skies and excellent visibility. It couldn't have been a better start to Operation *Tungsten*.

The main strike force was made up of 32 Barracuda dive bombers, divided into two wings, each theoretically consisting of 16 planes. To help the speed of flying off, there had

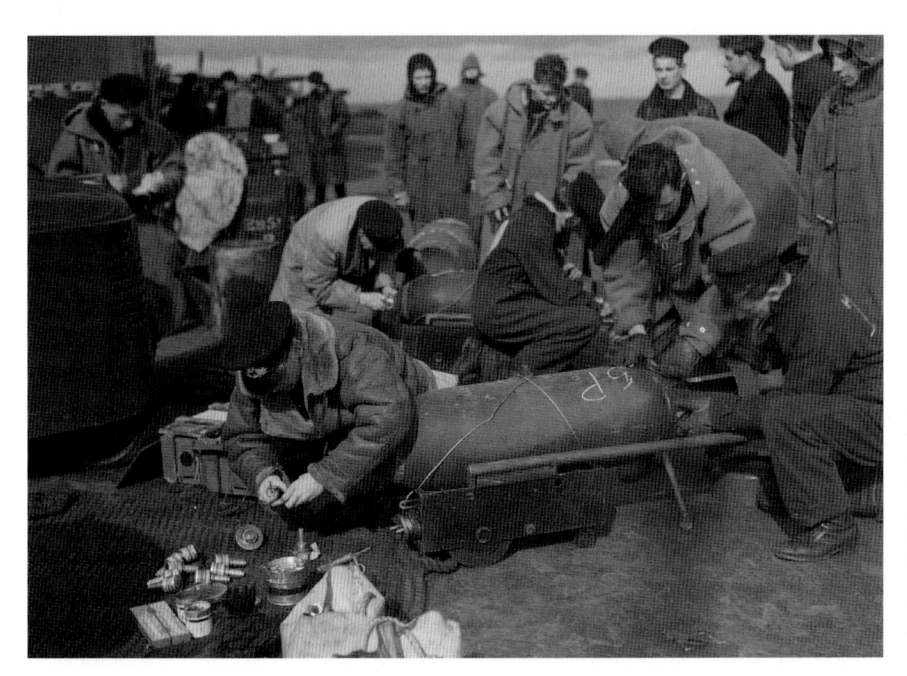

Fleet Air Arm armourers fusing 600lb AS bombs on the deck of *Victorious* before the launch of Operation *Tungsten*, on 3 April 1944. The chalked '5P' on the nearest bomb indicates that it is destined for Barracuda 5P of 827 Squadron.

been a bit of 'cross-decking' – the moving from one ship to another, so that both *Furious* and *Victorious* carried part of each wing. Using the two carriers simultaneously would greatly speed the take-off and assembly of each strike. The first of these, 8 Wing, was made up of Barracudas from 827 and 830 Squadrons, while 52 Wing, which would fly off second, consisted of 829 and 821 Squadrons. 'Top cover' fighters would be provided by the 21 Corsairs of 1834 and 1836 Squadrons, flying from *Victorious*. For escort during the flight, 40 Wildcats of 881, 882, 896 and 898 Squadrons launching from *Searcher* and *Pursuer*, and 20 Hellcats of 800 and 804 Squadrons from *Emperor*, would protect the Barracudas from the Luftwaffe. So, the strike was made up over 100 aircraft, more than half of which were fighters.

Finally, a combat air patrol (CAP) of 18 Seafires of 800 and 801 Squadrons operating from *Furious* would form a protective shield around the task force to safeguard it from enemy air attacks, while the 12 Swordfish of 842 Squadron embarked in *Fencer* would fly anti-submarine patrols around it. The whole complex operation had been planned by Vice Admiral Moore, who was now on board the battleship *Anson*, which formed part of Forbes' distant covering force. While he retained overall direction of the operation, due to radio silence direct hands-on control fell to Rear Admiral Bisset in the anti-aircraft cruiser *Royalist*, commanding Force 7. The plan called for the dive bombers to carry out their attack in two waves, preceded by the Hellcats and Wildcats, which would swoop in and strafe both the battleship and the flak batteries.

The Barracudas carried a mixture of ordnance: AP bombs, three 500lb SAPs and either three 500lb MCs or two 600lb anti-submarine bombs. All of the Barracudas were ordered to begin their dive from 10,000ft, and release their ordnance at 3,500ft. The idea was that the large bombs would pierce the battleship's armoured deck, while the smaller bombs would cause extensive damage to her superstructure, sensors and weapons mounts. The idea behind the anti-submarine ordnance was that they would be just as effective for this as conventional bombs, with the added bonus that if they missed the ship then they would explode in the fjord, where they might still cause underwater damage. Zero Hour, when the flying off began, was set at 0415hrs.

The Hellcats of 804 Squadron lined up for take-off on the small flight deck of the escort carrier *Empress*, at the commencement of Operation *Tungsten*. These ten fighter aircraft would form part of the second wave during that morning's attack on the *Tirpitz*.

During the voyage north the air crews all had the chance to study models of the Altenfjord, and so were familiar with the geography of the area. A final briefing was held at 0330hrs, and then at 0416hrs 11 Corsairs were flown off from *Victorious*. Unlike the other planes they had spent the night ranged on the carrier's flight deck, and so while the briefing was being held the flight deck staff were kept busy de-icing them. Still, they all took off successfully, and were followed eight minutes later by the 21 Barracudas of 8 Wing, launched simultaneously from *Furious* and *Victorious*. While they were taking off, the Hellcats and Wildcats were launched from the three escort carriers and formed up above the bombers. The second wave would follow an hour behind the first. By 0437hrs the first wave of the strike had formed up, and it set off towards the target, flying on an east-south-easterly course of 120 degrees. The flying time to the target was around 50 minutes.

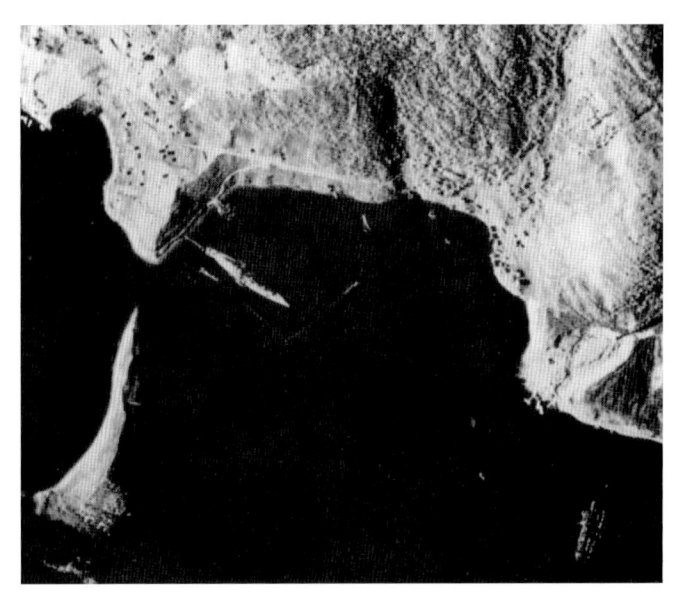

At first the strike force stayed low, below 4,000ft, to avoid detection by German coastal radar. Then, when they were 25 miles from the coast, the Barracudas climbed to their optimal dive-bombing height of 10,000ft. The Corsairs circled above them, while on the flanks of the dive bombers the smaller fighters had to circle and weave, to keep pace with the slower strike aircraft. They reached the coast at 0515hrs near the small island of Loppa, some 40 nautical miles north-west of their target. The route took them over snow-covered mountains and two smaller fjords, the Øksfjord and the Langfjord, both of which were used as destroyer anchorages. Sure enough, some crews saw two ships open fire, but they were well out of range. Then, 10 miles or three minutes' flying time from their target, Lieutenant Commander Baker-Falkner, who commanded the strike, ordered 830 Squadron to tuck itself in behind 827 Squadron. He planned to attack in a long single column of bombers.

The *Tirpitz* in her first mooring place in the Kaafjord, in the little bay of Barbrudalen, on the north-western side of the fjord. The photograph was taken by a British PRU flight. The battleship was screened by torpedo nets, and a walkway from her stern led to the spit astern of her, and a small boat dock. *Tirpitz* was in this mooring during Operation *Tungsten*, but in the spring of 1944 she moved to a second mooring, 300 yards to the south-east.

During Operation *Tungsten*, on 3 April 1944, *Tirpitz* was taken by surprise as she was putting to sea. This shows her after the attack by the first wave, manoeuvring in the Kaafjord, with her protective smoke screen only just beginning to cover the fjord. A few minutes later she was attacked by the second wave of Barracudas.

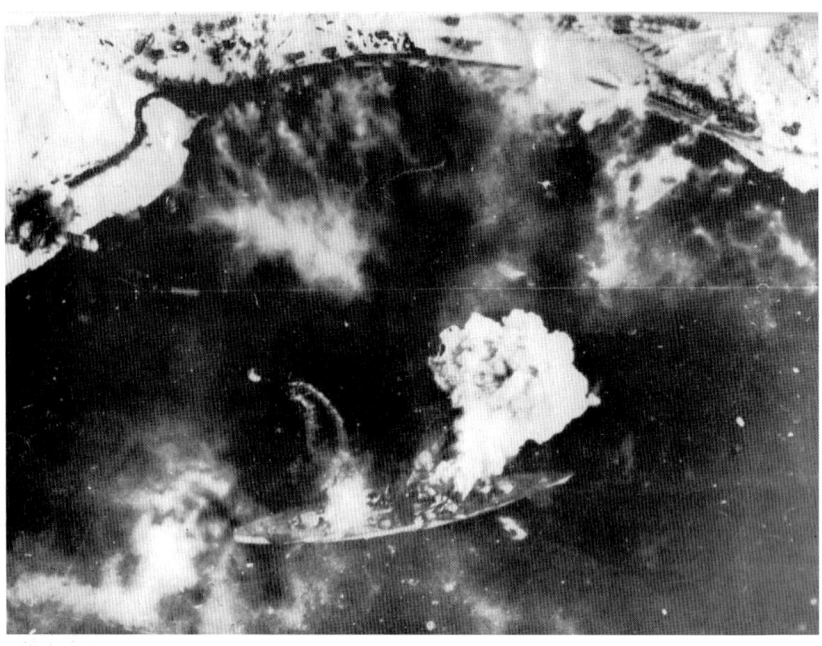

This photograph of *Tirpitz* was taken during Operation *Tungsten*, on 3 April 1944, shortly after the end of the first wave's attack. The battleship has been hit, and smoke is pouring from the port side of its forward superstructure. The battleship is moving slowly into the fjord, while the shore-mounted smoke generators are only just beginning to spread a covering layer of white smoke over the area.

A young New Zealand airman from 827 Squadron remembered flying towards a final ridge in front of the fjord: 'Then suddenly, with a surge we were over the top, and there beneath us lay the *Tirpitz*, and in exactly the place we'd been told to look for it.' For the crew of the battleship, the appearance of the aircraft came as a complete surprise. She was just about to slip her moorings and put to sea, to carry out speed trials near the seaward end of the Altenfjord, and many of her crew were on deck, getting ready to cast off. From the bridge, Captain Meyer sounded 'Action Stations', and the flak crews ran to their posts, while the order was given to start releasing the smoke screen. By then, though, it was too late. The British aircraft were upon them. As his Barracudas lined up to start their dive-bombing run, Baker-Falkner gave the order 'All fighters – anti-flak'. So, while the Corsairs stayed aloft, watching out for the Luftwaffe fighters that never appeared, the Wildcats and Hellcats swooped in low, shooting up anything they could find.

The Wildcats of 882 Squadron led the way, dropping down over the hills to fly up the fjord in a straggling line abreast, guns blazing. It was 0528hrs. The bullets from their 50-calibre Browning machine guns tore into the German sailors, trying to find cover on the battleship's exposed upper decks. The other fighters followed, and within seconds *Tirpitz* resembled a charnel house. However, this was only the start. A minute behind them, at 0529hrs, the first of the Barracudas began their attack. They swooped down towards the target in a ragged line, two or three planes wide. Most of the pilots were new to the job, even though the strike leader was an old hand and a veteran of the Taranto raid. So, while the official dive angle was 45 degrees, most left it a little late to start their dive from 10,000ft, and so had to dive more steeply. At 65 degrees, a dive steeper than the Barracuda was really designed for, a few pilots experienced a negative g-force, which made their job even harder.

The prescribed release height for the 1,600lb bombs was 3,500ft, but in the excitement most of the inexperienced crews held on a little longer, and most bombs were dropped from about 2,500ft. As soon as they released their ordnance, the Barracudas would bank, then try to dodge the flak which was now flying around them. Bombs of various sizes were hitting the *Tirpitz*, which soon became shrouded in smoke and flame. The dive bombers behind the first had to aim into the middle of what looked like a blazing inferno. Most crews watched as their bombs hurled down into this, but fresh explosions and flashes suggested they'd scored hits. As Baker-Falkner led his aircraft through a gap in the hills on the north-west side of the Kaafjord, he glanced at his watch. The attack had lasted exactly one minute.

During the strike, some of the air crew had noticed columns of white smoke rising from the shore. These were the smoke screen generators, started up too late to make any difference. However, the blanket would be in place by the time the next wave arrived over the ship. As the last flak guns fell silent the crew of the *Tirpitz* began to take stock. The attack had taken them completely by surprise, so only a few of the ship's flak guns had been able to open fire before the attackers had gone. Those that had done so had quickly run out of ammunition, as the handlers bringing fresh rounds forward were either hit or unable to bring them up from below decks. Both the strafing and the bombs had hit these flak crews badly, as well as the sailors on the exposed forecastle and quarterdeck, preparing to unmoor ship. Still, those who survived obeyed their orders and pulled their dead companions aside so they could slip the lines. That at least allowed the *Tirpitz* to manoeuvre before any more planes arrived.

Meanwhile, the second wave had taken off. The first Barracudas flew off from *Furious* and *Victorious* at 0525hrs – just as the first wave were approaching the target. The launch hadn't been straightforward – one plane from 829 Squadron remained behind with engine trouble, while another crashed into the sea just after take-off and its three-man crew were killed. That left 19 Barracudas in the strike, and these formed up as before, with the Corsairs from *Victorious* circling above them and the smaller fighters forming up on either side of the dive bombers. As they crossed the coast at Loppa they saw a column of black smoke ahead of them. It was the *Tirpitz* burning, 40 miles and 12 minutes' flying time away. On the way the strike commander, Lieutenant Commander Rance, ordered each squadron to form into its own column. He knew the flak crews would be fully alerted, so he planned to offer a less conspicuous target for the flak gunners to aim at.

Barracudas returning from their strike on the *Tirpitz* on 3 April 1944, photographed from the deck of the fleet carrier *Furious*. In the distance is the *Victorious*, with both carriers preparing to land their aircraft. This was done one plane at a time, with the deck crews having to clear it away before the next Barracuda made its approach. Priority was given to damaged aircraft.

Operation *Tungsten*

Force 7 (Rear Admiral Bisset, flying flag in *Royalist*)
Fleet carriers (2×): *Furious, Victorious*
Escort carriers (4×): *Searcher, Pursuer, Emperor, Fencer*
Light cruisers (2×): *Royalist* (flag), *Belfast*
Destroyers (6×): *Marne, Matchless, Meteor, Milne, Ursa, Undaunted*

First strike
8 TBR Wing: 12× Barracudas (827 Squadron) from *Victorious* (two with 1× 1,600lb AP, eight with 3× 500lb MCs, two with 2× 600lb ASs); 9× Barracudas (830 Squadron) from *Furious* (five with 1× 1,600lb AP, four with 3× 500lb SAPs)
11× Corsairs (1834 Squadron) from *Victorious*
10× Hellcats (800 Squadron) from *Emperor*
10× Wildcats (881 Squadron) from *Pursuer*
10× Wildcats (882 Squadron) from *Searcher*

Second strike
52 TBR Wing: 11× Barracudas (829 Squadron) from *Victorious** (four with 1× 1,600lb AP, four with 3× 500lb SAPs, three with 500lb MCs); 8× Barracudas (821 Squadron) from *Furious*** (all with 3× 500lb SAPs)
10× Corsairs (1836 Squadron) from *Victorious*
10× Hellcats (804 Squadron) from *Emperor*
10× Wildcats (896 Squadron) from *Pursuer*
9× Wildcats (896 Squadron) from *Searcher*

* There were originally 12× Barracudas in the wave, but one failed to take off due to engine failure.
** There were originally 9× Barracudas in the wave, but one crashed in the sea on take-off, killing its three-man crew.

Combat Air Patrol (CAP)
9× Seafires (801 Squadron) from *Furious*
9× Seafires (802 Squadron) from *Furious*
8× Wildcats (842 Squadron) from *Fencer*

Anti-Submarine Patrol (ASP)
12× Swordfish (842 Squadron) from *Fencer*

58   THE CAMPAIGN

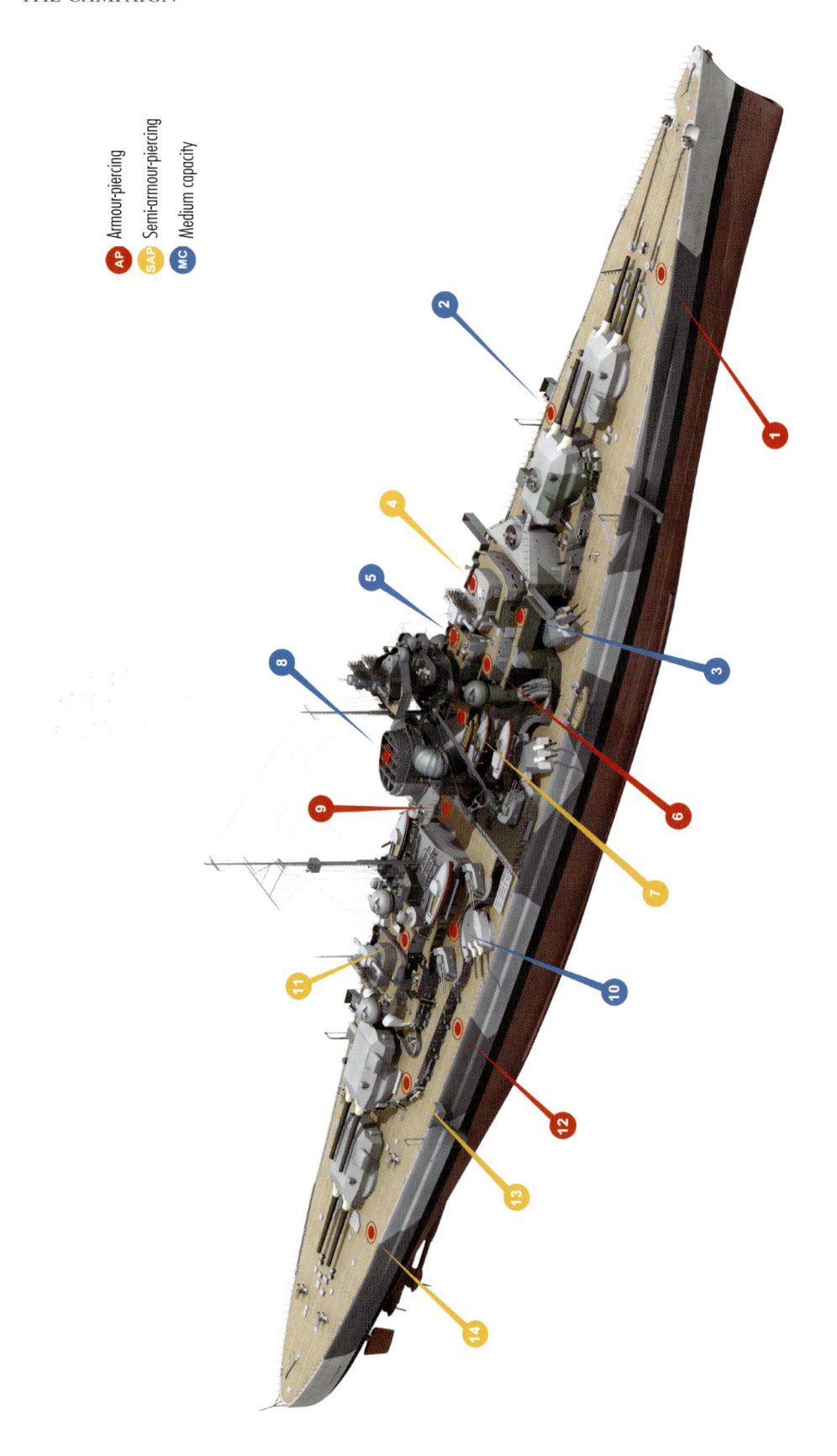

AP Armour-piercing
SAP Semi-armour-piercing
MC Medium capacity

OPPOSITE DAMAGE INFLICTED DURING OPERATION *TUNGSTEN*

This diagram is based on the Fleet Air Arm assessment of damage inflicted on *Tirpitz* during Operation *Tungsten* (3 April 1944), compiled a day after the attack. It replaced an earlier more optimistic account sent to the Admiralty immediately after the completion of the operation. In addition, considerable fire damage was reported in four locations – abaft 'Bruno' turret, around 'Caesar' turret and in the vicinities of secondary turrets PII and SIII.

First wave
A 1,600lb AP hit on starboard side of forecastle, forward of 'Anton' turret (**1**)
A 1,600lb AP hit on port side of catapult deck (**9**)
A 600lb AS (MC) hit on the funnel (**8**) [initially placed to port of funnel]
A 500lb SAP hit on the bridge (**4**) [initially placed starboard side of catapult deck]
One or two 500lb MC hits on port side of 'Bruno' turret (**2**)
A probable 500lb SAP hit on port side of after superstructure (**11**) [initially placed on catapult deck]
A probable 500lb SAP hit on starboard side of boat deck (**7**) [initially placed on catapult deck]
A probable 1,600lb AP hit on starboard side of foremast (**6**) [initially placed on catapult deck]

Second wave
A 1,600lb AP hit on starboard of after superstructure (**12**) [initially placed on hanger]
One or two 500lb MC hits on starboard beam, just inboard of SIII secondary turret (**10**)
A probable 500lb SAP hit on starboard side of quarterdeck (**14**)
A probable 500lb SAP hit on starboard side of 'Caesar' turret (**13**)
A probable 500lb MC hit on secondary turret SI (**3**)
A probable 500lb MC hit immediately forward of foremast (**5**)

In fact, despite the downgrading of the initial damage assessment, only three 1,600lb AP bombs hit the ship, at locations (**1**), (**6**), (**9**), and (**12**), as well as five 500lb SAP bombs at (**4**), (**7**), (**11**), (**13**), and (**14**) and four 500lb MC bombs at (**2**), (**3**), (**5**), (**8**), and (**10**). However, several near misses caused most of the flooding suffered by the battleship during the attack.

Once again, on reaching the Kaafjord from the north the Hellcats and Wildcats went in first, the former strafing the flak batteries along the north-western side of the fjord, while the Wildcats targeted the battleship herself. Rance noticed that the heavier flak batteries were setting their shells to burst at 3,000ft, but by then most of the Barracudas had dived through it and had released their bombs. By now the *Tirpitz* was manoeuvring slowly in the fjord, and when the second wave appeared she was lying across it, so that her starboard flak guns had a clear field of fire up the fjord. However, the air crews described her fire as light – they had more problems from the flak batteries on the shore. One Barracuda was shot down though – a plane from 829 Squadron, which was hit as it passed over the battleship. It dropped its ordnance, but crashed into the hillside on the south side of the fjord, exploding in a ball of flame. Then the fjord was clear again. Once again the attack had lasted no longer than a minute.

The *Tirpitz* looked a real shambles, with jagged, twisted metal everywhere, bomb holes in the deck, spouting smoke and flame, and everywhere the smell of burning. Below decks there was serious flooding, and the ship was listing slightly to starboard. Still, the damage control parties set to work, and soon the fires were extinguished and the flooding contained or stopped completely. Then the officers took stock. A total of 122 crewmen had been killed during the attack, and another 316 wounded. These included Captain Meyer, who was badly wounded as he watched the first wave attack his ship. His second-in-command, Captain Wolfe Junge, took over, and it was he who manoeuvred the battleship out into the fjord. While the ship looked a scene of disorder, the damage control reports proved encouraging. Much of the damage was largely superficial, and no bombs had penetrated the ship's armoured decks or put her guns out of action. Despite the mess, the *Tirpitz* was still operational.

Barracudas flying over the Altenfjord, on their way to the Kaafjord. During the Fleet Air Arm strikes of 1944, the Barracudas flew in at around 5,000ft, with the escorting Corsairs flying above them. They then dived to 3,500ft or less to release their ordnance – if they could see the Tirpitz *through her protective smoke screen.*

In all, the ship's Chief Engineering Officer reported that she had been hit by 12 bombs, and four near misses had caused further damage. One of these near misses from a 1,600lb bomb had caused most of the flooding, as its blast on hitting the water had ripped a hole in the hull below the waterline. Three of them hit the ship, but failed to penetrate the armoured deck, largely because they were dropped from too low an altitude. This deck was one deck below the upper deck of the ship, and although they had gone through this upper less-well protected deck, smashing up the wardroom and a galley, the ship's armoured citadel remained undamaged. While the other hits from the smaller ordnance had caused extensive damage to the battleship's superstructure and flak defences, none of these was seen as of critical importance. However, with so many of their comrades dead or wounded, the morale of the crew had taken a hefty blow.

Back on board the carriers the air crews felt they'd inflicted more damage than they actually had. The Barracuda crews all reported seeing the battleship on fire and that their bombs had hit her. They reported seeing explosions, smoke and flame, and all the signs of damage. From the radio report from the strike leader, Vice Admiral Bisset concluded in a signal to Forbes and Moore: 'It is certain that *Tirpitz* is badly hit by first strike.' The debrief of the crews confirmed this, and after studying photographs taken during the raid, Bisset concluded that *Tirpitz* had been struck by 17 bombs, including three 1,600lb armour-piercing ones, which landed near the forward superstructure. That evening, he signalled to his two superiors that 'I believe *Tirpitz* to now be useless as a warship.'

On board *Anson*, Moore had planned to send his planes in again the following day. Now, though, he concluded that there was no need to risk the crews, and he called off the attack. By the afternoon of 6 April the carriers returned to Scapa Flow, their arrival cheered by the other ships of the fleet. Celebratory signals arrived from both the King and the Prime Minister. The celebrations were premature. PRU flights over the coming days and weeks revealed that although *Tirpitz* had been badly battered, she was still afloat, and that the damage appeared largely superficial. So, on 13 April, the First Sea Lord, Sir Andrew Cunningham, called both Forbes and Moore and ordered them to carry out another attack. Admiral Fraser was reluctant, as he felt the efforts would be wasted, but eventually he acquiesced, and Moore was ordered to draw up fresh plans.

From *Planet* to *Mascot*

Part of Fraser's reluctance was that he was convinced that if the *Tirpitz* was only lightly damaged after a surprise attack, his naval airmen would have much less chance of success against a fully alerted target. This was particularly true in light of fresh evidence that the Germans were strengthening the anti-aircraft defences around the Kaafjord, and upgrading their chain of coastal radar stations. These were due to be fully operational by the end of June. However, he agreed to let Moore carry out another attack, codenamed Operation *Planet*.

It would use the same carrier force that had participated in *Tungsten*, except this time the escort carrier *Striker* replaced the *Fencer*.

The carriers sailed from Scapa Flow on 21 April, accompanied by Moore in the battleship *Anson*, and a screen of escorts. They reached their flying-off position on 24 April, and the crews prepared to launch the strike shortly before midnight. Then, late that afternoon word reached Moore that the weather had deteriorated over the Altenfjord and any chance of carrying out a successful attack had gone. So, Operation *Planet* was cancelled, and the task force returned south, managing only a small consolation prize of a successful attack on coastal shipping off Bødo, south of Narvik. On 15 May the Home Fleet tried again. This time the attack on the *Tirpitz* was codenamed Operation *Brawn*. The carrier strike against the *Tirpitz* would be carried out by *Furious* and *Victorious*. This time, no escort carriers would take part. In this operation, 28 Barracudas formed the main striking force, escorted by 28 Corsairs, four Seafires and four Wildcats. They took off successfully late in the evening, but as the aircraft reached the Altenfjord they found the whole area was blanketed in low cloud. The strike force was recalled, without even venturing near the Kaafjord.

Just ten days later, on 25 May, Moore and his carriers left Scapa Flow again, and three days later they were in their now familiar launch point to the east of the Altenfjord. This attack, codenamed Operation *Tiger Claw*, was similar to its predecessor in terms of scale, with just *Furious* and *Victorious* involved, but it was similar in outcome too. Once again the strike was cancelled due to bad weather, although this time it happened before the strike was launched, and the carrier group headed south again, its air crews taking out their frustration on coastal convoys near Ålesund.

Undeterred, the Home Fleet decided to launch yet another attack, codenamed Operation *Mascot*, which was scheduled to be carried out in mid-July. This time the meteorologists predicted fair weather and clear skies. In these northern latitudes the summer sun never properly sets, so the operation was timed to take place when the 'midnight sun' was at its lowest. The day before, Admiral Fraser had hauled down his flag as commander of the Home Fleet. His place was taken by his newly promoted deputy, Admiral Moore, who was a staunch advocate of naval air power. As in previous Home Fleet air strikes Moore played a major part in the planning. For Operation *Mascot*, he planned to draw on considerable naval

Operation *Mascot*

Home Fleet (Admiral Moore, flying flag in *Duke of York*)
Fleet carriers (3×): *Formidable, Furious, Indefatigable*
Battleships (1×): *Duke of York* (flag)
Heavy cruisers (2×): *Devonshire, Kent*
Light cruisers (2×): *Bellona, Jamaica*
Destroyers (16×): *Burges, Bulldog, Hoste, Inman, Marne, Matchless, Milne, Musketeer, Nubian, Scourge, Verulam, Vigilant, Virago, Volage*, plus *Algonquin, Sioux* (both Royal Canadian Navy)

Strike aircraft
8 TBR Wing: 12× Barracudas (827 Squadron) from *Formidable* (six with 1× 1,000lb AP, six with 3× 500lb SAPs); 10× Barracudas (830 Squadron) from *Furious* (six with 1× 1,600lb AP, four with 3× 500lb SAPs)
9 TBR Wing 12× Barracudas (820 Squadron) from *Indefatigable* (six with 1× 1,000lb AP, six with 3× 500lb SAPs); 10× Barracudas (826 Squadron) from *Indefatigable* (five with 1× 1,600lb AP, five with 3× 500lb SAPs)
18× Corsairs (1841 Squadron) from *Formidable*
12× Fireflys (1770 Squadron) from *Indefatigable*
18× Hellcats (1840 Squadron) from *Furious*

Combat Air Patrol (CAP)
12× Seafires (880 Squadron) from *Furious*
16× Seafires (894 Squadron) from *Indefatigable*
8× Wildcats (842 Squadron) from *Fencer*

Anti-Submarine Patrol (ASP)
3× Swordfish (842 Squadron) from *Furious*
2× Barracudas (830 Squadron) from *Furious*
2× Barracudas (826 Squadron) from *Indefatigable*

aviation resources, committing three fleet carriers to the operation – *Formidable*, *Furious* and *Indefatigable*. *Victorious* was no longer available, as she had been ordered to the Indian Ocean, so the newly completed *Indefatigable* took her place.

Operation *Mascot* would involve 48 Barracudas, flying from *Formidable* and *Indefatigable*, escorted by 18 Corsairs, 18 Hellcats and 12 Fireflies. Moore would command the fleet from his flagship *Duke of York*, while the carriers were controlled by Rear Admiral Rhoderick McGrigor, flying his flag in the *Indefatigable*. Once again the air crews practised their attacks over Loch Eribol, before the force sailed from Scapa Flow on 14 July. The attack was scheduled for the night of 16/17 July. By the late afternoon of 16 July the task force was in place, a little to the north of its position in previous operations. The Corsairs took off from *Formidable* at midnight, followed by the Barracudas, which were split into two wings. At 0135hrs, the strike force was fully assembled, and it set off towards the *Tirpitz*, flying at 50ft to avoid showing up on radar. There was no sign of enemy aircraft, and for once there was no low cloud to obscure the target.

However, this time, at 0200hrs, the Germans picked up the low-flying strike on their recently improved radar system, and the *Tirpitz* was warned even before the strike reached the coast. Just as importantly, a newly installed set of German electronic stations began jamming the British radio signals. A few minutes later, at 0210hrs, *Tirpitz* began deploying her smoke screen, which had recently been expanded by adding more smoke generators at the top of the heights overlooking the Kaafjord. Also, since *Tungsten* in April, the Germans had installed a mountaintop observation post on the crest of the high ground on the north-western side of the fjord, and it had a direct communications link to the battleship. Not only did this serve as a lookout, reporting on the course, number and height of the approaching planes, but the post also contained a flak direction team.

As for the flak itself, thanks to the arrival of new airburst shells, the *Tirpitz* was able to add the weight of her main and secondary guns to the flak barrage. In all, some 39 38cm flak shells were fired during the attack, as well as another 359 rounds from her secondary 15cm guns. While of limited use save as a deterrent, these larger shells added greatly to the strength of the flak barrage thrown up from the battleship by her dedicated 10.5cm flak guns. In addition her 3.7cm and 20mm guns were sending up streams of tracer, as were the flak batteries lining the fjord. It was into this maelstrom of smoke and fire that the strike aircraft began their attack, at around 0234hrs. As before it was the fighters who led the way, the Hellcats and Fireflies swooping down into the fjord to strafe the battleship and any flak batteries they spotted on the shore. In fact the target was completely obscured by smoke. The best the pilots could do was to fire into the murk. They did, however, manage to strafe the German destroyer *Z-33*, patrolling in the mouth of the Kaafjord, as well as a small patrol boat – a converted trawler – which duly ran aground.

Then, at 0249hrs, the Barracudas began their attack. Once again there was no sign of the battleship, but the dive bombers made their run, in batches of four or six planes at a time. Afterwards, only two pilots claimed they were actually able to see the *Tirpitz* through the smoke. Some air crews avoided releasing their bombs, as they found nothing to aim at, while others released their ordnance in the direction of the flak climbing out of the smoke towards them. All they had to show for their efforts was one near miss. However, other targets presented themselves – one Barracuda released its bombs over a flak position and another made an unsuccessful bombing run on the hapless *Z-33*.

Within 20 minutes it was all over. The planes climbed out of the fjord and headed back to their carriers. Two aircraft were lost during the attack – a Corsair and a Barracuda – but several other dive bombers were damaged, and were lucky to make it back to their ship. The Corsair crashed in the fjord, and the pilot was rescued and captured, while the Barracuda managed to reach the carrier group but was unable to land, and was forced to crash-land in the sea next to the *Indefatigable*. Her crew were rescued by a destroyer. One of the damaged

Corsairs of 1841 Squadron ranged on the deck of HMS *Formidable* being prepared for take-off during Operation *Goodwood*. Each of them carries a long-range fuel tank. Astern of the carrier, the heavy cruiser *Berwick* is deployed as part of the task force screen, providing extra anti-aircraft protection for the carriers.

Hellcats managed to land, but the aircraft was so badly damaged that it was written off, and thrown overboard. Yet again a Fleet Air Arm attack had ended in disappointment. Moore planned to repeat the attack the following morning at 0800hrs. The strike aircraft were actually ranged on deck for this second attack, when the appearance of fog, both around the carriers and in the target area, led to the attack being cancelled.

Tirpitz had survived Operation *Mascot* unscathed, and work continued on repairing the damage suffered during Operation *Tungsten*. Hundreds of civilian workers had cut away her damaged superstructure, repaired her guns, and patched the holes in her deck – often using wood and concrete if nothing else was available. Although her captain described her as fully combat ready, the battleship had never fully recovered from the damage she suffered from Operation *Source*, and more recently from *Tungsten*. At best, she could steam at 20 knots, which meant she could be overhauled by just about every surface warship in the Home Fleet. Still, at the end of July she left her moorings, and ventured out into the mouth of the Altenfjord, where she conducted various exercises, protected by a watchful screen of destroyers. When the Admiralty learned of this they feared that *Tirpitz* was ready to carry out operations again, and so once again she would be a threat to the Arctic Convoys. So, she had to be dealt with. By then, though, the Home Fleet was busy planning an even larger and more sustained operation. This time, the carrier group would keep launching attacks until the job was done.

Operation *Goodwood*

The Arctic Convoys had been suspended since May 1944, due to the coming of the long summer days. War materials were stockpiling in Britain, Canada and the United States, so it was imperative that they should resume in mid-August, when the days were beginning to get shorter again. Despite her reduced abilities the *Tirpitz* remained a potent threat to these convoys, particularly if she sortied under the cover of German aircraft. So the First Sea Lord, Admiral of the Fleet Cunningham, ordered the Commander-in-Chief of the Home Fleet to do what he could to sink the battleship, or at least to neutralize her. As a result, Admiral Moore and his staff set about planning what would become the biggest British carrier operation of the war.

This operation would serve a double purpose. Not only would it deal with the *Tirpitz*, but by putting to sea the Home Fleet could also cover the first Arctic Convoy of the season.

The 34 merchant ships of convoy JW-59 were due to leave Loch Ewe on 15 August, bound for Murmansk. They had a strong escort, including the escort carriers *Striker* and *Vindex*, and the Soviet battleship *Archangelsk* (formerly the British *Royal Sovereign*). However, the powerful carrier strike force could also support the convoy if required. On 18 August, Force 1 left Scapa Flow and headed towards the Arctic Sea. It consisted of Moore's flagship *Duke of York*, the fleet carriers *Formidable*, *Furious* and *Indefatigable*, and a screen of escorts. These were the carriers which had spearheaded Operation *Mascot*. Force 2 accompanied it, a much smaller group centred on the escort carriers *Nabob* and *Trumpeter*. Together, though, these carriers gave Moore the chance to launch an even larger strike than he had done during Operation *Tungsten*.

Just as importantly, Force 9 was also heading north – a group of two fleet tankers and their escorts, which gave Moore the ability to linger on station for several days. This reduced the risk of the whole operation being cancelled due to bad weather, and also allowed Moore to carry out flying operations for up to nine days. This meant that more than one strike against the *Tirpitz* could be attempted. On the evening of 20 August the carriers arrived at their flying-off position to the north-west of the Altenfjord, and as far as Moore could tell, their presence hadn't been detected. The first strike was scheduled for the following morning. However, bad weather intervened and the attack was postponed for a day. Moore used the opportunity to refuel his screen of destroyers and frigates, so that they could remain on station.

The plan was to carry out the strike with the Barracudas armed with a single 11,600lb AP bomb apiece. As in previous operations the Corsairs would provide 'top cover', along with the Fireflies and a squadron of Seafires. This time, though, the Corsairs also carried 500lb bombs, so they could dive-bomb the target if the opportunity arose. The Hellcats would provide close escort, but carried 500lb bombs as well. Meanwhile other Barracudas would fly on anti-submarine patrols around the task force, while Seafires and Wildcats would screen it from enemy air attacks. The large number of Seafires carried showed just how serious a threat

Operation *Goodwood*

Home Fleet
Commander-in-chief: Admiral Moore, in *Duke of York*
Second-in-command: Vice Admiral McGrigor, in *Indefatigable*

Force 1
Battleships (1×): *Duke of York* (flag)
Fleet carriers (3×): *Formidable, Furious, Indefatigable*
Heavy cruisers (2×): *Berwick, Devonshire*
Destroyers (14×): *Cambrian, Myngs* (flotilla leader), *Scorpion, Scourge, Serapis, Verulam, Vigilant, Virago, Volage, Whirlwind, Wrangler, Stord* (Royal Norwegian Navy), *Algonquin, Sioux* (both Royal Canadian Navy)

Force 2
Escort carriers (2×): *Nabob, Trumpeter*
Heavy cruisers (1×): *Kent*
Frigates (6×): *Aylmer, Bickerton, Bligh, Grindall, Keats, Kempthorne* (all 5th Escort Group)

Force 9
Destroyer (1×): *Nubian*

Corvettes (3×): *Poppy, Dianella, Starwort*
Fleet oilers (2×): *Black Ranger, Blue Ranger*

Air assets
12× Barracudas (827 Squadron) from *Furious*
12× Barracudas (820 Squadron) from *Indefatigable*
12× Barracudas (826 Squadron) from *Formidable*
12× Barracudas (828 Squadron) from *Formidable*
18× Corsairs (1841 Squadron) from *Formidable*
12× Corsairs (1842 Squadron) from *Formidable*
12× Hellcats (1840 Squadron) from *Indefatigable*
8× Avengers (846 Squadron) from *Trumpeter*
12× Avengers (852 Squadron) from *Nabob*
6× Wildcats (846 Squadron) from *Trumpeter*
4× Wildcats (852 Squadron) from *Nabob*
12× Fireflies (1770 Squadron) from *Indefatigable*
12× Seafires (801 Squadron) from *Furious*
12× Seafires (880 Squadron) from *Furious*
16× Seafires (887 Squadron) from *Indefatigable*
16× Seafires (894 Squadron) from *Indefatigable*

Moore considered the German bombers to be. Finally, the Avengers carried in the escort carriers would drop mines in the Kaafjord to seal the *Tirpitz* off from the sea.

At 0530hrs on 22 August, with the promise of better flying conditions to come, Moore made the decision to launch the strike at 0830hrs that morning. However, the continued bad weather led to a postponement, and it was 1100hrs when the Corsairs took off from *Formidable* and climbed above the carriers. The rest followed, and by 1150hrs the strike force was on its way to its target. It consisted of 31 Barracudas, drawn from all four squadrons, as well as 24 Corsairs, 11 Fireflies, nine Hellcats and eight Seafires. The Avengers were left behind on the escort carriers, as there were only enough mines for one operation. As the planes couldn't land with them if the sortie was aborted, and would have to ditch them in the sea, Moore decided to wait for better flying conditions before he used them. The strike force flew towards the coast at 500ft, and only started to climb to 10,000ft when it got within 15 miles of the coast.

However, the Norwegian coast ahead of them was blanketed in a thick low cloud, at 1,500ft. This meant it would be impossible to carry out a successful dive bombing, so the strike leader, Lieutenant Commander West, ordered the Barracudas and Corsairs to return to the carriers. The fighters pressed on, though, seeking out targets to attack. The Seafires strafed Banak airfield and a nearby seaplane base, the Fireflies did the same to flak positions around the Kaafjord, while at 1249hrs the Hellcats attacked the *Tirpitz*. The Germans were taken by surprise, so at first flak was relatively light. One Hellcat claimed to have hit the battleship just behind her forward superstructure, but otherwise she was unscathed. One of the Hellcats was shot down in the attack, as was a Seafire as it flew over Kolvik seaplane base. The only other loss of the strike was a Barracuda from 827 Squadron, which messed up its landing back on *Furious* and ended up ditching in the sea, from where its crew were rescued by a destroyer.

This attack, known later as '*Goodwood I*', was in line with Moore's tactic of carrying out 'teasing tactics' if the weather precluded the launch of a full-scale strike. It was repeated that evening, when in a sortie grandly known as '*Goodwood II*', six Hellcats and eight Fireflies from *Indefatigable* took off at 1830hrs, heading back towards the *Tirpitz*. Once again the Hellcats carried 500lb SAP bombs. They appeared over the Kaafjord at 1910hrs, and once more the low-flying fighters took the crew of the battleship by surprise. When they appeared the smoke screen still hadn't been deployed. Flying conditions were good, but still none of the bombs hit the ship. The fighters shot up other targets of opportunity on the way back up the Altenfjord, and all aircraft returned safely.

So far, *Goodwood* had cost Moore three aircraft, but this was partly mitigated by the fact that the Seafires patrolling over the task force had shot down two German reconnaissance flying boats. Much more serious was the operational loss of the escort carrier *Nabob*. The task force had been sighted by *U-354*, a Type VIIC U-boat commanded by Lieutenant Commander Sthamer. That afternoon, Moore detached *Formidable* and *Furious* to refuel from his fleet tankers, which were over the horizon to the west. He also sent Force 2 westwards, to refuel their escorts from their own fuel tanks. This unwittingly brought them within range of the U-boat, whose spread of torpedoes launched at 1755hrs hit the escort carrier *Nabob* and the frigate *Bickerton*. While the other escorts chased Sthamer, the crew of the *Nabob* fought to save her. Eventually, she limped off, protected by a screen of escorts. The stricken *Bickerton*, though, was a complete wreck, and had to be scuttled. This deprived Moore of the ability to launch his mine-carrying Avengers, so that part of the plan had to be abandoned. He probably found some consolation in the news that two days later *U-354* was sunk with all hands by depth charges dropped from a Swordfish operating from the escort carrier *Vindex*.

Nabob limped south towards Scapa Flow, protected by the rest of Force 2. Moore ordered his fleet carriers to regroup, and in the meantime, with one carrier at his disposal, he planned to launch another 'teasing attack' the following day. By dawn on 23 August both *Formidable*

On 22 August, during Operation *Goodwood*, the escort carrier *Nabob* was torpedoed by the German U-boat *U-354*. Ironically, *Nabob* was attached to the carrier group in order to provide anti-submarine air patrols. Despite listing to port and down by the stern the carrier made it back to Scapa Flow under her own steam, before being towed to Rosyth for repairs.

and *Furious* were still absent, so the attack would go ahead with just the Hellcats, Fireflies and Seafires from *Indefatigable*. Once again, however, bad weather led to the cancellation of the strike, as fog blanketed the area. Still, this allowed the detached carriers to rejoin the fleet, and so, in hope of better weather to come, Moore and his staff spent the day planning for a full-scale attack to be launched the following morning.

As dawn broke on 24 August it was clear that flying was still impossible. So the crews waited, until at 1330hrs Moore gave the order to go ahead. An hour later, at 1430hrs, the first of the strikes began taking off from the three carriers; '*Goodwood III*' was under way. This time 33 Barracudas formed the heart of the strike, made up from all four squadrons. Each carried a single 1,600lb AP bomb. The remaining operational Barracudas were deployed on anti-submarine patrol. Of the 24 Corsairs in the strike, five carried 1,100lb APs, while each of the ten Hellcats was armed with 500lb APs. Ten Fireflies provided dedicated 'top cover', as this time the Corsairs were ordered to peel off over the Kaafjord and attack targets of opportunity. In addition, eight Seafires took off to 'shoot up' Banak airfield, while others formed a combat air patrol over the task force. Conditions that afternoon were near perfect, and the air crews flying in at 500ft were able to see the coast from 60 miles away.

This time the German radar operators saw them coming, even before they climbed to their bombing height on reaching the coast. At 1541hrs the *Tirpitz* sounded her air attack warning, and as her crew scrambled to man their guns the smoke screen generators got to work. Meanwhile, as the strike aircraft flew over the Langfjord they came under attack from the flak guns of the destroyers anchored there. Over the Kaafjord the Germans were throwing up a strong box barrage at 3,000–4,000ft, but this diminished slightly when the fighters swooped in to attack the flak positions on the shore. It was now 1559hrs, and the Hellcats peeled off to attack the battleship. By now, however, she was completely obscured by smoke. Despite the heavy flak many of the pilots circled round for another bombing run, before making way for the Barracudas. All they had to show for it was one hit on the battleship's 'Bruno' turret. One Hellcat was lost during this attack, while a second Hellcat would go down while attacking a wireless station on the shore some ten minutes later.

Behind them came the five bomb-armed Corsairs, one of which mistakenly claimed a hit on the battleship with its 500lb bomb. Three of the five, though, were shot down, while a fourth was so badly damaged that it had to ditch next to *Formidable* after making it back to the task force. Behind the Corsairs the Barracudas were starting their attack. Again, almost none of the crewmen could actually see their target, and were reduced to aiming at the source of the tracer coming towards them through the smoke. The 33 Barracudas attacked in waves of five or six aircraft, and virtually all the pilots released their bombs from a height of around 4,000ft, well above the smoke and the box barrage exploding beneath them. They had to dive through it, however, and several of the aircraft were hit. One 1,600lb bomb struck the port side of *Tirpitz*, near the side of her bridge, but otherwise none of the bombs hit their target, thanks to the impenetrable smoke.

On the way home the strike aircraft attacked any targets they came across, from flak positions to patrol boats, destroyers and flak ships. Apart from the Hellcat that crashed during this phase, and the Corsair that ditched next to its carrier, all of the other surviving aircraft made it back. Many of the Barracudas were badly battered, though, and would have to be patched up before they could fly again. After the sortie, Moore counted the cost. He had lost six aircraft over the Altenfjord, and one more while landing on. In exchange he had reduced the flak defences surrounding the anchorage and scored two hits on the battleship. Of these, the 1,600lb bomb had pierced five decks, but failed to explode. The 500lb bomb dropped by a Hellcat had demolished the quadruple flak gun mounted on the top of 'Bruno' turret, but otherwise had inflicted no other damage. In all, *Tirpitz* had lost eight men dead and 18 wounded in the attack.

After the operation it was clear that the elderly *Furious* was suffering mechanical problems and running low on fuel, so she was detached early on 25 August. Moore took part of Force 1 over to the Faroes to refuel, while the carriers and their escorts did the same from the Force 9 fleet tankers. At 0300hrs on 29 August, the two parts of Force 1 were reunited 250 nautical miles west of the Altenfjord. They steamed inshore during the night, and by noon they had reached their old launching position, 80 nautical miles off the coast. The weather looked unpromising, but conditions soon improved, and at 1530hrs '*Goodwood IV*' began as the first aircraft took off from Moore's two remaining carriers, *Formidable* and *Indefatigable*. Twenty-five minutes later, after forming up, they set off towards the Kaafjord.

This time the strike force was made up of 26 Barracudas, each carrying a single 1,600lb AP bomb. Two Corsairs carried single 1,000lb APs, while three Hellcats were equipped with 500lb APs. Four other Hellcats equipped with target indication flares and 15 more

Operation *Goodwood III*, Kaafjord, 24 August 1944

On 18 August 1944 a British carrier force left Scapa Flow bound for the waters off the Altenfjord. There they launched the first of a series of naval air strikes against the *Tirpitz*, which was moored in the Kaafjord. This undertaking, codenamed Operation *Goodwood*, involved the launching of coordinated strikes from five aircraft carriers, supported by a screen of fighters. The first two strikes, *Goodwood I* and *Goodwood II*, were launched on 22 August, but low cloud hampered the first strike, while the second was little more than a small-scale bombing and strafing attack, carried out by Fireflies and Hellcats.

Two days later, on 24 August, the Fleet Air Arm tried again. This time weather conditions were more favourable, and a strike of 33 Barracuda dive bombers took off. Preceding them were five Corsair and ten Hellcat fighters carrying smaller bombs, while fighter cover was provided by 19 Corsairs and ten Fireflies. The attack began at 1559hrs DBST, as the fast bomb-armed fighters made their run, attacking at low level. By then, though, the *Tirpitz* was wreathed by her protective smoke screen, and by the time the first Barracudas arrived, the battleship was hidden by the smoke. Still, the attack went ahead as planned, with each wave of five or six Barracudas diving from 5,000ft to release their 1,600lb AP bombs at the spot where their crews thought the battleship lay.

The bombers had to dive through a heavy layer of flak, and many aimed at the source of the tracer from light anti-aircraft guns, emerging through the white smoke. However, only two bombs hit the *Tirpitz* during the attack. Several Barracudas were damaged, but miraculously none were shot down during the attack. Nevertheless, the effectiveness of *Tirpitz*'s smoke screen demonstrably showed that this sort of attack was unlikely to succeed. So, after one more attempt the operation was called off, and the Admiralty were forced to ask Bomber Command for their help in sinking the German battleship.

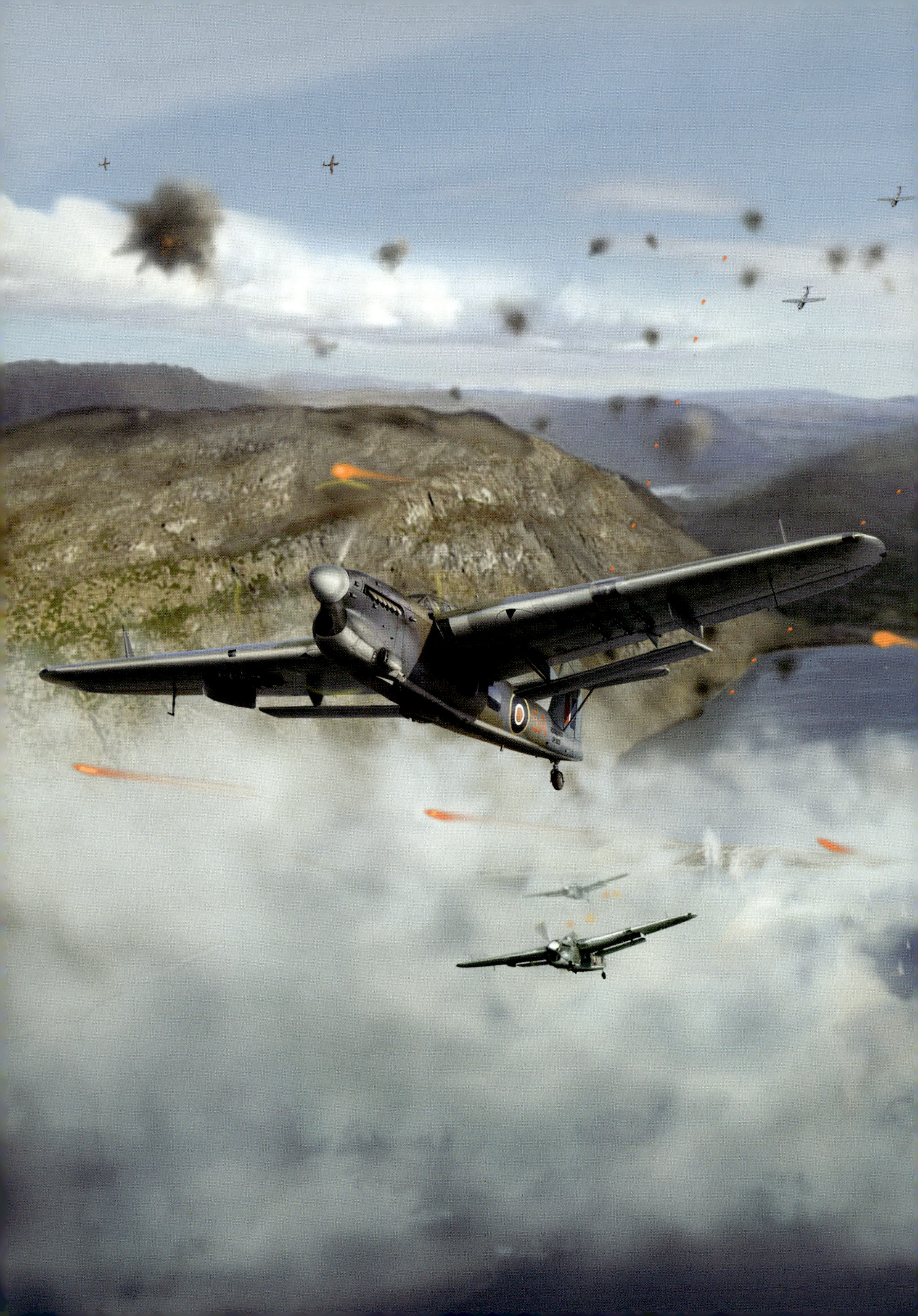

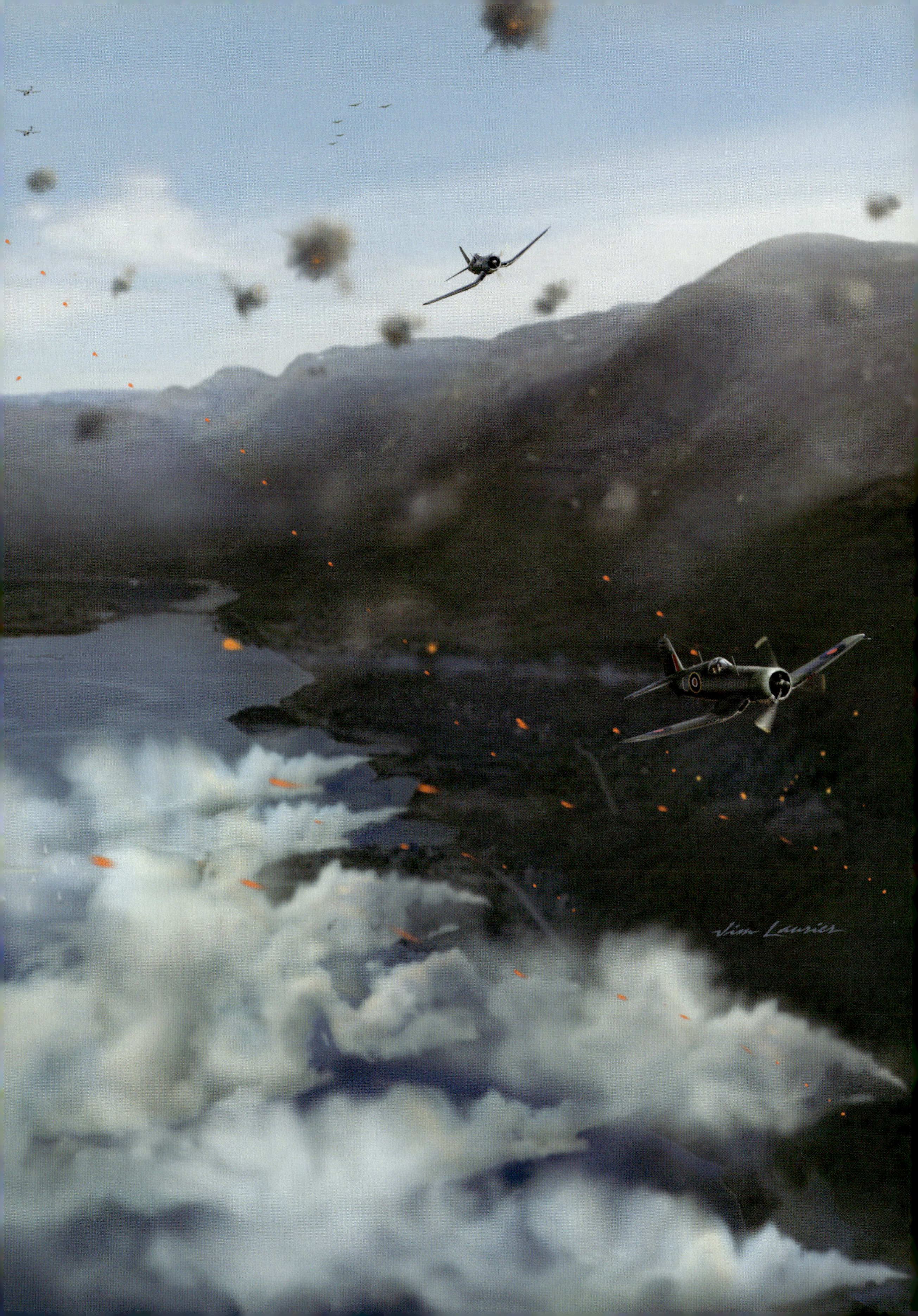
Jim Laurier

Corsairs flew as escorts, together with ten Fireflies. Seven more Seafires also took off to cause a diversion, by shooting up coastal shipping off Hammerfest. The aircraft were detected by German radar at 1640hrs, and thanks to a strong wind the strike made landfall some miles to the south of their usual spot over Loppa. For once they were approaching the *Tirpitz* from the south-west, rather than the west. Actually, this made almost no difference. The smoke screen was deployed long before the first aircraft appeared over the Kaafjord, and once more the air crews were attacking a target they couldn't see. The innovation of using four Hellcats to drop coloured smoke flares would have helped the dive bombers to identify the target, but by the time they arrived the *Tirpitz* was completely obscured.

At 1702hrs the bomb-armed Hellcats and Corsairs made their run, but all five bombs missed their target. Happy that no enemy fighters were in the area, the rest of the fighter escort and the flare-carrying Hellcats dropped down into the smoke to strafe the hidden battleship as best they could, or shoot up flak positions along the edge of the fjord. Then, 15 minutes later, the Barracudas began their attack, having formed a column several aircraft wide. They dropped their bombs from 3,500ft or above, and some kept diving until they were swallowed up by the thick white smoke. While the crews later claimed a score of two hits, in fact the *Tirpitz* emerged completely unscathed. This time a Corsair and a Firefly were shot down over the Kaafjord as they made their strafing run. Two more badly shot-up Barracudas made it back to their carriers, but were so badly damaged that they were ditched over the side.

Wing Commander J. B. Willy Tait DSO DFC (1916–2007) was the commanding officer of 617 Squadron, and the leader of the three Lancaster missions against the *Tirpitz* in 1944 – Operations *Paravane*, *Obviate* and *Catechism*. In all he flew over a hundred bombing missions during the war, but he is best remembered as the man responsible for the sinking of the *Tirpitz*.

On board the *Tirpitz*, the only material effect of these four Operation *Goodwood* attacks, apart from the loss of a handful of her crew, was the damage caused by an equally small number of bomb hits, the most serious of which was from a 1,600lb bomb that failed to explode. This damage, though, was easily patched. Less easy to replace was the ammunition she had expended. During the attacks she had fired off a total of 201 rounds from her 38cm main guns, 1,141 rounds from her 15cm secondary guns, and roughly 60 per cent of her smaller-calibre anti-aircraft rounds. In the late summer of 1944, as Allied tanks were racing through France towards the German border, the chances of replenishing all this ordnance looked slim.

After recovering their aircraft the carriers returned to Scapa Flow with an escort, while the rest of the Home Fleet set off to cover the transit of another Arctic Convoy, this time the homeward-bound RA-59. Moore's force finally reached its base in Orkney on 3 September. It was there that the Home Fleet's commander learned from Ultra signal intercepts that the damage of these raids on the German battleship had been negligible. So, gallant though it undoubtedly was, the Fleet Air Arm offensive against the *Tirpitz* had been a failure. *Tirpitz* still remained a threat to the Arctic Convoys, and by now it was clear that the Royal Navy lacked the ordnance needed to deal with her. It was now up to the RAF to take up the torch, and to deal the knock-out blow.

The Tallboy raids
Operation *Paravane*

Various alternatives were now considered. These included using fast twin-engined Mosquitos to attack the ship, launched from the Home Fleet's carriers. It was felt that they would be fast enough to confound the enemy's smoke screen and so have a clear run at the *Tirpitz*. However, they were all needed in the main theatre of war, so the use of them was denied. So too was another request to use American B-17 bombers, flying from Soviet airfields. They were required for the round-the-clock bombing of targets in Germany. So it fell to Bomber Command to do the job. That meant using the Lancaster.

Fortunately, since Bomber Command's last attempt on *Tirpitz*, new ordnance had been introduced which was particularly well suited to the task. These 'JW' bombs were mine-bombs designed to repeatedly rise and sink while moving laterally through the water. When they made contact with the underside of a ship they would explode. While this was ingenious, a much more effective piece of ordnance was the newly introduced 'Tallboy'. When dropped over land, this highly aerodynamic, hardened-steel 12,000lb bomb reached a supersonic

This rare photograph shows a 12,000lb Tallboy bomb being dropped from a Lancaster of 617 Squadron during a training exercise in August 1944, before the squadron carried out its three attacks on the *Tirpitz*. Thanks to a new precision bomb-aiming device, a high degree of accuracy could be assured, if only the aimer could see the target prior to the bomb's release.

EVENTS

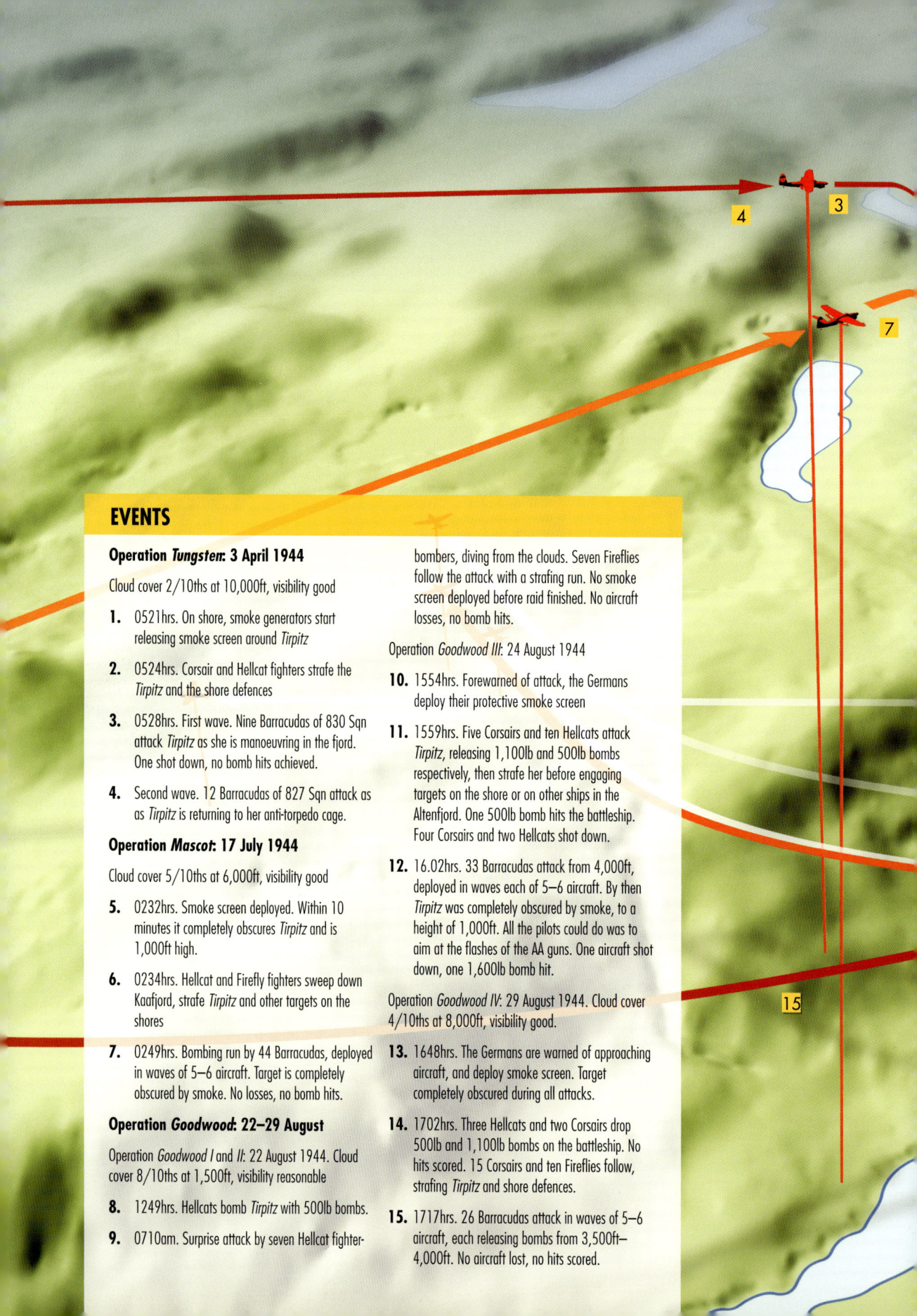

Operation *Tungsten*: 3 April 1944

Cloud cover 2/10ths at 10,000ft, visibility good

1. 0521hrs. On shore, smoke generators start releasing smoke screen around *Tirpitz*
2. 0524hrs. Corsair and Hellcat fighters strafe the *Tirpitz* and the shore defences
3. 0528hrs. First wave. Nine Barracudas of 830 Sqn attack *Tirpitz* as she is manoeuvring in the fjord. One shot down, no bomb hits achieved.
4. Second wave. 12 Barracudas of 827 Sqn attack as as *Tirpitz* is returning to her anti-torpedo cage.

Operation *Mascot*: 17 July 1944

Cloud cover 5/10ths at 6,000ft, visibility good

5. 0232hrs. Smoke screen deployed. Within 10 minutes it completely obscures *Tirpitz* and is 1,000ft high.
6. 0234hrs. Hellcat and Firefly fighters sweep down Kaafjord, strafe *Tirpitz* and other targets on the shores
7. 0249hrs. Bombing run by 44 Barracudas, deployed in waves of 5–6 aircraft. Target is completely obscured by smoke. No losses, no bomb hits.

Operation *Goodwood*: 22–29 August

Operation *Goodwood I* and *II*: 22 August 1944. Cloud cover 8/10ths at 1,500ft, visibility reasonable

8. 1249hrs. Hellcats bomb *Tirpitz* with 500lb bombs.
9. 0710am. Surprise attack by seven Hellcat fighter-bombers, diving from the clouds. Seven Fireflies follow the attack with a strafing run. No smoke screen deployed before raid finished. No aircraft losses, no bomb hits.

Operation *Goodwood III*: 24 August 1944

10. 1554hrs. Forewarned of attack, the Germans deploy their protective smoke screen
11. 1559hrs. Five Corsairs and ten Hellcats attack *Tirpitz*, releasing 1,100lb and 500lb bombs respectively, then strafe her before engaging targets on the shore or on other ships in the Altenfjord. One 500lb bomb hits the battleship. Four Corsairs and two Hellcats shot down.
12. 16.02hrs. 33 Barracudas attack from 4,000ft, deployed in waves each of 5–6 aircraft. By then *Tirpitz* was completely obscured by smoke, to a height of 1,000ft. All the pilots could do was to aim at the flashes of the AA guns. One aircraft shot down, one 1,600lb bomb hit.

Operation *Goodwood IV*: 29 August 1944. Cloud cover 4/10ths at 8,000ft, visibility good.

13. 1648hrs. The Germans are warned of approaching aircraft, and deploy smoke screen. Target completely obscured during all attacks.
14. 1702hrs. Three Hellcats and two Corsairs drop 500lb and 1,100lb bombs on the battleship. No hits scored. 15 Corsairs and ten Fireflies follow, strafing *Tirpitz* and shore defences.
15. 1717hrs. 26 Barracudas attack in waves of 5–6 aircraft, each releasing bombs from 3,500ft–4,000ft. No aircraft lost, no hits scored.

Fleet Air Arm attacks
Kaafjord, April–August 1944

TIRPITZ ANCHORAGES ●
- **A.** *Tirpitz summer anchorage*
- **B.** *Tirpitz winter anchorage*

KEY

△ Smoke generators

◎ AA guns

∙∙∙∙∙∙∙ Anti-torpedo nets

Kaafjord

terminal velocity, could penetrate up to 16ft of concrete and produced its own earthquake when it then exploded underground. It had already proved its worth in attacks on German rocket sites, and it was felt that it could be equally effective if dropped on a battleship.

Bomber Command realised that the Altenfjord was beyond the range of Lancasters operating from air bases in north-eastern Scotland. So it was decided to fly a bomber force to the Soviet Union, and base it in an airfield near Archangel. From there the bombers could reach their target if they were modified slightly with additional fuel tanks and the removal of their upper gun turret. Better still, by approaching the Kaafjord from the east, it was hoped that the attackers would avoid being detected by the German radar stations until it was too late to deploy the smoke screen over the Kaafjord.

The obvious choice for this operation was 617 Squadron ('the Dambusters'), commanded by Wing Commander 'Willy' Tait, based in Woodhall Spa in Lincolnshire. Their Lancasters had been converted to use the Tallboy, and the crews were used to unusual missions. Accompanying them would be 9 Squadron, commanded by Wing Commander Bazin, based in nearby Bardney. Their bombers could also accommodate the new bomb. In late August, 5 Group of Bomber Command were ordered to draw up plans for the attack, codenamed Operation *Paravane*.

Early on, it was decided that a Soviet airfield should be used. The original idea was to fly to forward bases in north-east Scotland, then bomb the *Tirpitz* before heading east to land on an airfield in northern Russia. However, the high risk of bad weather over the Altenfjord meant that this scheme was shelved on 11 September. Instead, the bombers would fly to Yagodnik airfield near Archangel, and launch their attack from there. The airfield lay in an island in the Dvina River, 12 miles south-west of Archangel and 610 miles from the Kaafjord. The only problem was getting there. At 1900hrs on 12 September, 18 fully armed Lancasters of 9 Squadron took off from Barney, accompanied by two Liberators carrying spare parts and ground crew, a Lancaster from 463 Squadron which was there to film the operation and a PRU Mosquito, to check that the *Tirpitz* was still where it was supposed to be. Another 20 Lancasters from 617 Squadron also took off from Woodhall Spa. The operation was under way.

This image was taken from a Lancaster carrying a film crew on 15 September 1944. Taken from about 20,000ft, it shows the opening stages of Operation *Paravane*, when *Tirpitz* was attacked in the Kaafjord by Lancaster bombers carrying Tallboys and JW mines. The bomber in the picture, part of 'Force A', is flying at approximately 15,000ft, flying up the fjord towards the battleship, having already released its Tallboy. The German smoke screen is already thickening, and beginning to obscure the target, which is just off the top edge of the photograph.

Air Vice Marshal Ralph Cochrane (1895–1977), the Scottish-born commander of the RAF's No. 5 Group, championed the use of his bomber squadrons in specialist precision attacks. The most famous of these was the Dambuster Raid of May 1943, carried out by 617 Squadron. He saw the potential of the Tallboy, and two of his squadrons were equipped to use the giant bomb when in August 1944 his group was ordered to sink the *Tirpitz*.

The flight path took them north over Lossiemouth, where the Liberators stopped to refuel, then on past Orkney and Shetland. Only one Lancaster had to turn back due to engine failure. From there they headed west over central Norway and Sweden, the Gulf of Bothnia and then Finland, before crossing into the Soviet Union west of Lake Onega. Before leaving, the crews had been assured that the weather would be favourable and visibility good. Instead, they found the whole region of endless forest, lake and swamp blanketed in thick low cloud, low mist and lashed by heavy rain. Most had been given the wrong radio frequencies too, so the crews had to navigate using outdated maps and dead reckoning. Consequently, only 23 Lancasters made it to Yagodnik. The other 14 Lancasters either landed on secondary airfields in the Archangel region or were forced to crash-land in the rare patches of boggy meadow they found.

The next day, Tait set out in an old Soviet biplane to look for the stragglers, while others flew on to Yagodnik after refuelling. He found five at Keg-Ostrov beside Archangel, and more at nearby Talagi, but others were as far away as Onega, 70 miles to the east. By the end of 12 September, 31 Lancasters had been gathered at Yagodnik. Six others – four from 9 Squadron and two from 617 Squadron – had to be written off due to damage. At least these would provide spare parts for the serviceable aircraft, several of which needed urgent repairs. During all this the Soviet servicemen they encountered were extremely helpful, doing whatever they could to help Tait gather his bombers together. The ground crews worked hard through 13 September, and by the following morning a total of 27 Lancasters were ready to fly. Of these, 20 were armed with a single Tallboy while the remaining six carried a payload of JW mine-bombs. The film unit Lancaster was also fully operational. Early that morning the PRU Mosquito inspected the Kaafjord, but reported that the area was covered in low cloud: the 0800hrs take-off was postponed for a day.

The day was spent playing football and being entertained by the Russians, who produced copious amounts of vodka for the British airmen. Meanwhile, Tait revised his plans. The two squadrons would form up together, then fly east over Finland, keeping below 500ft to avoid being detected by the German radar station at Kirkenes, 70 miles north-east of Murmansk. Then, over Lapland the attackers would split into two groups. Force A, with the Tallboys, and accompanied by the film plane, would climb to 20,000ft and approach the target in four 'gaggles' of five aircraft. Three planes of the first 'gaggle', all from 9 Squadron, would fly on ahead to check out the weather conditions over the Kaafjord before the rest of the Lancasters arrived. The six JW-armed bombers of Force B would fly in at 16,000ft.

Before dawn on 15 September the Mosquito set off for the Kaafjord, and at 0900hrs DBST (0700hrs Soviet local time) it reported that conditions there were favourable. Thirty minutes later at 0930hrs DBST the Lancasters took off, and headed west over the White Sea. On the way, six of the bombers were forced to turn back due to mechanical failure, but the rest continued on towards Norway without being detected. A little before 1200hrs Tait ordered them to climb, and 40 minutes later they spotted the Altenfjord ahead of them. Tait ordered Force A to drop down to their bombing height of 14,000–18,000ft. They were also spotted themselves, and as they neared their target they could see the smoke screen spreading out over the Kaafjord. Still, at 1256hrs the first 'gaggle' from Force A were able to drop their Tallboys before the *Tirpitz* was completely obscured. One of them – possibly the one dropped from Tait's bomber – hit the battleship. The other 'gaggles' were less fortunate and, although 17 of the 20 Tallboys were dropped, could only target the source of the tracer climbing towards them. A few bombers even made more than one pass, in the vain hope that a rift would appear in the smoke screen.

Force B had a plan which should have obviated the smoke. First they circled around, to keep out of the way of Force A's bombs. Their bomb sights were targeted at a feature on the hill on the north-west side of the Kaafjord, which was above the smoke. By adjusting their sights, they hoped to ensure that the JW bombs would land around the battleship. Most of them released their bombs according to plan, dropping them from a height of 10,000–12,000ft, but none of them caused any damage. By 1307hrs the attack was over and the bombers had turned back towards Russia. The one exception was the film Lancaster, which flew on to Waddington in Lincolnshire, landing there just before 2300hrs DBST, after a flight lasting almost 13½ hours. The others flew back to Yagodnik, where the Soviets welcomed them with a marching band and more vodka. The following morning most of the jaded airmen flew home to Lincolnshire, where they expected to learn if their mission had been a success or not. One Lancaster from 617 Squadron crashed near Nesbyen in Norway on the flight home, killing all the men on board.

In fact, of all the ordnance dropped that day, only one Tallboy hit the *Tirpitz*. It landed near the bow, on the focsle beneath the guns of 'Anton' turret. It went right through the armoured deck, and continued on to pierce the starboard hull of the ship below the waterline. There it exploded, causing extensive underwater damage. One officer likened the huge hole in the focsle to 'a barn door'. There was extensive flooding forward, with 2,000 tons of water flooding the forward compartments, while internal bulkheads were buckled by the blast. One Norwegian described the hole below the waterline on her starboard side as being large enough to sail a ship's boat into. The concussion from the 'earthquake bomb' damaged the ship's engines, turbines and much of her auxiliary machinery. It was five days before a PRU Mosquito could photograph the *Tirpitz*, and this showed that her bows were down in the water, and covered by some form of screen.

The full extent of the damage would soon be revealed through Ultra intercepts of German signals. On 19 September these reported that *Tirpitz* had been hit by a large bomb, but despite the substantial impact this had on the battleship's seaworthiness, official statements should say that *Tirpitz* only sustained light damage. At a meeting in Berlin on 25 September, presided over by Dönitz, it was estimated that it would take nine months to make the battleship seaworthy again. At that stage of the war this was far too long, so Dönitz ordered that she remain in Norway, serving as a floating gun battery to deter any coastal invasion. This meant that from that point on, *Tirpitz* was no longer considered a fully operational warship. A suitable spot had to be chosen for her, in an area worthy of being defended by her guns, but in an anchorage shallow enough that if hit, she could not be sunk. That way she could still serve as a static gun battery, even if her main decks were all but awash.

The Germans finally selected a spot in the Sørbotn Channel, off the small island of Håkøya, 3.5 miles west of Tromsø in northern Norway. At noon on 15 October, *Tirpitz* left the Kaafjord for the last time, and slowly made her way up the Altenfjord under her own steam, but aided by tugs. She could only manage 3 knots. Apart from a 25-mile stretch beyond the mouth of the Altenfjord, the route to her new anchorage ran through sheltered coastal waterways, protected from the sea by a barrier of islands. The Kriegsmarine were taking no chances, though, and as a wolfpack of U-boats patrolled offshore, a screen of destroyers and smaller craft escorted the limping battleship south towards Tromsø. By 1500hrs GMT the next day she was in place, lying off Håkøya. On 18 October she was spotted there by British reconnaissance planes. All her flak defences and smoke screen equipment

To fit the 12,000lb Tallboy into a Lancaster, the bomb bay doors had to be adapted so that they bulged out to accommodate its unusually large maximum diameter of 3ft 3in for the body of the bomb, and 3ft 6in for its tail fins.

EVENTS

After being crippled while anchored in the Kaafjord in September 1944, temporary repairs were carried out, allowing Tirpitz to be moved 120 nautical miles further south, to a new berth near Tromsø. It was acknowledge the battleship could never put to sea again – her new role was merely to act as a floating gun battery, to deter any attempted Allied landing in the area. While she was no longer a threat to the Arctic Convoys, the British had no idea how badly damaged she was. So, the air attacks continued. In late October the RAF carried out another major attack using Avro Lancasters, converted to carry the Tallboy bomb. Although this sortie – Operation *Obviate* – was foiled by low cloud obscuring the target, the two Lancaster squadrons earmarked for the operation were ordered to have another go. The result was Operation *Catechism*, and this time the skies over Tromsø remained clear. Even more surprisingly, the Luftwaffe failed to intercept the bombers. So, for the third time in three months, Tirpitz was attacked using Tallboys. This time her luck ran out. She was hit by at least three bombs, and mortally wounded. After 30 minutes she capsized and sank, taking almost 1,000 men down with her.

Operation *Obviate* (29 October 1944)

Cloud cover 8/10ths, 6,000ft. Visibility: Good. Bombing height: 14,000 feet

1. 7.49am The 20 Lancasters of 617 Sqn commence their attack, dropping Tallboy bombs from heights ranging from 13,000–15,000ft. Target almost completely obscured by clouds. No aircraft lost, but no bombs hit their target.

2. 7.55am The 17 Lancasters of 9 Sqn commence their attack, but again, visibility through clouds is poor, and three bombers failed to release their bombs, as their crews were unable to see the target. No aircraft lost, but four hit by flak. No bombs hit their target.

3. 8.05am The strike leader Group Captain Tait circles the area, watching the attack. Some bombers make more than one attempt due to poor visibility through cloud, circling round and following the same attack profile. Eventually, Tait orders the aircraft to withdraw.

Operation *Catechism* (12 November 1944)

Cloud cover 3/10ths, 18–20,000 feet. Visibility: Good Bombing height: 14,000ft

4. 9.42am the first wave of six Lancasters of 617 Sqn. released their Tallboy bombs from between 12,500 and 15,000 feet. After this, as his leading aircraft withdrew, Group Captain Tait circled round to watch the subsequent waves of bombers make their run. All 18 Lancasters of 617 Sqn. released their bombs in the space of three minutes, between 9.42 and 9.45am.

5. Just after 9.45am the first of ten Lancasters of 9 Sqn. released their bombs. The squadron's attack continued until 9.49am, by which time it was clear the Tirpitz was listing heavily. The final three Lancasters of the squadron elected to save their bombs, as their mission had been accomplished.

6. Apart from two, all the bombers in the strike crossed over the ship, and banked to port, to cross over Kvaloy island. from there they headed out towards the open sea. the two exceptions were Tait's Lancaster, which circled the area throughout the attack, and the photographic Lancaster, which also circled the target.

7. The *Tirpitz* had been hit by at least two Tallboy bombs, causing major damage to her. She began listing, and at approximately 10.04am a major explosion ripped through the bow of the battleship, as a magazine exploded. She then began to capsize, until only her upturned hull could be seen above the water.

Operations *Obviate* and *Catechism*
Off Tromsø, October–November 1944

KEY

◎ AA guns

KRIEGSMARINE SHIPS
A. *Tirpitz*
B. *Nymphe* AA ship
C. *Thetis* AA ship

RAF Units 🔴🟠
1. Operations *Obviate*: 37 Lancasters of 617 Sqn and 9 Sqn, in waves of 4–6 aircraft at 13–15,000ft
2. Operation *Catechism*: 38 Lancasters of 617 Sqn and 9 Sqn, in waves of 4–6 aircraft at 13–15,000ft

Kvaløya
Håkøya
Sandnessundet

In this photograph, taken during the opening moments of Operation *Catechism*, *Tirpitz* has received an initial hit amidships, and smoke is pouring from her superstructure. This was taken at around 0843hrs, from the 617 Squadron Lancaster flown by Flight Lieutenant Knights.

time conditions were favourable – really favourable this time – the bombers would be sent back to finish the job.

Operation *Catechism*

On 4 November, Captain Junge stood down as commander of *Tirpitz* and was sent to the Kriegsmarine's headquarters in Norway. His place was taken by his second-in-command, Captain Robert Weber, a gunnery specialist. By then dredgers were at work to reduce the depth of water under the battleship's keel, the smoke generators had arrived and were beginning to be installed, new flak guns were being emplaced, the torpedo nets had been laid and a direct phone link had been established to the Luftwaffe, so air support might actually arrive for once. Weber was confident that within three weeks the days would be so short that his battleship would be relatively safe from enemy air attack until the following spring. Until then, though, he needed low cloud and bad weather.

Bomber Command's 5 Group planners were conversely keen for a spell of clear and cloudless skies. The mere prospect of just such a spell was enough for 9 and 617 Squadrons to be ordered north again on 4 November, just in case these conditions might actually be met. Instead, northern Norway was swept by a winter gale. Then, on 11 November, the bombers were recalled to Scotland, as meteorological reports suggested that a spell of good weather was expected over Tromsø, which might last for up to two days. A Spitfire was dispatched to Tromsø, and reported that there were cloud patches over the target area. Although there were no guarantees, and this seemed far from favourable, the mission, now codenamed Operation *Catechism*, was confirmed. The crews were given a final briefing, and tried to rest before their departure early the following morning. The plan was largely the same as for Operation *Obviate*. The only difference was that a new intelligence report said that a squadron of German fighters had recently arrived at Bardufloss airfield, 42 miles south of Tromsø and almost astride the bombers' approach path to the target.

At 0259hrs GMT on 12 November the first of 32 bombers took off from Lossiemouth, Kinross and Milltown, the 13 operational bombers of 9 Squadron and 18 more from 617 Squadron accompanied once again by the Lancaster from 463 Squadron carrying the film unit. Once more they flew across the North Sea at 1,500ft, flying north, then veering towards Norway once they reached Shetland. The Norwegian coast was reached without incident, and the aircraft, widely separated in the darkness, now headed for their rendezvous point over Lake Torneträsk. Tait, who commanded the mission, was one of the first to arrive, and as he circled he saw other bombers straggling in. When all but two of 9 Squadron's bombers had appeared, Tait fired a flare pistol to signal that they should move off towards the target (the two stragglers returned to Britain after realizing they had missed the rendezvous). The sun was just beginning to rise over on the eastern horizon, but as they continued the light improved, until as one airman described it, the air was 'gin clear'. This could only be good for the bombing run, but the air crew also knew it would benefit the pilots of any German fighters scrambling from Bardufloss.

They climbed steadily to their prearranged bombing height of around 14,000–15,000ft, flying in 'gaggles' of four to six bombers, with 617 Squadron leading the column and 9 Squadron following behind. Tait's Lancaster was at the front. They spotted the Balsfjord, and banked to port to follow it towards the *Tirpitz*. They spotted the battleship 20 miles ahead of them, and this time there was no cloud to protect her – or a smoke screen. She appeared black, in contrast with the white snow-clad islands and coast around her. Tait felt she looked like a 'spider in her web', surrounded by her torpedo nets. The target might have been unprotected by smoke, but there was plenty of flak, including big orange air bursts from the battleship's 38cm main guns. The bomber crews held their nerve, and their course, although the flak intensified as they drew closer to their target.

It took five minutes to reach the bombing point after first spotting the target, and Tait noticed how the battleship lay with her bows pointing towards the north-east, so she was almost beam-on to the approaching bombers. The south-eastern side of the island of Haakøy lay about 400 yards off her port beam, while the side of the ship itself twinkled with flame as her flak guns fired at the approaching bombers. Her main gun turrets were trained to starboard, but the bombers were now too close for the big guns to bear on the attackers. Then they were approaching Grindøy Island, and the release point for the Tallboys.

The 18 Lancasters of 617 Squadron approached the target in 'gaggles' of from four to six bombers, flying at a range of heights from 12,650 to 16,000ft. This meant that some

This photograph of the *Tirpitz* was taken from 13,400ft during Operation *Catechism* at around 0844hrs on 15 November, from the Lancaster of 617 Squadron flown by Flight Lieutenant Knights. It shows the battleship belching smoke and flame, while a Tallboy explodes on the nearby island of Haakøy.

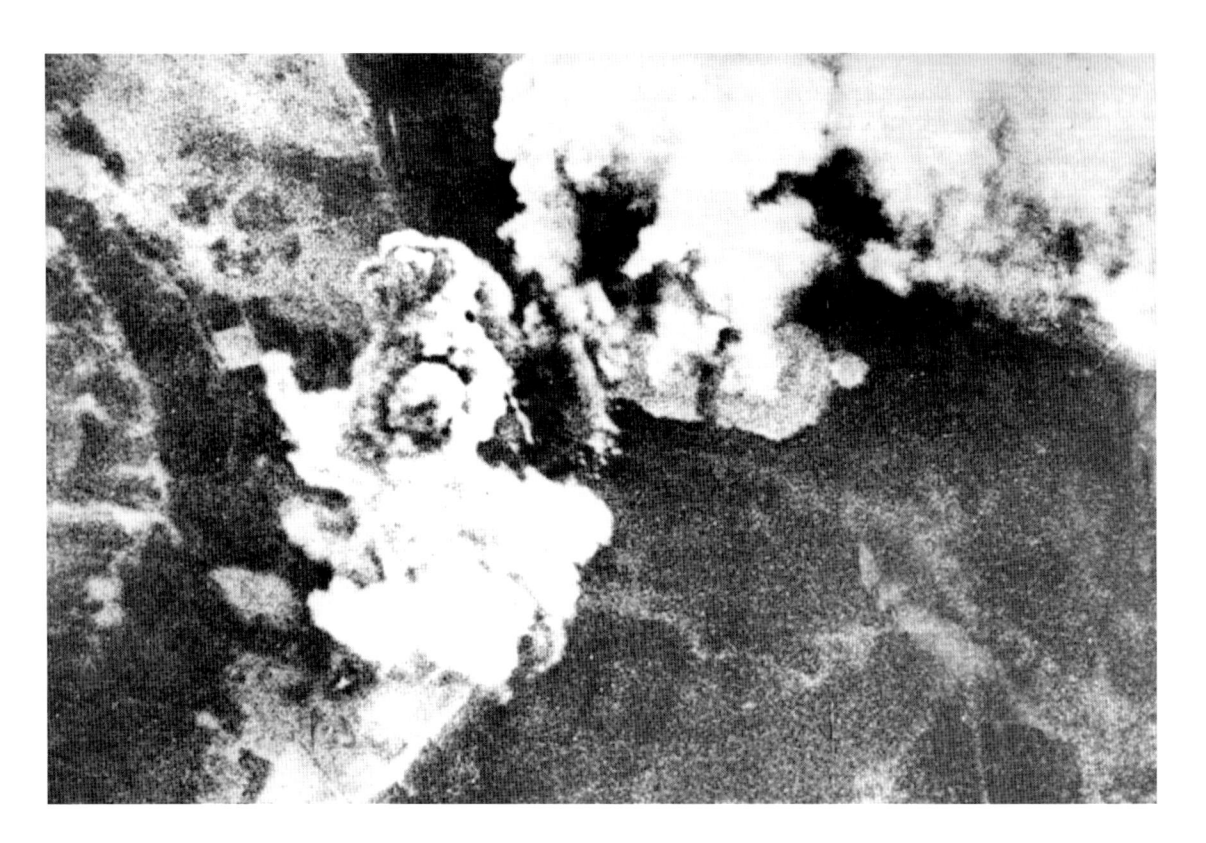

In this photograph, taken from around 16,000ft at 0849hrs during Operation *Catechism*, from the Lancaster carrying the film crew, the *Tirpitz* is completely obscured by smoke, as a large explosion erupts from her stern. This was the moment when 'Caesar' turret was blown out of the dying ship.

bombers were flying lower than their prearranged bombing height, in accordance with the 'gaggle' tactic of varying heights to make the approaching group of aircraft harder for flak batteries to target. Then at 0941hrs GMT the automatic bomb release mechanism triggered on Tait's plane, and his Tallboy began its descent. It took roughly 30 seconds to reach its target, and as Tait and his crew flew over the battleship, banking to port, they saw it head towards it. Other bombers reported that it had hit. By then the rest of the squadron were releasing their bombs too, and *Tirpitz* was now hidden in a pall of smoke, flame and spray from near misses. The film crew were busy recording all this, and their footage shows a big mushroom cloud appear near the bow of *Tirpitz*, probably from Tait's Tallboy. Other bombs can be seen to fall, then at 0943hrs another big hit amidships enveloped the ship in smoke.

Behind 617 Squadron, the 11 bombers of 9 Squadron added their contribution to the scene of destruction, with the first of their bombs falling at 0945hrs. By now the smoke was making it hard to see the target, so a few of the pilots went round for another run. The film plane was circling too, as was that of Tait, who was watching his aircraft finish the job he started. Then, at 0949hrs, it was over. The last of 9 Squadron's bombs had been released, and at least one major hit had been scored by the squadron. The smoke surrounding *Tirpitz* made it difficult to assess the damage. However, as the bombers departed, the battleship was clearly listing to port, and at 0949hrs a big explosion was seen, followed by at least one smaller one two minutes later. Tait led his Lancasters away towards the south-west, and the open sea. Only the film unit bomber remained, her crew disappointed that the battleship was still afloat. Then, as they watched, she heeled over to port, and then capsized. Soon only the red of her upturned hull was showing above the water of the fjord. The beast had finally been slain.

On board *Tirpitz* Captain Weber had plenty of warning of the approaching bombers, and his gun crews were ready for them. However, despite the increasingly frantic calls to Bardufloss, no air cover appeared. The Luftwaffe later blamed a 'clerical error' for this. So, apart from the shore-based flak guns, the *Tirpitz* was on her own. At 0802hrs local time (0902hrs GMT) 'Action Stations' was sounded, and at 0838hrs *Tirpitz* opened fire. None of the bombers were hit, and at 0841hrs local time (0941hrs GMT) the crewmen manning their stations on the upper deck watched as the first of a series of huge bombs fell towards them.

The first bomb landed forward, on the port side behind the funnel, astride the aircraft catapult deck. Another landed a little further aft, also on the port side. Both bombs ripped through the battleship's armoured deck and exploded inside her, causing extensive fire and flooding. *Tirpitz* began listing to port, but what really finished her was the near misses. Several bombs landed next to her in the water, and while their blasts caused underwater damage and flooding, they also blew huge craters in the seabed beneath her. Weber ordered his crew to deal with the flooding, and to evacuate the armoured citadel, but it was too late.

The ship was already listing 15 degrees, and the angle was increasing. Weber expected the ship to settle on the seabed, just a few metres below her keel, not knowing that the mud and sand beneath the keel had literally been blown away. Then at 0850hrs local time (0950hrs GMT) a huge explosion in the magazine for 'Caesar' turret ripped through the stern of the ship, and blew the 700-ton gun turret out of the ship. Moments later the list became more pronounced, until the battleship was lying on her side. At that point Weber gave the order to abandon ship. For most of his crew the order came too late. More, smaller explosions followed, and the heeling continued, until most of the superstructure was submerged. She hung there for a few moments, then rolled over completely.

Inside the hull, thousands of men were trapped, bulkheads collapsed, escape routes became jammed, the lights went out, and most of the young men inside the battleship's hull either died in the dark, or struggled to survive, kept alive by the slim hope that they might somehow be rescued. Very few were. Of the 1,700-strong crew of the *Tirpitz*, almost 1,000 were trapped inside her, or were killed at their posts. Of these, only 84 were ever rescued, escaping through holes cut in her hull during the days that followed. Meanwhile, all of the bombers returned safely.

Operation *Catechism*, Tromsø, 12 November 1944

After the damage suffered on 15 September 1944 during Operation *Paravane*, the *Tirpitz* was no longer considered combat effective. So, unable to undertake any more sorties, she was relegated to the role of a floating coastal defence battery, and moored in a new berth off Haakøy Island near Tromsø. It was there on 29 October that she was attacked by Lancaster heavy bombers of 9 and 617 Squadrons, flying from bases in the north-east of Scotland. On that occasion low clouds foiled the mission, codenamed Operation *Obviate*. Undeterred, Bomber Command waited for a more suitable opportunity. It finally came two weeks later on 12 November. The same two squadrons were involved in this mission, codenamed Operation *Catechism*, and this force of 30 Lancasters was led by Wing Commander Tait, the commanding officer of 617 'Dambusters' Squadron.

Flying conditions over northern Norway were perfect, and the *Tirpitz* was spotted while she was still 20 miles away. The bombers approached the target from the south-east, flying in 'gaggles' – groups of four to six bombers, operating in a loose formation, and at varying heights, to make it harder for flak gunners to target them. Tait and 617 Squadron led the way, followed by 9 Squadron – a force of 29 bombers in all, each armed with a single 12,000lb Tallboy bomb, and a 30th Lancaster, there to film the operation.

The attack began at 0841hrs, and the first Tallboy hit the battleship 30 seconds later. Soon she was half-hidden by a plume of smoke and flame, as numerous other bombs either hit her, or landed close by her in the water, causing underwater damage to her hull. The attack lasted just eight minutes, and by its end it was clear that the battleship was finished. She was listing heavily to port, and then as the bombers departed the first of two more explosions wracked the ship. As the lingering film crew watched, *Tirpitz* slowly rolled over and capsized, so that only her upturned hull could be seen above the water. This plate shows the aircraft of 617 Squadron flying over Haakøy Island after completing their bombing run, while behind them the Lancasters of 9 Squadron are dropping their Tallboys on the target. One 12,000lb bomb has hit the shore of the island – a detonation that left a crater which can still be seen there today – while others are falling around the battleship itself, which by now is in her death throes.

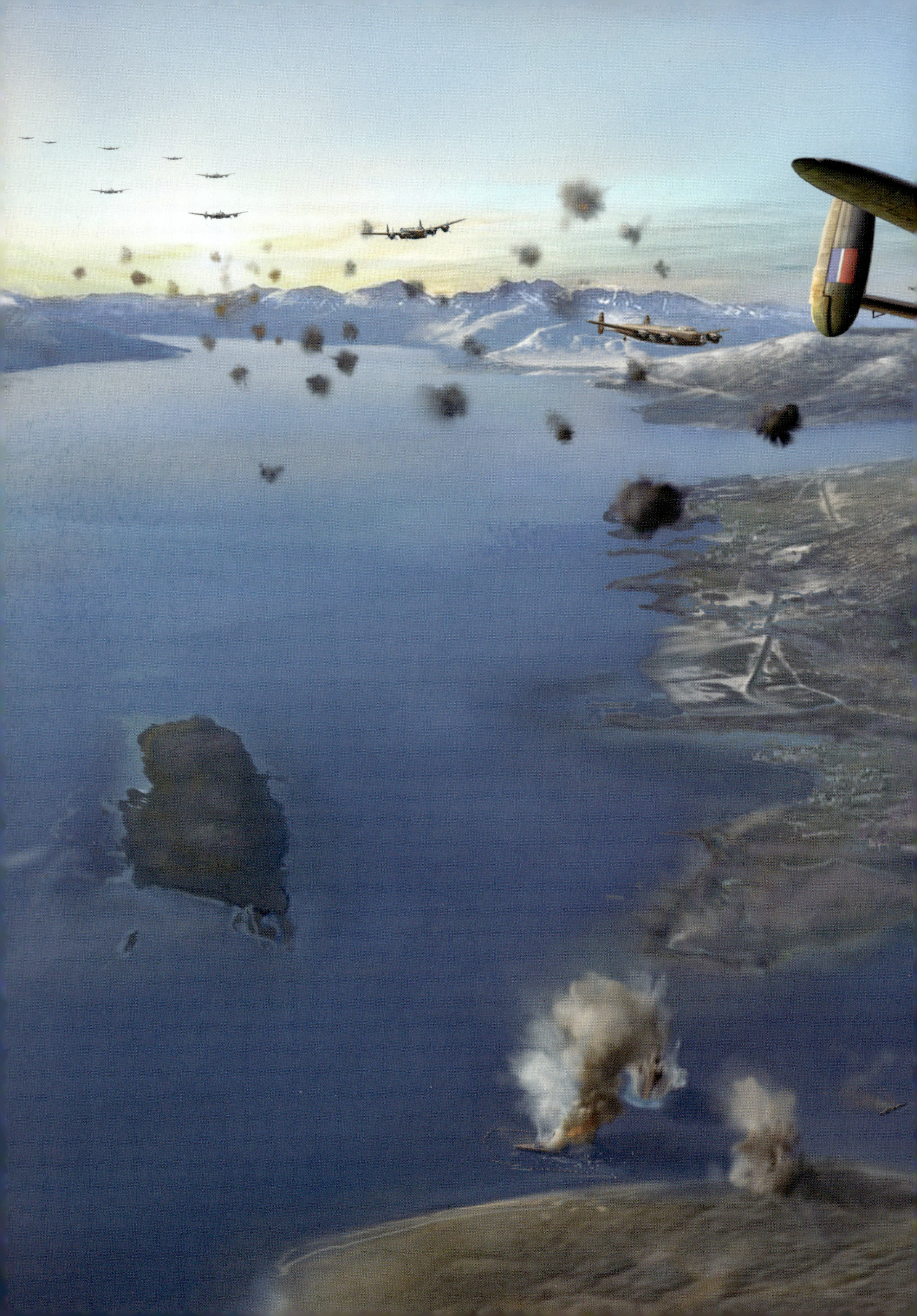

Jim Laurier

92 AFTERMATH AND ANALYSIS

In this diagram, based on information gathered by Bomber Command after Operation *Catechism*, the location of the Tallboy hits on *Tirpitz*, and many of the near misses, have been recorded, along with the order in which the bombs fell. Also shown are the location of the torpedo nets surrounding the battleship.
(Map by Nick Buxey)

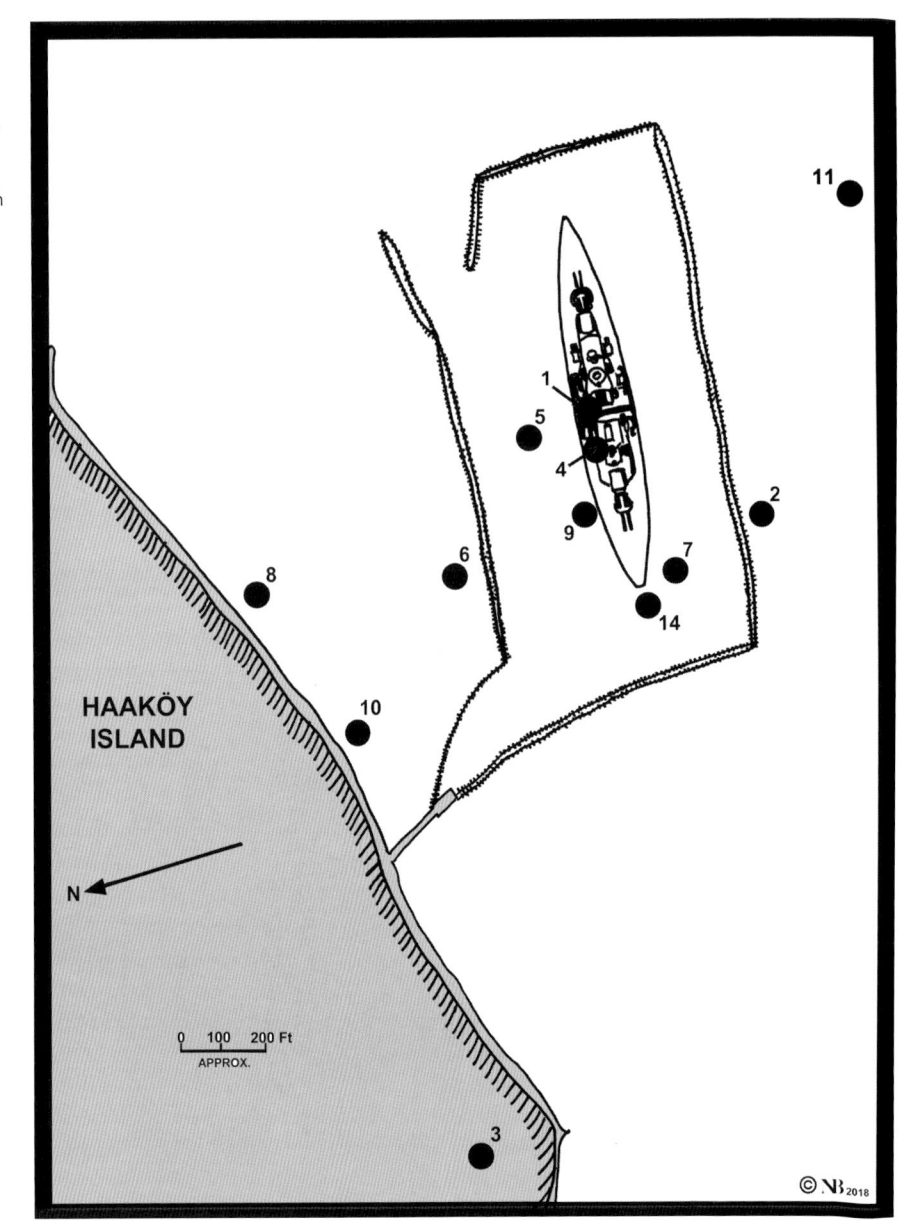

bombers might have a viable aiming point. Still, with insufficient problem-solving, hasty preparation, inadequately trained crews and low-performance aircraft, it is a real achievement that these strikes achieved what they did – a significant degradation of the German battleship's ability to function.

As for Bomber Command's attacks, the spring raids of 1942 proved costly, largely because the bomber crews, however well they had been briefed, were unprepared for the problems they encountered over the Faettenfjord. This was the first demonstration of the effectiveness of the battleship's smoke screen, and it foiled every attack. The bomber aimers had to fall back on dead reckoning – no easy matter while flying at speed up a high-sided fjord, through a wall of smoke. The intense flak took some of the air crews by surprise too. Its intensity is reflected in the relatively high losses encountered by the bomber crews during these attacks – roughly 12 per cent of the airmen who took part were either killed or captured. At least these attacks allowed the planners of Bomber Command's 5 Group something to evaluate, before attempting similar attacks again.

The real problem plaguing the British, however, was a lack of suitable ordnance. The 1,600lb AP bombs and 2,000lb 'cookies' used by the Fleet Air Arm and RAF respectively were powerful enough to inflict damage, especially the naval weapon. Unfortunately, this weapon was let down by manufacturing problems. If it had proved more reliable, and if the Barracuda crews had been able to score more hits, and in the right places, the *Tirpitz* might well have been destroyed six months earlier. However, it was not to be. So it was not until the summer of 1944, and the introduction of the Tallboy, that the British finally had the ordnance they needed to sink the German battleship. This took all the variables of luck and skill out of the equation. With it, even a few near misses could achieve a similar result to a direct hit or two.

In some ways these final operations – *Obviate* and *Catechism* – were something of an anti-climax. By then the *Tirpitz* was so badly damaged that she was no longer a threat to the Arctic Convoys, and with the Allies advancing on Germany from both east and west, the outcome of the war was no longer in doubt. However, what *Catechism* did achieve, apart from the final climactic destruction of the *Tirpitz*, was that it marked the passing of an era. It proved that even a powerful modern battleship was now no match for a bomber that carried the right ordnance. Although the writing had been on the wall for the battleship since 1916, this air campaign demonstrated that it was now a dinosaur on the eve of extinction. Airpower, both land-based and carrier-based, was the real arbiter of victory in the war at sea. The upturned hull of the *Tirpitz*, quietly rusting in a Norwegian fjord, now served as a fitting gravestone for that bygone era.

After the war, a Norwegian salvage company bought the *Tirpitz*, and set about salvaging what they could of her. Up to 1,000 bodies were interred in the battleship, and where possible their remains were recovered as the salvors worked their way through the ship.

FURTHER READING

A young German sailor peering upwards through a series of holes cut in the internal steel bulkheads of *Tirpitz*. Rescuers had to work their way into the ship from the upturned hull. For most of her crew, though, the rescuers were too late.

Bekker, Cajus, *Hitler's Naval War*, London (1974)
Bishop, Patrick, *Target Tirpitz: The Epic Quest to Destroy Hitler's Mightiest Warship*, London (2012)
Campbell, John, *Naval Weapons of World War Two*, London (1985)
Chesneau, Roger, *Aircraft Carriers of the World, 1914 to the Present: An Illustrated Encyclopaedia*, London (1992)
Cooper, Alan W., *Beyond the Dams to the Tirpitz: The Later Operations of 617 Squadron*, London (1983)
Drucker, Graham Roy, *Wings over the Waves: Fleet Air Arm Strike Leader against Tirpitz*, Barnsley (2010)
Forsgren, Jan, *Sinking the Beast: The RAF 1944 Lancaster Raids against Tirpitz*, London (2014)
Gardiner, Robert (ed.), *Conway's All the World's Fighting Ships, 1922–1946*, London (1980)
Grove, Eric, *Sea Battles in Close-Up: World War 2*, Vol. 2, Shepperton (1993)
Iveson, Tony and Milton, Brian, *The Lancaster and the Tirpitz*, London (2014)
Kennedy, Ludovic, *Menace: the Life and Death of the Tirpitz*, London (1979)
Llewellyn-Jones, Malcolm (ed.), *The Royal Navy and the Arctic Convoys: A Naval Staff History*, Abingdon (2007)
Mallmann Showell, Jak P., *Hitler's Navy: A Reference Guide to the Kriegsmarine, 1935–1945*, Barnsley (2009)
Peillard, Léonce, *Sink the Tirpitz!*, London (1983)
Roskill, S.P., *The War at Sea, 1939–45*, vols II and III, London (1954)
Smith, Nigel, *Tirpitz: The Halifax Raids*, Walton-on-Thames (2003)
Sweetman, John, *Tirpitz: Hunting the Beast: Air Attacks on the German Battleship, 1940–44*, Stroud (2000)
Walling, Michael G., *Forgotten Sacrifice: The Arctic Convoys of World War II*, Oxford (2012)
Whitley, M.J., *Battleships of World War Two: An International Encyclopaedia*, London (1998)
Woodward, David, *The Tirpitz*, London (1953)
Zetterling, Niklas and Tamelander, Michael, *Tirpitz: The Life and Death of Germany's Last Super Battleship*, Newbury (2009)

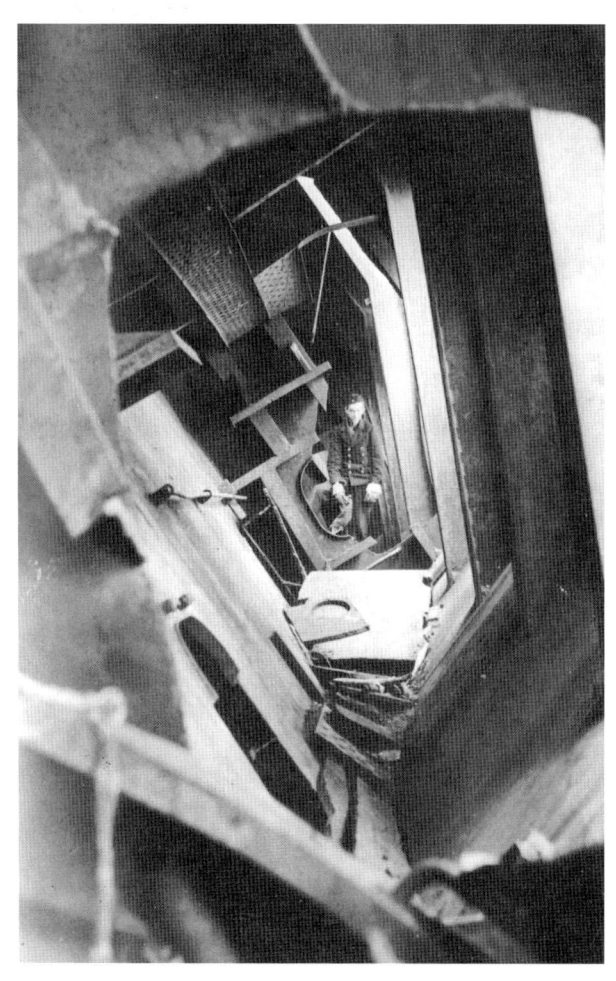

INDEX

Note: page locators in bold refer to illustrations, captions and plates.

air campaigns 4–5, 24, 29, 31–43, **36–37(35)**, **38**, **39**, **44(45)**
aircraft
   Arado spotter plane (Germany) 35
   Avro Lancaster bomber (UK) 8, **9**, **16**, 29, **40**, 41, 42, 43, **44(45)**, 46, 47, **47**, 50, 71, **71**, 74, 75–76, **77**, **78**, 80–81, **82**, 83, **86–87(85)**, 88
   Boeing B-17F bomber (US) 50–51
   Bristol Beaufighter fighter plane (UK) 43, 46, **47**
   Consolidated B-24 Liberator bomber (US) 74, 75
   Fairey Albacore torpedo bomber (UK) 9–10, **10**, 25, 34, **34**, 35, **36–37(35)**, **38**, 38–40, **39**, **44(45)**, 91
   Fairey Barracuda torpedo dive bomber (UK) 10, **10**, **14**, **45**, **52**, 53, 54, 55, **55**, 56, 57, **57**, 59, 60, **60**, 61, **61**, 62, 64, 65, 66–67, **67**, 70, 91
   Fairey Firefly fighter plane (UK) 11, 65, 66, **67**, 70
   Fairey Swordfish TBR plane (UK) 9, 65
   Grumman F4F Wildcat fighter plane (US) 54, 55, 56, **57**, 59, 61
   Grumman F6F Hellcat fighter plane (US) 2, 11, **11**, **53**, 54, **54**, 56, **57**, 59, 62–63, 64, 65, 66, **67**, 70
   Grumman TBF Avenger torpedo bomber (US) **64**, 65
   Handley Page Halifax bomber (UK) 8, **9**, 32, 33, **40**, 41, 42, **42**, 43, **45**, 46, 47, **47**
   Messerschmitt Bf 109 fighter plane (Germany) 24
   Messerschmitt Bf 110 fighter-bomber (Germany) 24
   Short Stirling bomber plane (UK) 8, **8**, **9**, 32
   Supermarine Seafire fighter plane (UK) 11, 54, 64–65, 66, 70

   Vought F4U Corsair fighter-bomber (US) 11, **11**, 54, 55, 56, 57, **57**, **60**, 61, **61**, 62, **63**, 64, 65, 66–67, **67**, 70
Altenfjord, the 51–52, **52**, 55, 56, 60, 74
Amatol 12, **13**, 15, **15**
anti-aircraft batteries 18, **(18)**19, 20, 23, 41, **48**, 52, 56, 57, 59, 62, **67**, 81, 92
Arctic Convoys, the 4, 17, 25, **26**, **26(25)**, 27, 31, 33, 48, 50, 52, 63–64, 71, 88, 89
armour-piercing bombs 12, **12**
armoured protection 12, **12**, 16, 18–20, 30, 59, 60
aviation design limitations 91

Barents Sea, battle of the **26**, **27**, 50
battleship role in modern warfare, the 93
Bomber Command 29, 31, 33, 40, 41, 47, **47**, 50, **67**, 80, **85**, 91, 92, **92**
bomber payloads 8, **9**, 10, 11, 12, 80
bomber routes and carrier launch locations 28
bombing techniques 41–42, **44(45)**, **71**, 75
bombs 9, 10, **10**, 12, **13**, **42**
   18in Mark XII torpedo 14, **14**, 35, **38**, 38–39
   500lb GP bomb 46, **46**, 47, 64
   500lb 'Johnny Walker' (JW) mine-bomb 15, **15**, 74, 76
   600lb anti-submarine (AS) Mark VIII bomb 15, **15**, **53**, 54
   1600lb AP bomb 12, **13**, **14**, **45**, 54, **59**, 60, 67, 71, 93
   2,000lb armour-piercing (AP) bomb 2, **12**, **13**, 32
   4000lb 'blockbuster' bomb 8, 12, **13**, 29, 40–41, 43, **45**, 46, 47, 50
   12,000lb 'Tallboy' bomb 8, 16, **16**, 29, **40**, **44(45)**, **71**, 71–74, **74**, **75**, 76, **77**, **78**, 80, 81, **83**, 84, **90(91)**, **92**, 93
   Mark XIX spherical contact mine 14–15, **15**, 42, 45–46, 47

British strategy 27–29, 33–34, 35–40, 41–42, 49–51, 54–55, 60–62, 63–66, 74, 76, 80–81, 82, 88–89, 91–92

'Caesar' turret 18, **19(18)**, **59**, 84, 85, **91**
camouflage **21**, 25, **32**, 33, 41, **43**, 49
carrier landings 57
chronology of events 6–7
Churchill, Winston 4, 27, 29, 31, 41, 48, 88–89
Ciliax, Vice Adm Otto 33, **33**, 34, 35, 40
Cochrane, Air Vice Marshall Ralph 75
construction 5, **5**, **7**, 12
Convoy PQ-17 6, **25**, **26**, 48, **48**, 49, 88
'Covering Force' for Arctic Convoys 48, 49
'cross-decking' 54
Cunningham, Sir Andrew 60, 63

damage assessment **58(59)**, 59–60
DBST (Double British Summer Time) 2, 76
Dervish Convoy, the 31
Dönitz, Adm Karl 27, 50, 77

experience of air crews 91

Faettenfjord, the **17**, 21, **21**, **22(23)**, 23, 24, 29, 31, **32**, 41, **43**, 45, 46, **49**, 50, 92
filming of operations 74, **74**, 76, 81, 83, 84, **84**, **85**, 89
Fleet Air Arm 9, 10, 12, 14, **14**, 15, **45**, **59**, 91
'fleet in being' naval doctrine 25–27, 29, 50, 88

geographical obstacles to attack 5, 21–24, **22(23)**, 29, 41
German attacks on Arctic Convoys 48, 48–49, 50
German naval strategy 25–27, **27**, **29**, 30, 31, 33, 34, 50, 77, 84–85, 88
graffiti **14**
gunnery exercises 33, 50

INDEX

Hassel, Ilse von 17, **18**
Hitler, Adolf 17, **18**, 25, 40, 49, 50, 88

invasion of the Soviet Union 30, 31

Junge, Capt Wolfe 59, 82

Kaafjord, the 2, 21, **22(23)**, 24, 29, **46**, **49**, **50**, 50–51, **52**, 53, **55**, 62, 66, **72–73**, 76
Kriegsmarine
  Admiral Hipper (heavy cruiser) 23, **23**, 30, 48, 50
  Admiral Scheer (cruiser) 23, **23**, **25**, 33, 43, 46, 48
  Bismarck (battleship) 4, 9, 14, 17, 25, 30–31
  Friedrich Ihn (destroyer) 34, 35, **35**, 39
  Lützow (cruiser) **25**, 48, 50
  Prinz Eugen (heavy cruiser) 23, **23**, 33, 46
  Scharnhorst (battleship) 51
  Tirpitz (battleship) 4, **4**, 5, **5**, 9, 10, 12, **17**, 17–23, **19(18)**, **20**, 21, **22(23)**, 24, 30, 32, 33–39, **34**, **36–37(35)**, **38**, 43, 48, **48**, **49**, 49–50, **50**, 51, **51**, 55
    as floating gun battery 77, **78**, 85
    sinking of **83**, 83–85, **84**, **86–87(85)**, 89
    strikes and damage **56**, 56–60, **57**, **58**, **59**, 66–67, 77, **82**, 88, 89, **89**, **90(91)**, 92

losses 4, 32, 33, **35**, 41, 46, 47, **47**, 57, 59, 62–63, 65, 66, 67, 76, 85, 92
Lucas, Lt Cmdr 34, 35, 38, 39, 40
Luftwaffe, the 24, 25, 48, 84, 88
Luftwaffe/Kriegsmarine rivalry 24, 27, 35

Mahan, Alfred Thayer 27
Meyer, Capt Hans 50, 56, 59
Moore, Vice Adm Sir Henry 52, 54, 60, 61, 62, 63, 64, 65–66, 67, 71

naval command structure 27, 50
naval defences 24, 27, **32**, 33, 41, **43**, 45, 46, 52, **55**, 60, **60**, 62, **67**, 77–80, **80**, 82, **92**
North Cape, battle of 51
Norwegian anchorages 21–23, **22(23)**, **24**, 25, 31, 41

Norwegian resistance, the **24**, 33, 40

Operations 6–7, 30, **50**, 61
  Catechism (November 1944) 16, **28**, 29, **70**, **78–79**, 82–85, **83**, **84**, **86–87(85)**, 89, **90(91)**, 93
  Goodwood I-IV (August 1944) 7, 11, **63**, **64**, 65, 66, 66–71, **68–69(67)**, **72–73**
  Mascot (July 1944) **61**, 61–63, **72–73**
  Obviate (October 1944) 7, **28**, 29, **70**, **78–79**, 80–82, **85**, 89, **91**, 93
  Oiled (January 1942) 6, 31–33
  Paravane (September 1944) 29, **70**, **74**, 74–77, 80, 89, **90(91)**
  Rösselsprung (July 1943) 6, 48, **48**, 50
  Source (September 1943) 6, **50**, 51
  Sportpalast (March 1942) 6, **28**, 33–40, **36–37(35)**, **38**, 39
  Title (October 1942) 6, 50
  Tungsten (April 1944) 2, 7, **11**, 14, 20, **52**, 52–61, **53**, **54**, **55**, **56**, **57**, **58(59)**, 64, **72–73**, 88, 91

performance 8, 9, 11
Pound, Sir Dudley 49
PRU (Photographic Reconnaissance Unit) 11–12, **30**, 31, 33, 41, **48**, **49**, 50, **50**, 51, 52, 53, **55**, 60, 76, 77, **80**, 81

Raby, Torstein **24**
radar capability 18, **20**, 24, 62, 81
Raeder, Grand Adm Erich 27, **27**, 30, 50, 88
RAF, the 51
  9 Sqn 29, 74, 76, **78**, 80, 81, 82, 83, 84, **85**
  10 Squadron 32, 41, 45, 46, 47, **47**
  617 Sqn 'Dambusters' 29, 50, **70**, **71**, 74, **75**, 76, 80, 81, 82, **82**, 83, **83**, 84, **85**
  832 Squadron 34, 35, 38, 39, **39**
raids of March–April 1942 40–47, **42**, **46**, **47**
range limitations 5, 8, **9**, **10**, **45**, 80
RDF (radio direction finding) stations 24
reconnaissance **10**, 11–12, **30**, **34**, 51
  see also PRU (Photographic Reconnaissance Unit)
release heights for bombs 41–42, **44(45)**, 46, 47, 54, 56, **60**, **67**, 76, 83–84

repairs 51–52, 63, **66**, **78**
Royal Navy, the 4
  HMS *Anson* (battleship) 61
  HMS *Formidable* (carrier) 67
  HMS *Furious* (carrier) **52**, 53, **53**, 54, 57, **57**, 61, 62, 64, 65, 67
  HMS *Hood* (battlecruiser) 4
  HMS *Indefatigable* (carrier) 67
  HMS *Nabob* (battlecruiser) 29, 64, 65, **66**
  HMS *Victorious* (carrier) 25, 27, 34, **34**, **35**, 49, 52, 53, **53**, 54, 57, **57**, 61, 62, 91

Schniewind, Adm Otto **29**
smoke screen defences 24, 43, 45, 46, 52, **55**, **60**, 62, 66, **67**, 70, **74**, 83, 91, 92
Soviet involvement 6, 11, 23, **48**, **49**, 51, 52, 64, 74, 76
speeds 11, **20**
strategic situation in the Norwegian sea, 1942–44 **26**
Sugden, Lt Cmdr 35, **35**, 39

Tait, Wing Cmdr Willy **70**, 74, 76, 83, 84, **88**
Topp, Capt Karl **31**, 38, 41, 50, **51**
torpedo nets 12, 14, 17, 21, **21**, 23, 25, 27, 41, **48**, **50**, **55**, **73**, **80**, 82, 83, **92**
Torpex 16, **16**
Tovey, Adm 33, 34, 48
training 21, 31, 38, 51, **71**, 91
Trondheimsfjord, the 21, 24, 42, 45, 50

U-boat attacks 25, 48, 49, 65, **66**, 77, 88
Ultra signal intercepts 34, 71, 77
underwater damage from 'earthquake' effect 15, 20, 45, 54, 77, 85, **85**, **91**

weaponry 18, **19(18)**, **20**, 23, **32**, 38, 46, 47, **48**, 56–57, 59, 62, 63, 67, 71, 80, 81, 82, 83
weather conditions 5, 6, 7, 29, 34, **35**, 47, 48, 50, 52, 53, 61, 63, 64, 65, 66, **67**, 74, 75, **78**, 80–82
Weber, Capt Robert 82, 84, 85
weights **9**
Wilhelmshaven launch 17, **18**, 31

X-craft midget submarines (UK) 51, 88

CW01213141

All rights reserved. No part of this publication may be reproduced, stored in a retrieval system, or transmitted in any form or by any means, electronic, electrostatic, recording, magnetic tape, mechanical, photocopying or otherwise, without prior permission in writing from the publisher.

The publisher makes no representation, express or implied, with regard to the accuracy of the information contained in this publication and cannot accept any responsibility in law for any errors or omissions.

The right of David Roberts to be identified as the author of this work has been asserted by him in accordance with sections 77 and 78 of the Copyright, Designs and Patents Act 1988. No part of this book may be reproduced in any form without permission from the publisher except for the quotation of brief passages in reviews.

A catalogue record for this book is available from the British Library.

This edition © This Day In Music Books 2020. Text ©This Day In Music Books 2020

ISBN: 978-1-8380783-1-7

The author and publisher gratefully acknowledge the permission granted to reproduce the copyright material in this book. Every effort has been made to trace the copyright holders of the photographs in this book but one or two were unreachable. We would be grateful if the photographers concerned would contact us.

Production Liz Sánchez and Neil Cossar
Design and layout by Gary Bishop
Album and singles artwork photography by Ian T. Cossar
Thanks to Dave Evely and all at Sound Perfomance. Printed in the Czech Republic

This Day In Music Books Bishopswood Road, Prestatyn, LL199PL

THIS DAY IN MUSIC BOOKS

www.thisdayinmusicbooks.com

Email: editor@thisdayinmusic.com

Exclusive Distributors: Music Sales Limited 14/15 Berners St London W1T 3JL

Foreword by Paul Rodgers

Every audience creates their own field of energy and has their own unique experience of the concert. There is an undeniable energy exchange between the fans and the musicians, this is what makes each night different. Performing live is always an uplifting and learning experience for me.

This book is by the fans, for the fans and because of you beautiful people. Thanks for taking the time to..... remember when.

I look forward to reading it.

Love Paul.

See you at the next show!!!

A

Bad Company

Manufactured in the UK

45 RPM
SSK 19416
(SS 70119)
S&K 19416 A
℗ 1979
SIDE ONE
STEREO

ROCK 'N' ROLL FANTASY
(Paul Rodgers)
Produced by Bad Company
WARNER BROS. MUSIC

Foreword by Simon Kirke

This book is dedicated to all the loyal fans who have followed us over the years — 50 + still counting! Thanks to you our music has survived + thrived — at any given moment somewhere in the world a Free or Bad Company song is being played.

Without you there would not have been us....

Thank you

Simon.

1954

Colin Bradley
St. Joseph's Infants/Junior School, Middlesbrough, UK

When did I first meet Paul Rodgers? Paul and I would have started school at St. Joseph's Infants/Juniors on the same day in 1954, having been born in 1949. We are close in age – both of our birthdays are in December and just 16 days apart. I suppose my earliest memories of Paul would be from perhaps 1956 or 57. We went on to attend St. Thomas' [Secondary Modern] on Highfield Road together, starting in 1961 when the school was very new, and gradually got to know each other more. Paul and I were very different kinds of personalities – he was very active and sporty, good at soccer and other physical activities like judo etc. I on the other hand, was hopelessly inept at any kind of sport, so I suppose it is interesting that it was music that eventually drew us closer together.

I was born into a family where music was a daily occurrence. My parents both sang as a couple, my Mam played a bit of piano, and all of my brothers and sisters (there were seven of us in total) could hold a tune. I was the youngest, having come along fairly late in my parents' marriage, so I spent a lot of time as a child in adult company. One of my brothers borrowed a guitar owned by a cousin and began to teach himself some basic chords to folk songs. I picked it up one day when I must have been about seven or eight-years-old, and it all started right there.

As a young child, I had been exposed to all kinds of popular music as a result of family gatherings such as weddings, birthdays etc., which invariably ended up in a sing-song session, so lots of the late 40s/early 50s crooner stuff like Vera Lynn, Nat King Cole, Rosemary Clooney, Doris Day, Sinatra etc. etc. Then came the phenomena of Elvis, Bill Haley, Buddy Holly etc. from the US, and of course our own musical trailblazers such as Lonnie Donegan, and it was really Donegan's skiffle thing that got me wanting to play the guitar in earnest. I was also listening to a lot of the early folk music stuff like Pete Seeger, and later on, Peter Paul and Mary and others. *Colin Bradley was a member of the 1960s group, The Road Runners, with Paul Rodgers*

1962

Paul Rodgers

St Thomas' Secondary Modern School, Middlesbrough, UK

I used to sit in class at St Thomas' Secondary Modern and watch the smoke billowing out of the steel works: that was my future.

Simon Kirke

When my family got its first TV, an old black and white set, one of the first shows I saw was *All That Jazz* which featured big bands playing swing music for the most part. I was fascinated by the drummer for some reason and it was at that moment I felt the pull, as it were, especially when he did a solo. I was enthralled and picked up a spare pair of my Mum's knitting needles and started tapping away on the electric fire.

Later I covered an old chocolate drop tin in paper and Scotch tape for a tom tom and had a couple of books of varying thicknesses for different pitches and spread them out on my bed. With a pair of sticks cut from a hedge - primitive days back then! - and with one earpiece dangling from a transistor radio, I played along to songs mainly from Radio Luxembourg and later Radio Caroline. Those pirate radio ships were a musical Godsend.

My first kit was a red sparkle Gigster: a four piece with a 12-inch cymbal. It cost 18 quid, which I borrowed from my dad and paid him back mowing lawns.

The first record I bought could've been 'Move It' by Cliff Richard and the Shadows, or 'Shakin' All Over' by Johnny Kidd and the Pirates, or maybe The Safaris' 'Wipe Out'.

My early idols? Elvis, Little Richard (I was a huge fan), Ray Charles, Otis Redding, Wilson Pickett. Al Jackson Jr. was my number one influence when it came to drumming. Then there was Buddy Rich, Ringo Starr, Charlie Watts and the three Motown drummers: Pistol Allen, Uriel Jones and Benny Benjamin, and Zigaboo Modeliste with the Meters too.

Ian Dalgarno

St Thomas' Secondary Modern school is where Paul Rodgers and I were both in the same class all through from 1961 up to 1965. He was very articulate and very bright. We weren't best mates, his close friends were Alan Delove and Paul Shields I think. Apart from being very creative, even back then, Paul was very competitive. I remember how we used to race bikes we'd made ourselves up and down the football field at school. His group played at the school assembly hall a few times. You could always tell he had something. Did I think he'd make a career out of music back then? Well, he's never had a 'proper' job, has he! *Ian Dalgarno is the former Mayor of Stockton-on-Tees and Thornaby*

1963

June Lipscombe

Back in the early Sixties, (I was June Hale then), Paul used to live next door in Saltersgill Avenue in Middlesbrough. I suppose I was one of the first fans to hear his music! I must have been about 14. We could hear him playing guitar and practising in the front room. Unusually for those times, my parents never objected. In fact, they really liked his music and the popular records of that time. We got on well, they were such lovely neighbours.

George Johnstone

I attended the same school, St. Thomas' Roman Catholic Secondary school in Middlesbrough, and Paul [Rodgers] was two years above me. His big friends were Mick Moody, who became famous in the music world also, and Colin Bradley. Together they formed a band together, The Road Runners, and would play at break times and even in school concerts and anywhere they were allowed to perform. I think Colin Bradley is resident in Canada now and featured on YouTube recently with Paul when he toured there solo. They were always in the music room practising when possible and tutored by a dedicated excellent music teacher, Mr Lawson.

As well as their dedication to music, both Paul and Mick proved to be excellent footballers but, alas, not Colin who seemed to prefer his music.

My memory of Paul, aided and abetted by Mr Moody, centres around the football pitch during a practice match where following an incident with myself they were both sent off and told to go home, as this was after school. The teacher concerned was a Mr. Joe Horkan.

So off they went. The game continued and there was plenty of time left to finish. On completion of the practice and returning to the changing rooms I found that all of my clothes had disappeared. Following a search, I discovered them in the shower, having been run under the water and completely sodden. As Paul and Mick Moody were the only two who had access to the changing area - it was all locked up and the teacher in charge gave them the key that they returned whilst the game was still in progress - it was blatantly obvious who was responsible! I had to travel home in my football kit, a journey that involved a long walk via where, I presumed, they would be gathering.

I decided to seek them out via the white bridge that spanned the beck and spotted them. Needless to say, words were exchanged and a small scuffle ensued and I gained my revenge by pushing Paul into the water. Then I continued my journey home - revenge completed!

Mick Moody, of Whitesnake fame, went on to make a career in music. Although I have never seen Free, I am fully aware of Paul's association with Brian May and Queen and everything else he has done. Paul Rodgers was always destined to go far within the music business. It is no surprise he has been a success and every time I hear 'All Right Now' it reminds me of him and how dedicated he was to his music and achieving that goal.

Paul, Mick and Colin might like to know that although several of the teachers at St. Thomas' at that time have sadly passed away, two I know are still around. Mr. Roe resides in Nunthorpe and Mr. Horkan in Ormesby. A lot of us have fond memories of those times and The Road Runners.

Lesley Willis

I've never actually met Paul Rodgers but I feel I know him quite well through his mother, Phyllis. I've worked for many years as a hairdresser for Richard Dye, in Middlesbrough. A regular customer, Phyllis Rodgers was the sweetest, most delightful woman you could ever meet. A good Catholic and proper down to earth Middlesbrough mum. She looked after a big family and brought them all up well in Grove Hill. I used to say to her, 'You must be so proud of Paul,' and she'd come back quick as a flash with: 'I am but I'm really proud of all of them.'

Bedford on keyboards and the TD teacher on saxophone. This was a closed event in the TD classroom.

Paul and I often met up to either listen to music or jam together. He had a number of other friends that were also musicians and he was part of at least one group, but I never saw him playing to an audience.

At this time (1963-66) just about every other street in London had a budding musician looking for a chance to play in a group. Whitefield had several of these school groups and I formed one called Shades Of Time, later known just as Shades. This was a four-piece, two guitars, bass and drums. Initially, I was a rhythm guitarist but as our bass player was not up to scratch, I was persuaded to take up bass and lead vocals. I traded in my beloved Watkins for a Framus 5/150 bass and apart from a few lessons, I was self-taught. Shades, along with the other school groups, began working the local circuit of youth clubs, schools and some of the smaller music venues. On two occasions we recruited Paul to play with us, on the first gig (a private party) we died a long and painful death! The audience was not receptive to blues and rock, although the second gig went okay, and we actually played two encores.

Our joint education in the blues would continue a year later when we began attending gigs.

1964

Colin Bradley

St. Mary's Boys Club, Sussex Street, Middlesbrough, UK
7 December, 1964

When myself, Mick(y) Moody and Paul [Rodgers] first got together to try and play stuff, it would have been early in 1964. So by then, the Beatles and the Rolling Stones were established and very much the happening thing. We tended to veer towards the early Stones kind of stuff, and then as a result became quickly interested in the artists that they themselves were covering. So atypically for kids of that age, we started getting into people like Little Walter, Willie Dixon, Howlin' Wolf, Muddy Waters and seeking out material that was kind of odd for our collective age bracket. At the same time though, we were obviously listening to pop radio and hearing bands like The Searchers, The Hollies, The Who and other similar acts that were enjoying chart success. So it really was a mish-mash of influences and inspirations. I still have the original book kept by my eldest brother Joe, who managed The Road Runners, which not only lists every show we ever did, including remuneration received and expenses incurred, but also catalogues our entire musical repertoire, totalling some 109 songs. It is interesting to see how the songs we were playing in our very early days subsequently morphed between genres as our musical tastes diversified. In the sunset days of The Road Runners, as the other members were yearning for a full-time musical career and my own intentions of staying close to home with a 'real job' became apparent, we were playing a lot of Otis Redding, Sam Cooke, Stax, Motown type things as convincingly as we could without a horn section. A big part of the ability to do that was because of Paul's remarkable voice, which could 'sell' that kind of stuff to an audience convincingly. The very first time it became apparent that Paul had a special vocal gift was when we worked up Little Richard's 'Long Tall Sally', and that was very early in the game. He could really shred those kinds of songs, like The Beatles' version of 'Money' too. Our old friend and mentor John McCoy recognised Paul's abilities in that regard immediately, and the story of his involvement with The Road Runners' development is well documented elsewhere.

The Road Runners' first gig? That was on December 7th, 1964 at St. Mary's Boys Club on Sussex Street in Middlesbrough. It was arranged by Vince Early, who was a school teacher at St. Thomas' and who used to run the boys club. We were paid fifteen shillings and had to plug our little amplifiers into a single overhead light-bulb socket via an extension cable. It's a wonder we weren't all killed. I remember it vividly.

Mick Moody
guitar

Paul Rodgers
vocals

Andy Fraser

I lived in London until I was about 22. I started classical piano tuition from the age of five (very precocious) until about 12 then got more interested in the guitar, The Beatles, and all the other great groups of the time. From about the age of 12 until 15 I was playing in blues bands playing Motown, Stax, and blues covers, scaring my mother to death, as I would get home at four or five in the morning after gigs, and I was 12.

1965

Colin Green

1965, Whitefield Secondary Modern School, Hendon, North West London, UK

My memories of Paul Kossoff? He and I attended the same school and we were almost in a band together. Around the age of 13 or 14 we became friends at Whitefield Secondary Modern. The school had a bit of a reputation of being tough, with the council estate boys going there. It was a good school overhaul with some great teachers, although back then discipline was strong and the cane was administered if you didn't toe the line. We had some now famous boys come from the school such as footballer Tony Currie, long-distance runner David Bedford, entrepreneur and cricketer David English, and of course Paul.

He was even then a bit of a rebel, so suited the school perfectly! I think Paul had been to a few schools and Whitfield was his last chance saloon. Around 1965 I became lead singer in a band called The Rest with four of my friends, which went on to be very successful in North West London playing Motown, soul and R&B. In 1965, we needed a lead guitarist and Paul came to audition. Unbeknown to me Paul was very into blues and rock, which reflected in his guitar playing and the volume at the audition, so unfortunately we had to turn him down for the band, which was a shame as even then he was a very good guitarist. Who knows, we may have changed history if we'd taken him on but, seriously, I very much doubt it.

Who knew then that he would become lead guitarist in a world renowned band like Free? Oh well, our loss I guess.

Colin Bradley

7 March 1965, The Catcote, Hartlepool, County Durham, UK

The first serious 'audition' type show was at Brambles Farm Club on 22 January 1965. The first proper 'pub' gig was at the Catcote in Hartlepool on 7 March 1965. Other venues that became regular gigs for us included the Acklam Steelworks Club, as well as numerous places in and around 'pit country' such as Wheatley Hill. In addition, we did a bunch of youth club dates like Joe Walton's Thorntree Youth Club, Whinney Banks Youth Club and many more.

Lesley Brownbridge

The Jubilee, Stockton-on-Tees, UK

When I was Lesley Gray back in the mid-60s I used to travel around the Stockton and Middlesbrough area with the group Paul Rodgers started his career in, The Road Runners. I was 16 or 17 at the time. We knew Joe Bradley, the manager and his brother Colin, the guitarist. My brother was Dave Gray, the group's roadie and every Saturday night he would take me with him to a dance hall called the Jubilee in Stockton. The atmosphere used to be fantastic and the place was absolutely packed. There were no tickets. Someone would take the money and put it in a little box at the top of the stairs as the crowds of people tried to get in. The songs they performed were mostly covers but all the music was dance music. Paul was very popular with the girls and I was always being asked by my school friends and girls at GEC where I worked to get them into the hall.

Paul was always up with the latest trends and fashion compared to the rest of The Road Runners. I remember he used to wear spats! He was a very confident performer. After the group had finished on a Saturday night we would all go off to Middlesbrough town centre to a nightclub called The Purple Onion.

When Joe Bradley died years ago, Paul sent condolences. He never forgot his roots.

Paul Rodgers

That Otis [Redding] thing. His voice leapt out of the speakers when I first heard 'Respect' or 'Mr. Pitiful'. Otis, Elmore James, Albert King, Sam & Dave became my teachers.

Paul's inspiration: Otis Redding

1966

Colin Bradley

The Road Runners line-up looked like this: Colin Bradley, Mick(y) Moody, Paul Rodgers and a drummer called Malcolm Cairns who was introduced to us by Vince Early. Cairns did not last long and was replaced by Dave Usher. In June 1966, Paul switched to front man/vocalist and Bruce Thomas joined on bass. Bruce was a work-mate of Mick Moody's at the Middlesbrough local paper, the *Evening Gazette*.

The much commented-upon colour photos of the band were taken by my brother Joe, in and around this house, which was in Norton. He had no photographic aptitude whatsoever, but those photos taken with an old Kodak Brownie were really quite something.

Here are some examples of the songs The Road Runners played:

High Heel Sneakers (Tommy Tucker – 1963)
What A Shame (Rolling Stones – 1965)
Louie Louie (Kingsmen – 1963)
Mr. Tambourine Man (Byrds version 1965)
For Your Love (Yardbirds 1965)
Confessin' The Blues (Rolling Stones version – 1965)
Black Girl (Leadbelly)
Oh Carol (Chuck Berry)
Around and Around (Rolling Stones)
Heart Full Of Soul (Yardbirds)
In The Midnight Hour (Otis Redding)
Soulful Dress (Sugar Pie DeSanto)
Sha la la la Lee (Small Faces)
Shotgun Wedding (Roy C – 1965)
Getting Mighty Crowded (Betty Everett 1964)

The gig diary lists a total of 134 shows between December 1964 and November 1966, when I left the band. They continued to play into early 1967 before leaving Middlesbrough for London. When Paul stopped playing bass guitar and switched to front man doing lead vocals, and we recruited Bruce Thomas to play bass, the dynamic in the band changed. Paul, Mick(y) Moody and Bruce were set on leaving Teesside and moving to London to give full-time music a shot. Drummer Dave Usher was also persuaded to adopt this plan, and so I was the only member not committed to it. I agreed to leave and let them do their thing. I soon found a gig in another local band, and they went off to London, signed up with the Cana Variety Agency, changed their name to The Wild Flowers (the Summer of Love in 1967 had taken hold), and commenced the grind of one night stands up and down the country in a clapped out Ford Thames van. It didn't last. The rest is history if you read Paul's story.

What became of The Road Runners band members? Dave Usher lives in Ireland and has been a drummer in scores of part time bands for his entire life. He made his living as an HGV driver, but plays drums to this day.

Micky Moody was a member of Whitesnake (along with David Coverdale, also Teesside born), and has enjoyed a lifelong career as a sideman, studio musician and singer song-writer in his own right. These days he performs in a duo with his wife Ali Maas as well as in a number of other band projects, and lives in Twickenham.

Bruce Thomas played with Quiver, who for a while were associated with The Sutherland Brothers. He subsequently joined Elvis Costello's Attractions and was eventually inducted as a member of the Rock and Roll Hall of Fame. These days he still plays bass and has also carved out a career as a writer, having published books on his musical career as well as martial arts and boxing.

Original drummer Malcolm Cairns passed away several years ago.

As for yours truly, I enjoyed a 47-year-career in the engineering and construction business, whilst playing in bands continuously for my entire life.

Selmer Musical Instruments Ltd

MARK VI Tenor, completely overhauled, relacquered	130 gns.
MARK VI Alto. As new	115 gns.
SELMER Mk. VI Soprano, absolutely as new	85 gns.
Selection of S/H Clarinet Outfits	15 gns.
KARL MEYER Tenor Outfit	52 gns.
CONN 10M Tenor, c/o, relacq. Beeson pads	120 gns.
CONN Cornet	38 gns.
MARTIN Trumpet	58 gns.
KING 2B Trombone, lacq.	39 gns.
KING Symphony Silversonic Trumpet, dual bore	125 gns.
VOX Escort Guitar	£21
FUTURAMA III Guitar	£19
GIBSON 335 with BIGSBY	145 gns.
FUTURAMA II de luxe, immaculate	20 gns.
HARMONY H77 Guitar	85 gns.
GRIMSHAW, 2 P/up	50 gns.
HOFNER Senator Guitar, perfect	£22.10
FRAMUS Bass	37 gns.
WEM 3 P/up de luxe with Bigsby	75 gns.
GRETSCH GUITARS, large selection from	£110
GUILD Starfire. Now only	110 gns.
RICKENBACKER Solid, 3 P/up	118 gns.
HOFNER Artist Bass Guitar	£30
GRETSCH 'Country Gent.', as new	180 gns.
GIBSON L.5, with De Armonde Pick-up	250 gns.
BURNS Split Sonic Guitar	£41
GIBSON 330	135 gns.
FENDER Jaguar, as new	135 gns.
BURNS Left-hand Bass	£28
CHET ATKINS Hollow Body Guitar, immaculate condition	145 gns.
GRIMSHAW, 2 P/up, semi-acoustic with Bigsby	45 gns.
BURNS JAZZ GUITAR	75 gns.
HOFFNER Verithin, Stereo	£66
HOPF Guitar with de Armonde P/up, absolutely as new	52 gns.
FENDER Bassman Amp, bargain offer	£110
BURNS Double 12 Amp., now only	53 gns.

STOCK OF ACCORDIONS AT BARGAIN PRICES

REPAIRS AND OVERHAULS A SPECIALITY. FIRST-CLASS WORKSHOPS, SKILLED CRAFTSMEN
HIRE PURCHASE — PART EXCHANGES

114-116 Charing Cross Road, W.C.2. TEM 5432. Open 9.30-6 Weekdays. All day Saturdays (Thursdays after 1 p.m. until 6 p.m. Repairs and payments only)

The Selmer music store was a Mecca for guitarists. While working as an assistant at the London shop in 1966, the 16-year-old Paul Kossoff served Jimi Hendrix

Paul Kossoff

Sixteen-year-old Paul Kossoff recounted a story about Jimi Hendrix visiting the Selmer [guitar store in Charing Cross Road] and he described Hendrix as 'looking and smelling strange.' He went on to claim that he was the only assistant to step forward and offer his help, and they watched 'wide-eyed' as the young American 'took down a right-handed model, flipped it over and played it upside down with no problem.'

Derek Carter

22 April 1966, The Refectory, Golders Green, London, UK

Having performed a couple of concerts together ourselves, Paul Kossoff and I began attending a few gigs to expand our awareness of the blues. One I recall was to see John Mayall with Eric Clapton at The Refectory in Golders Green. Paul was in awe afterwards: he did not stop talking about Clapton for days.

By this time Paul had left school and after briefly working with his father got a job as an assistant at Selmer's music shop on Charing Cross Road in London. Selmer's was a Mecca for guitarists, so he was clearly in his element. Around the same time he had formed Black Cat Bones, a pure blues band.

Derek Carter with his 1964 Fender Precision bass

I left school in 1966 to start as an apprentice photographer with the Shell Photo Unit on Warren Street, London. One morning whilst waiting for the Tube at Golders Green Station, I spotted a familiar face, it was Paul on his way to Selmer's. We shared our underground trip on the Northern Line catching up and chewing the fat, so to speak. This later became a regular event and helped to pass the tedious daily rush-hour trip.

At this point in time, I had been in and out of various groups, still playing bass. One day, I mentioned to Paul that I wanted to upgrade my bass guitar (at that time a Hagström Kent) to something better, preferably a Fender. So the suggestion was this; if he came across something that would fit, could he let me know? A few weeks later, Paul called me up at home to tell me that he had a Fender Precision in the shop and I was welcome to try it out.

The next day I left work early and went straight over to Selmer's with my Hagström in hand. Paul greeted me with his warm impish smile, then off he went and returned with a long black guitar case: the silver Fender logo immediately caught my eye. Three clicks of the latches, the lid raised, and it was love at first sight. There she was, a 1964 Precision, Olympic White, a few dents and dings but otherwise perfect. I ran my hands up and down the neck, twiddled the knobs, checked the action and promptly asked to plug in. After a few riffs and more knob twiddling, I was sold, or more to the point that bass was sold. We worked out a great deal, my Hagström in part exchange and the rest in cash. Thanks Paul, I owe you!

1967

Paul Rodgers

There are many singles that have kind of been milestones, turning points in my life. 'Hey Joe' by Jimi Hendrix is one of those. He brought the blues to life and blew away everything in its path. He delivered the story with his voice and guitar in an understated but completely masterful way. It's like you're there with him walking down the street in another world – like watching a movie. There are some low-pitched female voices in the background doing 'oohs' and 'aahs', almost like angels watching over the unfolding story. The sad but inevitable foolishness of mankind. I like his throwaway ad-libs on vocal, and his guitar never aimed at being flash – getting the point across and all the more brilliant for it. Jimi baby could sure nail your soul to the wall when he got it right.

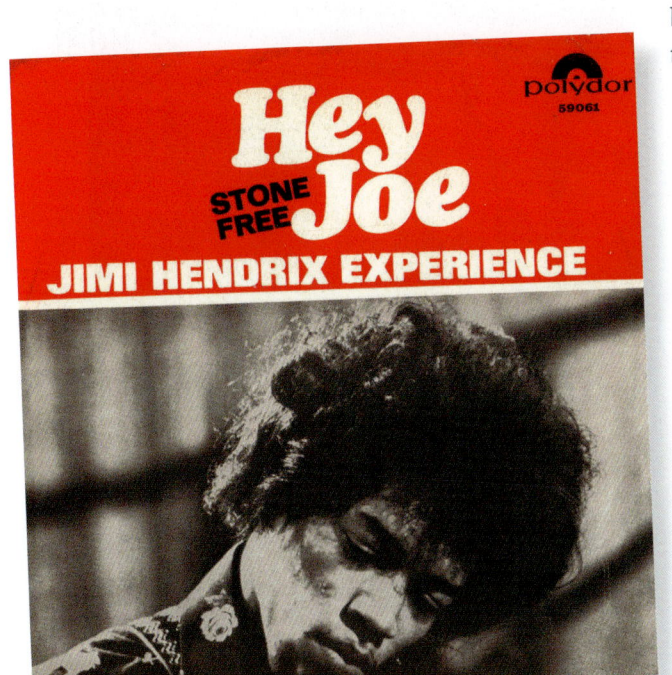

Andy Fraser

Age 15, I joined the Bluesbreakers. I was very excited to be playing with such musicians and respected them as my elders. I felt especially close to Mick Taylor, as he was only 19 and the next youngest. I used to sneak off and share a joint, something John Mayall would have fired us for, as he was a Bemax and

John Mayall's Bluesbreakers, with Keith Tillman (second from the right), who Andy Fraser replaced. Pictorial Press Ltd / Alamy Stock Photo

Corn Flakes kinda guy, nothing like his image suggests. But I held them all in high esteem, considered them my seniors, and learnt all I could.

A major influence on me was meeting Alexis Korner. I had gone to college after being expelled from school for refusing to cut my hair, and became very close with Sappho, Alexis' daughter. I spent a lot of time at their home, playing his guitars, listening to his records, and getting educated in the music industry. Alexis was like a substitute father. My own was an asshole. Alexis did everything humanly possible to educate me, share his experience, get us a manager, then get us with Chris Blackwell's Island Records, absolutely the best label for us. Then he had us open gigs with him. Can't give the guy enough credit. He was a fun guy, very intelligent, spoke about 15 languages, and thought I rolled an excellent joint. I spent so much time there with Sappho listening to his blues records, it was the best education I could have had.

Paul Rodgers

Going to the clubs. The Kirklevington and the Purple Onion, you heard the records and the live bands too. The Who, Cream. Jack Bruce three feet in front of me playing his harmonica. Marshall stacks, sweat running down the walls. The real deal.

Derek Carter

6 October 1967, The Marquee Club, London, UK

I went to see my old school friend Paul Kossoff with Black Cat Bones at the Marquee in 1967, when they supported Ten Years After. It was Friday Night Blues, as I understand, a new type of gig for the Marquee. Although the large audience were there primarily to see Ten Years After, both bands were excellent and I stood there in awe and was proud to see Paul receiving the appreciation he deserved. It was the first time I saw him playing a Les Paul and he made that axe sing! I'd never seen Ten Years After before and they were amazing, especially Alvin Lee. But he was no way comparable to Paul Kossoff... apples and oranges!

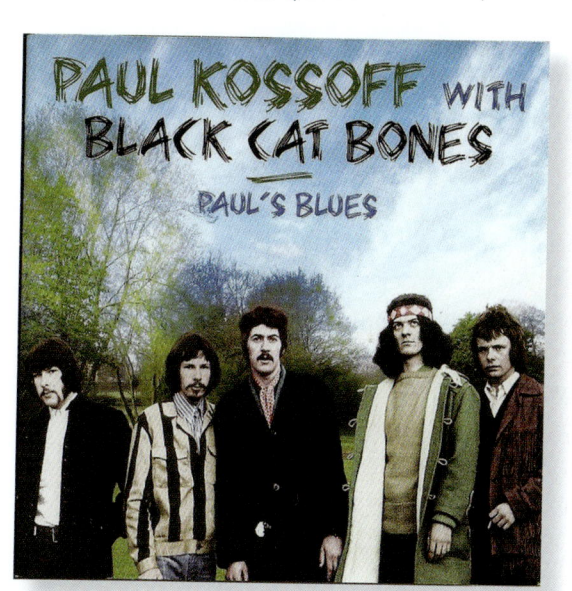

Deep down I wished that I was on bass backing Paul that night, but such is life. For Paul, Black Cat Bones turned out to be the stepping stone into Free, and the world would never be the same!

1968

Caroline Ingledew

Everybody used to say I must be Paul Rodgers' twin sister! We were actually cousins but we shared the same looks. I had his eyes and his dimple! He was a bit older than me and a bit bossy.

Simon Kirke

I first met Paul Kossoff at a pub called The Nag's Head in Battersea, London.

I had gone there on a whim because I was intrigued about this band called Black Cat Bones. I thought it was a great name. When I got there I guess they were about half way through the first set. The band was just above average I guess, but the guitarist was really special. He was quite small but he played with such a passion that he got my attention straight away.

During the break he came to the bar and I complimented him on his playing and asked if he would like a drink. This was Paul. As an aside I said, 'I really don't think your drummer is very good...' and he said with a smile that this was the guy's last gig with them that night. They were holding auditions for drummers tomorrow at the same pub.

Koss added: 'If you want to try your luck then you are welcome to come along.' So I did show up the next afternoon, played on a couple of the Black Cat Bones' songs with them and got the job. A few months after I'd met Koss and joined Black Cat Bones he told me that he'd jammed with this great singer from the band called Brown Sugar and he wanted to start a band with him. He was a little tired of playing the same old blues standards with Black Cat Bones.

So we went up to North London to this big house where we met Paul Rodgers and played a few songs, and that really was the start of Free.

Koss knew of this bass player who was friends with Alexis Korner, who was one of the godfathers of the blues scene in London at that time.

Alexis told us about this great little bass player, even though he was only 15, and said he was just absolutely stunning. He had just left John Mayall's Bluesbreakers and was playing at a club the next night. So the three of us went down to the club and saw Andy Fraser for the first time. He really was that good. We met him backstage afterwards and asked if he would be interested in joining a band. And a few days later we had our first rehearsal at the same pub that I had met Paul Kossoff at a few weeks before.

Andy Fraser

The other three were looking for a bass player, they tried many and were unhappy. When I left the Bluesbreakers, Alexis [Korner] had talked with Mike Vernon, the owner of Horizon Records, a little blues label, who mentioned Koss and crew were looking for a bass player. Koss came around to my mum's house, we jammed a little, and suggested we all get together at the Nag's Head pub, in Battersea, which had a little blues club upstairs where we could rehearse when it was closed. It was instant magic. We all knew it. Alexis promised he would try and show up, but it was his birthday, and a party was being held for him, but he did make the last 15 minutes, and immediately got it. He christened us Free after his band, Free at Last.

In a busy year, Paul Kossoff makes his recording debut, alongside Simon Kirke, when the duo play guitar and drums respectively on bluesman Champion Jack Dupre's latest LP.

Mike Vernon

Well, I was impressed with both Koss and Simon in the days of Black Cat Bones. They were part of a Champion Jack Dupree album on Blue Horizon back in 1968 entitled *When You Feel The Feeling You Was Feeling*, which has recently been re-released on CD as part of *The Complete Blue Horizon Sessions* series that included a couple of previously unreleased titles, with the band in high spirits. I had seriously considered signing the band to the label but backed off at the time. A few years later I did get involved with Koss, Paul Rodgers, Andy Fraser and Simon Kirke when they first rehearsed as a 'new' quartet that were not yet named as Free. Although that might not be totally correct chronologically. We rehearsed at Ken Colyer's club and talked about doing some demos. They sounded great! Never got to that though as Chris Blackwell snapped them up; a smart move on his part. The Black Cat Bones also played on several occasions at The Blue Horizon Club in Battersea. Always a great show!

Simon Kirke

Roehampton, South West London, UK

We always congregated every Monday night at Andy Fraser's mum's house in Roehampton. We brought round albums that we thought the others would like. Andy had a really nice stereo system in his room. I still remember what it was: a Leak Stereo 30 Plus amp with a couple of Wharfedale speakers. We'd be sprawled on the bed or sitting on the floor, the four of us, smoking a bit of dope, and we'd really listen. We listened to Motown, Otis Redding. I believe we even listened to a bit of Mozart once. It was just bouncing what we liked off the other three people. And I really believe that cemented us as musical brothers. It wasn't strictly blues-slash-rock, there were always other elements involved.

Mick Austin

15 June 1968, The Nag's Head, Wollaston, Northamptonshire, UK

Back in June 1968 a friend of mine informed me that Alexis Korner was about to play a gig at our local pub. The public house was The Nag's Head in the small village of Wollaston, Northamptonshire. The venue was one of the last places on earth anyone would imagine to go and see rock and blues bands. If my memory serves me well I think we arranged transport with a friend. Arriving at the Nag's Head, the first thing I noticed was a large old Citroen car standing by the back door of the pub, and this turned out to be Alexis Korner's vehicle.

    Access to the room that the bands performed in was via some fire escape metal steps. On entering the room you paid your money at the door (five shillings or 25p at today's value), your hand was stamped with ink for re-entry. Once inside you were greeted by darkness and a plain timbered floor. The stage was small, about one foot high, and ran the width of the venue, but when considering that a discotheque covered half the stage one can only imagine how bands using Hammond organs and Leslie tone cabinets managed to fit on the platform. But they did, on many occasions. The windows in the room were boarded up and the whole place was painted in matt black paint so even during the day the room was dark. The stage was the only illuminated part of the room. A Marshall amplifier stack stood to the right, fronted by battered and torn fabric and at the opposite side was a large Vox bass amp. Centre stage was a beat up blue pearl Premier drum kit that had obviously taken a good spanking from the owner during its lifetime!

The opposite end of the room was where the bar was situated, it was a small concern and difficult to get served at, due to the number of people attending these great gigs. The band's dressing room door was slightly to the left of this bar, and an old fashioned four-panel door, seen more commonly in Victorian houses, led down two or three steps to a passageway, beyond which was the living accommodation for the pub landlord. This passage was glazed down the left hand side by small window panes and a very wide ledge which served as seating to watch Free and many other bands that played there. Waiting for Alexis Korner to perform, we were serenaded by a man known as 'Jork'. He was responsible for suggesting that Bob Knight (the Nag's landlord) should diversify into promoting blues and progressive bands away from Bob's normal interest in Atlantic soul and Tamla Motown bands. Jork played records of the time, mainly progressive, blues and rock. I recall Alexis making his way through the crammed, smoky room (cigarette and other substances being in-vogue and indoors during the 1960's!) and he was followed by a young boy, about 10-years-old with a head of hair which stretched down below his shoulders. The boy sat on top of Alexis Korner's amplifier during his set. How surreal, I thought, that such a young lad should be out so late and in such a den of iniquity. To this day I have no idea who he was but he was obviously close to Alexis. Alexis stepped onto the stage, with his familiar black cheroot cigar dangling from his mouth and a vintage Guild semi-acoustic guitar hanging around his neck.

He sat down and in his leisurely style began to explain to the audience what they were going to hear from him during his set. It's worth mentioning that anyone that was privileged enough to watch and listen to Alexis Korner in a small club would understand me when I say that even if he just talked all night it would have been a pleasure. The man knew everyone and when he spoke, wow – that voice. It came as no surprise that during his later years he became almost as famous for his voice overs on television advertisements as he did as a blues performer.

He rambled through his set in his laconic style. At the end he told us that in the second set 'Things would liven up' and went on to explain that he had brought a band with him. I assumed that the second set would be less of the solo blues renditions and would lean more towards rock when he performed with a backing band. How wrong I was!

We returned to the downstairs bar to have a drink and step outside into the warm summer air to relieve our lungs of that stuffy smoke-filled room for 30 minutes. When we returned in readiness for his second set, I was right at the front of the stage. Slowly the band members walked through the crowded room towards the stage. First to step up was a long, straight-haired muscle-bound man dressed in a red singlet and brown corduroy trousers, who sat behind the drums. I still recall him taking a few strokes of the snare drum and I instantly knew (being a drummer myself) that this bloke wasn't taking any prisoners.

Next up was a 19-year-old in Levi 'stay pressed' trousers and plain blue shirt. When he spoke to the drummer I noticed he had a North East accent. He adjusted the mic stand as the bass player stepped onto the stage. This boy was so young! He could only have been 15 or 16-years-old. In his black trousers and a white shirt and a well beaten Gibson EB3 bass guitar, he said nothing and looked a little nervous as he adjusted the controls on the Vox amp mentioned earlier. Last to arrive on stage was a very short young man. His entry through the audience was far more conspicuous, he appeared to almost drag a sunburst Gibson Les Paul with the strap dangling from the instrument. As he mounted the stage he was standing about three feet away from my face, but being so short (maybe just over five foot tall) I was staring straight into his eyes. There was the soon to be famous beard and lion's mane hair, a pigeon chest, jeans, collarless shirt, pin-striped waistcoat and fingers filled with cheap but decorative rings. At this period of time it was popular with the 'hippy' fraternity to read Tolkien's *Lord of the Rings* and I instantly thought he reminded me of the character Gimli, the axeman dwarf! He turned to his amplifier and clicked the main amp switch, hit a stifled chord and I just knew this was going to be loud.

'Ready?' the singer checked with the rest of the band. They all nodded and the drummer played the short intro into 'I'm a Mover'. God he really hit those drums like I'd never seen before. The song was played at such a steady pace, it was blues, it was rock, it was funky, it was mind blowingly tight, even danceable, it was Free!

As they progressed through the set: 'Moonshine', 'The Hunter', 'Over The Green Hills', 'Walk in my Shadow', 'Going Down Slow' and a string of other blues standards, they were magnificent. Kossoff with his contorted facial expressions and guitar so loud it was practically on the verge of constantly controlled feedback, was showing off his now famous guitar vibrato for the first time. So many would emulate his style in the years to come. Paul Rodgers, that voice, somewhere between Otis Redding and heaven. On larger stages than this his antics with heavy microphone stands would become a learning curve for lead vocalists but in the Nag's it was virtually impossible with such a low ceiling, and with the crowd so close to the edge of the stage someone would have been killed.

Andy Fraser's bass playing was also so totally original, playing chords a lot of the time to fill in the gaps during Kossoff's solos, his rhythmical swaying to the timing of each song lasting throughout his time with Free. Simon Kirke, sweating, hair stuck to his face, facial contortions in competition with Kossoff, looked as though he would be equally at home in a boxing ring as sitting behind a drum kit!

The end of the set finally arrived, they appeared totally drained, sweat-covered and looking tired. 'More! More! More!' we all cheered. Luckily in the confines of a small club it was pretty pointless trying to make a dash for the dressing room, getting off stage wasn't an easy option… 'OK', Rodgers shouted, 'One more', and after a quick unheard comment to the rest of the band they slid into the slowest version of Robert Johnson's 'Crossroads' I ever heard, apparently their standard encore number in those early years.

At the end of the song Alexis Korner introduced the band, I'd heard of none of them and just to add insult to injury when he introduced Paul Kossoff all I remember thinking was 'David Kossoff? The guy on TV?' I didn't realise then that the guitarist was his son.

The band were finally allowed to get off the stage and I recall lots of back patting and 'thanks' as they made their way through the audience back to the dressing room. We all filed to the exit to make our way home. We had prearranged to meet up for our lift home at the old Lyric Cinema in Wellingborough, which housed another night club called the Lynton Hall Palais. Here the likes of Joe Cocker, Yes and a string of other hopefuls would learn their trade to perfection. The doors opened to the club and out rolled our friends. 'Christ! It was a great band in there tonight' they claimed. We wasted no time in informing them that they'd made a fatal mistake in not travelling the extra couple of miles to the Nag's Head, where they had literally missed the best band in the world!

Mick Crane

The Fantasia Pub, Northampton, UK

I'm from Kingsthorpe, Northampton and I saw the band in a local pub, at one of their 'try out' gigs before they 'made' it. I went with two or three school mates, we were all around 14 or 15 years-old at the time. Unfortunately, I have very little memory of that gig I saw with a few mates, but what I do remember is the band playing at The Fantasia pub in Northampton before they 'made it.' I believe in the early stages, bands did try out gigs in smaller venues to test the water.

A few years later my school mate Dave had a copy of *Free Live* and asked me if I'd like to go round to his house a couple of streets away and listen to it. I was hooked there and then: it was 'Mr. Big' that did it for me.

I'm 66 now and still impressed with Paul Rodgers, his voice and the original band's sound.

Mick Austin

September 1968, Jordens Record Shop, Wellingborough, Northamptonshire, UK

Having seen the unnamed band at Wollaston, the very next day (Saturday) I, and no doubt every other person that had attended the Nag's Head gig in Wollaston were at their local record store to try to find a record album. I'm sure they, like me, had great difficulty in obtaining a recording, because when I asked for the new album by The Alexis Korner Band it took forever as the manager filed through all the new releases to inform me that 'no such band exists'. After trawling through the music papers for a few weeks trying to identify who these amazing musicians were, the name 'Free' suddenly began to appear in reviews. I continued searching, still unsure of who the hell I was looking for! When I returned to the record shop, purely to buy *Diary Of A Band Volume One* by John Mayall's Bluesbreakers, out of the blue the manager informed me that the band I had been looking for previously were called 'Free'. I enquired if there was a record available and he told me he had a single. I immediately bought it and took it home. It was on the Fontana label. Having placed it on the turntable, I waited for the track to start... It was awful! This definitely wasn't the band I had seen at the Nag's Head.

To this day I have no idea who this other band called 'Free' were, but they obviously dropped the name once the *real* Free came on the scene. It probably took another week or two until I heard through the grapevine that the real deal, and the album I wanted, was called *Tons of Sobs*. I still recall putting the record on and observing the cover by Mike Sida: Mickey Mouse in a glass coffin jumped out at me and everyone else I imagine, and the sepia tone photographs of the band would confirm that this was The Alexis Korner Band I had witnessed a month or two ago. I've read that *Tons of Sobs* was recorded in October 1968 and 'The Hunter' recorded and added to the album in December 1968.

I saw them during summer so the time frame of seeing them performing live and obtaining the 'Sobs' album makes it a very small window that they were going around without having a name. At the risk of name dropping I know Mike

Vernon was responsible for suggesting that Andy Fraser take the role of bassist in the band. Mike, who I recorded an album with in one of my bands, had used Paul Kossoff and Simon Kirke on a Blue Horizon release called *When You Feel The Feeling You Was Feeling.* I've asked Mike if he could recall the dates but he wasn't sure when Rodgers, Kossoff, Fraser and Kirke became Free, but he did remember that Paul Kossoff appeared on one of his solo albums and on the album *Fiends and Angels* by Martha Valez recorded in 1969, which also featured Jim Capaldi on drums. He also confirmed that Paul Kossoff played on Capaldi's *Oh How We Danced* album.

Months after their first appearance in Wollaston (it must have been Spring/Summer 1969), Rodgers, Kossoff, Kirke and Fraser returned to the Nag's Head, very definitely called Free.

Alexis Korner

One of the things that impressed me most about Paul Kossoff, as a very young player, was that he knew when not to play. It made him exciting.

Alexis Korner, 1971. Alamy Stock Photo

Andy Fraser

Chris Blackwell [at Island Records] wanted to christen us The Heavy Metal Kids. Well we were not going to have any of that. I remember being in my mother's living room, and the four of us wrote out 'Free' and 'The Heavy Metal Kids' and put it on the little mantlepiece, and we looked at it and we said 'nah'. So, as the leader, it was my job to call up Chris Blackwell and tell him 'nah', and he took his time and then he said, 'well if it's not The Heavy Metal Kids, I don't think Island will be interested' and I slammed the phone down on him. Five minutes later he calls back and he says 'sorry', and we had a great relationship ever since.

I think Chris Blackwell and I have integrity, and although they weren't great deals by today's standards, they were okay by those standards and they were always pretty clear. I remember our first job, because they had in-house management and an agency, and we did a gig for like 20 quid or something somewhere, and I showed up the next morning with change in my pocket and put it on the table – and they went 'you can hang on to that for a while'. *Andy Fraser talking to Terry Rawlings in 2013*

Stephanie Jones

The Railway Hotel, Bishop's Stortford, UK

I was Stephanie Latham back then. I used to live in Bishop's Stortford, Hertfordshire when I was growing up and when I was sixteen The Railway Hotel, which was just round the corner from where I lived, opened a blues club in their barn. It was run by a guy called Steve Miller and it was called Rambling Jack's Blues Club. I think membership was about five shillings and then you paid another five every time you went to see a band.

I can't remember the exact date but it was late spring or early summer 1968 and myself and my friends,

Stephanie saw Free at Rambling Jack's

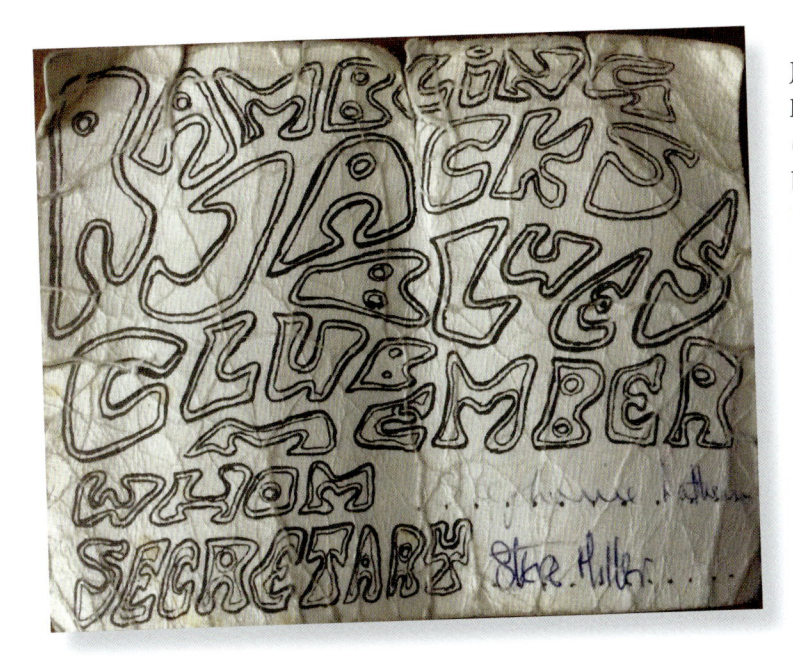

Jo Burnard (nee Raven), Marilyn Paget (Stark) and Sue Southern (Elliott) went along to see the band, but it appeared they had been replaced by a band we'd never seen before. It turned out to be Free and we were blown away by them. Paul Kossoff's guitar playing was incredible and Andy Fraser could certainly find his way round that bass. After they had played Paul Rodgers came up to us and asked if we had had a good time and did we think they had gone down well. We told him that they'd been amazing and we went to see them several more times at Rambling Jack's during 1968 and 1969.

Another place they played near us was The Barn Ballroom, Little Bardfield, Essex. The organisers used to put a coach on from Bishop's Stortford to Bardfield on a Saturday night and a crowd of us would head off there, particularly when we knew Free were playing. They were such a friendly, down to earth group of guys and would come and sit with us during their break and chat. Such wonderful memories.

Less than a year later, I remember buying *Tons of Sobs* from a record shop called Stevens in South Street, Bishop's Stortford when it first came out and played it over and over.

Tons of Sobs recording

October 1968, Morgan Studios, Willesden, North West London, UK

By the end of October 1968, having been given the name Free by Alexis Korner, Paul Rodgers, Paul Kossoff, Simon Kirke and Andy Fraser had recorded their first album, *Tons Of Sobs*, for Island Records and, although it was not released until the following year, the album documents their first six months together and contains studio renditions of much of their early live set.

Produced by Guy Stevens, the majority of the album was recorded over the course of a few days at Morgan Studios. All of the four band members were under 20, and the youngest, Andy Fraser, was just sixteen-years-old.

Martin Leedham

The title of Free's first album, *Tons of Sobs,* is both a term for delta blues wailing and a cockney term for loads of money, which is ironic considering the album only cost about £800 to produce. Recorded over five separate days during October 1968, the process was delayed to enable the band to record a studio version of live favourite 'The Hunter'. Originally the album was going to include the Fraser/Rodgers composition 'Visions of Hell', since released on the remastered version.

The band didn't waste any time getting down to business when it came to song writing. The first rehearsal was held upstairs at the Nag's Head in Battersea and saw the creation of the first original Free songs. Paul Rodgers had already penned 'Over the Green Hills', originally a complete song until producer Guy Stevens decided it worked better as a split track opening and closing the album. 'Walk In My Shadow' and 'Worry' two of the albums harder, rockier tracks had also been pre-penned by Rodgers and were accepted with enthusiasm by the other members. That initial rehearsal also saw the foundations being laid for the first Kossoff/Rodgers composition 'Moonshine', a dark and eerie track in which Rodgers sings about leaning on his own tombstone and waiting for the dawn. It was a far more sinister lyric and vocal performance than any Rodgers would manage again and is, in truth, far more menacing than anything the current crop of goth rock bands could conjure up.

The writing partnership of Andy Fraser and Paul Rodgers was responsible for the majority of Free's material and their first joint composition was also created at that first rehearsal when they penned 'I'm A Mover'. It would remain a vital part of Free's live show right up until the closing tour in 1973 and was the first instance of that classic Free sound which has been described elsewhere as 'four flat tyres on a muddy road'. Whilst that description doesn't really do them justice, it gives an idea of the overall sound: Hard driving powerful blues with a prominent bass line, explosive drum fills and rich, heartfelt vocals all topped off with Kossoff's unique 'crying' guitar. Of the other tracks Free were working up for the album, the 'The Hunter' was the pre 'All Right Now' live favourite and the studio version differed very little from the way it was played live. 'Wild Indian Woman', probably the weakest song on the album, was still a fine tune. 'Sweet Tooth' gives a little hint of the more commercial side of Free that was to come with its catchy chorus. If you listen carefully, you can tell that

Rodgers was suffering from a cold during its recording. Not that it lessened his performance. The pure blues of 'Going Down Slow' probably formed the inspiration for later lengthy tracks such as 'Mr Big'.

It was a glorious time for British rock in 1969 with the likes of Deep Purple, Led Zeppelin, Black Sabbath and Uriah Heep all arriving on the scene, but the teenagers recording Free's first album may have recorded a better debut than all of them. It's just a pity no-one noticed at the time.

"I'd turn the lights down, close my eyes and imagine I was on stage. It was the only way I could get a feel for it."

PAUL RODGERS

"Guy Stevens was instrumental in getting our first album together. 'Just go in there and do your normal set.' Those were his exact words. The whole album was cut in two days, with a couple more to mix. He was very endearing... when he wasn't hurling himself around the studio spilling wine everywhere!"

SIMON KIRKE

"Except for Koss, who had done a few sessions for Bluesman Rambling Jack, we had never been in a studio before, so we were real green. The sterilized atmosphere minus an audience really threw us. Guy Stevens who was the producer and can be described as somewhere between a genius and a mad-hatter on speed, eventually said just play your live set, which we did, and they recorded it."

ANDY FRASER

"They were so easy to work with because they were such good musicians."

ANDY JOHNS (TONS OF SOBS ENGINEER)

ROCK 'N' ROLL FANTASY

Steve Miller

Steve Miller, who sadly died of cancer on 9 December 1998, began his musical career in the early sixties, gigging with numerous blues and R'n'B outfits, and sometimes backing visiting American musicians. By the end of the decade, he had become an in-demand session player, guesting on albums by the likes of Alexis Korner, John Dummer and Daddy Longlegs. In 1968 he was playing in a band called British Delivery and running a popular blues club in Bishop's Stortford, Essex, and was invited to attend the *Tons of Sobs* recording sessions by Paul Rodgers.

'An exceptional player, we were good mates.' is how Paul rated the man who contributed thumping piano to those Morgan Studios sessions.

Paul Kossoff

The first album we just went in and played everything we did, sort of live and straight off, almost. The second album was much more of a studio album. We were beginning to form some sort of way of doing things, things we carried through to the following albums.

By the time the debut LP went on sale in March 1969, Free had begun to gather a devoted following through their successful live appearances – regularly playing five or six nights a week. Fans at the small blues clubs up and down the UK that had witnessed them live were increasingly asking record stores the same question: 'Is there an LP by this group called Free?'

Vic Wells

Redcar Jazz Club, Redcar, North Yorkshire, UK

In 1968, my friends and I went to the Redcar Jazz Club in the Coatham Hotel on the seafront to see Jethro Tull. The Redcar Jazz Club unbelievably attracted all of the top rock bands every Sunday night. Unfortunately Jethro Tull didn't turn up.

The compere, Roger Barker apologised and said there was a band staying at the hotel after performing at the Coatham the night before, but they hadn't really been appreciated. They were called Free.

The Coatham Hotel ballroom every Saturday evening had a live band and the resident band called Government, with, would you believe, a lead singer called David Coverdale belting out soul music. This was very popular with teenagers that liked to dance. Regarding the Jazz Club, it was in the ballroom of the Coatham Hotel.

The ballroom had its own entrance from the side street, but was also accessed from the hotel, where the acts emerged. The stage backed onto the hotel. The auditorium was laid out with long tables stretching from side to side. Along the right, looking from the stage were the main bars. Above the bars was a balcony. This could be accessed from the main auditorium. Interestingly, the risers on the stairs were uneven, coming as a shock after a few drinks!

That Sunday night, the Jethro Tull 'no show' announcement didn't go down too well with the faithful.

The replacement band came out, led by a guy with shoulder-length hair, mutton-chop sideboards, a short skinny-rib sweater, Levi's and knee-length boots, namely Paul Rodgers. He was followed by the lead guitarist wearing a full length coat. I seem to recollect it was leather. He immediately took up his position, leaning back against the bank of speakers. Typical Paul Kossoff. They were followed by drummer Simon Kirke and bass guitarist Andy Fraser. They complemented each other perfectly.

Almost from the first chord of 'The Hunter' everyone was convinced and wanting to see Jethro Tull was a distant memory. That was the first of many Free gigs I enjoyed.

One downside was when Free had a hit single with 'All Right Now', their next gig at Redcar Jazz Club attracted a lot of teenyboppers.

I also remember seeing Paul Rodgers later at the Jazz Club with his short lived band Peace. My recollection of that gig is very sketchy. I seem to remember it was a four-piece with Paul doubling up on lead/rhythm guitar as well as lead vocals. The set was low key, more melodic, and a little disappointing compared to Free.

When the Coatham Hotel was later sold to British Steel (whom I worked for at the time), the ballroom was turned into a carpeted drawing office, but the riser mismatch was not rectified. It seemed very surreal working in an open plan, carpeted drawing office knowing the building's history.

Po Powell

Royal College of Art, London, UK

Hipgnosis was in its infancy and Alexis Korner, who I got on famously with, said: 'I've got a new band called Free. These young kids, they're amazing.'

The next thing I knew Brian Morrison was involved and he called me up and said 'Can you do some photographs of these guys?' I lived round the corner from the Royal College of Art and I met them there and took a whole load of photographs of them on the steps of the Royal College of Art, down in Cromwell Road. And then I think we went up to Hyde Park, but sadly I don't have those photographs anymore and I don't know where they've gone.

I also photographed them at a gig they did at the Revolution Club with another band called Love Sculpture and I took photographs of both of them. Love Sculpture was Dave Edmunds' band. Sadly, I have no idea where those pictures are either!

That was my first encounter with Paul Rodgers and Simon Kirke and everybody. They were very young indeed. I remember Simon Kirke saying to me 'Have you tried these marijuana cigarettes?' Which of course I had and they hadn't!

Oliver Gray

10 November 1968, The Progressive Club, Norwich, Norfolk, UK

The Progressive Club was a tiny back room behind the Bedford Arms in the city centre. It had previously been called The Cat Trap Club. A local promoter called Gerry Welsh, who ran the place, contacted me and asked if I could do a write-up in the student mag to encourage students to go there. Free was one of the first bands to play there and I duly attended with

Oliver Gray wrote about Free in his University mag

a bunch of my mates. It was incredibly rammed and hot, with a stage so low that it was hard to see the band, but the gig was intense and full of excitement. Above all, they were all so young - pretty much the same age as we were.

I wrote a piece about his venue for the university mag and Gerry Welsh was very pleased. Other bands we saw at the Progressive Club included

```
                    -PLUG-
     Olly is now about to pull a plug out.
He's doing so because he's recently met
somebody who deserves very much to succeed
This person's name is Gerry Walsh, who owns
and manages the Progressive Club in Bedford
Street. At his own expense, Gerry has taken
over and done up an old trad dive and
reopened it five weeks ago as a Blues club.
Of course, you've all seen the notices in
the Union about it, but if if you haven't
got round to paying a visit, try it.
Some of the bigger forthcoming attractions:
SUN 10th.NOV:   FREE.
FRI 15th.NOV:   DEVIANTS.
SUN 17th.NOV:   BLONDE ON BLONDE(?)
FRI 29th.NOV:   PRETTY THINGS.
SUN 15th.DEC.   KEEF HARTLEY.
Which is a pretty impressive line-up for a
club so young. The biggest disappointment
so far is that American hit-maker Robert
Parker, booked for tonight has work-permit
trouble and will be unable to appear. He will
be replaced by CLOUDS, who are reputedly very
good. Gerry is determined to get Jethro Tull
at any price, and there is a distinct poss-
ibility they might appear before Christmas.
If not, definitely next term.
     The most interesting point is that if
response is favourable, Gerry will be only
too happy to open the club every night for
somewhere for Students to go who are fed
up with the Union bar and the standard
student haunts. Of course, you can't manufact-
-ure a haunt just like that, but think on
this: plenty of space, colourfully decorated,
good atmosphere, the best and cheapest juke-
box in Norwich, and Red Barrel 2/4d a pint..
........Blimey, why did we ever go to Backs?
Gerry Walsh wants to appeal to the Univer-
sity; now you appeal to him to get on with
this idea but quick!
```

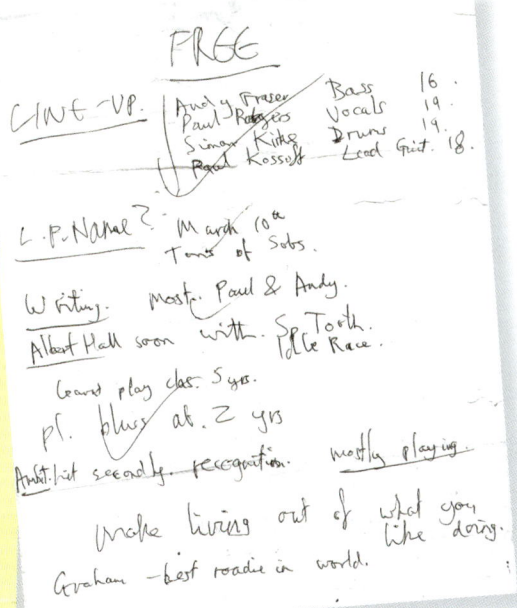

[Handwritten notes:]

FREE

LINE-UP: Andy Fraser — Bass — 16
Paul Rodgers — Vocals — 19
Simon Kirke — Drums — 19
Paul Kossoff — Lead Guit. — 18

L.P. Name? March 10th Tons of Sobs.

Writing. Mostly Paul & Andy.
Albert Hall soon with Spooky Tooth, Idle Race.

Learnt play clas. 5 yrs.
pl. blues at 2 yrs.
Ambit: 1st secondly recognition. mostly playing

make living out of what you like doing.

Graham — best roadie in world.

The Deviants, Jethro Tull and a great band from Birmingham called The Locomotive.

When Free played at the Uni a few months later, we were able to experience the band in all its glory.

1969

Paul Daniel

My first experience of Free? I think it was 1969. Pre-showtime. In the upstairs lounge of a suite in the Coatham Hotel on Redcar's seafront. A Sunday night, the night for bands at Redcar Jazz Club.

I leant on the fireplace, balancing my notebook. The band were sprawled around the room, working on a song. It turned out to be 'Baby, Be Me Friend' [or 'Be My Friend' as it ended up]. And even in its unstructured form, it sounded brilliant.

I was a young reporter working for the *Middlesbrough Evening Gazette* and thought I'd chance my arm by interviewing my favourite singer. Paul [Rodgers] was really kind to give me half an hour, even going through the names and ages of his brothers and sisters, vital information when you're trying to get the news desk to appreciate its worth.

The story's intro chronicled Paul's elevation from his first performances at St Mary's Youth Club in Middlesbrough to the beginning of Free's iconic status in 1969. I was chuffed with the piece. But it never saw the light of day, 'spiked' by my news editor through 'lack of interest'.

So you can imagine how chuffed I was to convince the Gazette to use another interview Paul gave me, scarily 25 years later! I've kept the cutting and, if I say so myself, it's a good read!

Today, it's a treat to look back on 50 years following his career. The best rock blues singer? I Can't think of a real rival.

Those Free concerts at the Jazz Club were brilliant. With a supposed 650 capacity in what was the hotel ballroom, the place literally rocked. It wasn't all glory nights. The terrible decline of Paul Kossoff was so sad to watch. And it was public. I can never forget Koss standing centre stage for his solo in 'All Right Now', arms aloft, screaming.

But on the good nights, it was brilliant. 'The Hunter', 'Fire and Water', 'Wishing Well'. Wow.

Then came Peace, Paul's first bad after Free. I've been lucky enough to follow his career right from those embryonic days. Bad Company, fronting Queen and the terrific solo tours. And now he's pitching it full circle, with Free Spirit. Just perfect.

One more thing. In 2010, six months after retirement, I was sitting in a consulting room at James Cook University Hospital in

Middlesbrough after being diagnosed with head and neck cancer. I was told: 'This is the best you'll feel for the next three months.' I said: 'Will I be able to see Paul Rodgers at the Newcastle Arena in May?' The consultant said he didn't know. I did. I'm All Right Now. Sorry, couldn't resist that.

Oliver Gray

23 January 1969, University of East Anglia, The Barn at University Plain, Norwich, UK

I was the music correspondent for the student magazine at UEA. I've still got my notes from an old interview with Free. Judging by the terrible writing, I was obviously drunk!

When Free eventually played at the university, I knew I had finally found my kind of music. Paul Rodgers was so macho, doing impossible splits in his skin-tight trousers, manipulating the microphone stand like no one before, and barking out the songs in a voice and style which would be copied for decades. The sparseness of their music appealed: the bass used almost as a lead instrument, the hard but unfussy drums and the trebly vibrato style of the unhealthy-looking, disgracefully unkempt guitarist. He stayed at the back of the stage, leaning back against the amp and pulling grotesque faces, but otherwise avoiding guitar hero poses. This was Paul Kossoff, and it was Paul I homed in on for the interview, because I was intrigued that this wild man could be the son of the gentle and benign David Kossoff, who I had often heard reading Bible stories on the radio.

The report in *Ollipop* gives a good idea of the naive style of the column:

Andy Fraser, Free's bassist, is a mere 16-years-old, and very accomplished too. The lead guitarist (the bristly one on the right my notes said) is Paul Kossoff. He studied classical guitar for five years and had been playing blues for two. Paul and Andy do most of the writing.

On March 14th, their first LP emerges, entitled Tons of Sobs (yes, they hate it too!).

They were terrifically together on stage, but will they come across well on record? We shall see. Career-wise, nothing particularly exciting is coming up, which is sad. Ambitions? A hit, they say, is not the greatest objective, merely recognition and the chance to make a living out of what they enjoy doing.

I saw Free a number of times over their career and watching the decline of Paul Kossoff was heartbreaking. On the final occasion, at the Colston Hall in Bristol, on 15 October 1973, he collapsed twice onstage and the show had to be curtailed. That is one of the many reasons why I am unashamed in not being interested in drugs. People like Hendrix, Kossoff and Cobain, who destroy themselves before they get to scratch the surface of their potential, are the high-profile cases, but what about all the other thousands of ruined lives?

Sandy McAllister

22 February 1969, Leeds University, Leeds, West Yorkshire, UK

I first saw Paul Rodgers, Paul Kossoff, Simon Kirke and Andy Fraser in 1969. I used to go on a Saturday night to the Leeds University Hop. The event was held every week, term time. I used to take my younger sister Maz to all the concerts even though she was three years younger than me. We called ourselves 'Groupies' without the sex.

We loved the groups we saw and paid our seven shillings and sixpence for our tickets. That was a laugh. Sometimes at these kind of events they used to take the whole ticket off you so you didn't give it to someone else! You were not allowed out of the show sometimes. We were controlled in those days, probably because there wasn't a lot of security and definitely no mobiles.

I saw Free again on Saturday 22 November that same year when they appeared with Christine Perfect (now known as Christine McVie). They were one great rock band with the fab singing of Paul Rodgers and guitar playing of Paul Kossoff. I can't remember what the songs were they played, but the show must have been good as I wanted to go see them again. I was with my sister Maz and George, her boyfriend (later to be her husband). Me and Maz asked them if they wanted to go to a party we were going to, but they declined.

I do have all their autographs, which I keep taped to my L.P. *Tons of Sobs*.

Sandy invited all the members of Free to a party

Lucy Piller

One Stop, Central London, UK

I first heard the voice of Paul Rodgers when I was taking a lunch break and walked into a record store called One Stop in the West End of London. The band's album *Tons of Sobs* had just been released and it was scattered all over the shop windows and the music was heard in the streets. At that moment I knew I needed to hear more and went in the store to hear the whole album, and from that moment on I was hooked.

It would be impossible to say which song meant the most to me, and most fans say the same, but my mother once commented about a Free song called 'Moonshine' on their first album *Tons of Sobs*. She said it was so morbid, and talked of death, she didn't like me playing it, yet I loved it because of the haunting melody. So maybe that one means a lot to me.

Rab Sneddon

I heard 'Walk in My Shadow' from the *Tons of Sobs* album and for me it had everything – it literally struck a 'chord' and it gave me a lifelong love of the band and their music.

A young Paul Kossoff backstage. Photo by Lucy Piller

Tons of Sobs

Tons of Sobs, the debut album by Free, was released in the UK on the 14 March 1969 on Island Records.

The album cover design proved to be a source of anxiety for the label responsible for marketing the record in America.

Album artwork photography by Ian T Cossar

Simon Kirke

'I just remember this cold, damp day in Barnes cemetery, lugging this plexiglas coffin around with Mickey Mouse and other dolls and artefacts and just wondering what the fuck we were doing there, and couldn't we just all slope off to the pub? But it is still one of the most recognisable album covers around.'

The packaging was completely changed by A&M for US release, and featured individual pictures of the band members on the front cover with a group shot on the back. One reason for that decision could have been the silhouette of Mickey Mouse in the bottom right of the British front cover – a lawsuit from Disney would not have been the best way in which to kick off a young band's US career.

Paul Rodgers, vocals
Paul Kossoff, lead guitar
Andy Fraser, bass guitar
Simon Kirke, drums

SIDE ONE
1. OVER THE GREEN HILLS Pt. 1 0:45 (Rodgers) Blue Mountain Music Ltd.
2. WORRY 3:27 (Rodgers) Blue Mountain Music Ltd.
3. WALK IN MY SHADOW 3:29 (Rodgers-Kossoff-Kirke-Fraser) Lupus Music Ltd./Universal Music
4. WILD INDIAN WOMAN 3:39 (Rodgers-Fraser) Blue Mountain Music Ltd.
5. GOIN' DOWN SLOW 8:19 (Oden) Leeds Music Corp.

SIDE TWO
1. A MOVER 2:49 (Rodgers-Fraser) Blue Mountain Music Ltd.
2. THE HUNTER 4:14 (Jackson-Jones-Wells-Dunn-Cropper) Universal Music Publishing Ltd./Warner Chappell North America
3. ...SHINE 5:03 (Rodgers-Kossoff-Fraser-Kirke) Lupus Music Ltd.
4. SWEET TOOTH 4:54 (Rodgers) Blue Mountain Music Ltd.
5. ...GREEN HILLS Pt. 2 1:57 (Rodgers) Blue Mountain Music Ltd.

Front cover photography: Mike Sida
Inside cover photography: Richard Bennett Zeff
Piano Thumping: Steve Miller
Recording engineer: Andrew Johns
PRODUCED BY GUY STEVENS

MIKE VERNON

March 1969

I recall Paul Kossoff's involvement in a Sire (US) Decca (UK) project that took place in Decca #2 Studio featuring a young singer from New York City, Martha Velez. Head of Sire Records, Seymour Stein (who was also a partner in Blue Horizon) had been in touch asking me to make an album with Martha that should, if possible, feature some famous UK musicians. Martha was being touted at that time as the next Janis Joplin or Grace Slick. She was very good.

Putting this project together took quite a while but eventually everything fell into place. Four days of recording with different rhythm sections that included Jack Bruce and Mitch Mitchell; Dave Bidwell and Andy Silvester (Chicken Shack); Gary Thain and Keef Hartley and Jim Capaldi with 'Honk'. Featured guitarists were Eric Clapton, Stan Webb, Rick Hayward (Jellybread), Spit James (Keef Hartley Band) and Paul Kossoff. Others involved included Brian Auger, Christine Perfect, Mick Weaver, Chris Mercer, Johnny Almond and Duster Bennett.

The final results were very exciting and following the initial release of *Fiends & Angels* in both the US and UK during 1969 press reaction was extremely encouraging. The album was subsequently re-released on Blue Horizon in late 1970 retitled as *Fiends & Angels Again*.

At the time of release none of the musicians involved were named on the album artwork, but gradually the participants' names were leaked.

CHRIS JOHNSON

30 March, 1969, The Argus Butterfly pub, Peterlee, UK

I have a signed copy of Free's first album, *Tons of Sobs*, which they signed before a gig at the Argus Butterfly in Peterlee.

I'm from Hartlepool originally and during this period my friends and I would either visit Redcar Jazz Club or the Argus Butterfly on Sunday nights. We had seen Free a few times previously and I was keen to buy *Tons of Sobs* when it was released. My album had been loaned out to a friend and returned the night we went to the Argus, which is why it was with me. The Argus Butterfly was a typical sixties pub with a fairly small concert room at the back, probably used for bingo sessions. It was part of a large council estate with a small parking area at the rear, which is where we would park up (being Monkey Hangers in Pit Yacker Land meant we had to be very careful and ready for a quick getaway!)

On this particular night as we were chatting in the car a transit type van pulled up and some lads, who we took to be the band, climbed out and went into the pub through a back door. Brian Rattigan, one of my mates, had got caught short and as the pub was not yet open decided to chance his arm and followed the band into the pub to look for a toilet. After a few minutes he came back and we took the album inside to be signed. I recall they were a bit coy about signing as we got the impression that Island [Records] weren't very confident about it being a success.

A week earlier I'd seen Led Zeppelin play at the Argus Butterfly. Happy days!

Lucy Piller

4 May 1969, The Country Club, Belsize Park, London, UK

I was living in East London with my parents and up until 1969 I'd been listening to The Beatles, The Bee Gees, Manfred Mann, Joe Cocker, Georgie Fame, Small Faces, Jose Feliciano, Canned Heat, Status Quo, Beach Boys, Dave Clark Five.

If they were a good band and had a great sound I was listening to them. Then in 1969 I was into the Rolling Stones, Fleetwood Mac with Peter Green of course, Desmond Dekker, Booker T & The MGs, The Hollies, David Bowie, Jethro Tull and many more, but after I heard Free I was introduced to more progressive underground music. Those bands included Pink Floyd, Traffic, The Nice, T Rex, Deep Purple, Atomic Rooster, Uriah Heep, Hawkwind, King Crimson and East of Eden.

The first time I saw Paul Rodgers was on the 4 May 1969. Free were playing at a dance club I used to attend called Caesars, in Belsize Park. I used to go to dance there on Saturday nights. When I noticed Free were appearing there on a Sunday, the club changed its name to The Country Club, with tickets priced at eight shillings and sixpence.

Photo by Lucy Piller

The Country Club was a low single-storey prefabricated building situated in a cul-de-sac, just a short, five-minute walk from the London Underground station. I travelled there alone from East London to West London and although I arrived dressed like a mod, the freaky-looking way-out people waiting in line made me feel very welcome. I wanted a seat as close to the stage as possible, but not wanting to stand out I sat in the second row. I would say that there were about 300 people inside the place, which had a bar at the back. I remained seated until the DJ announced: 'Here are Free' and in walked four little people in long maxi coats, wide bell-bottoms with guitars in hand as they walked, or rather it looked like they marched, from the back of the club and took to the stage. After removing their coats, they put them near the amps and Free began to play.

The actual show and content I cannot remember, but I do remember how I felt when it ended. I was completely overwhelmed, I walked back to the station, took the lift down to the station, and waited for my train, I was in a trance, I just stared at the advertising hoardings across the track with no thoughts but numbness, and I was not stoned, trust me! I sat on the train, as it went into the tunnels staring out to the blackness thinking, that was the most amazing experience of my life, and I can still feel the rush of excitement all these years later.

My parents supported me and my love of music when I was young, they knew I was going to see Free perform at just 16-years-of-age, but they were very proud of me taking all those photos of this new British Blues Band.

You Can All Join In

Many people's introduction to Free was when they heard 'I'm A Mover' while listening to the Island sampler *You Can All Join In*. The compilation album, which unexpectedly made the UK Top 20 in June 1969, was a favourite among British music fans who wanted a blast of the latest bands Island Records were championing, at the bargain price of 14 shillings.

The Island 'family' was small enough and obscure enough to be gathered together in a park one morning for the cover photo of *You Can All Join In*. Paul Kossoff was the only member of Free not to be featured on the album's cover art, which shows the likes of Richard Thompson, Sandy Denny, and not all the members of Jethro Tull.

Groovesville! The now demolished Wake Arms pub

Barry Morris

1969, The Wake Arms, Epping, Essex, UK

I was around 14 and living in Ilford and I heard 'Woman' from the Island sampler *Nice Enough To Eat*. Me and my mate found the other Island sampler *You Can All Join In*, which featured 'I'm a Mover', and from that we discovered *Tons of Sobs*. As a result, we started following them at gigs. The first was at the Wake Arms, Epping. Unfortunately someone in the band was ill, so Sam Apple Pie did the gig but I remember Paul Rodgers got up with I think Kossoff and did a couple of songs, it was brilliant.

   A couple of months later we saw the full band at the same venue, they were just awesome and after that I attended Free gigs at The King's Head, Romford, The Cooks Ferry Inn, Edmonton, The Lyceum, London, as well as other venues that I can't remember. They were the greatest live band I ever saw and at that time I saw them all.

   After Free split I saw Bad Company many times and I've seen Paul many times solo too. He is absolutely brilliant and an inspiration. When I think, I was 14/15 when I first saw Free but they weren't much older. Brilliant band, which has had a massive effect on my life. I will never forget them.

David Crewe

I saw them at a gig in a pub called The Wake Arms, in Epping, Essex. The back room was called Groovesville! The sweat was running down the walls and the sound of the bass thump rattled your rib cage!

Pete Dawson

The first time I heard Free? Probably when I bought the Island record sampler *You Can All Join In* on the original label design, various artists, with 'I'm a Mover' on it.

I saw Free a couple of times but most memorable was at the Isle of Wight Festival, Afton Down in 1970. They played an afternoon set, one of my favourite bands of the seventies. Absolute icons. I have most of their albums on vinyl, including *Tons of Sobs*, which is my favourite, but *Fire and Water* is commonly regarded as their best. I still have the framed original Island posters of Free, and I have to say they are absolutely so cool.

If you like that old school bluesy rock listen to 'Mr Big' with headphones. *Tons of Sobs* is probably as close as you would get to a live set, it is as raw as you can get and probably why I like it so much. I think Andy Fraser was only 16 at the time and the rest were not that much older. *Tons of Sobs* first pressings are well sought after on the original pink Island label.

David Tangye

I can remember seeing Free at Lancaster University, many moons ago. I was a 20 year-old regular at Lancaster University. The Main Hall had mainstream bands playing on Friday nights. I used to go down with my pals from Cumbria. Free were a great live band. *David Tangye was the former Personal Assistant to Ozzy Osbourne*

Gered Mankowitz

Mason's Yard, London, UK

This was one of the last sessions at my studio in Mason's Yard and is pretty typical of my style at that time. I had been working on these dramatic, angular close-up portraits with punchy lighting for some time and they had become my trademark look for that period. I was at school with Paul Kossoff, who was a wonderful guitarist but had a terrible weakness for drugs and regrettably died in America in 1976. His father David Kossoff was a very well known character actor, who worked a great deal with my father in the 50s.

Photo by Gered Mankowitz © Bowstir Ltd. 2020 Mankowitz.com

Alastair Smith

1969, Dunelm House, Durham, UK

I spent a great half an hour sitting on a table with Paul Rodgers in the band room at Dunelm House in Durham in 1969 when Free played there. We talked about the music scene on Teesside. It was the same room where he and Andy Fraser wrote 'All Right Now' in 1968.

My background is based around Teesside, where I lived until I left Durham University in 1971. Being a month older than Paul Rodgers I was very much involved with the same music scene in the Teesside area as Paul. Musicians such as Mick Moody, Terry Popple and Paul Rodgers were playing with local bands that I would see at pubs, working men's clubs and nightclub venues.

Well known bands would visit the area and play at places like Mr McCoys, The Kirklevington Country Club, The Redar Jazz Club and a few formal night clubs.

I started at Durham University in September 1968 and soon realised that the Durham University Students' Union at Dunelm House held events every Saturday night for students and their guests. The bands that played there were the top gigging bands of the time, Family, Joe Cocker, P P Arnold, Idle Race, Spooky Tooth, The Edgar Broughton Band amongst them, and of course Free.

It would have been around the end of 1969 that Free were booked to play their second gig at Dunelm House, the first had not been a success and had led to a bit of trouble in the audience. It was a gig that I wanted to see as a musician friend of mine, the late John Whittingham, who played in a local band from Middlesbrough, had played guitar in a band with Paul Rodgers for a while and knew him quite well.

On the night of the gig I managed to get into the band room about 45 minutes before Free were due on stage. Paul Rodgers and I started talking after I had mentioned John Whittingham and soon we were sitting on a table talking about our hometown Middlesbrough, not 25 miles down the road. During the conversation I noticed that Paul Kossoff was standing in the corner looking very detached and quiet. I thought that it was nerves but found out later that it was something a lot deeper.

During our conversation the door opened and a police inspector and a couple of officers came into the room and asked for the band's attention. The inspector started by mentioning the trouble at the last Free concert in Dunelm House and requested that if there was any sign of trouble the band were to cease playing and return to the band room. On his way out the police officer noticed a quite sizeable lump of a substance known to be used by musicians on the table. He looked at it, made mention that he had spotted it, but said that he would ignore it as it would no doubt cause trouble if the band didn't play that night. A close call.

It was later that I was told by someone on the Students' Union music committee that the room was where Paul and Andy had written 'All Right Now' which became their hit later on. The gig went well and Free played a terrific set.

I saw Free play quite a few times after this but always remember this gig as the best.

Roger Smith

27 June 1969, The Bay Hotel, Whitburn, Tyneside, UK

During 1968 and into 1969, Free were slowly building up a following, mostly by playing at small clubs throughout the country. Their first gig in Sunderland was at the Bay Hotel on the seafront at Whitburn on 13 January 1969. Promoter Geoff Docherty, who had just started to stage gigs featuring national bands at the Bay, booked them following a recommendation by a musician friend. That first Free gig in Sunderland was poorly attended because, at that point, few people in the North East had heard of them. However, Geoff Docherty realised their potential and decided to keep them in his pocket for a later date. He planned to put them on as a support group alongside a band that would potentially pull in a good crowd.

The opportunity for Docherty to rebook Free came five months later in June 1969. Tyrannosaurus Rex, a duo consisting of Marc Bolan and Steve Peregrin Took, were due to appear at the Bay Hotel on 27th June and Geoff wanted Free as the support band. The popular 'alternative' DJ, John Peel had been plugging Tyrannosaurus Rex on his underground radio programmes and consequently the show was a sell-out.

By the time Free started their set early in the evening the Bay Hotel was filling up but was by no means crammed. What happened next turned out to be the spark that ignited Freemania in Sunderland and the North East.

Geoff Docherty received a couple of messages that Marc Bolan and Steve Peregrine Took were having trouble with their motor and would be very late. By this time the Bay was packed. Most of the audience was sitting on the floor waiting for Tyrannosaurus Rex to perform and people were getting impatient.

Geoff, knowing that it would be quite a while before Tyrannosaurus Rex's arrival had to do something. He persuaded Free to go back on stage and do another set.

Free took to the stage again, this time to a full house. The return of the band was greeted with a flood of cheers. Free performed another great set to the delight of the audience and went down a storm.

The 800 or so people in the Bay that night must have told others about the gig. Word quickly spread throughout the Sunderland area about a fantastic band called Free. By the time the band did another gig for Geoff Docherty, this time at the Locarno Ballroom (also known as Fillmore North), on 12 September 1969 the town of Sunderland was ready for them. Thousands of people turned up to see Free that night. Three thousand lucky fans were let into the Locarno whilst many more were turned away because the venue was full to capacity.

Thereafter, any time that Geoff Docherty booked Free to play at the venues that he promoted – the Locarno and Top Rank Suite in Sunderland and the Mayfair Ballroom in Newcastle – he could be sure that the gigs would be sell-outs. Perhaps that was just as well because Free, realising their popularity in the area compared with elsewhere in the country, hiked up their fees for North East gigs. In effect, they started charging significantly more for their performances in Sunderland and Newcastle than for gigs elsewhere, including London.

David Woodley

I think the reason Free's first concert at the Bay was so poorly attended was the way the advert appeared in the *Sunderland Echo*. It read 'Tonight FREE'. I saw it and thought 'Nah, it couldn't be.' If I remember right it was on a Wednesday, and Wednesdays were free admission. I believe that was why they didn't pull a crowd that night. The next day at work somebody said 'Hey, Free were on at the Bay last night!' I was gutted! I had heard both their albums from a friend. I did later get to see them at the Locarno when they recorded *Free Live*.

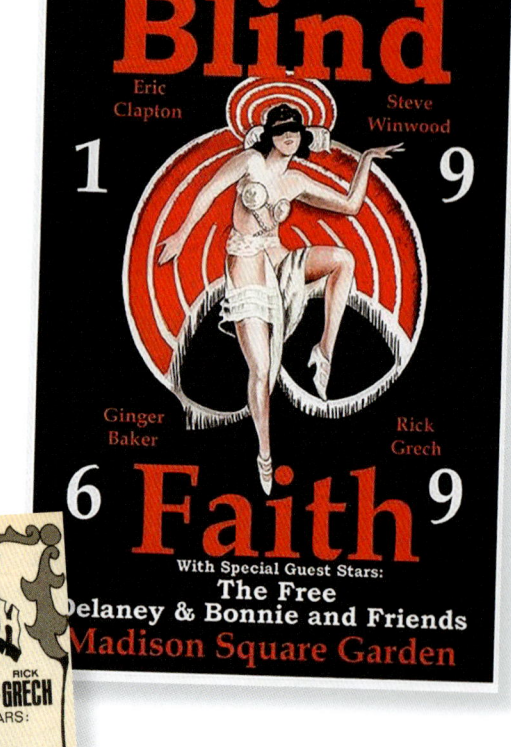

First US Tour

During the summer of 1969 Free embarked on their first trip to North America, opening for the newly formed (and short lived) Blind Faith at Madison Square Garden, New York City. Other shows included support slots for Jethro Tull, Tom Rush and British singer Terry Reid.

Paul Kossoff

Blind Faith came to see us and we were dead nervous, what with them sitting twenty yards away. Afterwards Clapton came round and said, 'How do you do that tremolo?' I looked at him and said, 'You must be joking' cause that's exactly how I felt – I thought he was taking the piss, but he wasn't.

Andy Fraser

Kossoff was a born comedian. Because it was cold in England, Koss would often wear a very long coat. He could go into character, for example 'Ena Sharples' from the long-running English soap series *Coronation Street*, an old woman with an attitude, and proceed to take any of us apart, by telling the truth, but in character. The funniest thing!

Gary Grainger

30 August 1969, Isle of Wight Festival, Woodside Bay, UK

Free perform at the second Isle of Wight Festival, an event headlined by Bob Dylan and The Band.

Free used The Who's amps and cabinets (Hiwatt, not their usual Marshalls) but Simon Kirke didn't use Keith Moon's drums because The Who let them play their set as their slot had been missed. Some of the earlier bands had overrun their allocated time - Edgar Broughton for one!

It was all a bit hurried with Free being allowed to play in that slot and Paul Kossoff's sound was a bit cleaner at the start of their set. But I think it was Bob Pridden (The Who's sound man) who went onstage and told Koss to 'turn up' if he wanted, which he did, and his guitar was singing then! Not sure he was used to that much volume (2x100watt Hiwatts - he was only usually using a 100watt Marshall at the time) so, unusually, he was standing away from the speaker stacks!

But Free played a great set and then The Who played a blinding show. They were two of my favourite bands, so it was great to see them back to back.

1969 Isle of Wight Festival photos by Malcolm Colton

Derek Carter

30 August 1969, Isle of Wight Festival, Woodside Bay, UK

In 1969, I enthusiastically attended the Isle of Wight festival, to experience one of the greatest performances of a superb band. I was very proud to see my old schoolmate and fellow musician [Paul Kossoff] with thousands of screaming fans.

Free's set was all too short, just three numbers. I was about 150-200 metres from the stage, left side. I had binoculars so I could zoom in on Koss. Paul Rodgers had red trousers and a yellow top, Koss had a fringed suede/leather vest and was sporting a goatee.

It might have been a short appearance but it was a memorable one. The only downside was my car was broken into and all my possessions were stolen, sleeping bag, food drink and all!

Nick Riffed

My dad was in the book publishing business. Every year they used to have a bit of a do at a house in Marlow, by the Thames. Various writers and celebs used to turn up for lunch, booze and sometimes an impromptu game of cricket whilst others would mess about on the river.

David Kossoff had just had a book published and was chatting to my dad, who was a great fan of his acting, when he turned and asked the nine-year-old me what type of music I liked. I told him I liked Jimi Hendrix. He said his son, Paul, played guitar in a band and that I should listen to his new LP.

I asked if he was as good as Jimi Hendrix. He replied that he couldn't really say. That was the first time I'd heard of Kossoff or Free.

Paul Kossoff

I like it when the music is moving in slow waves... rising and falling.

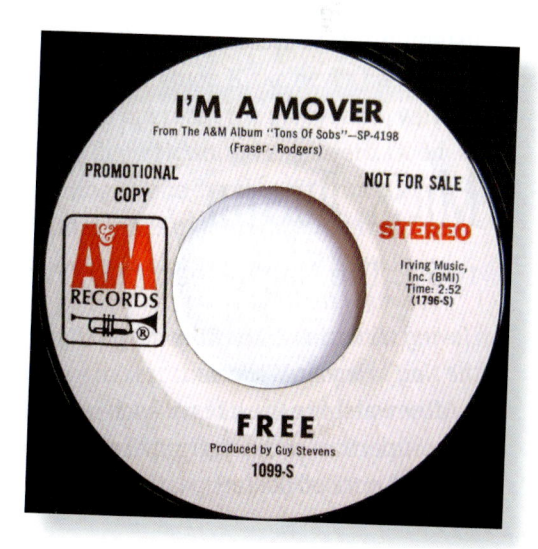

Ludwig Super Classic drum kit with a Ludwig Suprephonic snare drum, it was a big improvement tonally on his old Premier kit. The Super Classic was, and still is, a very desirable drum kit and tuned to his requirements the sound was phenomenal. I believe he recorded *Tons of Sobs* with the old Premier kit and the second album using the Ludwig kit, so you be the judge.

It was early so I went back down to the bar, on the way down it was possible to see the band sitting in the dressing room via the long window. They were eating and chatting, it was apparent that the door scenario was over.

About an hour later the Nag's Head yard began to fill with people arriving by bus from Wellingborough. It was time to get pole position at the front of the stage before it was impossible to move in there. I had been explaining to my younger cousin what a great treat he was in for as we climbed the stairs again for the gig. I knew it was going to be stuffed in there. It was heaving at the first gig and I reasoned that if everyone attending that gig had told a friend just how great Free were then the audience had to double on this second appearance. It must be remembered that this was 1969 and still pre 'All Right Now'. To many, Free were still an unknown quantity, excepting those that had witnessed them playing live in 1968. We all went to see them on the strength of *Tons of Sobs*.

They stepped onto the stage looking so much more confident. Simon Kirke was still wearing the red singlet t-shirt and the brown corduroy trousers but this time wearing expensive riding boots! Andy Fraser and Paul Kossoff looked much the same as they did at the first gig. Kossoff was now playing the plain-topped Gibson Les Paul which became legendary.

It didn't take more than five seconds when they stormed into their first number, 'The Hunter', to realise they were no longer just another blues band. Their new equipment made the whole thing sound better, their confidence shone through and the amount of gigs they had obviously played made it all sound polished and precise. The one thing Free had at that time over other bands was they understood the art of dynamics, they understood how to use volume without it becoming just a huge noise, they wrote great riffs with gaping holes in them and it's almost impossible to describe that in such a small venue how important that style works. I hate getting technical about music but Free along with maybe Led Zeppelin understood dynamics way before many other bands. The musicians that followed learned from them and today every rock band has emulated that approach. Lynyrd Skynyrd openly admitted that they were totally influenced by Free and in the way they constructed songs. You only have to listen to 'Sweet Home Alabama' to understand where that technique came from. Watching Free in a small club was not only audible, it was also physical, take a song like 'I'll be Creeping'. Free were the loudest band I ever saw in a small venue but the silence between the riffs could make you lose your sense of balance, one moment it was blasting out your eardrums and within a second it vanished and within another few seconds the power was there again. A physical thing not every musician mastered. Free managed it every time, but in a small venue like the Nag's Head it was much more pronounced.

Free were not only great in their own right they understood how to control sheer volume and power without it becoming just noise. This second gig staggered me completely. They looked so sharp, they had already began to distance themselves from being just a blues band. They now used everything in their tool kit and although the second album was a couple of months off being released they were playing mainly their own songs which tightened the whole set up. My younger cousin Dennis had never really seen a live band before and standing directly in front of Paul Kossoff's amplifier probably wasn't the best place to start! As Kossoff threw himself into the guitar solo during 'The Hunter' I yelled in his ear 'Fucking brilliant or what?!' I was confused by his bland expression with his hands motioning towards his ears. I guessed he was gesturing to tell me he couldn't hear me. It was only once the band reached the end of the song that he looked at me while Paul Rodgers was introducing the second song and said: 'My hearing's gone!'. I had to drag him out through the heaving audience into the fresh air at the top of the fire escape. After a few minutes he said he was OK and it was almost a fight to return to the front of the stage. Luckily it was the era of 'Peace & Love' and fighting was considered something of a taboo, after all the first Woodstock was happening at around this time.

More or less all the second album's songs were within the set now. At one point during the first set I recall them playing 'Free Me' when Simon Kirke damaged his snare drum (hardly surprising) and as he repaired the drum he sang harmonies from the drum stool and Andy Fraser proved himself to have a quality singing voice. They proved to everyone that day that they were not just amazingly good at playing rock, they were now capable of playing soft acoustic material to a very, very high standard. With the drum repaired they immediately stormed into 'Mr Big'. The song had obviously been in the set list months before it was added to the album *Fire & Water*. Some of the *Sobs* material was still in the set: 'I'm a Mover', 'Walk in my Shadow' being obviously well received numbers. The blues was being pretty much buried by the amount of great songs they were writing. At one point, a few people in the audience, between songs, started yelling to hear 'Going Down Slow': A perfectly reasonable request for any diehard *Tons of Sobs* fan. They did play the song, but it was clear as day that all the members of the band, except Paul Kossoff maybe, thought that they had far more to offer than 12 bar slow blues. But that didn't stop Kossoff ripping up the place during his solos.

The first set finished, the band retreated to the dressing room and the audience made their way downstairs to the bar of the pub. We got our drinks and sat down and within a few minutes the band appeared and sat at our table: Paul Rodgers to my left, Paul Kossoff to my right and Simon Kirke and Andy Fraser sitting opposite. I have to explain here that I had another cousin that lived in Kent at the time and during those days, decades before the internet and mobile phones, people kept in touch via the Royal Mail. I corresponded frequently with her. It also has to be remembered that Free, although being an amazing band, were still relatively unknown. That said, a few fans were asking for autographs from them during that interval. As I was trying to inform Dennis that I had received a letter from our cousin in Kent, he gestured for me to pass the envelope so that he may read the correspondence. As I handed him the letter, I recall Andy Fraser moving his head to one side to allow for him to grasp it, as he did so Paul Kossoff snatched it out of my hand and signed it! I didn't actually ask for his autograph but thank God he did. I still have the piece of envelope with Kossoff's signature written in biro on it. To my eternal regret I have to say I didn't make conversation with any of the band, they appeared busy talking to each other across me and to have interrupted to simply tell them I thought they were the best band I had ever witnessed would only have duplicated what about 20 other punters had already informed them as they signed odd pieces of paper, posters and *Tons of Sobs* albums.

With hindsight these were heady days indeed, they will probably never happen again. If you didn't live through them I can only try to explain why hero worship didn't really exist back then. We were spoilt rotten with music, everything was in forward gear, one week it was Free drinking at the same table, the following week you may well have been drinking with Supertramp, Rod Stewart and the Faces, Uriah Heep or Wishbone Ash, Bob Marley and The Wailers, Mott the Hoople.

Free were just one band amongst so many that were on a heady road to stardom and fame, they hadn't reached that point where they had become unreachable, they were just one of so many musicians that were challenging what had gone before musically. Free were my favourite live band but in the context of fame, it ceased to be celebrity fame for many years in the late 60's and early 70's. Even legendary bands like Cream and Jimi Hendrix were approachable back then, my ex-wife sat on the lawns of De Montfort Hall in Leicester eating ice cream and chatting to Hendrix himself! Times were about to change though as venues got bigger so this social freedom with bands began to end, it didn't happen overnight but it was definitely on the wane.

The next time I saw Free the album *Fire & Water* had just been released and that change in being able to actually sit and talk to bands was coming to an end. At the Nag's, providing you arrived early enough, you could watch the van turn up and these (now) famous people would pile out and you could be helping unload their equipment for the gig. Free played The Drill Hall in Northampton during 1970, they had moved up yet another gear, the venue was bigger but they were still playing with Marshall stacks and acoustic drums with no mixing desk to be seen. At the Drill Hall they would have a couple of support bands; they were progressing fast to becoming a huge success.

Richard Wyatt

27 September 1969, The Vandike Club, Plymouth, UK

My mates and I went to the Vandike thinking it was free entry to the club. Free were playing that night! I was so impressed I went and bought *Tons of Sobs*.

Dave Hansell

1969, Edward Herbert Building, Loughborough University, UK

I first saw Free in 1969 at Loughborough University, then again in 1970 at the same venue.

Before the first gig I didn't know much about the band but was advised to go by my roommate, Jack Delap, who was on the University entertainment committee. The chair was fellow student Rob Dickins. We knew that Rob's dad [Percy Dickins] was at the *New Musical Express*, and his elder brother, Barry, was already into promotion. Rob later went into a great career with Warner Bros: No wonder we got some great bands at Loughborough.

Both gigs were in the Edward Herbert Building, which in those days housed the Students' Union Offices, the Union Bar and two sports halls, where the gigs were staged.

I was just knocked out by that first gig – I had never seen or heard anything like it before. I remember that as soon as I got home for the Christmas vac,

ROCK 'N' ROLL FANTASY

I looked for *Tons of Sobs* at my local record store in Wimbledon. They didn't have it in stock, but ordered it for me. I remember driving my parents mad, playing it over and over again. They were probably very glad to see me return to Loughborough in January!

Lucy Piller had Paul Rodgers sign the front of her 1969 diary

Free

The group's second album, simply titled *Free*, was released in the UK in October 1969 on Island Records just seven months after *Tons of Sobs*. The recording sessions had taken place in the first half of 1969 at Morgan Studios and Trident Studios, produced this time by Chris Blackwell. Like its predecessor, it failed to chart.

   Despite the LP's lack of sales at the time, this release was notable for a growing reliance on the Paul Rodgers and Andy Fraser songwriting partnership. Unlike *Tons of Sobs*, *Free* included no covers and nine original new songs.
   The album was also significant for its striking cover art, designed by American photographer Ron Raffaelli, known for his fine art and erotic photography. Raffaelli also acted as official photographer for Jimi Hendrix in 1968 and went on to photograph major acts such as the Rolling Stones, The Doors and Led Zeppelin. His work has appeared in hundreds of magazine layouts and over 50 album covers.
   Raffaelli created the *Free* cover depicting a woman photographed from ground level leaping across a blue sky in what appears to be a shining starry cat-suit. The band's name/title is printed in tiny lettering at the top of the cover, which on later CD's rendered it almost unreadable.
   The cover is featured in the *book 100 Best Album Covers*.

Simon Kirke

Andy Fraser's bass playing on 'I'll Be Creepin' was fantastic. I always felt that, pound for pound, Andy had the most talent of the four of us. He was quite advanced for his age and, in many ways, a lot like John Paul Jones of Led Zeppelin – someone who could play a number of instruments well and was a strong but quiet influence.

Martin Bobbe

Paradiso, Amsterdam, The Netherlands

One Sunday afternoon in 1969 I was sitting on the floor in Paradiso, Amsterdam, Holland, waiting for a friend, when they put on the side A of the second album, *Free*. 'I'll Be Creepin'' had me swinging on my ass. 'Songs Of Yesterday' sealed the deal and made me a fan for life. Boudisque at the Haringpakkerssteeg in Amsterdam was my regular music dealer. I bought most of my Free albums there. Only one serious musical weekly was published in Holland at the time, which was called *Oor* (Ear). It had good interviews and reviews and Boudisque took out ads with new releases for every issue.

    Andy Fraser's distinctive bass lines in those two songs made the final decision to choose the bass guitar over the guitar very easy for me. His jumping octave in a rhythmical pattern like a flea adds flourishes that go against the rhythm in between. It's got an instant swing and makes you wanna jump up and dance. His style was unique.

    I've been playing the bass in various semi-pro and hobby bands close to 50 years. He's been my main inspiration and my number one choice on my fave bass player list ever since.

Jerry Ewing

Editor: *Prog* magazine

'Songs of Yesterday' is the perfect example of Free taking a very mellow route. I mean their debut album *Tons of Sobs* had a bit of an earthy, youthful swagger to it as quite rightly it should have done given that they were steeped in a bit of blues, soul, bit of R n' B. But *Free*, the follow-up, was a much softer album, almost melancholic in a way which might have surprised a few people. There's only two or three really up-tempo groovy songs on there, the rest of it displays the mellower side of the band and 'Songs of Yesterday' is probably the best example of that on the album.

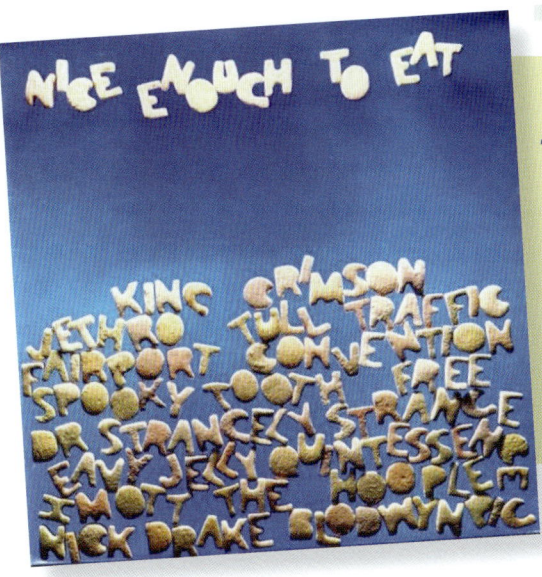

Nice Enough To Eat

Island would continue the policy of releasing sample LPs featuring their roster of up and coming artists. *Nice Enough to Eat*, released in November 1969, was the second compilation to showcase Free, with 'Woman' the track chosen this time.

Marilyn Rowland

30 November 1969, The Roundhouse, London, UK

I remember seeing Free perform live at the Roundhouse, Camden, in November 1969 when I was 18-years-old. I have been a huge fan ever since. At the time I was living with my parents in Southgate, North London. I had finished college and was working as a retail assistant in the Jaeger store in Regent Street, London. I couldn't yet buy albums because we had no record player - just a radio and a tape recorder!

At the Roundhouse, I have no recollection of having anyone with me, but who knows!

Free were all brilliant: talented musicians and an exciting performance. The vibe was great. Lots of fans by the stage but, nearer the back of the hall, lots of empty space and people milling around. I do remember being shocked at people having babies strapped to their backs and wondering how they were coping with the crowds and the noise! Some of them will be grandparents now - I wonder if they remember being taken to a Free concert all those years ago.

Sandra Banks

December 1969, Art College, Maidstone, UK

Sadly, I only saw Free twice. The first time was with my cousin Mick Austin and the second time was at Maidstone Art College where I took the photographs on pages 70 and 71. I was Sandra Waite back then but Bill Banks (now my husband) saw them more than I did, he recalls early gigs at Maidstone when they would arrive in an old Ford Transit. At one of the gigs the stage was constructed from large boxes which started to move about as Paul Rodgers was strutting around and his microphone lead got jammed between those boxes, severely restricting his movements until the roadie was able to free it. On another occasion Bill's band were supporting Free and his guitarist wanted to know what the settings were on Paul Kossoff's Marshall amplifier. At the end of the show the guitarist went rushing up to Kossoff's amp to see the settings, but the roadie saw him and quickly moved the settings before he had time to make a note.

Mick Austin and Sandra Banks

Julie Scott

December 1969, Art College, Maidstone, UK

Free have been a special part of my life since I first heard *Tons of Sobs* in 1969. I was 16 and had just started college in Chatham, Kent. I became friends with Dallas and two guys, Lindsay and Lex. Lindsay's older brother, Geoff, had recently heard Free on the Island Records sampler *You Can All Join In* and on hearing the track 'I'm A Mover' we decided they sounded like they could be a great live band. We all gathered together and listened to their debut album *Tons Of Sobs*, a brilliant bluesy rock, soulful album, and immediately agreed seeing them live was a must.

The opportunity quickly came when, in December 1969, a mutual friend, Andy, booked them to play at Maidstone Art College and we made sure we got tickets. The five of us travelled to Maidstone by bus, high in anticipation. We made our way to the front of the makeshift stage and waited. We were so excited when these four young men just strolled out, plugged into amps and played. From start to finish I was completely blown away by the impressive combination of talent. Paul Rodger's gritty, raspy voice, Paul Kossof's superb guitar riffs, Andy Fraser's fantastic bass lines and Simon Kirke's steady beats just all fitted perfectly and I was hooked! We all travelled home that night squashed into Andy's dad's van, discussing our great evening.

1970

Robert Lazenby

1970, St. Mary's Youth Club, Stockton-on-Tees, UK

My first hearing of Free was on one of Island Records' sampler albums, possibly on *You Can All Join In* released in 1968. I later purchased the second album, just titled *Free*, with its stand-out track, 'I'll Be Creepin'. I bought it from a record shop that was right next to the Globe Theatre on Stockton High Street.

In October 1969 I heard they were playing at a youth club, which I frequently went to, St Mary's on Norton Road, Stockton-on-Tees. I booked for January / February 1970 and tickets were twelve shillings and sixpence in old money and of course I purchased one with a few of my friends. You knew this was not just any old band and I was unaware at the time that Paul Rodgers was a local lad. Apparently Free used the St Mary's Youth Club as a practice gig, which might explain why it does not come up on the usual Free gig lists. I think they played St Mary's a few times and weren't alone in using the venue: David Coverdale (another local lad) fronted Rivers Invitation performed there, as did Bronco (fronted by Jess Roden) who I saw later in 1970.

Seeing Free, you could tell they were going places and I remember there were posters on sale at five shillings and sixpence.

In his multi-colour patchwork boots Paul Kossoff was leaning precariously back and forth against the two Marshall cabinets on that stage. I was unaware how young the band were and not much older than myself. I was nearly 16 at the time.

At the end of the gig I remember Paul Rodgers saying 'there is transport outside' going to various local areas.

My first proper gig and a memorable one at that.

These days I drive past St Mary's quite a lot and still can't believe that I actually saw Free in there and that is 50 years ago now: quite incredible really. I had been told the band got paid £150 for that gig but I don't know how accurate that is. I saw Free again in 1972 at Middlesbrough Town Hall and *Free Live* is a constant companion in my car's CD collection.

Free

live at Maidstone Art College and The Drill Hall, Northampton

copyright Mick Austin

Photos by Mick Austin and Sandra Banks

Marlène Rivet

February 1970, Continental Hotel, Lausanne, Switzerland

In February 1970, I was barely 18-years-old and that year, I had this enormous chance to attend the concert by Free in an establishment in the basement of the Continental Hotel near the train station in Lausanne in Switzerland. I remember that it was a Swiss production house named Good News Production which brought these rock groups to Switzerland for concerts and particularly in the cities of Lausanne and Geneva.

A bulletin with the programme and the names of the artists was published regularly with the names of the groups that were scheduled to perform on stage. When we went to Geneva to see Free with a friend, because they had played in Lausanne and in Geneva, we hitchhiked! It was one of the first rock concerts I attended.

There were about 200 people in the room and the stage was quite small with everyone seated very close to the stage. Another concert by the group had been organised in a small club in Geneva called The Black Bird. During this same period, many rock groups had also performed in Switzerland: Taste, Black Sabbath, East of Eden, Mott the Hoople, Writing on the Wall, Stone the Crows, Renaissance, Rare Bird, Jody Grind, Terry Reid, Spirit of John Morgan, Toe Fat, Sweet Water Canal, Atomic Rooster and many more.

I have a very good memory of Free and was so lucky to see them at their beginnings. I remember their way of moving on stage, especially that of Andy Fraser, and I always remember the good sound from the Gibson guitar by Paul Kossoff.

As for the hoarse voice of Paul Rodgers, it was a pleasure to listen to it. His voice has hardly changed and he is still an extraordinary singer. I think Free was very avant-garde at the time. A mythical and fabulous group from the 70s.

Fire and Water recording sessions

After less than two years together, and set against a background of constant touring, Free somehow found enough time to work up and record the songs for their third album, *Fire and Water*. The first two tracks laid down were 'Remember', a reworking of 'Woman By The Sea', an unused song from the *Tons of Sobs* recording sessions in 1968, and an early version of 'All Right Now' which the band laid down on 11 January. With sessions lined up in between a packed gig schedule, the tracks were recorded throughout February, with a new version of 'All Right Now' added right at the end of the sessions, on 8 March. It was apparently only the second stereo single released in the UK (the first being Bowie's 'Space Oddity'), which accounts for the rather separated stereo balance. Mixing was done straight after that, and an album master delivered to Island on March 11th.

Richard Digby Smith

February 1970. Morgan Studios, Trident Studios and Island Studios, London, UK

Chris Blackwell engaged Roy Thomas Baker, an engineer at Morgan Studios in Willesden, North West London to start work on Free's third album. A hit was surely due soon. Roy Baker was later to become the engineer/producer for Queen and *Bohemian Rhapsody* would be his greatest achievement. But back in 1970, along with producer John Kelly, additional sessions at Trident studios and also at Island, the third Free album, *Fire and Water*, was in the can.

Free were in desperate need of a hit and so too, no doubt, Island. The title contender from the album was 'All Right Now' but the problem was with the length of the song. At five minutes 35 seconds it was far too long for radio airplay. Three and a half minutes was the norm, with the possible exception of the Animals' 'House of the Rising Sun' at almost four and a half minutes, radio stations simply wouldn't give the air-time. So, out with the razor blades and the splicing tape and enter Andy Johns. Having already worked with the band on their debut album *Tons of Sobs* he was best placed to work alongside label boss Chris Blackwell, in studio two. Andy had in his head the perfect edit: take out the second verse and shorten the guitar solo. Just a smidgen over four minutes. Done.

A few weeks later, I remember all the band members walking into Island Records' reception, heads held high, a victorious swagger in their steps. The guys were on top of the world. Island's belief had paid off. The single reached No. 2 in the UK and was No, 1 in about 20 territories around the world.

Andy Johns

Kossoff would pretty much just sit and smoke big joints. They used to make fun of Koss because he'd pull a lot of faces; he never combed his hair or anything. And they would laugh and Koss was a pretty sensitive chap and I think it used to upset him a bit. But he was just the most wonderful guitar player. Never really made any mistakes, had this fantastic sound, and that man's vibrato! Still to this day, someone will play something and I'll go, 'Man, that's almost as good as Koss!'

Mike Vernon

It was in the early months of 1970 when I took the decision to make an attempt at recording my own solo album. By that time the distributorship of the Blue Horizon label had moved from CBS to Polydor. The label had lost Fleetwood Mac to Immediate and then to Warners; I was no longer in charge of John Mayall's production as he moved to Polydor (US) and Ten Years After had also moved to Chrysalis. The so-called British 'blues boom' had been drifting into decline and I realised that it would not be long before Blue Horizon might become redundant unless we made some major changes. We signed Dutch rock band Focus and had immediate success with their product, so I figured it was time to get 'stuff' off my chest and make my own recorded contribution to the label's catalogue. Maybe not a great idea in hindsight? The Mike Vernon *Bring It Back Home* project was recorded at Polydor's small 'in house' studio in Stratford Place in Central London, with Andy Stephens and Carlos Olms in charge of the engineering tasks. The rhythm section consisted of Kenny Lamb, John Best, Paul Butler and Rick Hayward (Jellybread) with the addition of their former leader Pete Wingfield. Four additional musicians were drafted in as featured soloists: Laurence Garman, Dick Parry, Rory Gallagher and Paul Kossoff. Paul features on the song 'My Say Blues' and did a really good job with some great guitar work. Rory also played on a track - my version of a Doctor Isaiah Ross classic entitled 'Come Back Baby'. As it turned out these two songs are probably the strongest on the album. Have to say that I felt good about the results, especially 'My Say Blues', but sales were poor and reviews not overly enthusiastic. Glad I took the jump though!

Chris McCauley

6 March, 1970, The Lyceum Ballroom, The Strand, London, UK

I sat cross-legged on the floor, quite near the stage. When Free had finished their customary one-hour 15-minute set I left with my spine still tingling and I made my way to the Tube in a kind of trance.

After that I tried to get to as many shows as I could and to this day I never miss a Paul Rodgers concert if he is playing in my area (within 100 mile radius). Free are still far the best band I have ever seen.

Bumpers

Island records released *Bumpers* in 1970, with the cover art by Tony Wright, his first sleeve for Island. The 19 track double album featured 'Oh I Wept' by Free along with tracks by Traffic, Spooky Tooth, Mott the Hoople, King Crimson and Cat Stevens.

Julie Scott

6 March, 1970, The Lyceum Ballroom, The Strand, London, UK

On the train up to London we wondered what the weekend held for us. My friend Lindsay's brother Geoff had managed to get tickets to see Free again. The Lyceum, an all-nighter, was a very laid-back affair with the crowd either sitting or lying on the floor! Keef Hartley Band, Crazy World of Arthur Brown, East of Eden and Mandrake also played sets that night but as soon as Free walked out you could hear a buzz from the crowd. The sets didn't disappoint, with tracks like 'Woman', 'Walk in My Shadow', 'I'm a Mover' and the hauntingly beautiful 'Don't Say You Love Me', to name a few.

In the early hours of the morning, and having had a remarkable evening, we left the Lyceum and hung around London all day patiently waiting to get to the Rag Ball. We paid the princely sum of seven shillings each, with a promised disco and bar to boot. The bar definitely beckoned after our long day waiting! Audience were the support act that night, along with other rag ball shenanigans. Free gave another stunning set and the crowd were raucous. Geoff remembers Paul Rodgers cadging cigarettes from Heather, with which she cordially obliged. At around midnight we walked back to Victoria station to catch the milk train home, jubilant and shattered!

Shane White

21 March 1970, The Vandike Club, Plymouth, UK

I was 18. I was into Simon and Garfunkel, The Moody Blues and suchlike, and had never been to any sort of a live gig before other than school concerts. Late developer, I guess.

A couple of mates said they were going to see a group in Plymouth, did I want to come? I wasn't sure it was 'my sort of thing', but tagged along anyway. The group was called Free. Never heard of them.

We drove into town, then on through the back streets until we arrived outside a rather run-down place that looked a bit like a church hall, with a queue of people outside who definitely didn't look like church hall sort of people. We joined the queue, got to the door, paid our seven shillings and sixpence and walked into a whole new world.

Inside, the hall was big enough for about three hundred people at most. It was dimly lit, hot and smokey, with a bar on the left and a stage at the far end that looked far too small to be of much use. It was filled with speakers, amps, drums and mics, but there didn't seem to be room for much else.

To the right of the stage behind a high desk, a DJ who looked exactly like the Milky Bar Kid was playing totally unfamiliar records, and to this day I couldn't tell you what they were but they sounded pretty good to me. Around the walls were huge reproductions of Aubrey Beardsley prints which gave the whole place a slightly decadent, sophisticated air. So cool to a naive teen.

The place was about half full, so we made our way to the middle of the room and settled on the floor. We didn't have to wait long. From the first number, I was smitten. Paul Rodgers was completely compelling, rough and raw voice, the classic freak look, he set the template for how I wanted to be from that point onwards. Kossoff's guitar seared through the whole place accompanied by his trademark grimaces, and the whole effect was completely overwhelming.

Did I say that the stage was small? Andy Fraser's bass stack was placed right on the edge of the left hand end, only about three feet above the floor level. By the end of the evening I was sitting on the edge of the stage leaning against the speakers, lost in a whole new world.

After that, the Vandike became a major part of my life. I was introduced to music ranging from Edgar Broughton to Fairport Convention, and from ELP to Black Sabbath, but that first life-changing evening with Free is the one that I'll always remember. Best night ever.

Gerald Edmonds

The Vandike Club Plymouth. I was at this one - never forget my mate picked up the tickets and dropped mine off at home, my dad, dear of him, said as I walked through the door 'Alan stopped by and left you a free ticket to see a magician at The Guild hall'.

Mike Hobbs

22 March 1970, The Greyhound pub, Croydon, UK

That Sunday was already a red letter day. Mike Binns and I had tickets for the afternoon show of The Nice at Fairfield Halls, Croydon. It was the start of the Easter holidays. I was just sixteen.

We took the train from Horsham to Croydon and settled in for some extensive virtuoso keyboard bashing from Keith Emerson. He didn't disappoint. 'America' was the highlight, burning Stars and Stripes and dagger stabs to the organ both present. We reeled out as the light started to fade.

Special entrance fee to the Greyhound to see Free, claimed the leaflet distributor. Where is it? Just over the road. How much? Only six bob (30p). Twenty five per cent discount. Seemed a bargain.

Because we didn't have much to spare after the entrance money, we joined the queue to get in very near the front. So we got good places near the stage – mosh pits weren't quite so riotous in those days. Probably because everyone was stoned. As were we: we'd been smoking all day wherever we could. The atmosphere was great. The Greyhound epitomised a certain type of sweaty blues/rock club, one which needs protecting.

I knew a little bit about Free. Their first album had been so popular at school that our band, for which I used to sing very badly, used to play 'I'm a Mover' and 'The Hunter'. So I was predisposed to like them. But I didn't realise they were going to be that good.

What was so amazing about them? Basically, it was the way they seemed to leave spaces between the notes so that the music loped along. Kossoff, swaying over his guitar, was at that time a master of underplaying, whereas Fraser bubbled like his bass, making it almost a second lead instrument. And sure, they could be heavy: Kirke's drumming made sure of that, driving Kossoff and Fraser to wild heights.

And Rodgers? Just one of the great blues/rock voices, who commanded the songs effortlessly. He also knew how to command the stage, with the right touches of showmanship. I was in awe. His demeanour was rather like a midshipman leading an assault on a French privateer in the Napoleonic wars. The bell-bottoms undoubtedly helped. As did being so close, watching them go to work right before our eyes. Rodgers and the band took no prisoners. Through a haze of smoke, the audience responded with wild enthusiasm.

As well as the songs we knew from the first and second albums, they also played material they were recording for their next (breakthrough) LP. I can only now recall 'Fire and Water', 'Mr Big' and 'All Right Now' individually but the whole set was dynamite.

The particular reason, I think, was that this was Free's moment. There's always a spell just before big success strikes when a group is at its powerful best. They know it, and soon enough the crowd knows it too. Poised on the cusp of greatness, everyone can enjoy the feeling.

I saw Free again about a year later, at the Colston Hall in Bristol, and they were very good, fully on terms with the larger venues they were now playing. Rodgers was still excellent, but it wasn't quite the same for me. Nor was it when

I saw Bad Company at The Valley, Charlton Athletic's football ground, in 1974. Inevitably, as you move further from the stage, some of the magic is lost. Bad Company were a great band, but they weren't Free at the Greyhound.

Best six bob I ever spent.

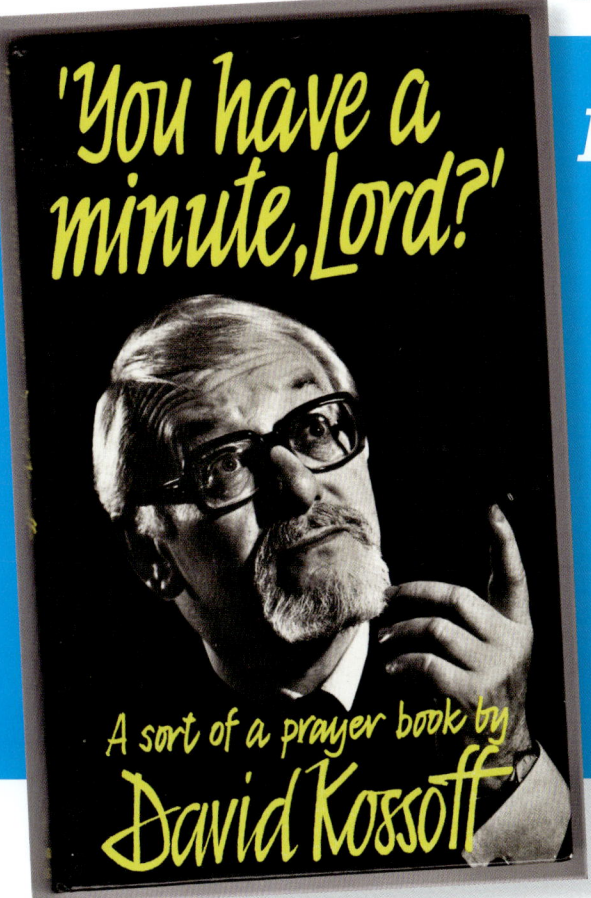

David Kossoff

That was a night, that show in Croydon.
That was a night!
You left 'em for dead, you slayed 'em.
Lucky you had a high stage, and big roadies,
or they would have torn your clothes off.
Worshippers they were, followers, the faithful.
And you played that night, my Paul, to
show 'em they'd chosen right.

Extract from 'Words for Paul' from his father David Kossoff's 'You Have a Minute, Lord?'

Richard Jolliffe

13 April 1970, Cooks Ferry Inn, Edmonton, North London, UK

Wonderful gig at Cooks Ferry Inn, Edmonton in 1970 for 9 shillings! They played with so much passion.

Chris Cantor
1970, King's School, Canterbury, Kent, UK

I was 15-years-old and seated in front of a bass cabinet with a school band playing all the gems of the day. On came 'Walk in My Shadow' [from *Tons of Sobs*]. That instantly converted me to Free and bass as an instrument. I never get tired of playing it. Fortunately for my limited skills it is an easy line - but so good. Saw Free at the Albert Hall and Fairfield Halls, Croydon. (Also Peace, at the Rainbow, Finsbury Park.)

My favourite band member was Andy Fraser but now I'd rate Kossoff and Rodgers above him, and Kirke was also damn good. Free was the only band whose albums I bought as they came out.

Nig Greenaway
1970, Student's Union, Reading University, UK

First saw Free at Reading University for seven shillings and sixpence.

As teenagers, music was vitally important to my mates and me. We'd work hard to find new music as there wasn't a great deal of decent stuff played on the radio. However, there were a couple of shows such as *The Perfumed Garden* that were almost mandatory listening.

We'd buy records and listen to them together or lend them around the group – seldom buying the same album to maximise what we could listen to. In the record shops you could listen to an album in the booth before listening to another one which you would actually buy. Some of those listenings almost turned into parties with at least one booth that had a door being filled with cigarette smoke from the top and right down to the floor after a few of us had gone through the process.

In this way, a couple of my mates had obtained Free's first album *Tons of Sobs* and *Free*, which came out later in '69. My brother also had the second single 'Broad Daylight'. None of these releases really bothered the charts.

All of us were of school leaving age, and about to get our first jobs and we were extremely fortunate that there were a number of music venues that we could get to that weren't too far away. The main one that we used was the Students' Union at Reading University which being on the university circuit of the late 60s/early 70s put on a lot of upcoming bands. None of us actually attended the uni but we had a mate who could print NUS cards, giving us cheaper entry and more to spend on beer.

On a Saturday night, the students' bar was open but you were not allowed to take drinks into the hall. I managed to perfect the art of smuggling in six bottles of Newcastle Brown under my coat while still showing the stamp on the back of my hand to gain entry.

The hall was always crowded and we had to get there in good time to claim a spot on the floor somewhere towards the front. The difficulty was keeping that space as you had to leave to go to the loo or get more beer. This all had to be managed in shifts that were timed so no one missed the main act.

After all these years, I cannot recall all the songs Free performed but I know I particularly enjoyed 'The Hunter' at the end. That was a Booker T and the MGs number and what we did not know at the time was that Free wanted their own number to round out their shows. The result was them writing 'All Right Now', which rushed up the singles chart to No.2. in 1970, with the LP *Fire and Water*, which contained an extended version, also reaching No.2 in the album chart.

Andy Fraser

4 June 1970, BBC TV *Top of the Pops*, London, UK

Free appeared on the BBC British TV weekly music show *Top of the Pops* on 4 June 1970 performing 'All Right Now'. Andy Fraser stood grinning with his hands folded above his bass until he joined in for the first chorus.

'I wanted to turn down *Top of the Pops*. I just couldn't see us on the same stage as some band like The Sweet.'

Christine Sands

When did I first become a fan? From the minute I saw Paul Rodgers on *Top of The Pops* singing 'All Right Now', at the grand old age of 10. Still love him now.

Fire and Water

The band's third album, *Fire and Water* was released on 26 June 1970. In many ways this month was the band's most momentous. The album would mark a significant breakthrough for Free and the single 'All Right Now' would become a pop rock classic. The widespread commercial success gave the band their first chart placings. The album and single would go on to peak at No.2 in the British charts. Only the seemingly ever-present 'In The Summertime' by Mungo Jerry prevented Free bagging a chart-topper in the summer of 1970. US success followed quickly with *Fire and Water* rising to No.17 on the *Billboard* chart and around the world 'All Right Now' introduced the band to a rapidly expanding audience.

Album artwork photography by Ian T Cossar

Andy Fraser

We were grounded in blues, rock, and wanted to keep it as an underlay to more original things. That was our first step in a forward direction. Not always successful, but generally moving in the right direction to something that was totally us. We kept reaching for the horizon until we imploded. Me personally: I always want to keep moving forward, discovering, keeping it an adventure, and not re-doing one's old party tricks until you get stuck in some past decade. *Fire and Water* probably nailed it at our best, and opened many doors with 'All Right Now'.

Luke Morley (Thunder)

Although I adore 'All Right Now', my favourite Free song is actually 'Oh I Wept' from the *Fire and Water* album. For me, it has everything in it that makes Free Free. Incredible restraint. The space in it. Amazing how little they all play on it. Normally in a rock band you want to play all the time. That's how you start as a kid. Economy is something you learn, but Andy Fraser was only 15 when they started. It's a very unusual song. There's a very unusual little guitar part and the bass part is typical Andy Fraser. Rodgers kind of croons it. He doesn't put his foot down. And you feel like they've got plenty more in the back pocket.

I think the reason Paul Rodgers is such a fantastic singer is that he has that natural ability to sound great. You are born with that taste, it's inbuilt. You can't really learn it.

Hipheads, Roundheads and Cavaliers

Barry Cain remembers how 'All Right Now' became a focal point of two strands of culture, music and fashion.

When I was 15, skinheads ruled the roost on my manor and they kept the streets mean. They were everywhere, and some were real bastards. I used to frequent lively East End pubs like the Green Gate in Bethnal Green, the Blind Beggar, site of Ronnie Kray's hit, in Whitechapel, The Black Boy by Stepney Green tube station; full of skinheads in mohair.

And the dancehalls, sumptuous palaces with sweeping balconies and huge dance floors like islands in seas of blue carpet – Streatham Locarno, the Tottenham Royal, the Lyceum in The Strand, The Boathouse by Kew Bridge, full of skinheads in mohair.

And the clubs, flashier and louder than the pubs and dancehalls – Tiffany's in Shaftesbury Avenue. Room At The Top in Ilford, The Bird's Nest in Muswell Hill; full of skinheads in mohair.

Always in suits, two-tone tonic mohair suits. Always fitted Ben Sherman's and college ties. Always a silk handkerchief in the top pocket. Always. You couldn't get in otherwise.

When I went to these places I made sure I was with friends I knew were cool. Sensible minds, don't push it, even with four pints of light and bitter steaming in their heads. Four was the best number. Deviation from that number could be a problem,

The music was everything, and the girls of course. A dance to a dandy duet in dream time and a kiss did it for me. Smooching to 'I'm Gonna Make You Love Me', the smell of Harmony in her hair, tongues, the gentle sway, the faraway sound of fists being thrown and broken glass shoved into faces. There were rip roaring, vicious, deathly fights – fuelled by amphetamines, lager and ska – every Saturday night.

While these working class cavemen were fighting in the dance floors in suits and outside the dance halls in boots and sta-prest, the predominantly middle-class hippy – fuelled by acid, dope and Hendrix – was getting it on internationally through the promotion of peace and love.

Both movements began in 1967 in the UK and flourished like Roundheads and Cavaliers through '68 and '69. By the time of the Isle of Wight Festival, during a sweltering August Bank Holiday weekend in 1970, both movements were in decline, their fall hastened by songs like 'All Right Now' released in the early summer of that year.

'All Right Now' was a crossover record, uniting the tastes of the skin and the hippy. It was the ninth best-selling single in the UK that year, nestled cosily between 'Back Home' by the England World Cup Squad at eight and 'Yellow River' by Christie at ten. There were very few 'rock' singles in the Top 100, maybe four, or five if you include Creedence Clearwater Revival, and to make the ten was unheard of.

They even played it in the dancehalls. This was a hippy band you could party to, sing along to a la 'Hi Ho Silver Lining' or 'Hey Jude'. This was music on another path.

Yep, Free were instrumental in creating the hiphead, a crossbreed. You could spot a hiphead anywhere – longish hair, flared jeans, open neck Ben Sherman and mohair suit jacket. In, out, shake it all about. I loved the style of skinhead, I loved the ska and the Motown and the soul. But I loved The Beatles, Leonard Cohen, Bob Dylan, The Doors, Ten Years After and, of course, Free more.

ROCK 'N' ROLL FANTASY

As Jimmy, our trumpet player, and I went back out towards the van to make sure everything had been successfully unloaded, two hippy-type girls approached us. They were dressed as if they'd just come back from Woodstock and looked too young to be university students. 'We haven't got tickets' they began. 'Can you get us in with your band? We can pretend to be your girlfriends. We'll be really nice to you until Free goes on stage.'

Could we refuse an offer like that? Well, we did refuse because the students guarding the door were watching and had already let our *real* girlfriends through.

Before we took to the stage for our first set, Rod our vocalist announced that Free had arrived in the building: 'Hey – that Paul Kossoff is a right worky-ticket. Nobody was there to unlock the back door and let him in so he was hammering away with his guitar case. I thought he was going to break the plate glass!'

We played the opening set of the night to a growing crowd who were clearly excited about Free's forthcoming performance in just over an hour's time. At the end of the set Jimmy and I find a spot to the left of the stage where we can watch the other bands. As we were waiting two familiar figures came rushing over to us. It was the two hippy chicks that had asked us to get them into the gig. 'You thought you were so big not letting us come in with you, didn't you. Well guess what? We got in with Free. They're not stuck up like you two fuckers. They're better musicians and nicer people than you'll ever be. You thought you were so clever, didn't you?'

The tirade went on and on with no sign of it abating, but there wasn't much Jimmy and I could say so we beat a hasty retreat and headed for the 'green room'. This was, in fact, a cafeteria with a sizable dining area, which has been put off limits to the general public for the evening. There were quite a lot of people in the room – some of Sneeze, some student-types, other hangers-on and, of course, the four members of Free. At one stage Jimmy and I sat at a table with Paul Kossoff and Simon Kirke. A middle-aged man approached and addressed Jimmy and me.

'Hi there – I've got a record shop in the city and wondered how you'd feel about coming down tomorrow morning to sign a few LPs and...'. Jimmy interjected; 'I think you should be talking to the two guys on the other side of the table. They're in Free. We're just the support group.' Embarrassing pause. 'Oh no.... It would be great if your group could come as well.' Smirks all round and the red-faced record shop owner backed away.

When Free took to the stage they certainly lived up to their reputation. After they'd finished, Sneeze had to do the 'tough act to follow' bit and play another set. The crowd's reaction wasn't as bad as we'd anticipated and there were still a lot of people around the stage during our set. One of the benefits of having a good-looking vocalist with a great image.

Sneeze's gig with Free had a positive effect on our band. We were all very impressed with their musicianship and, in particular, their stage presence. Over the next few months our bass player (Stodge) and drummer (Brian Gibson) became a lot tighter as a unit; Stodge started to emulate Andy Fraser's stage movements and some of our songs were slowed right down to become a lot heavier and beatier.

After our dressing down, Jimmy and I pledged that we would let any female into a gig that asked, in future. It still puzzles me today why those two girls hunted us down for that ear-bashing. After all, they'd achieved their aim of getting in to see Free, with the added bonus of meeting a couple of their idols in the process.

Alan Davies

5 July 1970, The Greyhound, Croydon, UK

It was 1970. I had hooked back up with a couple of old friends (we had drifted apart) and they invited me to go to the Greyhound in Croydon (the one opposite Fairfield Halls) to see the band. I lived at that time in a little village called South Godstone and friends that I reconnected with were already going to the Greyhound. I had seen Free on *Top of the Pops* and liked the sound and song 'All Right Now'.

It was a Sunday night and from memory the entrance fee was 15 shillings and sixpence (77.5 new pence).

This was my first live music experience. Free came on and wow! The atmosphere, the smells (possibly patchouli oil, possibly something different) and the general good-natured way everybody was enjoying the experience was just great. The people jammed into the hall were up standing on tables around the perimeter of the hall, jigging about until a couple of the tables collapsed, to great laughter. Nobody was hurt and Free played on.

After seeing the band, I went out and purchased their albums from a small local record shop in Caterham valley.

I was, and still am, hooked on Free, but I never got to see them again.

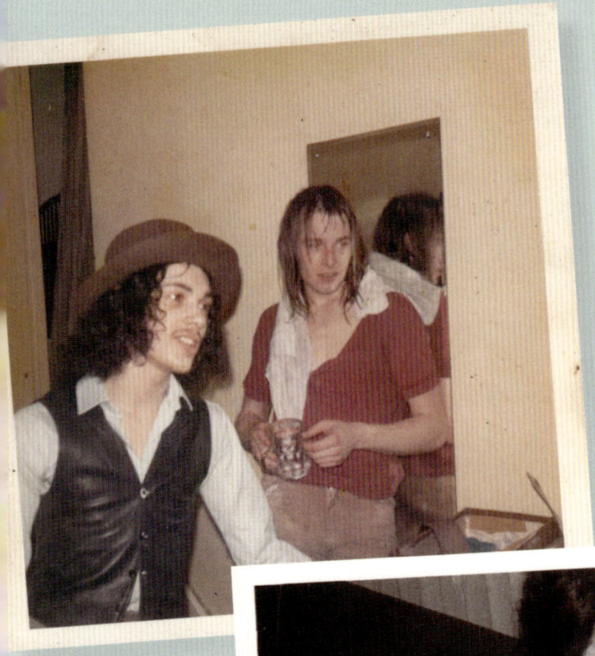
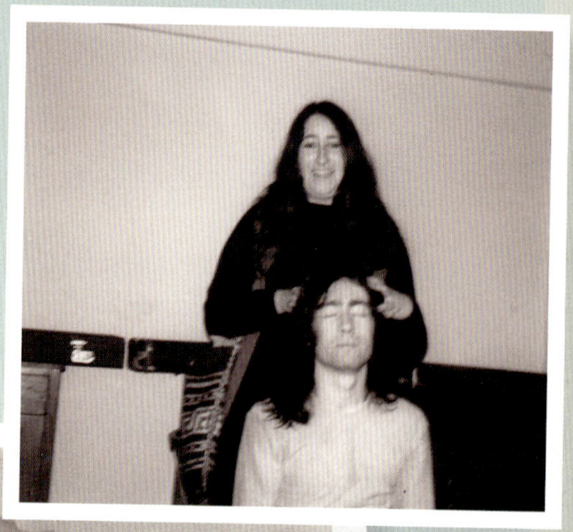
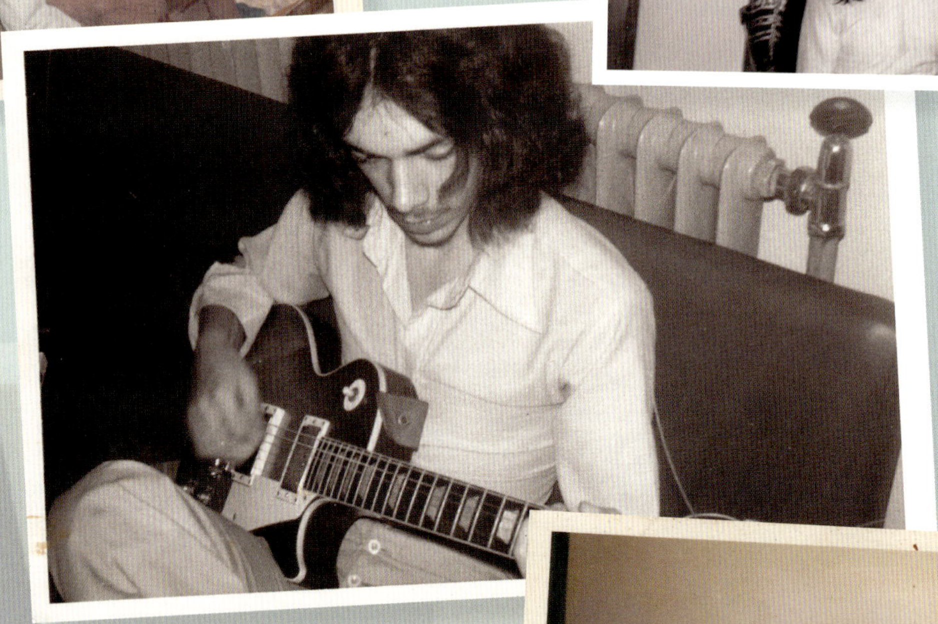
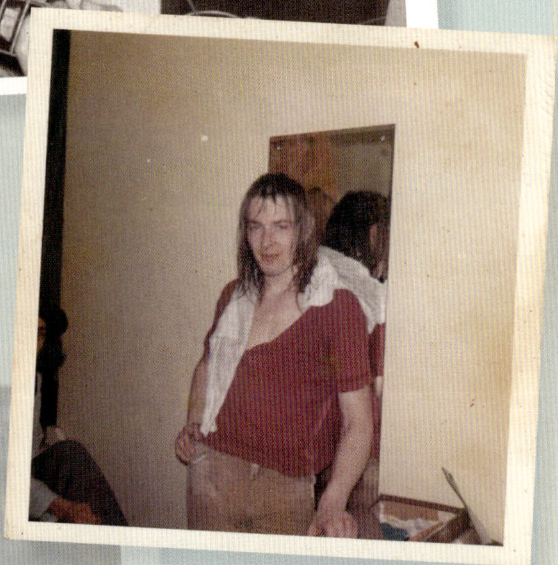
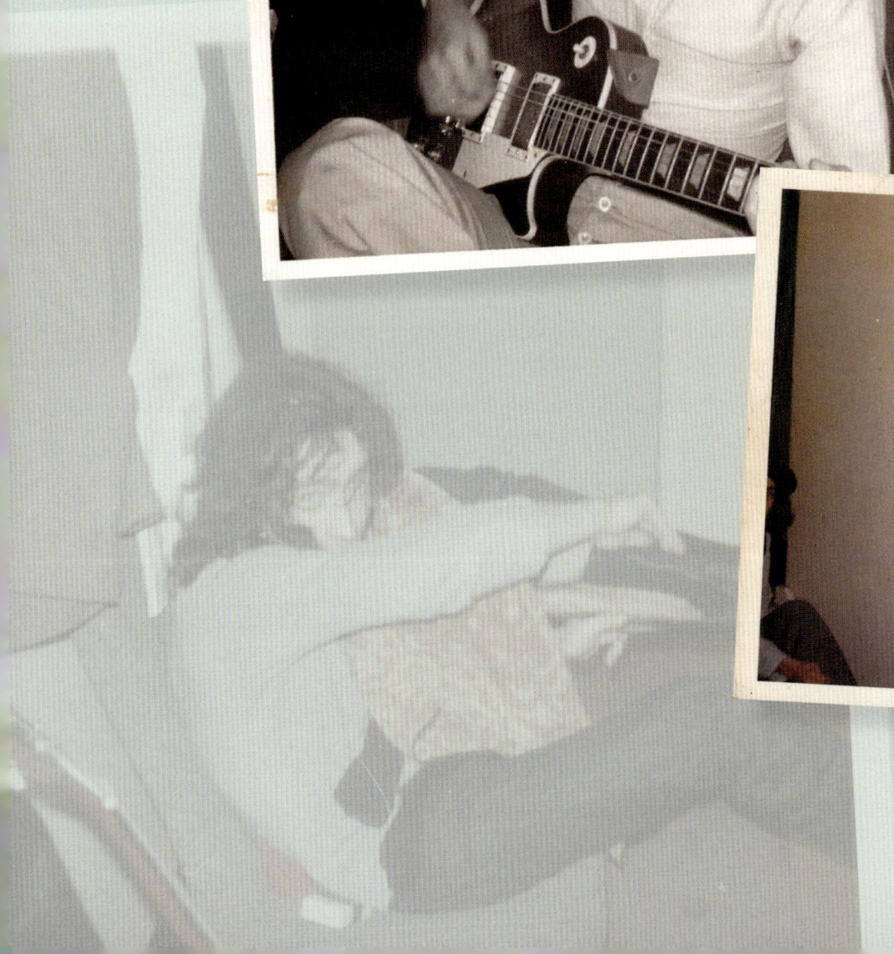

Free backstage after a show with Lucy Piller. Photos by Lucy Piller

Robert Tolley

7 July 1970, McIlroy's Ballroom, Swindon, UK

When we discovered that Free were playing at McIlroy's Ballroom in Swindon, my brother and I decided that this was too good an opportunity to miss.

So at 5:30 pm we were sat outside the door, first in the queue. We had been there about 20 minutes when a tatty old Maxi pulled up in front of us and out got Paul Rodgers, Andy Fraser and Paul Kossoff. Paul Rodgers asked if we were OK and which was the way in. We then shook hands with them and settled down to wait for the doors to open. Simon Kirke was, it turned out, already inside the venue. Before long we started to hear the strains of 'Wild Indian Woman' as the soundcheck.

The gig was absolutely electric and the place was packed to the rafters, as they say, with so many people that those at the back were leaning against large plate-glass windows that were actually bowing with the pressure. Thankfully, we were up the other end touching the stage, right in front of Paul Kossoff.

Free just blew us away, and the one memory that has been with me ever since was that iconic stance of Paul Kossoff, leaning up against his Marshal stack giving that pained look as he felt every note.

At the end of the gig we again got a handshake from Paul Rodgers.

I never had the opportunity to see Free again, although my brother did, two years later in Cheltenham on the Heartbreaker tour, the lucky bastard! However, I have seen Paul Rodgers and Simon Kirke several times in Bad Company and also Paul when he did the Free Spirit tour, again right down the front.

My other outstanding memory was meeting Andy Fraser on 26 July 2013 and getting a photo with him and getting him to sign a copy of *Heavy Load: The Story of Free*.

Long Live the music of Free.

Oliver Gray

15 July, 1970, Spektrum Club, Kiel, North Germany

I was on my 'year abroad.' Finally, Free came to Kiel, playing in the tiny Spektrum Club. 'All Right Now' had just been released and no longer did they have the attitude of 'just doing what we enjoy doing' - Free were 'up for it' in a big way. My freeze-frame of that night is of a lascivious Paul Rodgers pinching the bottom of a girl who walked across the corner of the stage. She turned round and delivered a mighty slap to his extravagant stubble. Paul Kossoff played a blinder but looked ill, ill, ill.

The band that we worshipped was Free. Although, in some ways, it was hard to justify this. The band was a hairstyle disaster area, with only one member out of four being really well-smoothed. Andy Fraser, the bassist, had an awful poodle-cut, singer Paul Rodgers' locks, though long and flowing, were coarse and unacceptably wavy, while Paul Kossoff....well!

Drummer Simon Kirke, however, was the man. His hair was blond, straight as a die and fell forward to completely obscure his facial features as he walloped his drums in a wonderful minimalist fashion, for which he has never really been given the right amount of credit for. He was the role model: That was what we were trying to look like as we swayed on the dance floor, and do you know, we probably didn't do badly.

That Tuesday night, at the Spektrum club, it was the first time I heard 'All Right Now'. The entire band looked hopelessly out of it and played like angels. On the way home, I became involved in a bizarre episode which involved getting arrested for fly-posting. It was a genuine mistake, since what I was actually doing was the opposite, i.e. *removing* a poster of Free from a wall in order to put it up in my bedroom. When all this was explained, I was released amidst much hilarity.

The next weekend, we hitched to Copenhagen and ended up in the Tivoli Pleasure Gardens. Eager for further pleasure, we tried to impress some young girls by taking them repeatedly on the Big Dipper, but eventually impressed them much more by pretending to be members of Free on a night off from their European tour. Dark-haired Jochen Schmidt, slightly dishevelled from repeated goes on the 'Ruschebeen', was Paul Rodgers and I, of course, was Simon Kirke. Just for one night, we got a mild feel for what it must have been like to be in a pop group. Because yes, the girls believed it and yes, they were impressed.

Jon Kirkman

24 July 1970, Granada Studios, Manchester, UK

My earliest memory of Free, like most people, would be 'All Right Now'. That

Lucy Piller

10 August 1970, The King's Head, Romford, UK

By this time I was taking photos at gigs. I used a Kodak Instamatic back then, I hated it as it had these press on flashes which gave four flashes, it drove me nuts. One good thing: I developed all the photos myself in a dark room in my youth club.

In the late 60s and early 70s it was so easy to take photos from the audience, no rules at all, Even going back stage when the band were unknown, I just went back and knocked on the door and in I went. How times changed over the years. Once the band were well known, the tour manager would bring me back to take photos, pulling me out of the crowd of screaming girl fans.

1970 Isle of Wight Festival

A couple of weeks after the giant Woodstock festival, the Isle of Wight staged its own equivalent.

Between 26 and 31 August 1970, Joan Baez, Joni Mitchell, Jimi Hendrix (his last ever UK appearance), Ten Years After, John Sebastian, Donovan, Jethro Tull, Miles Davis, Family, Taste, Mungo Jerry, Emerson, Lake and Palmer, The Doors, The Who, Spirit, The Moody Blues, Chicago, Procol Harum, Sly and the Family Stone, Richie Havens and Free all appeared at what was the third Isle of Wight Festival. Estimates for the size of the crowd attending topped 600,000.

Just a few hours before Jimi Hendrix took to the stage, Free appeared on the Sunday afternoon. Their set, captured for posterity on video, was a turning point for the group. Free put in a blistering performance and with the latest album *Fire and Water* just released, the crowd sang along to their first hit single, 'All Right Now'.

Lucy Piller's backstage photos and a page from her diary of gig dates she attended in the Summer of 1970

FREE – 31 July – Lyceum. 23/- with Helen Cokeh took photos
CURVED AIR – 31 July – 23/- 7.30 – 12. – ANDY GIRLS
Strawbs – 31 July – 23/- 7.30 – 12. – HAIR –
Mathews Southern Comfort – 2 August. Roundhouse ③
Humble Pie – Implosion – 8-10.30 8/- ⑤ IMPLOSION
MC5 – Saw Steve & Friend, Denise Shoults ⑤
Michael Chapman – Went with Linda ⑤ IMPLOSION
May Blitz – ② ⑤ Implosion.
Brett Morvin & the Thunderbolts – ⑤ IMPLOSION – ROUNDHOUSE
GNIDROLOG – 10 Aug. Romford – Kings Head 7.30 – 9. Paul 15/-
FREE – 10 Aug – Kings Head – 9.50 – 11pm Paul, 15/- LUNCH WITH BAND
Emerson-Lake & Palmer – I.O.W 29 August.
Chicago – I.O.W 29 August
WHO – IOW
DOORS – IOW
TEN YEARS AFTER – I.O. WIGHT
FAMILY
FREE – Isle of Wight 30 August
MOODY BLUES – IOW
JIMI HENDRIX – IOW

Photos and handwritten note by Lucy Piller

Andy Fraser

Quite the experience! To play in front of what I am told exceeded half a million people requires matching the vast energy thrust towards you and returning it in performance. We were exhausted afterwards.

Alan Lewendon

Isle of Wight was my first festival. I hitched down with two schoolmates. We were picked up by two Dutch journalists in a 2.8 litre Capri. Most of the trip was around 100mph. They dropped us in the middle of the New Forest outside their hotel. We were lucky enough to flag down a bus and made it to Lymington Pier, sleeping on the pavement, catching the first boat in the morning. I remember being disappointed by the sound system at the Isle of Wight. I've seen the films of Free playing there and it's clear - the sound system didn't do their performance justice.

Lucy Piller

The 1970 Isle of Wight Festival 'Message to Love' was *the* most memorable music event of my life without a doubt. I went with my friend Linda. We took the train, then a ferry across to the island. It was a very hot weekend and a lot of walking was involved but it was so much fun meeting people (hippies) on the way. We only took sleeping bags with us but when we arrived at the festival, joined up with some people and shared their tent: those days everything was shared. Only one night I was in a tent, the rest was under the stars.

It was a sea of people, the most amazing sight ever seen – with many people lighting their lighters or candles to show themselves out there in the hills. To see so many historic bands from the USA and UK was great and to see my band Free taking the stage in front of so many people was mind blowing.

I had waited many hours for Free to take the stage, I badly wanted to go right to the front to capture some photos. But, I knew if I'd done that I would never have found Linda and my boyfriend Paul again.

Seeing the response of the audience when they hit the stage made me feel so good inside, like, wow look at everyone digging this amazing band and I know

Lucy Piller and Paul Jupp – IOW 1970

them. I was so far back, they looked like peas on a stage. But the sound was loud and very powerful. I remember singing along with all the songs – very loudly!

The Festival left me with so many memories which seem to get stronger as I age. The smell in the air was pure pot. You didn't even need to inhale to get stoned!

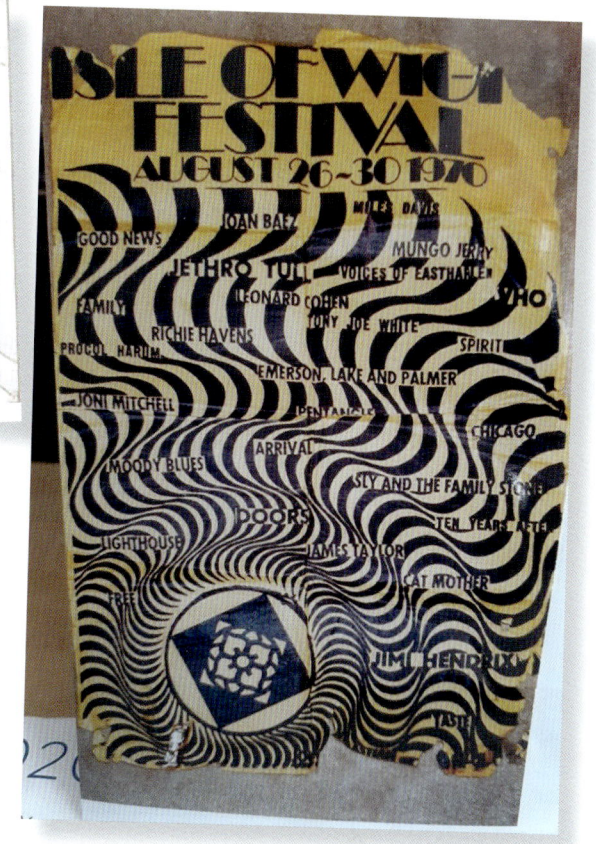

Pete Dawson

Derek Dye was my friend, we were at school together, and we both hitch-hiked to the Isle of Wight Festival in 1970. A weekend ticket was the princely sum of £3.00, purchased I believe from HMV Stevenage. If you bought the weekend ticket that included Friday, Saturday and Sunday you got Wednesday and Thursday free as an extra bonus.

So, of course, we arrived a lot earlier and spent one night under a makeshift tent made from Fisons fertiliser bags, and then another night on the beach at Alum Bay, famous for its coloured sand.

The weather was fantastic and the toilets were dire! Everything ran over schedule. Us fans were meant to vacate the viewing area every day but things got ridiculously late. I seem to remember not leaving one night, the Sunday, I think.

Free played Saturday afternoon in glorious sunshine. They were at that time riding the crest of a wave after their success with the hit single 'All Right Now', and of course the much longer version we were treated to which found its way onto the album *Fire and Water*.

Paul Rodgers I can clearly remember dressed all in black: Such a great voice. Paul Kossoff grimacing in his distinctive style, he played a Gibson I think. Simon Kirke face contorting in a style I still mimic in the kitchen!

My whole Isle of Wight experience was something I shall never forget. Even though I saw Jimi Hendrix, The Doors and The Who, there were two bands that I found outstanding, one being Free and the other Rory Gallagher with Taste.

When the sunshine and excitement was over, we were forcibly removed from the site because we had overstayed our welcome. The weather changed dramatically on the Monday, by which time we were trying to source fencing to keep us dry!

Barry Cain

The Doors and Ten Years After both played on the Saturday at the Isle of Wight festival along with the first ever performance by Emerson, Lake and Palmer while The Who performed the whole of *Tommy*. Won't forget that night in a hurry, even if it was fifty years ago. Nothing could top that.

But Free did. Oh boy, they did.

My mate Tony and I were staying at a hotel three miles from the Afton Down site. None of that camping malarkey for me. The idea of sleeping in a tent surrounded by 600,000 mighty strange strangers didn't appeal, so we booked a room at the all-inclusive Totland Bay hotel. The room turned out to be in the beach annexe. The sea was yards from our door and every morning we'd run straight out into the water because the weather was glorious.

We dined regally, drank Campari and soda on the hotel balcony and smoked Sobraine Black Russian cigarettes. I had a few bob from doing a nightly cleaning job after school at offices in Pentonville Road opposite my estate. I was barely 18 and flush. Never flash.

The walk to and from Afton Down was fascinating and always full of incident. As we melted into the crowd that edged along the road, we really did think we were stardust and golden, mohair jacket notwithstanding. Yep, I wore my hiphead outfit to the festival everyday – suit jacket, clean Sherman, Levi's, Dr Martens. Everyday. Nobody cared.

After a hearty breakfast in the hotel restaurant on Sunday morning, and necking a few cheeky Camparis, we made our way back to the garden for the final day with Hendrix topping the bill. Free were due to do a 'matinee' performance.

Before we reached the site, I found a phone box. I decided to ring home to see if I'd had my A Level results through. I'd taken History and English Lit and knew I'd fucked them up. I was shit at exams but always managed to scrape through. They scared the bejesus out of me. I knew I wasn't gonna make it and had been too scared to ring before.

'Have they arrived?'

'Yes,' said mum.

I feared the worst.

'Well?'

'You passed!'

I couldn't believe it.

'What were the grades?'

'Two Es.'

Who gives a shit? No bloke I knew from my council estate took CSEs let alone A Levels. They called me Prof. Me, the boy with two Es, fucking Prof. By the time I reached the site, I was I was on cloud cuckoo land where I ruled like Jack The Lad. My jacket was tied around my waist and I was hot to trot. Two fucking Es. Prof. The world was my oyster.

'You look happy.' She looked around 20. Twisty black hair, red and green poncho, twisty black eyes, red and green tie dye shirt, twisty black smile.

'Just got some good news.'

'Care to share it?'

'I passed my exams.'

'Congratulations. What degree did you take?'

'Er, English Lit.'

'Really? I'm studying physics. One year left. I'm at Warwick. Where did you go?'

'Er, Sheffield.'

'Mind if I ask what you got?'

'Er, a first.'

'Wow!'

'With honours.'

'You genius. Let's celebrate.' She handed me a joint.

Free strolled onto the stage. We snogged all the way through their set. It was like being down the Streatham Locarno only we were lying on the floor under a blanket and she wasn't wearing any Harmony. For the first two songs of their set – 'Ride on a Pony' and 'Woman' – we settled for tongues in each other's mouths. 'The Stealer' and 'Be My Friend' stole over the crowd as I tentatively began exploring her breasts.

'Mr Big' 'Fire And Water' and 'I'm A Mover' followed while Albert King's 'The Hunter' got the crowd going. My hand started to move south. I was heading for unchartered territory.

Then it was 'All Right Now' and I was hoping she would undo my flies but it never happened. Still, 'All Right Now' never sounded so good.

We stopped for the encore, Robert Johnson's 'Crossroads'. They gave Cream a run for their money and we swayed to the rhythm. I never did find out her name. I remember a band called Heaven preceded them and Donovan followed.

I remember they were beset by technical problems. I remember Paul Rodgers wore black. I remember the whole crowd singing along to 'All Right Now' like they were in the The Globe in Whitechapel Road. I remember someone mentioning that Paul Kossoff was 19 and bassist Andy Fraser was a month younger than me. I remember they were funkier than other hard rock bands, as bluesy as Peter' Green's Fleetwood Mac and as rocky as, well, Peter' Green's Fleetwood Mac. And Paul Rodgers looked so much the dreamboat rock star that he might just as well have gone the whole hog and changed his name to Paul Todgers.

I remember the crowd adored them. But most if all, I remember exploring unchartered territory under that blanket.

Yep, I couldn't get enough of her love...

Julie Scott

13 September 1970, Fairfield Halls, Croydon, UK

What would turn out to be my last opportunity to see Free live was on the 13 September 1970 at the Fairfield Halls, Croydon. My uncle, who lived nearby, purchased tickets and became chauffeur for the evening. Friend Lindsay and I attended this event, which was seated. Mott the Hoople were the support.

As soon as Free walked onto the stage a mighty roar went up, and we knew we were in for a treat. 'I'm a Mover', 'Be My Fiend', 'Fire and Water', 'Ride on a Pony', 'Mr. Big', 'Woman', 'Walk In My Shadow', 'All Right Now', 'The Stealer'. This couldn't get any better, it was pure musical genius at its best.

John Hall

16 September 1970, The Top Rank Suite, Sunderland, UK

There are three things a man does not forget: his first beer, his first real girlfriend and in my case my first rock 'n' roll show. I was very fortunate that my first gig ever was the Indoor Festival of Music at the Top Rank Suite in Sunderland, 16 September 1970, promoted by Geoff Docherty. Free were billed as the headliner with Deep Purple, then there was Principal Edwards Magic Theatre, Cochise and Yellow. Not yet 15 and still at school, I can still remember how excited I was to be going to the show, which was billed as starting at 7.30pm and finishing at 2am – wow, how cool was that? I was just beginning my rock 'n' roll journey.

Tickets were purchased at Bergs, our local Bicycle Shop, which also sold records and tickets for local rock 'n' roll shows. So for the princely sum of just one pound, me, and couple of school friends Pete and Telford, went along with Pete's older brother and a friend to our local theatre of dreams.

Purple had some transportation problems and so Free went on first. *Fire and Water* had been released in June, they had played the Isle of Wight Festival, 'All Right Now' had reached No.2 in the charts and they had appeared on *Top of the Pops:* very heady times for a band still barely in their 20's.

So that Friday night I got the No. 41 bus from the top of our street in Ryhope into Sunderland, arriving at about 6:30 as many people were boarding in the opposite direction returning home from work. There was already a long queue outside the venue which was across the road from the bus station. Two middle-aged women in front of me passed a comment on the line of hippies waiting outside the venue. That just raised the excitement level for me as I crossed the street and joined the line of cool people. I think the venue opened around seven, and after we had handed in our cool-looking tickets we all filed in and sat cross-legged on the floor, as you did in those days. I don't remember much about the first band Juice, but enjoyed the second band Cochise and bought their album the following week. A pattern I was to repeat over and over again in subsequent years. Next up were Principal Edwards Magic Theatre. A pretty sensational name for a band. I recall there were a lot of them - sort of prog rock and maybe a bit mad.

The preliminaries over, we waited for the main acts. Free were massive in Sunderland. *Fire and Water* was out and the single 'All Right Now' had been high in the charts all summer. Only right that they would headline. I recall an announcement that Deep Purple's van had broken down on the motorway and so Free had agreed to come on next. The band went down a storm with the partisan crowd.

Free were at the height of their powers with Paul, Koss, Andy and Simon all in great form. Can't remember the entire setlist but I'm pretty sure it included 'Fire and Water', 'I'm a Mover', 'Songs of Yesterday', 'Mr Big', two quieter numbers 'Be My Friend' and 'Heavy Load', plus the classic 'All Right Now'. I think they closed with 'The Hunter', which was an absolute anthem in Sunderland. Paul would later remark, with some humour, that 'even when ABBA played Sunderland the crowd would demand 'play the fuckin' Hunter', in our quaint local dialect.

If you ask any Free fan from the time I am pretty sure they'd say that 'Mr Big' and 'The Hunter' were their favourite songs and to this day I still get goose pimples when I hear the opening chords of the live version of 'The Hunter'.

Deep Purple finally made it to the gig, a bit late, but also played a great set with tracks from their *Deep Purple In Rock* album plus some earlier material. They closed with 'Black Night'. A sensational end to a sensational evening. I got separated from my friends and later learned that they left early as a parent had come to give them a ride home. I walked back the three miles by myself, not a care in the world and still glowing from the experience, finally making it home at about 2.30am.

Five bands for a pound and an evening that changed my life.

Richard Digby Smith

September 1970, Island Studios, London, UK

I assisted Andy Johns on the *Highway* sessions, along with Bob Potter, Island's latest recruit as a trainee engineer. Despite the critical acclaim of tracks like 'Stealer' and 'My Brother Jake', *Highway* was not as big a success as hoped and the band began to fragment.

Peter Hennessey

19 September 1970, Boxing Stadium, Liverpool, UK

Living in Liverpool, I heard 'All Right Now', bought *Fire and Water* and then spent 70p for a ticket to see Free, supported by Mott the Hoople, Amazing Blondel and others at the Liverpool Boxing Stadium on 19 September 1970. I was 16 at the time and went with my 14-year-old brother. Free were astoundingly good, they were about my age and they had me hooked!

I went to see them, again in February 1971 at the same venue and they were even better! Twelve months later I saw them for a third time and they were just unbelievably good. Even their tickets were good. The first one had a design featuring an American policeman, which I copied to poster size and had on my bedroom wall.

I'm still hooked. I was devastated when they split up; but went to see Bad Company a couple of times and have seen Paul Rodgers on many occasions.

John Burton

October 1970, St. George's Hall, Bradford, UK

I heard 'All Right Now' on Radio 1 and I was hooked! Then I saw that Free were touring and were playing at the Bradford St. George's Hall that night, so took myself off to town and found someone outside the concert hall selling his ticket, fortunately at cost price: ten shillings. So I bought that, and in I went.

I clearly remember, before any encores, Paul Rodgers asking the audience that night: 'Do you want any more music?' A somewhat redundant question under the circumstances!

Highway

Released just six months after *Fire and Water*, *Highway* was recorded hurriedly in September 1970 to capitalise on the band's successful showing at the Isle of Wight Festival and their summer-long hit single 'All Right Now'. Critically and commercially, *Highway* generally failed to attract the positive reviews and sales of its predecessor. Produced and engineered by Andy Johns, the album surprisingly eventually stuttered to a disappointing No. 41 in the UK album charts and 190 in the US *Billboard* 200.

Island Records boss Chris Blackwell originally wanted 'Ride on a Pony' as the single release from *Highway* but the band overruled him and 'The Stealer' was selected. The track would go on to become a great favourite of some fans, but it wasn't able to drive sales of the album and although it hit No.49 in the US it failed to chart at all in the UK.

HIGHWAY
1. THE HIGHWAY SONG (Rodgers/Fraser/Kossoff)
2. THE STEALER (Rodgers/Fraser/Kossoff)
3. ON MY WAY (Rodgers/Fraser)
4. BE MY FRIEND (Rodgers/Fraser)

All songs published by Blue Mountain Music Ltd.

Produced by Free

Side 1
473 182-0

℗ 1970 Island Records, a division of Universal Music Operations Ltd.
© 2016 Island Records, a division of Universal Music Operations Ltd.

BIEM SDRM LC 01846
STEREO

Album artwork photography by Ian T Cossar

Andy Johns

I remember when I did the *Highway* record and it came out, the album cover was kind of obscure. You couldn't really see who they were and it was very pastel and there were these very finely spaced pixels. I remember reading one review in some rag that said, 'New band called Highway sounds just like Free.' So I went into the record company with the album cover and said, 'Who the hell is responsible for this?' And Chris Blackwell looks up and says, 'I am.' And I go, 'Nice job!'

Tommy Smith

1970, Kelvin Hall, Glasgow, UK

I was just 15-years-old and had just left school. I went to Kelvin Hall, Glasgow with two friends. We were already ecstatic after hearing 'All Right Now' and I'd bought *Fire And Water* thinking that was their first album. I was into ear-shattering stuff like Led Zeppelin, Sabbath, Deep Purple etc., so this album was a revelation. Sort of bluesy/soul.

One mate I had kept coming up with albums that were a bit obscure for 1970 and my rock tastes. *Mad Shadows, Thank Christ For The Bomb, Live Taste* and other great music. I asked him if he had heard *Fire And Water.* 'Yep', he said, 'the third album by Free'. Third? I immediately went to our local record shop for the other two.

Most of the concert at the Kelvin Hall was made up of tracks from *Fire And Water* plus 'The Hunter' and one or two early songs. The highlights for me, apart from Paul Rodgers' mic stance, was Andy Fraser's bass lines on 'Mr. Big'.

I tried to see them again at the same venue on the release of *Free At Last* but that tour was cancelled. Never again was Free to be witnessed live. Great memories though.

John Howard

1970, University Students Union, Sheffield, South Yorkshire, UK

I've seen Free, Bad Company and Paul Rodgers with Queen live. However my lasting memory was seeing Free at Sheffield University Students' Union in 1970. I was a 17-year-old sixth form student in Sheffield at the time. I didn't have a ticket for the gig but myself and a friend watched the gig from outside in the darkness. The Union concert room had a large glass window behind and above the stage. We looked down on the band through the rear window. I can still remember Paul, dressed in jet black, mic stand in hand, leading the band through songs from *Tons of Sobs* and *Fire and Water*. It was a clear, cold frosty night but the music thudding through the glass kept us warm. Paul was and still is my all time hero. His voice is unique and timeless.

Brett Capman

Paul Rodgers' voice and the primal grit of the band did it for me. One of the coolest band names ever.

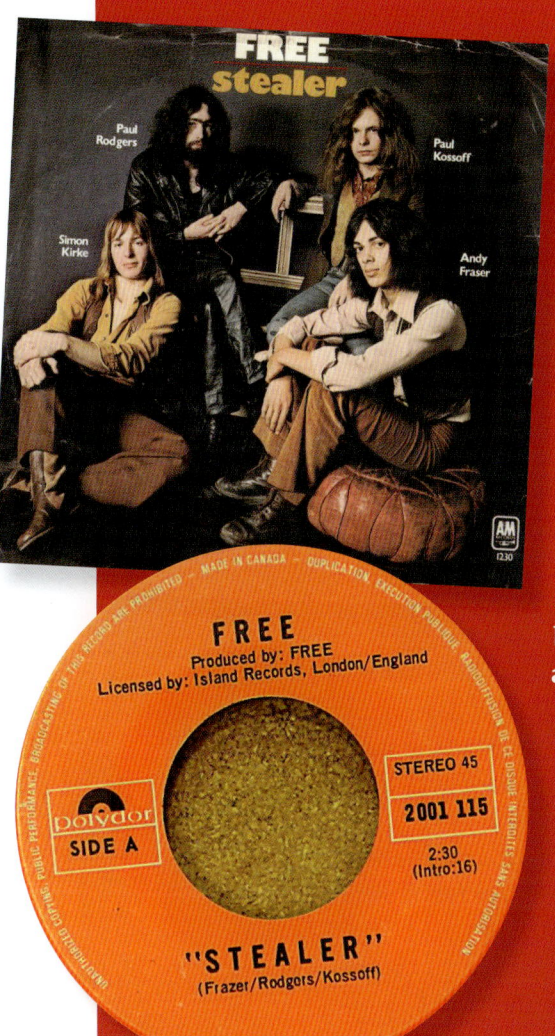

Andy Fraser

Andy Johns was one of my favorite people. Only a year older than me, we worked in the studio on a lot of Free recordings, both as teenagers. I loved his energy, always up, keen, ready to go, full of enthusiasm. He was the engineer the night we wrote, recorded and mixed 'The Stealer' in one session. Then ran up to the top floor where Chris Blackwell of Island Records had an apartment, woke him up, and said 'you gotta get down and hear this'.

Andy Johns

Kossoff was out in the studio playing the riff from 'The Stealer' and we didn't know what we were going to do because we only had eight songs. He was playing the riff, and it's a great riff, and I said, 'Well, let's do that.'

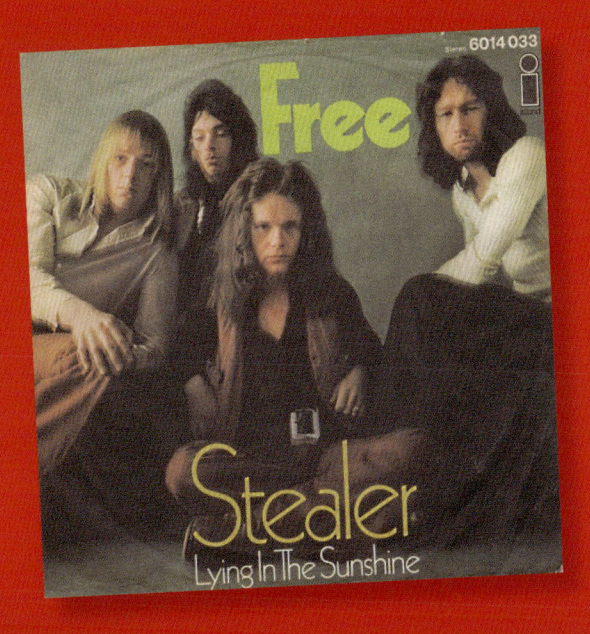

Les Davidson
(Guitarist)

It was a band where there was just bass, drums, and guitar. Paul Kossoff would make his guitar parts sound as big as humanly possible, and there's a track called 'The Stealer' which was quite a big hit for them, and I would always think what Paul would do to set up and start the track and it comes from a kind of Robert Johnson blues background, yet he takes it into that kinda 60s style of blues rock.

Nig Greenaway
1970, Nag's Head, High Wycombe, UK

Having seen Free six months or so earlier at Reading University, for seven shillings and sixpence, the band was riding high in the charts when we next saw them in 1970. This was at the Nag's Head in High Wycombe and the cost was 12 shillings - 62½p in today's money! The reason for the increase in ticket price? 'All Right Now'.

Free thus became more of a household name. Once somebody made the charts, we often felt that they had sold out a little by becoming 'commercial', although I don't think we ever accused Free of that crime!

I recall that the room at the Nag's Head was a fair size and we managed to get to a reasonable position. I remember hearing 'All Right Now' but the number that really did strike me was 'Mr. Big', which I just thought was out of this world.

I never got to see Free again but they were great - moving around the stage just about all of the time. Paul Kossoff was gurning as he squeezed out some brilliant sounds from his Les Paul. They were a fantastic band!

A few years later 'All Right Now' was still gathering new fans. I remember one of my mates at the original gig brought his son round to my place for dinner about the time that the Levi's advert was using the song on the telly.
As usual, I put on some music including that song and I was really chuffed to be complimented on my taste by my mate's son for playing some 'new' music - which just goes to show that a good song and good music never goes out of style.

Mick Austin

1970, The Drill Hall, Northampton, UK

At The Drill Hall in Northampton during 1970 Free had moved up yet another gear...

'All Right Now' was climbing the charts and it was patently obvious to me they knew exactly where they were going. I did feel a certain loss of what was once 'mine' being appreciated by thousands, I suppose all of us Free fans felt the same back in 1970 but they deserved every bit of success they were enjoying. By the time they played The Drill Hall there was a certain amount of the audience that had watched them on *Top of the Pops* and decided to go and see them: 'All Right Now' changed the whole ball game, suddenly there were screaming girls (screaming at pop stars was still in vogue even then) but the majority of the audience were hardened Free fans. I don't seem to remember if alcohol was served at this particular gig but I definitely do recall everyone drinking Coca-Cola, this was pre plastic bottle Coke and served in those iconic glass bottles.

The venue had supplied a light show for the bands, with strobe lights and a lot of weird stuff going on, more in the context of Pink Floyd. Free took to the much larger stage, amid the flashing lights. The applause went up and they hadn't played a note!

Right at the beginning Paul Rodgers lifted my spirits when he grabbed the microphone stand and began speaking. I assumed he was going to thank the audience for their welcome, he didn't, he immediately asked for the 'Pretty lights' to be turned off! The place was plunged into almost total darkness save for the red power lights on the amplifiers. A few words were uttered from the light show operators before the house lights came on, it was rather like watching them play in your sitting room...

'That'll do' Rodgers exclaimed and they ripped straight into the first song, which if I recall correctly was 'Fire and Water'. Free didn't need fancy lights, the experience was the music.

Their popularity might have risen but the band and their equipment looked pretty much the same, albeit a bit road worn. The exception was Simon Kirke, who was now playing what became his familiar Gold Ingot Hayman drum kit.

Paul Rodgers now had the space to hone what became his stage craft, the microphone stand was now an integral part of the show. He threw it around like a baton major in a carnival band! Evidence of how much shorter their set was compared to their Nag's Head appearances became apparent by an almost total dedication to playing most of the tracks from *Fire and Water* and a couple from what was to become the *Highway* album. They still had the energy in spades and continued to play at a considerable volume but it was still controlled to perfection, as they retained that quality of great dynamics. They punched their way through the songs, 'pretty lights' or not it didn't matter.

They were awesome and had transferred their small club presence to the bigger stage, not a trace of a blues band at all now, they were a band in their own right. They played their last number and retreated from the stage to the dressing room, the audience yelling for more. Within a couple of minutes they returned, I nudged my friend and said: 'Here we go…. 'Crossroads''.

Then they moved on yet again and Simon Kirke stormed into the funky drums that introduced 'All Right Now', and the place went absolutely wild. Those Coke bottles I mentioned earlier were now being beaten on the timber floor in time with what had been the cowbell on the single or the claves on the album version. The song would become their anthem as had 'The Hunter' before it. Kossoff was bending notes like a crazy man and it was obvious that Free were enjoying themselves and their new found popularity outside the blues/progressive market. It was a rewarding time for them, financially and musically I imagine, but part of me missed the access to them. Not once did it stop me from looking forward to each album as they were released, they were wonderful composers and had that amazing gift of making songwriting appear easy. It looked like they had a bottomless pit of creativity.

The band exited the stage, once again to rapturous applause and shouts for more. They had played the whole set without proper lighting but it had no bearing on the excitement they could seemingly create from nowhere. As we left that night and drove home the 10 miles or so, my thoughts kept going back a couple of years when they'd arrived with Alexis Korner at that tiny pub in a tiny village, virtually unknown and their future path to worldwide success uncertain. Free had accelerated at such a pace in such a short time and yet the sound was the same. they seemed to understand what they could let go and what they needed to retain to push themselves even further up the ladder. Breaking so much new ground in such a short time, it was almost breathtaking.

Recently, I had a phone conversation with a drummer friend that supported Free at the Northampton Drill Hall just prior to 'All Right Now' taking off. He played in a band called Phoenix and recalls that the dressing room was sealed off and he recalls them rehearsing constantly in the dressing room from the time they arrived, until they took the stage, and once again as the equipment was being loaded back onto their van! He said that was his only experience of seeing Free but still maintains that they were the best band he ever witnessed and were true perfectionists and totally enthusiastic in their goal to be a great band.

SIMON KIRKE

Free slogged around the country for about two years, doing hundreds and hundreds of dives and little clubs. It wasn't until our third album was released - that we had the big hit and all that groundwork, all that slogging around the country paid off.

ALISON JANE HARRISON

I saw Free live at The Mecca, Sunderland many times. They were talented musicians. I once saw Paul Kossoff fall and stumble onto the drums. I remember them being well liked and loved. Very happy times.

SANDY McALLISTER

24 October 1970, The Refectory, Leeds University, Leeds, UK

Saw Free for the second time at the University Hop in Leeds and that was 24 October 1970. They were appearing with a group called Aquila I think. They completed a great concert and were well received by the crowd. At the end we went backstage and asked for their autographs.

Paul Kossoff fancied my sister Maz and wanted her to stay but we had to go to catch the last bus home. Funny that!

A while later we saw them again, this time at the Gaumont Theatre in Bradford. I managed to climb on the stage and sat on the floor in front of Simon Kirke's drum kit. Those were the days - loved it and so glad I lived through that time.

I'm still a Rock Chick. I bought all their albums and fell in love from afar with Paul Rodgers. I remain a fan after all these years.

Simon Kirke

Well, we'd been working for two years fairly solidly around England and Europe and we'd had a couple of singles out and two albums which had done fairly well, you know, but nothing phenomenal. Then 'All Right Now' came along and was a hit in just about every major country, and it opened up the market incredibly and we found that we were playing to countries that normally we wouldn't have gone to. We've been around England, you know, six or seven times, we've had our own concert tours but we started in the little clubs - the blues clubs - and then sort of graduated I suppose to ballrooms and concert halls.

Andy Fraser

We've never really rehearsed for the whole time we've been together, and when we feel aggressive, we are aggressive, when we feel mellow, we are mellow.

Paul Kossoff

The way we started we just played and played. The first year we'd play 12 or 13 nights in a row all over England with maybe a couple of days off and then the same, and that lasted for a year and we never had a holiday once. That way, you played it to people and you would develop musically on stage, and you build a good, strong, honest following rather than hype.

Paul Kossoff.
Photo by Lucy Piller

Paul Kossoff's guitars and amps

Paul's guitar of choice was a Gibson Les Paul for the most part of his career, and he was one of the people responsible for the spike in popularity of that guitar that occurred in the years following his death. He mostly played late 1950s models, which are now considered to be the best Les Paul guitars ever made – often referred to as 'The Holy Grail' Les Pauls. His most iconic guitar is perhaps the one with clear coat finish that appeared on *Top of the Pops* show, and at the Isle of Wight Festival.

When Free went on their first tour, Paul started using Marshall Super Lead 100w 1959 played through Marshall cabinets equipped with G12H speakers. Later on he mostly used Marshall Super PAs (as seen during the Isle of Wight gig in 1970), but he was also seen using Super Bass heads.

Also worth noting is that he allegedly used a Selmer Treble and Bass Fifty on the band's biggest hit 'All Right Now' from the third album. If so, that amp probably pre-dates his first Marshall, and it is somewhat safe to believe that Paul bought it while working at Selmer's music shop in the late Sixties.

Photo courtesy of Bonhams

John Pagliaro

25 January 1971, Carnegie Hall, NYC, USA

I was a mere 13-years-old and a neighborhood band from Brooklyn where I lived, Sir Lord Baltimore, was playing at Carnegie Hall, NYC. At the time me and my best friend Tim had formed a band and music was everything for us. We took a bus and train to New York City and waited online to purchase tickets in person at the box office. There was chatter outside Carnegie Hall about the headliner Free, however I had never heard them.

Soon after, we went to the show and the band we actually went to see was absolute trash and very unrehearsed. Then the headliner, Free, came out and I'll never forget our reaction. This rich soulful voice resonated through the most prestigious music hall in NYC. From that moment I realised I witnessed something very special. The band was incredibly tight and Kossoff had a killer sound that blew us away (both of us played guitar).

For me, that night was beyond special. I've been a fan of Paul Rodgers since, and not a day goes without listening to his music. I've seen Paul numerous times in every venue I could get to from New York to Florida. At one show I introduced myself to Lucy Piller and purchased the book *Heavy Load* and convinced her to have Paul sign it, which he did. It reads 'For John - Fly Free, Paul Rodgers' and I'll cherish it 'til the day I die.

John Ruggiero

5 February 1971, Victoria Hall, Hanley, UK

When I was 16 I started to get into what I would call proper music. I had a few albums, one was *Revolver* by the Beatles, but I didn't really see The Beatles as part of this proper music. My record collection at the time consisted of, *John Barleycorn Must Die*, Traffic, *Benefit*, Jethro Tull, *Deep Purple in Rock*, *Every Good Boy Deserves Favour*, Moody Blues, *Time and a Word*, Yes, Emerson Lake & Palmer and *Fire and Water* by Free. Later in 1971 I got *Highway* by Free.

I loved the cover of *Fire and Water* and still do to this day. The members of the band looked so cool and sort of moody. Free were playing that blues/rock vibe which I immediately took to and the voice of Paul Rodgers was mesmerising. His voice was so good: rock, soul, blues - he could do it all. I started to get into the more complicated stuff of ELP and Yes, which I

'I am a massive Free and Bad Company fan': Stoke City professional footballer, John Ruggiero

FREE DATES FOR 1971

Friday Feb 5th .... Victoria Hall, Stoke
Saturday Feb 6th .... Liverpool Stadium.
Sunday Feb 7th .... Fairfield Hall, Croydon
Monday Feb 8th .... Oxford Town Hall.
Thursday Feb 11th .... Plymouth, Guild Hall.
Saturday Feb 13th .... Hull City Hall
Sunday Feb 14th .... Sunderland Empire.
Monday Feb 15th .... Green's Playhouse
Tuesday Feb 16th .... Music Hall, Aberdeen.
Thursday Feb 18th .... Portsmouth Guild Hall
Friday Feb 19th .... Coolston Hall Bristol
Saturday Feb 20th .... Nelson Imperial Ballroom
Sunday Feb 21st .... Guildford Civic Hall
Monday Feb 22nd .... Brighton Regent Theatre
Tuesday Feb 23rd .... Leicester De Montfort
Wednesday Feb 24th .... Birmingham Town Hall
Friday Feb 26th .... Sheffield Oval Hall
Saturday Feb 27th .... Newcastle City Hall
Sunday Feb 28th .... Bradford. St. George's H.
Sunday March 7th .... Lyceum Ballroom. London

****
****

enjoyed but the rock/blues thing was what made the biggest impression.

When I read that Free were playing my home town, I knew I had to get tickets. I asked my best friend Billy Allen if he fancied it and together we booked tickets. Victoria Hall, Hanley, Stoke-on-Trent on Friday 5 February 1971. The cost was 15 shillings, so 75p in new money.

We were in the stalls, row 16, so pretty close to the stage. The atmosphere was amazing, such a buzz of excitement and like nothing I had experienced before. We had a proper DJ playing music before the bands came on but I can't recall who the support band was. When the lights went down I remember everyone shouting out 'Wally, Wally' and to this day I've got no idea why or what it was supposed to mean!

It was an amazing show, the band at their prime, so tight and rock solid.

The songs I remember most from the set list that night? 'Mr Big', because the live version was always stretched out to show off the bass playing of Andy Fraser. I also recall 'The Hunter', which I later found out wasn't a Free song. It got everyone out of their seats. Then, as soon as you heard the drum intro you knew it was 'All Right Now' and that was again stretched out and it really showcased Paul Kossoff's guitar work. His playing was so intense you could see the pain on his face. However the star of the show was Paul Rodgers. What stood out for me was how perfect his voice was. I think it was Jimmy Page who said that he had never heard him sing a bum note ever. To think that even today his voice has never changed and it's still as good new. He is the best blues/rock singer that has ever lived.

Later that year the *Free Live* album came out so it was like a reminder of that gig. Lucky for me I was able to see Free on another two occasions. Sunday 20 February 1972 and again Monday 9 October 1972 both at the Victoria Hall.

When Free split up I also remember seeing Peace which was fronted by Paul. They were supporting a band at the Victoria Hall. It was great to see him playing live again. Of course Bad Company came along and the rest is history.

As you would imagine I was a massive Bad Company fan and have followed most of what Paul Rodgers has done, including his collaboration with Queen. I remember watching Queen + Paul Rodgers doing 'All Right Now'. Brian May really nailed the Kossoff solo, it was such a tip of the hat to him. I'm sure May and Roger Taylor enjoyed playing Free / Bad Company songs more than their own stuff.

Ian Oakley

6 and 7 February, Fairfield Halls, Croydon, UK

I bought tickets to see Free and Mott the Hoople at Fairfield Halls in Croydon UK. I was 19 at the time. Free really stood out for me, especially the vocals and Paul Kossoff's outstanding high notes screaming out. I can still see the image of them on stage, Andy Fraser a mass of hair, rocking from side to side to the bass beat, Paul Kossoff leaning slightly forward, one foot in front of the other.

Some people tried to get onto the stage and security staff were bundling away. Paul saw this, finished his song and said, 'Hey! If some of you want to come up here and dance then that's okay'. About a dozen people took him up on it - there was no mass invasion, it was all very civilised. I bought *Free Live!* when it came out and read the footnotes about where part of it was recorded, Fairfield Halls! I still have that album.

Andy Cross

13 February 1971, City Hall, Hull, UK

I first heard Free in 1969 when my sister Carol was dating a guy called Andy Hall, who brought a copy of *Tons of Sobs* to our house. We sat down and listened to it and I was hooked. In 1971 I saw Free for my 15th birthday, a present from a friend, with Amazing Blondel as the support band. I was on my own at the concert that night and two things really stuck in my mind. Paul Kossoff's presence on stage and his playing blew me away - he was the first rock guitarist I had seen live - and also, Paul Rodgers' voice.

The venue was Hull City Hall - not the best place for loud, electric music, and then a year later to the day (as both gigs were 13 February) at The Top Rank, Sunderland. Again both Pauls were fantastic. I do remember Koss having to go off because he had no power and the audience were getting upset until he returned back on stage, to a huge roar from the packed crowd. Andy Fraser played some piano in one part of the gig - a great night for all.

Paul Kossoff is the only guitarist who moves me to tears with some of his playing. 'A God in *my* eyes' not Eric Clapton.

John Hall

14 February 1971, Sunderland Empire, Sunderland, UK

My second Free gig. This time Free appeared at the Sunderland Empire, supported by Amazing Blondel. I think I can remember local famed promoter Geoff Docherty introducing Free. I have in my head Geoff coming out and saying he couldn't ask them to play anymore as they were knackered!

Having attended my first ever gig (Free of course in 1970) and this Sunderland Empire performance, I would see the band three more times, Peace in 1973 with Mott the Hoople, then Bad Company three times in 1974, including a majestic show at Charlton Athletic's The Valley football ground which featured The Who, Humble Pie, Maggie Bell and Lindisfarne, as well as Paul with Bad Company.

Here we are 50 years after that, my first ever Free show. I moved to Canada, then to the USA and have seen Paul Rodgers something like 18 times in total, finally meeting my hero in person on a rock 'n' roll cruise in 2018.

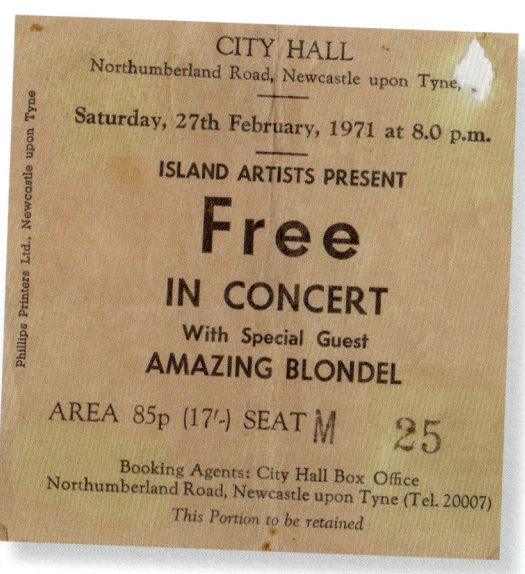

Christine Killen

27 February 1971, City Hall, Newcastle, UK

I have many, many memories of the number of times I have seen Paul Rodgers. These include him with Free, Bad Company, The Firm, Queen and his solo tours. However the memory I treasure most is the first time I saw him with Free. This was Saturday 27 February 1971 at the City Hall, Newcastle-upon-Tyne.

I still have the ticket. Seat number M25. The support band was Amazing Blondel. The ticket cost 85p (17 shillings in old money).

I was 15-years-old and absolutely blown away. He was amazing, his voice sent shivers running down my spine. I didn't want the concert to end. I was just getting into music and I knew that after that night I had become a fan and would follow his career. I would make every effort to see him in concert as many times as I could.

My two friends said we would have to leave before the end to get the last bus. I refused. We missed the last bus and on a cold February night we had to walk 12 miles home.

His voice still blows me away, he is still amazing, he still sends shivers running down my spine.

Graeme Harrison

27 February 1971, City Hall, Newcastle-upon-Tyne, UK

Free were the first band I saw at Newcastle City Hall back in the 70s, when I was about 16 and I was lucky enough to see them another three times I think. Some say that the City Hall was where 'All Right Now' was apparently penned. *(it was actually Durham's Dunelm House).*

Seeing this band blew me away and they are still one of my favourite bands. What I remember is Paul Rodgers strutting about with his mic, pure genius. Throwing it up high in the air and always catching it, never once dropping it. Also the crowd were pushing forward as they always did and one of the bouncers was getting a bit rough with a fan and I recall Paul pushed the security guard with the base of the mic stand!

I can see him now, in his scooped-neck stars and stripes long-sleeved flared t-shirt. His jeans were homemade flares with a triangle of denim sewn in on the outside from the knee, with studs up both sides of each flare to his waist. He was also wearing desert boots.

Paul Kossoff was great, but I then knew nothing of this band so I didn't really appreciate what was going on at the time. They always finished with 'The Hunter' and I loved the guitar on that song, and the bass on 'Mr Big'.

Still go and see Paul Rodgers whenever I can.

Brod Selwood

1971, St. Mary's University College, Strawberry Hill (theatre), Twickenham, UK

Saw them live and close-up at Strawberry Hill College in Twickenham in 1971, when they had released 'All Right Now'. The stage was about 1ft high and the room was packed and rocking. A fan from then on in.

Tony Walsh

1971, St. Mary's University College, Strawberry Hill (theatre), Twickenham, South West London, UK

Both Free and Deep Purple were virtually house bands at Simms at different times because they played so often. Simms was college slang or jargon for anything associated with St Mary's College.

Strange to think that Free originally came to Simms as part of a deal to get a band (now long defunct) called The Spirit of John Morgan and first appeared in a disco slot in the old chapel. Hard to think of one of the leading rock bands of the period starting their life on the college circuit as a disco warm-up band on a Friday night at Simms.

That first booking – which I think was £25 - led to Free being booked as the first act on the Saturday night concert roster. It was apparent from the first night that disco was never going to be their metier, but we were so impressed and booked them for three more gigs – I think at the princely sum of £50.

We booked our bands through NEMS and we mainly got recommendations through attending clubs and venues around London – the Marquee etc. - and reading *Melody Maker*, *NME*. We kept a close eye on new releases especially albums and then tried to book bands early for concerts. The main Saturday night concerts took place in the Theatre on the site of St. Mary's University College, Strawberry Hill, but the first Free gig was held in the Old Chapel, part of Strawberry Hill Old House, which had been converted into a student bar a few years earlier. With Mick Jagger's father (Jo) lecturing at St. Mary's and the Stones, The Who (Pete Townshend lived in Twickenham) always around Richmond, Twickenham and Kingston was a hotbed of music back then. Simms (St Marys) was one of the great college venues at the time as rock bands started to appreciate the power of the student market in the late sixties and the costs and difficulties of playing live in central London.

Long story short, by the time the third Free booking came around 'All Right Now' was released and riding high in the singles chart - *Fire and Water* went to No. 2 in the very competitive album charts in the UK and the band also headlined at the legendary Isle of Wight Festival. We did receive a call during the week from (I think NEMS) thinking they might wish to renegotiate the £50 deal – as the band were reputedly charging over £1000 a gig by then - but we were wrong. In fact the band offered to come for free – literally, not a pun – if we would allow John Peel to record their set in our theatre for his then highly influential Sunday afternoon Radio 1 show. Of course we said yes, but as a gesture offered the band and roadies free beer and sandwiches from the bar!

The John Peel Show for the BBC was a major breakthrough and the guys in Free had asked to use the 'theatre' at St. Mary's because the acoustics were so good. We got to know the guys in Free very well for a time.

A couple of years later when I was at my parents' home in Bradford, West Yorkshire, Free headlined at St George's Hall. My younger sister who was – and still is – a great fan wanted to go and mother asked me to take her (worried about too much sex and drugs as well as rock 'n' roll). At the end of the concert I went backstage to see if I could get an autograph for my sister and happily the band remembered me and I got invited into the dressing room for a drink and autographs.

My Brother Jake

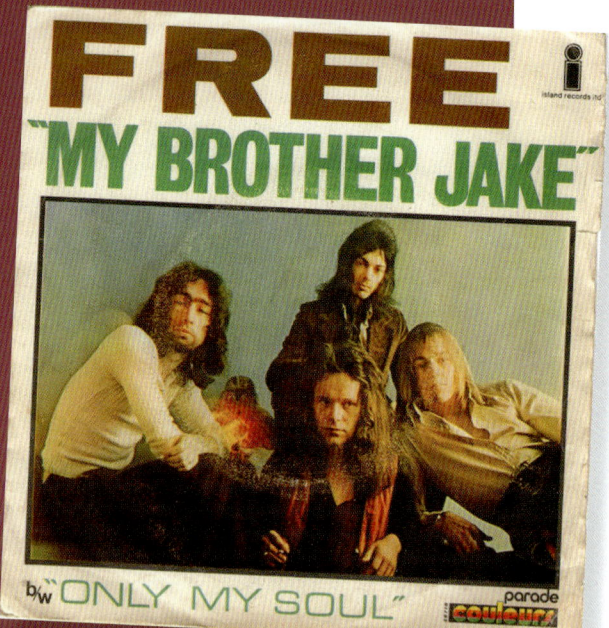

Released 23 April 1971, 'My Brother Jake' gave Free their second UK hit single when, boosted by an appearance on *Top of the Pops* on 13 May, the song peaked at No.4 on the UK chart.

Simon Kirke

'Jake' was very cheeky and all Andy Fraser, with pub piano, a jaunty beat and lyrics about someone pissing their lives away. Who couldn't relate to that?

Bob Mortimer (comedian)

I had a girlfriend from when I was about 13 until I was about 20. I was in love with Andy Fraser and she fell in love with Paul Rodgers. And then seven years later she copped off with Paul Rodgers' brother called Jake. So the only Free song I don't like is 'My Brother Jake'! But all the rest I adore.

Andrew Toplass

First heard Free when Alexis Korner played 'My brother Jake' on his radio show which came on after the charts on a Sunday night. Many many years ago.

Niall Brannigan

It was our mutual love of Free which first drew me to Des. He was a new student in Guildford, the Surrey town where I lived, and walked into my local pub. I later found out he was an orphan, a foster child. A child of care, as two friends put it. They are also children of the care system.

Looking back, it's incredible that, by then, September 1974, Free had already broken up and I'd seen Bad Company twice, in their first few months as a band.

Des became my closest friend and, despite two marriages (me) and a troubled time (him) we stayed friends for 44 years. It didn't matter what happened, it was Free, Bad Company or Paul Rodgers that glued us together.

Niall Brannigan and Des, aka 'Jake'

In my teens, I taught myself to play drums, wanting to sound like Free and Bad Company's Simon Kirke – rock solid, pushing the band from behind the beat, simple, dependable. Des taught himself to play guitar and saved up enough to buy a Gibson Les Paul Gold Top, exactly like his hero, Paul Kossoff. For a short while, Des joined the band I was in, with my brother, and we had a great time playing the songs of Bad Company, Faces, Badfinger, Cream and Free.

But neither of us had seen Free play live.

I had met Paul Rodgers though.

When I say 'met', I mean I bumped into him. It was early 1974. Paul was living in Guildford and one day, I turned a corner and walked right into him. We both did the classic English thing of apologising ('Hey, sorry, man,' he said) and went on our way. I'd walked about four paces when I realised who he was. I turned, watching him walk down the hill, and debated what to do. Did I chase after him? Did I shout? I desperately wanted to tell him what he meant to me, how many times I'd played his albums, how many times I'd played drums to 'All Right Now', how I thought he was the best singer, ever. But I did none of those things.

When I told Des the story, not long after we first met, he grabbed me by the arms in excitement.

'Where?' he said.

'It doesn't matter now, he's moved,' I said, as he shook me.

'No, just show me.' So I took him to the street corner and he made me tell the story again, in full detail. We decamped to our favourite pub and he quizzed me, again and again, soaking in every detail. For the next 44 years, if I beat him in a quiz, or knew a piece of music trivia he didn't (rare), he would say, 'All well and good, Mr. B, but you are the one who let Paul Rodgers get away,' and we'd collapse, laughing.

It was 1997 before I got Des to a Paul Rodgers gig, at the Shepherd's Bush Empire. We were with my girlfriend (now my wife, whom he adored) standing downstairs. Paul and his band played a terrific set, ending with 'All Right Now'. It was during this song that we noticed three guys in front of us. The one in the middle had one arm in the air, a half-full pint glass clutched in his hand. His two friends were leaning into him, drunkenly holding him up. Des took a few steps to the side, and began to laugh.

'He's asleep!' he yelled. All three of us laughed so much, and it was one of those shared memories we never forgot.

Des passed away in March 2018, aged just 61. My wife and I organised the funeral, as he had no one else, apart from his foster-brother, who I never knew about, a pastor who presided over the service, now one of my closest friends.

I asked Des's landlady if he mentioned any songs he wanted played at his funeral. Luckily, he had, so we played 'Hallelujah' by Jeff Buckley and 'Sad Café' by the Eagles during the service. But I couldn't let him go without making sure there was some Free to see him off. And so 'My Brother Jake' rang out in the lovely chapel, as the coffin disappeared.

Just 10 weeks later, my wife and I saw two consecutive nights of Paul Rodgers' Free Spirit tour, in Birmingham and London, and sang every song, holding each other. When the band started to play 'Be My Friend', my favourite Free song, I couldn't hold back the tears, thinking about so many happy times, so many gigs together, so many dinners, pints of beer, glasses of wine, and laughs.

Why did I choose 'My Brother Jake'?

Because Des is Jake. Paul wrote it about Paul Kossoff and his struggles with addiction. But Jake is Des.

'Hat, shades, head in a daze.'

RIP, my friend.

Yoshi Hoshina

1 May 1971, Sankei Hall, Tokyo, Japan

From the early 1970s to the present, I have experienced an estimated 2,500 rock concerts in Japan, helped by the fact that I have been a music journalist since 1973.

Still in the top three of the best live shows I have seen is the unforgettable Free performance in 1971. I was a high school student who lived in a rural area at the time, before I began my career. I listened to all Free albums and had become a big fan, so I skipped classes and went to Tokyo on Saturday 1 May at Sankei Hall, an all-night event called 'Rock Carnival # 4', a rock concert series by promoter Kyodo Tokyo.

Free played in Japan only twice, on April 30th at the Kanda Kyoritsu Auditorium and the day I saw them at Sankei Hall. Rumours that the live performance on the previous day was so wonderful were spread by word of mouth by rock fans and then tickets sold out. The exact start time of the concert was jeopardised by a tense situation where 300 fans who could not enter were involved in a skirmish with attendants. It wasn't until around 3:30 a.m that Free came up on stage and started with 'Fire and Water'. The atmosphere was tense and aggressive. Paul Rodgers swings the microphone stand and shouts soulfully, and Paul Kossoff's guitar sounded like crying vibrato, absorbing his guitar sound all over his body while leaning on a

Paul Kossoff and Simon Kirke in Japan. Japanese rock critic Yoshi Hoshina bagged a signed LP when Free flew into Tokyo's Haneda airport at the end of April 1971

David Roberts 1971

Like everyone else, I had been impressed by 'All Right Now' a year earlier but by 1971 I hadn't much of a clue about anything else Free had done. The Island Records double album sampler *El Pea* changed all that. Remember, in those days rock, folk, blues or anything not pop wasn't given much of an airing on TV or radio. So, sampler albums, such as this one, featuring Island artists like Traffic, Jethro Tull, Fairport Convention and Emerson Lake & Palmer were great ways for labels to introduce people like me with limited student resources to a whole new world of music. From the get go, I absolutely loved the track chosen by Island to showcase Free: 'Highway Song'. It cleverly showcased all the band's individual attributes perfectly. But it was the story that first sucked me in. "The farmer had a daughter..." sang Paul Rodgers and the song became ridiculously easy to sing along to. And it was probably one of the first pieces of music where I appreciated how underproduction could create such a powerful sound. Bass, guitar and drums all have their own space with apparently much less overlap than I'd been used to. Less was definitely more in Free's case. Of course, I soon discovered that nearly everything they did followed that same template but 'Highway Song' is still my most listened to Free song, according to my iPhone.

Marshall Amp. Simon Kirke, with dishevelled blond hair and cheerful face, looks like a red demon and strikes a thumping powerful beat. Andy Fraser's playing style is very unique with melodic funky phrasing and a soulful feeling for the sound. He shook his entire body to the left and right, making steps across the stage as he enjoyed himself. I cannot believe that he was 19 because his playing style is not like that of a teenager.

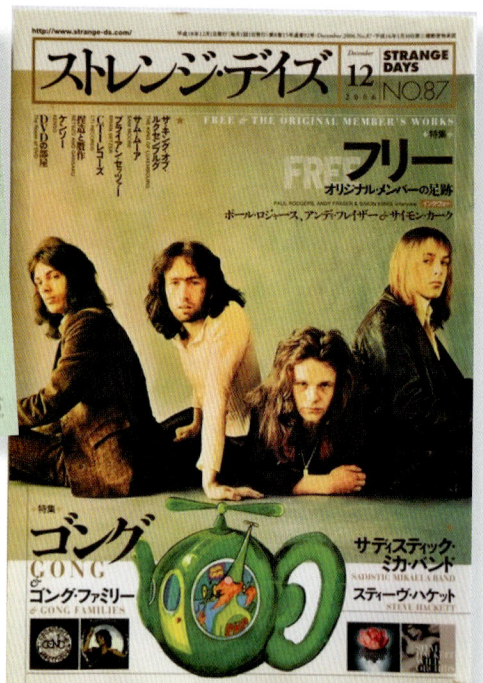

For their encore, 'Crossroads', the rotary stage began moving before they could complete their set and their performance was dramatically abandoned amid confusion and much noise from the fans.

As a first experience for teenage Japanese rock fans, including myself, of witnessing real British rock live, the concert left a strong exciting impression. The big effect it had, changed my life and I went on to work in the music business.

Steve Mulligan

9 May 1971, Randwick Racecourse, Sydney, Australia

I saw Free at Randwick Racecourse in Sydney. They played before Deep Purple and were brilliant. They have always been my favourite band – Little Feat come a close second. Paul Kossoff: what a great guitarist.

David Lowrie

9 May 1971, Randwick Racecourse, Sydney, Australia

I went to Randwick Racecourse in Sydney on 9 May 1971 to see Deep Purple, Free, Manfred Mann and the Aussie band Pirana. Very much loved Free even though Koss could not play. I remember seeing him plug in aided by a roadie but inexplicably that was the last I saw of Koss. Fellow musician friends of mine agree with this account. At the end of the show Paul Rodgers hurled his mic stand into the wings of the stage on his left. Andy Fraser was unbelievable on bass.

Paul Rodgers

The Australian audiences have really been nice. We had no idea, you know, what to expect but it's been great and when you get on stage you do realise it's the kids that have come for you. They're the kids who are buying the album and want to see you, and although it's only for an hour you've got to try and get the other people and their various motives.

Yeah, it is exhausting, but I mean it's worth it to play once you get on the stage after all the hassle is over, and the stage, and the lights, and the equipment, and you're there, it's worth it. Does the work suffer? Well, no, it tends to express what you've been through. I mean, if you feel mellow because you've had a nice flight with a nice sunset then that's how you play it, but if there's been a lot of hassle the gear tends to suffer, like Andy says.
What are we intending to do when we get back to England? Rest!

Nig Greenaway

May 1971

I saw Free on and off during the early 70s and with the success of each new album we thought it would last forever but then stories in the music press touched on Paul Kossoff's dissatisfaction of the blues side of Free hitting the buffers. Then the stories began to appear of his drug problems. Today with the advent of the internet we all know of the trials and tribulations that were going on behind the scenes within Free and Paul Kossoff but back then it was rather more sketchy and you tended to have to read between the lines to reach a verdict. Yet when the headlines appeared explaining Free were about to split I wasn't surprised at all. The speed at which they had reached stardom and merit for what they had achieved was gob-smacking: Kossoff was appearing in polls as one of the world's greatest guitarists alongside the likes of Jimi Hendrix, Eric

Rock fan Nig Greenaway and his friends weren't surprised when they read reports that Free might split

Clapton, Jimmy Page, Jeff Beck and Frank Zappa. Of course, no one but Free fans could understand that if you were going to vote it should be considered on a technical or musical basis and I tired of reading letters directed to the music press of the 'ridiculous notion that Paul Kossoff could rub shoulders with the likes of Jeff Beck'. Kossoff contributed to the sound of Free in a massive way. He played for the song and not technical 'know how', rather as Ringo Starr contributed to the Beatles. Apparently these accolades to his skill as a guitarist didn't sit well on his shoulders and his confidence suffered. I read of his falling off stage more than once due to drug-induced accidents, the cancelling of gigs and almost total unreliability. Added to all this negative press was the fact that so many bands arriving on the music scene had virtually stolen Free's approach. They must have felt they were in competition with themselves!

Free released the live album which contained screaming girls at their gig, a bad omen although they still appeared to be working hard. Suddenly it seemed Free were done. There were names being bandied about during this split of the band - Peace and Toby were two - but nothing materialised. Sharks, on the other hand, did release records. It was only when the album *Kossoff, Kirke, Tetsu, Rabbit* appeared that it seemed Free were still bubbling around, but although there were some good tracks on the album it wasn't Free. Then Andy Fraser did a couple of albums with some great tracks but once again, although it was still in the same framework of the Free style of songs without Kossoff's guitar, Simon Kirke's drumming and Paul Rodgers' voice (although Andy Fraser did an admirable job of the vocals) the old trademark wasn't there.

Free Live!

Free Live! was rush-released by Island Records in September 1971 after the group had broken up five months earlier. The album was recorded from gigs comprising some of the band's most memorable UK performances at The Locarno, Sunderland and Croydon's Fairfield Halls. Engineer Andy Johns could only use two tracks from the Sunderland gig ('The Hunter' and 'All Right Now'), but utilised crowd noise from the night to create seamless links between tracks. The album closes poignantly with 'Get Where I Belong', the last of four studio tracks recorded by the band before they split.

The album cover replicated an authentic airmail envelope with stamps depicting all four band members. The design quickly became a talking point and classic for its originality.

Selim Sünter

Growing up in Turkey, I was around nine or 10 and it was the *Free Live!* LP that my brother had that really got me connected.

That was a very interesting concept for me as it was designed as an envelope. As you know, there are four 'stamps' on the sleeve and each one had the face of a band member. Remember at that time we had nothing to see or watch too much about rock music. So LP covers were something I examined deeply from an early age. I remember looking at Paul Rodgers' photo and thinking he could be from an Arabic background and Andy Fraser from an Indian. Simon Kirke looked so pale and pretty, or should I say handsome. Paul Kossoff had an innocent and pure look. I always wanted to be like them, a hippie I thought. But my teacher never let me grow my hair. She cut my hair two times in the class with scissors just to humiliate me and force me to go to a barber. It was not even close to long hair when she did that. I guess we were raised like soldiers in those days.

I was playing that *Free Live!* record so much that one day I failed to put it back in its cover and it kind of melted on the turntable from the sun's rays. Scared and worried, I put the record back in the pile with the others and tried to hide the incident from my brother. He was a collector but not a fanatic music listener such as me. I guess he did not notice until now. Yes, it could still be pretty much listenable after that incident all those years ago, although now I hope my brother did not sell it on ebay or some other internet market!

I am very happy to be able to express my feelings about this band, which provided me with one of my milestones in life.

Billy Sloan

September 1971

My all-time favourite Free track? That's a tough – if not impossible – question. How do you choose just one? But if pushed, it's got to be the version of 'Mr Big' from the *Free Live* album. It's got everything.

It kicks off with that almost lazy Kirke drum beat ... leading into Kossoff's guitar intro. As soon as you hear that voice – surely *the* greatest in UK rock history – you know you're listening to something very special.

As the song unfolds, it's easy to focus on each individual who is playing out of their skin.

Two and a half minutes in, Paul steps back vocally to make way for one of my favourite guitar solos, which is fuelled by Kirke's spirited drumming.

Just when you think things can't get any better, Fraser steps up to the plate – around 4.15 – to lead the song to a thrilling climax with a stunning bass solo.

Rodgers' 'whooo' at 5.21 is vindication we're hearing something very special indeed.

It's the one track I keep going back to. Unbeatable!

I've kept all my ticket stubs, signed albums, photos and set lists, etc. I'm a bit of a magpie. I've also got a few pictures taken alongside the great man. But my most prized possession is that second crucial purchase, *Free Live* in 1971, signed: 'Best wishes Billy – Paul Rodgers'.

Phil Ault

1971, Island Studios, London, UK

Although I'd assisted on a few sessions for *Free At Last*, they were just sessions like any other and I've no memory of them. However, I was ever present on the Kossoff, Kirke, Tetsu and Rabbit album which was important in bringing Free back together for the final *Heartbreaker* project. Initially it was Kossoff and Kirke, together with engineer Richard Digby Smith (Diga!) and myself in studio two at Basing Street. This was the smaller studio, downstairs, generally considered the better of the two for mixing, but just as good for recording, as long as it didn't involve an orchestra or the Luton Girls Choir.

Typical of most bands of the time, the agenda read:

1. Book studio.
2. Turn up at studio, preferably with instruments.
3. Decide what to do.
4. Drink tea and discuss what to do.

The duo did have a few ideas for songs, so we set them up so they could jam some ideas, but it became very clear that two musicians weren't going to achieve much alone. Then, still on the first day, a truly serendipitous event occurred in the shape of a Japanese bass player called Tetsu. I'd wandered up to the front desk and he was there asking if there was any session work available, and although the receptionist was humming and hahing (but not in a musical way), I dived in and asked him to hang on a minute. Half an hour later he was in the studio, and it was obvious he knew how to play. A band was born, or at least having labour pains. For such a quiet person, Tetsu bonded very quickly, and the whole project gained momentum. Not many days later John Bundrick, commonly known as 'Rabbit', also appeared as if out of nowhere, and his keyboards and vocals added another dimension. He was the opposite of Tetsu, personality wise, being a lively American, and was the secret ingredient for the album. The whole crew were so easy to work with, as I knew Koss and Simon already were easy going and full of talent. Koss did have a substance problem, but it never made him anti-social. It wasn't the best album in the world, with hindsight, but it was half decent, and paved the way for Paul Rodgers to become involved.

Richard Digby Smith

1971, Island Studios, London, UK

Because of the lack of success of the *Highway* album, an inevitable, albeit brief separation occurred. The band had, after all, been together for over four years, joined at the musical hip as teenagers.

Drummer Simon Kirke and guitarist Paul Kossoff combined forces with Texan keyboard player John "Rabbit" Bundrick and Japanese bass player Tetsu Yamauchi to record the *Kossoff, Kirke, Tetsu, Rabbit* album, released on Island Records in 1972. Having worked with Rabbit as the keyboard player on several Johnny Nash sessions and working as an assistant engineer on Free sessions for Highway, I was first choice, along with some additional engineering from fellow Island staff engineer Tony Platt, to engineer this hybrid album. Vocal duties were shared out between Simon and Rabbit, with one contribution from Paul Kossoff on the wistfully hypnotic track 'Colours'. This was an altogether thoroughly enjoyable album to record. Gone were the pressures of trying to repeat and better the previous glories of Free.

Oct 1971

A letter from Andy Fraser dated 8 October 1971 to British Free fan Lucille Bannard, who was living in Israel at the time. In the letter Andy talks about his new group Toby and seeing Paul Rodgers in his new group Peace.

Dear Lucille,

I'm glad you're enjoying Israel and I hope sometime that we might be able to come and play out there. Since "Toby" has been together we have played a tour of Germany, and one gig at Norwich - St. Andrews Hall, It was great, although the audience was a lot better than us. Tomorrow we play in Stoke-on-Trent, should be good.

I saw "Peace" the other day and I thought the first time they played, (She was a Lady) was really good, and P.R. was singing good and playing nice guitar but some people thought that

I've seen Koss & Si, around quite a bit and they always look happy enough.

As far as my music goes its Jazzy, P.R.'s is very heavy and loud. Oh yeah and Graeme married Gwyn, I think P.R.'s married too.

Hope all goes well for, Istanbul & India

Andy and "Toby"

1972

Lynne Gibbs

City Hall, Sheffield, UK

Saw them at City Hall, Sheffield in the seventies. Paul Rodgers' stars and stripes flares and fantastic voice will stay with me forever!

Richard Digby Smith

January 1972, Island Studios, London, UK

Early in 1972 the original Free line-up got back together in the studio. This was to record the *Free at Last* album.

To now be sitting in the engineer's seat about to commence the recording of Free's fifth studio album was to me a dream come true. During the *Highway* and *KKTR* sessions, I had established a solid relationship with the band members. I remember one time going to Andy Fraser's house, listening with him to his record collection: Aretha Franklin, James Brown, Wilson Picket. This was the kind of music these guys grew up on. Same as me.

Listening to and recording one of the greatest British blues/rock vocalists, guitar solos of exquisite passion and soul, combined with the tightest of drums and bass, to the extent that even to this day, I am still a massive fan of Free.

Julie Scott

10 February 1972, Royal Albert Hall, London, UK

My friends Geoff and Heather saw Free for the last time at the Royal Albert Hall, London in February 1972. Geoff recalls it was the only time he ever heard Free perform 'Crossroads' live. In his words 'I can still recall that I enjoyed every minute of every time I saw those four guys with a magic combination of talents'.

Peter Smith

1 February 1972, The City Hall, Newcastle, UK

If you asked a teenage gig-goer from the North East of England in the early 70s to name their favourite live bands, they would probably have said Free, Family, and possibly Stray. All three of those bands played in the region a lot at the time, and were great live, building a strong fan base as a result.

Sunderland in particular is where Free had a strong cult following, playing lots of gigs at the Bay Hotel and Sunderland Locarno (or Fillmore North). I was just that little bit too young to catch some of those early gigs, and was very jealous at the time of some of my slightly older mates who told me how great Free were live.

Free existed only for a brief few years at the end of the 60s and beginning of the 70s and yet their shows and records are still spoken of today. There was a unique emotional groove to their music that set them above others, and gave them a different feel to the heavier bands of the time like Deep Purple, Black Sabbath and even Led Zeppelin. This came from the combination of Paul Rodgers' soulful vocals and Paul Kossoff's bluesy guitar.

The first time I got the opportunity to see Free was at a gig at Newcastle City Hall in early 1972. This was something of a comeback concert, as the band had broken up briefly in 1971. The City Hall was packed but the gig was abandoned due to a power failure. Support came from Bronco featuring Jess Roden, who managed to complete their set by performing acoustic versions of some of the songs. Free took to the stage, but again there were problems with the power, and they had to cut their set short, promising to return later in the month.

Free did return for two nights on the 21st and 22nd of February, with one of the nights being a free concert for ticket holders from the original gig. I went along to the new gig and saw Free play a full set, and they were amazing; every bit as good as my mates had told me. I'd end up seeing them three times in the same month. Live favourites for me were 'The Stealer', 'Mr Big', 'All Right Now' and, of course, 'The Hunter', which was always the encore.

Paul Senior

3 February 1972, Sheffield City Hall, UK

I first saw Free at the Sheffield City Hall while still at school. First five gigs in the space of two months were Family, America, Groundhogs, Wishbone Ash, Free and Mott the Hoople. These were followed by Deep Purple, Black Sabbath, Humble Pie, Lindisfarne, Genesis, Led Zeppelin and Beck Bogert and Appice.

I had bought *Free Live!* the year before, which blew me away, then bought all other albums and played them to death.

My favourite two bands were Free and Mott the Hoople. It may just prompt you to go onto YouTube and search for Free – Sheffield City Hall 1972. It is on there. And you may just hear applause from a 16-year-old Sheffield lad called Paul Senior.

Peter Smith

13 February 1972, Top Rank, Sunderland, UK

Support came from Vinegar Joe featuring Elkie Brooks and Robert Palmer, who I had seen the previous year in the band Dada. I went along with a few mates from school, and we arrived early, sitting cross-legged on the dance floor; as you did in those days. Vinegar Joe were a great live band; Elkie was very much the raucous rock chick singer, with swirling gypsy skirts, and quite a raunchy stage act. Her vocals were complemented by Robert Palmer's more soulful approach. I saw Vinegar Joe quite a few times around that period; they were very popular, but didn't achieve anything like the great success that Elkie and Robert went on to in their own right.

The place went crazy for Free. I recall being crushed near the front of the stage, concentrating on watching Paul Rodgers and Paul Kossoff. These guys seemed so much older than me, but they were actually pretty young at the time. Paul Rodgers was an incredible front man; lots of throwing the mic stand around, and a great vocal performance. Kossoff would really wring the notes out of his Les Paul. He has influenced so many people, including Joe Bonamassa, who owns one of Kossoff's original guitars. The set list is likely to have included 'Little Bit of Love' (which was a single at the time), 'My Brother Jake', 'Travellin Man', 'Ride on a Pony', 'Be My Friend', 'Fire and Water', 'Songs of Yesterday', 'Mr Big', 'All Right Now', and 'The Hunter' as the encore.

TERRY BUNTING

18 February 1972, University of East Anglia, Norwich, UK

I was in first year of sixth form at my local grammar school when a few of my classmates and some other friends went to see Free at the University of East Anglia in Norwich.

Tickets were £1, but what made the gig unusual was that instead of being in the university assembly hall (as historical gig lists state), it actually took place in a two thousand capacity marquee in a nearby park.

The reason for this was because during the first couple of months in 1972, Edward Heath's Conservative government was in a pay dispute with Britain's coal miners. This resulted in the miners going on strike. To preserve the nation's coal reserves, the Government restricted the country's power supply to a three-hours-on, three-hours-off timetable. The power outage would have occurred halfway through any gig played on that night, so the university decided to hold the show inside a marquee, with power being supplied by diesel generators behind the tent. The support band were called Junkyard Angels, and we all sat on the grass inside the tent.

I clearly remember parts of Free's performance, and, being a young guitarist myself, Koss was awe inspiring. Funnily enough though, what really sticks out in my mind was when Andy Fraser sat down behind the piano, and with no announcement they launched into 'My Brother Jake' - which really got the place rocking.

That week will also stay forever in my memory as it marked my first ever performance as a musician - and I've played around five thousand gigs since then!

Free are one of my all-time favourite bands, I still listen to them regularly, and teach their songs.

PETER ATKINSON

19 February 1972, Middlesbrough Town Hall, UK

One of my first memories of Free was watching my two older brothers preparing to see them live at Middlesbrough Town Hall around about 1972. The buzz in our house was electric. And even though I was only ten, and knew I couldn't go, I still pestered my brothers to somehow sneak me in to the gig. Alas it was not to be.

The first time I actually saw Free? It must have been 1970 when the whole family crowded around the TV to watch them perform 'All Right Now' on *Top of the Pops*. A special day that lives long in the memory. The sound of Free had been around our house for the previous three years. *Tons of Sobs* and *Fire and Water* were always laid open next to the stereo while my eldest brother strummed and practised away on his electric guitar. The sound of these two albums became background noise forever cemented in our childhood and we all still talk and discuss their unique sound to this very day, and make our annual trip to the Free Convention in Newcastle. The sound of Free will be forever etched in our memories. It's shaped our lives, our nights out and who we stand for musically. Once Free are in your head, you can never get them out, thank God!

I finally got to see Paul Rodgers perform live in the 1980s when he played Middlesbrough Town Hall, then with The Firm and several times since with Bad Company. It's an Iconic moment when your hero is stood before you, playing the songs of your life.

What was special about the music of Free? I'll let my older brother Tom answer that. He has followed, played and studied Free for the past 50 years.

Tom Atkinson

Free wore their heart on their sleeve, with Paul Rodgers' voice creating a hint of danger when he wanted. He didn't know how to hit a bum note. Free conveyed feelings in a masculine way. Believable. Understated. Never any over-the-top flash. Slow burning, Free always allowed a song to build to a crescendo. With Paul Kossoff's open chords and sustained vibrato and Andy Fraser melodically ducking and diving between it all, it was richly harmonic. The syncopated interplay between bass and drums created a funky 'push – pull 'effect, all sat on Simon Kirke's muscular, metronomic time-keeping. Not bad for two guitars, a time-keeper and a singer.

My special memory? Our mother had just returned home from the local further education college in Middlesbrough, where she was studying book-keeping with other parents wanting to better themselves. She had her back to us while she was cooking tea for me and my brothers. 'I was chatting to one of the other mothers today about you four,' she said.

I was in my mid-teens in the early 70s, playing guitar for a popular band on the north east social club circuit, blasting out as much 'Free' as we could get away with.

'.....and our Thomas,' she recounted to the other mother,'.. plays in a group'.

It was a big deal back then.

'Oh.' said Phyllis, mother's new coffee partner. 'What's their name?' 'Aviary Jim' she announced, looking for a glint of recognition.

'My eldest lad sings in a group...' Phyllis unassumingly added. 'What a coincidence. 'What are they called...?'

Cue soundtrack: 'All Right Now'.

Billy Sloan

24 February 1972, Green's Playhouse, Glasgow, UK

Musically, I was a bit of a late developer. Strange when you think I've spent more than 40 years as a music journalist and broadcaster.

I didn't buy my first single and album until the summer of 1971 when I was 15. Positively ancient by today's standards, where every kid has a music collection on their tablet or phone.

Again, the Boys Brigade played a part in my musical education. While at B.B. camp in Wales, I used up most of my two-week pocket money buying the single, 'Won't Get Fooled Again' and the album, *Live At Leeds* - by The Who – from Woolworth's in Rhyl. A proud moment. Both records blew me away.

A few months later, I'd saved up enough cash to buy my second album, *Free Live!* complete with the Air Mail-style envelope sleeve design where each stamp was a picture of a band member. That record blew me away too.

I attended my first ever gig – The Who at Green's Playhouse in Glasgow – on October 21, 1971. It sounds dramatic to say it, but it was a real moment of awakening. From that night on, there were not enough hours in the day to listen to records and go to see live bands.

So when Free were booked to play Green's Playhouse on February 24, 1972, I bought a ticket for the princely sum of 40p - a lot of cash for a 16-year-old. I've still got my ticket stub in which the group are billed as 'The Free'.

I remember everything about the gig apart from the support acts. In those days, nobody was interested in seeing the warm-up bands; we just wanted the headliners. I didn't know any better which was a real shame because the show was opened by Traffic followed by John Martyn. If only I'd been more switched on.

Free played a stunning set opening with 'I'll Be Creepin'' and followed by hits such as 'My Brother Jake' and 'All Right Now'.

Highlight of the gig were the tracks I'd discovered on *Free Live!*, 'Ride on a Pony', 'Mr Big', 'Be My Friend', 'Fire And Water' and 'The Hunter'.

What struck me, even as a 16-year-old was the sheer virtuosity of each band member. Paul was a sensational singer. What he did appeared effortless. By his side was Paul Kossoff who looked – and sounded – every inch the guitar hero. Andy Fraser didn't just play bass as a rhythm instrument; his lead lines really enhanced the songs. His blistering solo on Mr Big remains one of my favourite Free moments. And just when you thought it couldn't get any better, Simon Kirke had such a distinctive drum style, you knew instantly who it was.

Every band usually has a couple of members who really stand out. But with Free there wasn't a single weak link. Each musician was a performer at the very top of his game.

Green's Playhouse was a crumbling building in Glasgow city centre. It had a capacity of 3500, which made it the largest cinema in Europe. Primarily still a picture hall in the early 1970s, film screenings would be set aside to make way for concerts. In terms of being an ideal location in which to showcase live music, Green's was totally unsuitable. For a start, the stage was 25ft off the floor of the stalls. So an artist – standing at the front vocal microphone – would look straight into the first balcony. Above that was the Upper Circle, the cheapest seats in the house. You almost needed breathing

Paul Kossoff - 'Every inch the guitar hero.' Billy Sloan. Photos by Lucy Piller

apparatus to watch a gig from way up there. The stalls audience were on ground level, looking up the nose of the performers. But it didn't matter. Despite its size, Green's Playhouse felt incredibly intimate. The venue boasted *the* greatest, most vocal and discerning, audience in the UK. If the Glasgow audience embraced you, you were made for life. In a *Melody Maker* poll in the mid-1970s, the venue – which became the now-legendary Glasgow Apollo in 1973– was voted No. 1 place to see a band in Europe, if not the world.

I'd have gone to the Free show with one of my mates from school. The venue didn't have a Box Office, so we purchased our tickets from House Of Clydesdale, an electrical store nearby. You had to walk past all the washing machines, refrigerators, vacuum cleaners and irons – into the back shop – to purchase tickets. For real hot gigs – such as The Who or the Rolling Stones – you had to queue outside the store overnight to be assured of a ticket.

As a fan of Paul Rodgers, if I had to nominate my favourite live performance it would have to be that first show for the reasons mentioned earlier. But another stand-out gig for me was at Barrowland in 2007 … recorded for the Live In Glasgow DVD. I also saw Queen with Paul Rodgers at The Metro Arena in Newcastle, which was great too. *Billy Sloan is a music journalist and broadcaster, BBC Radio Scotland*

Mick Austin

1972, De Montfort Hall, Leicester, UK

It took a few months of what appeared to be half-hearted attempts to knock up a stunning band when the music press headline was 'Free To Reform'. I recall all Free fans were on a high and itching to see them back together. We all waited to see the advertisements for the planned return tour, when it was finally arranged the nearest date for me was De Montfort Hall in Leicester.

We arrived early at the venue, at that time De Montfort Hall still wasn't a seated venue but it was a big hall and the place was stuffed with people. This time Kossoff was using four Marshall stacks as was Andy Fraser, Simon Kirke's gold Hayman kit was in evidence and a much bigger PA system was in situ for them. The electric piano was a new instrument which wasn't normally on stage or the bass pedals beneath it. At this stage of rock concerts it had become synonymous that bands would often be accompanied by some stirring introduction music such as 'The Dam Busters' theme or similar classical music. I remember thinking: 'please God, I hope Free don't begin to emulate trends and fashions. I wasn't disappointed. The band strolled onto the stage in what would have been silence had it not been for the exhilaration of the audience - they went wild. After a minute of switching amps on and generally preparing to play they were ready, Simon Kirke attired in the same riding boots I saw him perform in at The Nag's Head, Paul Kossoff still wearing Levi jeans, and his now famous waistcoat and the plain topped Les Paul slung around his neck and Paul Rodgers in studded jeans. Andy Fraser had dispensed with the Gibson EB3 bass and appeared to be drowned by the size of his new weapon, the Gibson ES 335.

'Good Evening' Rodgers shouted, 'It's good to be back' and they ripped into 'Catch a Train' from the *Free at Last* album. I, and a few other members of the audience, had been discussing at the bar prior to the gig whether they would still be the same band sound wise as they had been before the split. A lot of bad press had dogged them before and during the split. I needn't have worried, all the ingredients that made them so unique were still there. The songs, which I had not heard before indicated another shift in gear, as was their habit. It was loud, it was clean and the old dynamics were still there, this was Free and I mentally breathed a sigh of relief that they still had it.

For the first time Andy Fraser played piano on some of the songs, using bass pedals, it was, yet again, a great move on their part. Far from inviting an extra keyboard player, which would have seemed odd, in their true 'we can do this alone' attitude they played superbly. They excelled as a three-piece with a superb singer. Sadly behind the scenes Kossoff was 'going off the rails' again and the music papers were printing stories of his unreliability and drug abuse. On this particular night he behaved perfectly and never put a foot wrong, he looked so happy to be playing within the band. It was Free at its best once again. The second split came pretty quickly and without so many dramatics, the stories began to emerge as much on the grapevine as in the press of Kossoff's fall into drug-fuelled mayhem. It was obvious this really was the end of such a talented bunch of songwriters and musicians. Free ended the De Montfort gig with a string of encores, 'All Right Now', 'The Hunter' and other old favourites but I left the gig feeling I wouldn't be seeing them ever again. I still have no idea why but I was right and now with hindsight and interviews with Free members they also knew it couldn't last. In my lifetime I've watched some amazing talented musicians playing together live, all of them superb bands, but Free had something special. Nothing to do with technicalities, stage antics, drama, light shows and all the other paraphernalia we have got used to with modern bands. Free were simple, uncluttered, clean, dynamic and loud and some 50 years after first seeing them I still uphold they were the best band I ever saw live.

Ralf-Erik Sjöström

21 March 1972, Turku Concert Hall, Finland

Free played two gigs in Turku, Finland. The following day they played in Helsinki. The concert in Turku was my first and it changed my life forever.

In the winter of 1972 my 14-year-old brother, Pär-Henrik Sjöström, asked me if I would be interested in going to a concert with him. I was ten at the time. We had begun listening to rock music in the autumn of 1971, the first albums being Creedence Clearwater Revival: *Pendulum*, Santana: *Abraxas* and Deep Purple: *Fireball*. I was very flattered that he was willing to take me, his ten-year-old brother, with him to our first rock concert, so I said yes.

I asked him what band we were going to see and he answered 'Free'. I did some thinking but the name Free did not mean much to me. Then he played me 'All Right Now' and I liked it. He bought the tickets and I remember that they cost 8 FIM at the time (slightly over 10 Euros in today´s money). Our places were on the left side in the front row, seats number 13 and 14. Turku Concert Hall is the home of the Turku Philharmonic Orchestra with a capacity of 1002 seats and good acoustics.

The day of the concert came and I was very excited. I knew that I would most likely be the youngest attendant and I also knew that some of my brother´s friends would be there. This made me a bit nervous but on the other hand I knew that I could keep a very low profile and not disturb my brother and his friends.

We entered the Hall and I could not believe my eyes when I saw the stage. At the back was the drum kit on its platform, a shiny Hayman kit, if I remember correctly, and printed on the bass drum was the classic rounded Free-text. The cymbals were almost in a vertical position. It was not a large kit, rather a compact one.

To the left was a row of three Marshall amps on top of six cabinets and to the right was a similar row of Marshall-amps. Far left and far right in the front of the stage stood two stacks of speaker cabinets, for the vocals and drums presumably.

The supporting act for Free on these two concerts in Finland was John Martyn. He came on stage with a brown acoustic guitar and a chair, sat down and started to play and sing. Since I did not know his music at all it was a bit difficult to make anything out of it. I thought that the songs were quite difficult to get a hold of and I probably was not that keen on concentrating as well as I ought to have. I would imagine that he played songs from the album *Bless the Weather*, released in 1971.

After John Martyn had finished there was a short break. The older ones in the audience probably went for a smoke, I sat in the hall and waited. I grew more and more excited.

Then Free came on stage, plugged in the instruments and Paul Rodgers said good evening and presented the first song as a new one called 'Travellin´ Man'. That is the precise moment that forever changed my life. Can a band sound this good, this loud and so full of energy? Of course I did not have anything to compare with but I like to think that I started at the very top, with the best band there was.

As I sat on my chair I had Andy Fraser in front of me at a distance of one or two metres. He played a big white (or nearly white) Epiphone bass and I remember how he slid along the stage as he played. He had some kind of bowling shoes on his feet and he was sliding back and forth as he played. He was dressed in a pair of brown velvet jeans and a white t-shirt. The thing that amazed me most was his way of playing. When Paul Kossoff took a solo, Fraser played the bass like a rhythm guitar and, when needed, he himself took solos on the bass. He defined bass playing for me, he became the standard to who I compared all other bass players. They were mostly dull, except for Jack Bruce. Simon Kirke sat behind the drums, solid as ever. His kit was well tuned and sounded tight with the bass drum kicking deep and the snare whipping. He laid the foundation for the rest of the band, and he hit hard and precise.

To the right stood Paul Kossoff, barefoot and dressed in a pair of jeans and a shirt. He was often very close to the amps and totally in his own world, with his eyes closed and miming with his mouth as he made his Les Paul cry. His playing is something that I have never heard the like of since. He made the guitar a part of himself and he sang so beautifully that it nearly hurt. And he could make the guitar sound better than anyone else.

In the front stood Paul Rodgers, the best frontman ever. He carried around his microphone stand as he sang. He held the band together with a firm hand and his voice had so much power, so much authority that it was nearly unbelievable. He was already a true superstar, and by far the best singer I have ever heard live. His phrasing is so unique, his sound so raw and yet so soft when needed.

I do not remember exactly which songs Free played that evening but as I mentioned they kicked off with 'Travellin' Man'. At some point there was a piano brought on stage which means that they at least played 'My Brother Jake' and probably also 'Heavy Load'. I know that they played 'All Right Now' (since it was the only song I was familiar with) and I am also quite sure they played 'Soldier Boy', 'Fire and Water', 'Ride on a Pony' and 'Mr Big', and probably, also, 'I´m a Mover'.

    That evening in March 1972 was the beginning of a lifelong relationship with everything that has to do with Free. I know that this is the case for so many other Free fans. Those of us who get their magic are forever loyal. We live our lives with Free present in some way every day. I cried when Kossoff and Fraser died, it was like losing close friends you had known for your whole life. I was so proud and happy to get in touch with the Free band members as a grown man and tell them how much their music has meant to me. And the magic of Free´s music has been passed on to my children.

Kenney Jones

When I was in the Small Faces, and more when I was in the Faces, our paths crossed with Free a fair bit. They supported us on one of our American tours [the sixth Faces US tour: 21 April 72 to 30 April 72]. We'd always been fans of Paul's voice, big time. One terrible memory I have is when one of their roadies fell asleep in the back of one of those big equipment trucks and died.

    We loved Paul Kossoff's guitar playing but the whole band in its entirety. I was great friends with Simon Kirke. One of those bands we had a mutual respect for. As drummers, Simon and I got on really well. I lived on Kingston Hill and had a studio with only drums in it. He'd say to me, 'Can you show me how you did that thing?' I'd say: 'Only if you show me how you do your wonderful press rolls!'

Al Orsini

April 1972, Los Angeles Memorial Coliseum, USA

My first concert was Woodstock '69. I was 14! I saw Free in 1972 at the L.A. Memorial Coliseum, I would have been in the 11th grade.

Free at Last

Having reformed Free in January, the four members saw their fifth studio album, *Free At Last*, released in May 1972. The nine-track LP featured the single, and future classic, 'Little Bit of Love', which enjoyed a 10-week run on the UK chart, peaking at No. 13. *Free at Last* also became their highest chart placing album in the UK since *Fire And Water*, when it sneaked inside the Top 10 at No.9.

Paul Kossoff

Free At Last: I really didn't want to do it. Or rather, I wanted to do it, but I really couldn't take it. It was very unpleasant. There was a lot of pressure on me. Paul wanted to get me well and I believe he figured that if he got me up and playing that would do it. And there was pressure from Island. I didn't stand a chance. I had to do it. They sort of dragged me out of my pit.

Hazel Taylor

I got into Free when I was 14 and was hooked. I remember going to Virgin records sitting on floor cushions listening to *Free at Last.* Love the track 'Child', it's so beautiful. I have loved Free ever since. Disappointed that I never got to see them live but their records are totally sublime.

Rob Nottingham

May 1972, Some Kinda Mushroom, Chesterfield, UK

I got into Free in about 1972 after hearing 'Little Bit Of love' in a pub I was too young to be in. I just thought 'what a great track' and wanted to know more about them. So, the next day, I went into a record shop called 'Some Kinda Mushroom' in Chesterfield after school and bought the record, which then got me into buying the albums and the music papers *Sounds* and *New Musical Express*. When I eventually read that they were splitting up I was absolutely gutted. I then ordered *The Free Story* limited-edition album album which had to be ordered, so when I was told it would be in after three days I broke out of school to get it.

Laurence Tressler

I got into Free rather late. I always regretted it. It was around the middle of 1972 and at the time I was a T.Rex and Slade fan. I looked forward to seeing *Top of the Pops* once a week, listening to Radio 1 and following the pop charts as much as I could, but the serious progressive stuff just didn't do it for me – well not then anyway.

A song started to be played on the radio called 'Little Bit of Love'. It was great. An amazing guitar sound, a good band performance, but the singer, he was something else. I found myself singing along to it every time it was played. Apparently it was by a band called Free. I'd never heard of them. I delved a bit and discovered that they had recorded some great singles, including, of course, 'All Right Now', which I discovered was amazing, with a killer guitar solo. This was the song that got me into air-guitar and whilst we are on the subject, surely 'All Right Now' is the greatest air-guitar song of all time.

Dave Nichols

First time I came across the band and the biggest impression on me? Hearing Paul Kossoff's guitar for the first time, about 1972 as a 14-year-old.

Kevin Reynolds

9 October 1972, Victoria Hall, Hanley, UK

Just 13-years-old. This was my first ever live gig!

I went to the gig with my (older) best friend Dave. Dave had spent months indoctrinating me into the love of Free. We spent every weekend in his bedroom playing *Tons of Sobs*, *Highway* and *Fire and Water* on rotation on his Dansette record player. We sat cross-legged on his bed listening to the music and scrutinising the album covers.

A few weeks before the gig I had purchased my first ever album – *Free Live!* I still have this album. The sleeve is not quite as white as the day I bought it, but has all the signs of a well-played, well-loved record. I can still see the distinctive Island Records label turning slowly at 33 and ⅓ rpm.

I'd pored over photographs of the band playing live in the *NME* and *Sounds*. I tried to imagine what the experience would be like.

In the run up to the gig I remember asking Dave: 'What should I wear?' and 'How loud is it going to be?' I also wanted to know: 'What do you do at a gig?' Dave's reply involved something called 'freaking out'!

In terms of what to wear. I've never been a fashion guru but it was important to get this right... I opted for loon pants, a red top with flared sleeves and a beanie hat on top of my long blonde locks - I had lots of hair back then! The red top was chosen because I'd seen Paul Rodgers wearing something similar in a magazine!

Dave's dad dropped us off at the venue – my dad would be outside at the end to collect us.

Despite the listing on the ticket the support was actually a band called Hackensack (who were also signed to Island Records). This was my first live experience (discounting Freddy and the Dreamers in pantomime when I was six!). I was excited but also nervous.

I've only just realised after digging out the original tour programme that I never actually saw the 'classic' line-up that night as Andy Fraser had left the band. I obviously saw them with the addition of Tetsu and Rabbit. I'd forgotten this fact but can imagine that at the time I was probably slightly upset as I'd memorised Andy's bass solo from 'Mr Big' and was really looking forward to seeing him perform it live.

My first impression? I couldn't believe how loud it was! You could *feel* the bass and the drums in your gut. To be honest, 48 years later, I have no memory of the actual gig itself but I do vividly recall that moment when the house lights when down and the band were about to take the stage. The hall went black apart from the light from the corridor at the side of the stage. Through the glass in the door I could see the shapes of the band as they waited to come on. I cannot express the feeling of excitement and anticipation. Even today that memory gives me goosebumps. This was my first gig and I was about to see my idols.

Peter Smith

11 October 1972, Locarno, Sunderland, UK

Free returned to play in Sunderland only a few months since their last gig in the town. I have a programme from that time which doesn't actually list the Sunderland gig, but it does mention local gigs at Newcastle Mayfair, Durham University and Redcar Jazz Club. However, I'm certain that I bought it at a gig in Sunderland Locarno, which was presumably added as an extra date after the programme was printed.

By this time new tracks from *Heartbreaker* will have featured in the set, including the future hit, 'Wishing Well'. My memories of this Free gig are much hazier than those of the gigs I saw earlier that year, which suggests to me that it didn't reach the same heights, both in terms of performance and audience reaction. I don't remember the place being packed. The programme lists support as coming from Smith Perkins and Smith, who were an American soft rock / country band. The next time I was to see Paul Kossoff and Andy Fraser it was as part of their own individual bands, and in the case of Paul Rodgers and Simon Kirke as members of Bad Company.

Paul Clarkson

18 October 1972, The Dome, Brighton, UK

Finally got to see Free live in 1972 but I first became aware of the band in the summer of 1970 when I was 13 and they released their single 'All Right Now'. That great guitar intro by Paul Kossoff hooked me in as soon as I heard it along with the bluesy soulful voice of Paul Rodgers.

On the back of this I saved up my pocket money and went and bought the LP *Fire and Water*, it cost me around £37s/6d. I got it home and saw that it only had seven songs on it which was very different from all the other LPs we had in the household, I was very tempted to put the arm straight on to the last song on side 2 which was 'All Right Now' as it said 'long version': How exciting was that? - I'd never seen that before, but I decided to play the LP as nature intended from the opening song 'Fire and Water'. To my delight every song was as good as the single. Coming out of the 60s, I was used to three minute songs and 14 tracks to an LP, but this was totally different. It changed the way I looked at music and I realised there was something other than the Hit Parade.

I still followed the mainstream as most teenagers did back then but I had my eye on other up and coming groups that were being formed out of the 60s groups such as Led Zeppelin and Deep Purple. It wasn't long before *Sounds* replaced *New Musical Express* and *The Old Grey Whistle Test* replaced *Top of the Pops.*

Then in 1972, having seen so many great groups at The Dome in Brighton I saw that Free were to play there on 18 October. It wasn't the original four-piece line up, as Andy Fraser had left and been replaced by Tetsu Yamauchi on bass and John 'Rabbit' Bundrick on keyboards - they had played on the LP *Kossoff, Kirke, Tetsu and Rabbit* during the band's first split in 1971.

They started their set with 'The Stealer' and played most of the songs from *Fire and Water* and *Free at Last*. I had read in the music press about their live sound, particularly the fact that when watching them you were looking for the second guitarist. Paul Kossoff, sporting a shorter haircut, had such a unique style that it was as if he was playing both rhythm and lead. Not sure if he was in a bad way that night but he hardly moved from his spot right in front of the amps. Paul Rodgers had his usual swagger and fabulous stage presence, Simon Kirke, head down as usual pounding out the beat. The encore was of course 'All Right Now'.

After the gig along with my friends we stayed behind to see if we could get some autographs. Paul Kossoff was standing on the stage in exactly the spot he'd been playing all night. He signed my poster and said with a cheeky grin: 'How did you lot get in here?' and then added, 'the rest of the band are in that room over there'. So we went over and the rest of the band signed autographs for us. A great evening and a fabulous memory to look back on.

Of course I was disappointed not to see Andy Fraser in the group, but I didn't have to wait long to see him as his new band Sharks were support to Roxy Music on 11 April 1973.

So at the time, Free became my second favourite band behind The Beatles and still are to this day, I now have their entire back catalogue, including the box set *Songs of Yesterday.*

The autographs I obtained on the night of the Free gig were thrown away by my mum, who had no idea of their importance, luckily I managed to keep the tickets safe.

Phil Ault

October/November 1972 Island Studios, London, UK

Because I was involved with so many other sessions I can't recall the actual reforming of Free, only that I ended up assisting on most sessions for what would be the *Heartbreaker* album. There was no Andy Fraser of course, but I suspect he was one of the reasons for the initial break up, judging by comments at the time. The songs were strong, but there weren't that many of them. The album credits Andy Johns as producer and engineer, but I distinctly remember Richard Digby Smith at the controls for some tracks - notably 'Come Together In The Morning', which proved to be difficult. This was mainly because Koss was not in a good place with his addictions, and trying to overdub his guitar part took hours and hours. I have a strong mental image of working into the early hours in studio one (the upstairs big studio!), with five Marshall cabs on their own in the recording space - four were in action (and maybe the Leslie cab mixed in, can't be sure) while the fifth cab was used to prop up Koss. We were just about to call it a day because Paul seemed likely to fall over, when he insisted 'No! One more, I can do this!' He then pulled off the brilliant take which is on the record, and he did the whole track in one take, and carried on playing. Luckily there was blank tape at the end of the song and we left it running, as we knew it was a bit special - full of pain and emotion. This gave us a problem. We wanted to keep all of it, but were lacking a good 20 seconds of backing track. Engineers will try anything once, so the following day we all reconvened, set up the band, trying to replicate from memory all the mic positions, desk eq. etc., to attempt to match the sound and levels of the backing track, and drop the whole band in for an extended outro! Sheer madness, as so many things could go wrong, but amazingly it worked a treat. Remember, in those days you only got one shot at stuff like that, there was no cutting and pasting bollocks.

Mixing the album down in studio two wasn't as much fun. Koss had disappeared from the project by this time, replaced by Snowy White, and at the end, Island boss Chris Blackwell thought the mixes could be better, so Andy Johns remixed them. I'd worked with Andy before and was used to his mood swings. He was a bloody good engineer, if a little different from most. I remember the 'Wishing Well' mix very clearly, as Andy didn't have enough fingers, so I ended up mixing it with him, mainly in charge of vocals and drums. My difficulty was the toms, which in those days were mixed in with the cymbals on a stereo track. We wanted to highlight the toms so I had to learn the drum part and get the pushes just right, as well as cutting vocals in and out to keep the mix as clean as possible. It was a really good learning curve as I was about to start 'real engineering' myself, rather than just assisting.

1973

Andy Fraser

'The break up of Free? It was totally appropriate, because although we'd been brothers in arms, comrades, a gang, we had each other's back, it was the best thing any of us had ever been involved in, we all loved it, we all fit together really well, the chemistry was such that we had what we call a fifth member. But at some point in time, that fifth member departed.

What happened is, for me and Paul Rodgers, we're like A and Z as far as personalities. I suppose I'd say I was 'the sensitive gay boy', although it took me a couple of decades to come to terms with that, and Paul was like your northern street fighter, you know, but we found common ground. And when you do I think you invite the most amount of people in. We learnt from each other and we needed each other to help complete each other's ideas, but by the time we'd learnt to write songs by ourselves we started going in different directions and although I felt things were going as we wanted them, Paul felt that we had done things my way and now we were gonna do things his way.

I wanted to strengthen my voice, and the only way to do that is put your arse on a stage and start at the bottom. And I think likewise with Koss he wanted to strengthen his guitar playing, and likewise you've gotta get up there and see what it takes. And I credit him for having the balls to do that, but then when we saw what was happening to Koss we said, if for no other reason, we need to get back together because this guy is dying. And although that was the motivation, it wasn't enough to prevent him from slow suicide basically.'

Larry Turner

January 1973, Albuquerque, New Mexico, USA

I saw Free in Albuquerque, New Mexico in 1973 when I was 16 years old. It was the second rock show I ever attended (the first being Badfinger a year earlier). This show left an indelible impression on me, even though I was high as a kite (as was most everybody else in attendance).

The headliner act was Traffic, who I loved, but I really came to see Free. The first song I remember hearing by them on the radio was 'All Right Now'. I'd rushed to buy the *Fire and Water* album and discovered that this great song wasn't even the best on the album. To this day I believe the album is towards the top of the pantheon of all time rock masterpieces.

Heartbreaker

Released in January 1973, *Heartbreaker* was Free's sixth and final studio album. It featured the new line-up minus Andy Fraser, with his bass and keyboards work being shared by Tetsu Yamauchi and John 'Rabbit' Bundrick respectively. Yamauchi and Bundrick, along with Leigh Webster and Wendell Richardson, were all required to tour in support of the album. Paul Kossoff's struggles while recording *Heartbreaker* increased to an extent that made the 1973 tour impossible.

With the album and hit single 'Wishing Well' both going Top 10 in the UK there was no sign that the fanbase were losing interest in Free. There was even a sign that the band were steadily increasing their popularity in the US when *Heartbreaker* hit No.47 on the *Billboard* album chart.

The opening act in Albuquerque was a guy named John Martyn, who I'd never heard of before. He sat on a chair and sang while playing an acoustic guitar plugged into an Echoplex. I'll never forget it. It was hypnotic and mesmerising and I instantly became a lifelong fan. So sorry he's gone.

Traffic closed the show and, as expected were outstanding. I remember being impressed by the musical versatility of Stevie Winwood more than anything.

As for Free, who played in between, it was a big let down to be honest. It wasn't the same guys that were on the *Fire and Water* album cover, other than drummer Simon Kirke and, of course, Paul Rodgers on vocals. The new bass player did a good job, along with Simon, as the rhythm section, but I thought the guitarist used too much wah-wah pedal and didn't really come close to pulling off the Kossoff parts. The piano player seemed too animated and was a bit of a distraction. Paul Rodgers nailed the vocals, though, and single-handedly saved the show. Lots of charisma, a workhorse, and that voice!

I was able to see him again in the 80s with Jimmy Page in the band The Firm. He was phenomenal then, too.

I think I own everything Paul Rodgers ever recorded and to this day, when anyone asks who my favorite rock singers are, I answer 'Paul Rodgers, Robert Plant and Chris Cornell.'

Jenny Price Jennings

My best memory of Free? After college in 1973, going to Look 'n' Listen record shop in downtown Johannesburg. Sitting on bean bags and asking Moolah to play records. Heard the *Heartbreaker* album, loved it, bought it, still have it. 'Wishing Well', my all time favourite.

Tommy Taylor

Tommy Taylor has been a professional drummer, vocalist and songwriter for 52 years. Here he describes his gradual discovery and immersion in Free when 'there became no other band to touch them' on hearing Heartbreaker. His fan worship, which began as a teenager in Austin, Texas, concludes with a drummer's appreciation of Simon Kirke.

I was the original drummer in Christopher Cross and played all of the drums on the debut album. I played for the last 36 years off and on with the guitarist Eric Johnson and have contributed to every one of his records.

I worked with numerous blues, rock, rhythm and blues artists of note all over the world. I used to think I was the world's biggest Free fan... before I heard of Lucy Piller.

Tommy Taylor aged 13. Photo by Todd Jagger

I liked 'All Right Now'. We learned it and played it the week it came out. I was 13 playing clubs and dances and frat parties. A friend had the 8-track of the record with the lady on the front simply called 'Free'. We listened to it a lot. I loved the guitar tone - the rhythm tone - the way the guitarist used single notes in the rhythm parts and the riffs, like on 'Woman'. The sound was different -no one sounded like that.

I played a gig with some other local groups, one of whom did original bits. We were all mostly cover groups but this group played a good bit of their own material. I knew all of their original songs. They played a song I'd never heard. When they came off the stage, I asked the guitarist what this song was. He said 'that's the new one by Free - 'The Stealer''. I was wowed for sure.

The very next morning I went in search of the album with that song on it. I had to hear it again. I found *Highway* in the record bin at a local discount store that had a good selection and I immediately bought it and took it home and put in on the player. From the opening notes of 'The Highway Song' I was entranced. There was that guitar sound again, like in the chorus, 'But it was a long....da boo da da...way...from this high road.' Those notes 'da boo da da'... that's the sound...I must know more.

As the record progressed I grew more and more spellbound and I just became like a racehorse with blinders on, nothing else existed. Every track was like a drug. It was winter time and *Highway* is most definitely a winter album, it became a comforter. Mind you I was only 13 at this point.

It remained part of my go to arsenal of music, I was a fan. You hear about what is popular or what someone turns you on to. Free weren't very successful in the US after 'All Right Now'. My chance hearing of the 'Stealer' was a complete happy circumstance. My band learned it but it wasn't popular. We never heard about subsequent releases. When I turned 16 and got my permit we had 8-track players in the cars and I began frequenting a tape exchange place. I saw a tape with really cool graphics that said *Free At Last*. I thought, 'Oh wow, that must be Free!' I'd never heard of it. I still loved *Highway* and actually found a copy of that as well. How bad could it be? I'd risk it. I put in *Free At Last* in my car and I was transported to another universe. There was something completely disjointed and unpolished about it in comparison to *Highway*, but it had a power and energy and emotion that completely decimated the meter. I couldn't believe it. 'Catch A Train', 'Soldier Boy', 'Travelin' Man', 'Little Bit of Love', how come this record was unknown? When 'Goodbye' came on I was moved to tears. I decided right then I had to know everything about Free.

Of course, there was no internet back then. All we had was the big discography book at the record store called *Phonolog* that had every record in print by every artist. I quickly went and wrote down all of the titles and set out to find them. Shortly after, a copy of *Heartbreaker* showed up at the tape store and by this point there is no other band there is only Free - for a good period of time nothing graced my turntable but Free and the occasional Hendrix or Todd Rundgren - for a break possibly, but it was Free, Free, and more Free. People thought I was crazy. I didn't talk about anything but Free. Musicians knew, but no one else even knew who they were.

Heartbreaker was another mind blower, but it was different with the keyboards and I could tell things were a bit different in the bass. The records were tough to find. I think I ordered them all. They were still in print but not stocked. I finally had the whole catalogue and it was like an encyclopedia - the reference. I could see that for *Heartbreaker* the line-up had changed. Still great! Then *The Free Story* came out and the *Live Heartbreaker* at Sunderland. I lost my mind - I'd never heard a guitar solo with that much emotion ever. Paul Kossoff said more in one note than all the other guitarists said in a career. I learned every vocal of every song, note for note. I could sing right along with Paul to the point that I couldn't hear a double track. Rodgers became my vocal mentor via those records.

I was drummer in an R&B type horn band but my friends were in rock bands. I made them learn Free songs so I could stand up and sing Paul Rodgers. I wanted to see them live. I did more research and realised that Free was no more and there would be no chance of ever seeing them live. I was however pleased to note that Bad Company was coming on - it wasn't Free but I did like them, because I was so enamoured with Rodgers' vocals.

I had a rough time being a teenager because I had already sort of outgrown my school chums, because I played professionally at such an early age - school was tough and it was hard to find a place. Free kept me sane. I honestly believe that. They were like a blanket - an anchor of sorts - the safety net.

Fast forward and I'm friends with a guitarist who manages a cool record shop and I turn him on to Free and he can get JEM imports and we got the whole catalogue and also Koss's solo record on import - Molten Gold, that's the band again: Koss even more emotional than before. I could go on and on but I was there way, way before it was fashionable. Now Free is super highly regarded by everyone. Finally they have their day. Pity Koss wasn't around to see it. God bless them all.

As a drummer, the thing is and what I didn't go into was, how infectious and artistic Simon Kirke's playing with Free was. I call him the Van Gogh of rock drums. He doesn't owe anything to anyone. A total original. You can't find any influence in his playing.

By the time *Free at Last* came around he was breaking all the rules - he was not just a drummer - he was an orchestrator. My friend Jim Casey has had an opportunity to speak with Simon a few times. He mentioned me to Simon once and Simon said, 'Tommy Taylor? Great drummer!'

Jim called and left me a message on my answering machine. I couldn't believe it was real. Simon - there's no one like him. He is one of my biggest influences ever.

Koji Yoshida

In 1973 or 74, a Japanese FM station aired the whole *Free Live!* album. I recorded it on my open reel tape recorder. I fell in Love with *Fire and Water*. Then I made my friend play it during our school lunchtime music hour.

Neil Waite

My birthday present from my parents in 1973 was a copy of K-tel's *20 Power Hits*, a compilation album featuring the 'real' groups, unlike those *Top of the Pops* fake artist releases that at some point caught us all out. Just like listening to John Peel many years later, this moment was a milestone in my musical education. Thursday night viewings of *Top of the Pops* in the early '70s represented my staple diet of music, predominantly of the glam rock variety. At the tender age of seven, the record made me realise there were many amazing artists that were clearly not in my field of vision.

My birthday present that year introduced me to artists such as The Who, Jeff Beck, Faces, Nazareth and Edgar Winter, as well as the familiar Mud, Elton John and Suzi Quatro. The track that stood out the most, however, was Free's 'All Right Now'. That heavy rhythmic Les Paul power chord chop combined with Paul Rodgers' beautifully toned but powerful vocal made it a song to listen to over and over again.

This early initiation to Free was exciting but, being of limited age as well as limited finance, it wasn't something I was able to pursue through back-catalogue exploration. That would come later. I'm sure I would have discovered their six fine studio albums earlier if not for the late '70s tidal wave called Punk. A tidal wave I willingly got swept away with. The accessibility and DIY approach, with the help of a daily dose of John Peel, was something that dominated my early teens. It was inevitable that Free would be put on hold for a while.

I eventually rediscovered Paul Rodgers and Free in the late '80s, along with associated projects such as Bad Company, Peace, KKTR, Back Street Crawler and The Sharks. I remember listening to *Fire and Water* for the first time expecting the full version of 'All Right Now' to dominate my enjoyment. How wrong I was. Their famous two-chord hit, for me, although remaining brilliant, was overshadowed by the rest of the album. Much bluesier, giving Paul Rodgers a platform to show the amazing versatility and range of that soulful voice. This was the start of a long and continued love affair with Free and Paul Rodgers. The band would command my listening through the 1990s. A short official video release featuring, among others, Germany's *Beat-Club* and Granada performances, would only cement my love for the band, who were visually exciting as well as audibly so: Simon Kirke's drumming, with expressions of contorted focus; the young Andy Fraser, consistently rocking back and forth; Paul's stomping command of the stage; and Paul Kossoff's incredible guitar work, leaning back on the amp stack, grimacing. It all made for compulsive viewing.

Sharks

Andy Fraser formed Sharks in September 1972. The initial line-up who signed to Island Records consisted of Fraser (bass, piano), Snips (real name, Steve Parsons) (vocals), Chris Spedding (guitar) and a Canadian, Marty Simon (drums).

During January - February 1973, Sharks set out on a UK tour, playing clubs and universities. To promote the band, whilst touring, guitarist Chris Spedding customised his Pontiac Le Mans, fitting a shark fin on the roof and fibreglass teeth on the grill. On the way back to London from a gig in Cleethorpes on 19 February 1973, the car skidded and hit a tree. Fraser suffered injuries to his wrist and, during recuperation, had second thoughts about the band. After a short break, the band went back on the road in March and April, opening for Roxy Music, although Fraser had some difficulty playing with his injury. On 17 March, they made an appearance on the BBC Two programme, *The Old Grey Whistle Test.* The tour ended on 15 April, in Cardiff.

Sharks' debut album, *First Water*, was released in the same month, to critical acclaim, but Fraser left shortly afterwards.

Album artwork photography by Ian T Cossar

ALBUM	TRACKS	ALBUM	TRACKS
TONS OF SOBS	SIDE 1 1. OVER THE GREEN HILLS - PT 1 2. WORRY 3. WALK IN MY SHADOW 4. WILD INDIAN WOMAN 5. GOIN DOWN SLOW SIDE 2 1. I'M A MOVER 2. THE HUNTER 3. MOONSHINE 4. SWEET TOOTH 5. OVER THE GREEN HILLS - PT 2 PRODUCED BY: GUY STEVENS ℗ 1968 ISLAND RECORDS, A DIVISION OF UNIVERSAL MUSIC OPERATIONS LTD.	**FREE LIVE!**	SIDE 1 1. ALL RIGHT NOW 2. I'M A MOVER 3. BE MY FRIEND 4. FIRE AND WATER SIDE 2 1. RIDE O... 2. MR. B... 3. THE ... 4. GET ... PRODUCED BY: FREE AND ANDY JOHNS ℗ 1971 ISLAND RECORDS, A DIVISION OF UNIVERSAL...
FREE	SIDE 1 1. I'LL BE CREEPIN' 2. SONGS OF YESTERDAY 3. LYING IN THE SUNSHINE 4. TROUBLE ON DOUBLE TIME 5. MOUTHFUL OF GRASS SIDE 2 1. WOMAN 2. FREE ME 3. BROAD DAYLIGHT 4. MOURNING SAD MORNING PRODUCED BY: CHRIS BLACKWELL ℗ 1969 ISLAND RECORDS, A DIVISION OF UNIVERSAL MUSIC OPERATIONS LTD.	**FREE AT LAST**	SIDE 1 1. CATCH A TRAIN 2. SOLDIER BOY 3. MAGIC SHIP 4. SAIL ON 5. TRAVELLING MAN SIDE 2 1. LITTLE ... 2. GUARD... 3. CHILD ... 4. GOOD... PRODUCED BY: FREE ℗ 1972 ISLAND RECORDS, A DIVISION OF UNIVERSAL...
FIRE AND WATER	SIDE 1 1. FIRE AND WATER 2. DON'T SAY YOU LOVE ME 3. MR. BIG 4. HEAVY LOAD SIDE 2 1. REMEMBER 2. OH I WEPT 3. ALL RIGHT NOW PRODUCED BY: FREE AND JOHN KELLY ℗ 1970 ISLAND RECORDS, A DIVISION OF UNIVERSAL MUSIC OPERATIONS LTD.	**HEARTBREAKER**	SIDE 1 1. WISHING WELL 2. COME TOGETHER IN THE MORNING 3. TRAVELLIN' IN STYLE 4. HEARTBREAKER SIDE 2 1. MUDD... 2. COMM... 3. EASY ... 4. SEVEN... PRODUCED BY: FREE AND ANDY JOHNS ℗ 1973 ISLAND RECORDS, A DIVISION OF UNIVERSAL...
HIGHWAY	SIDE 1 1. THE HIGHWAY SONG 2. THE STEALER 3. ON MY WAY 4. BE MY FRIEND SIDE 2 1. SUNNY DAY 2. RIDE ON A PONY 3. LOVE YOU SO 4. BODIE 5. SOON I WILL BE GONE PRODUCED BY: FREE ℗ 1970 ISLAND RECORDS, A DIVISION OF UNIVERSAL MUSIC OPERATIONS LTD.		

CLIENT: ISLAND
SUBJECT: FREE

ISLAND STUDIOS

15 IPS ☒   7½ IPS ☐   DOLBY ☐   NAB ☒

Richard Digby Smith

1973, Island Records, Basing Street Studios, London, UK

On a photo shoot for the *Back Street Crawler* album cover, Paul took this Gibson Les Paul out into the side alley next to the Basing Street studios. He took the guitar lead and 'plugged' it into a dustbin!

That photo of Paul plugged into a dustbin was to be the album cover and was to signify the defiant nature of the man in a most humorous way, which was typical of him. The alley cat, rebel of a guitar player. He sounded like no other and wanted an image to match.

Back Street Crawler

Paul Kossoff released his first solo album *Back Street Crawler* in 1973 which featured contributions from his former Free band mates as well as Yes drummer Alan White, Scottish singer song-writer John Martyn, English singer Jess Roden and Trevor Burton from The Move.

Side one on the original vinyl edition is given over entirely to one song. The seventeen and a half minute opus 'Tuesday Morning', side two features four more tracks, 'I'm Ready', 'Time Away', 'Molten Gold' which has Paul Rodgers on lead vocals, Andy Fraser on bass and Simon Kirke on drums and the final track 'Back Street Crawler (Don't Need You No More)'.

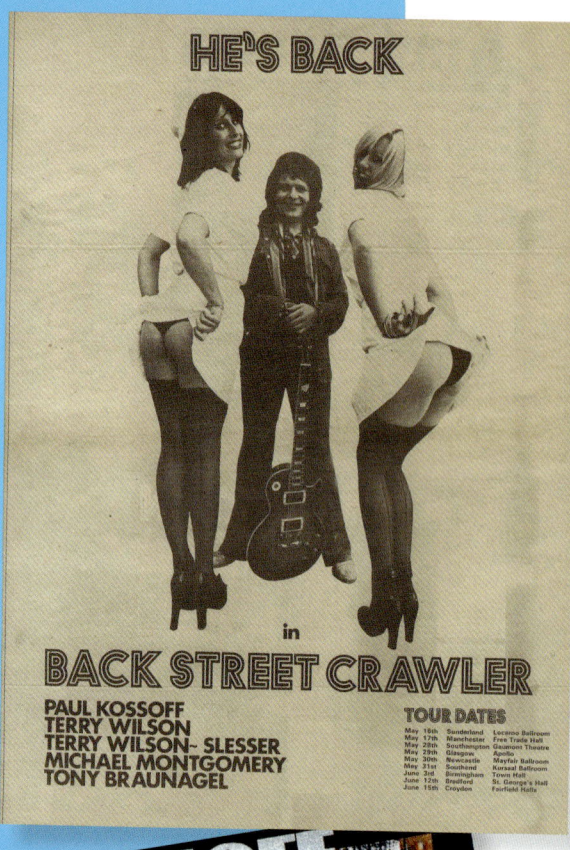

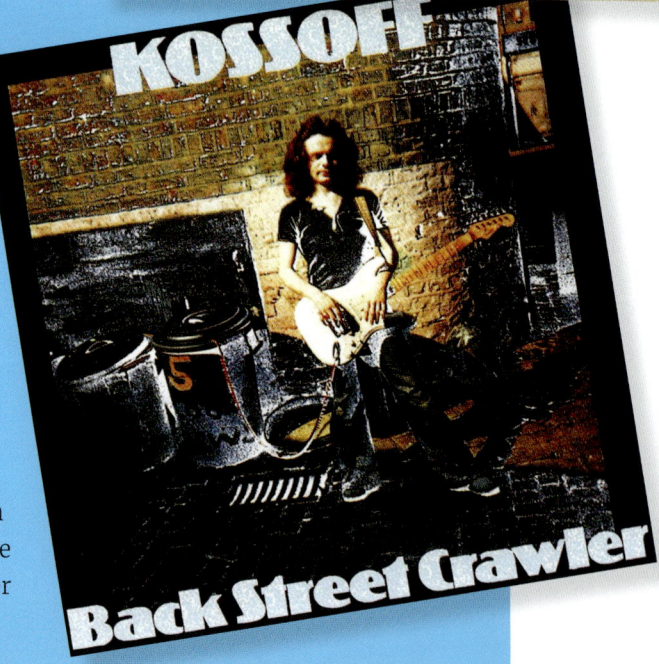

Summer 1973

FREE SPLIT, BAD COMPANY FORM

Andy Fraser

I love that band, I love what we did. I thought what we expressed then was honest, it had integrity and was in the moment. We're equally matched in a way and held each other in check. So all of that I wouldn't change.

Ritchie Blackmore

The only band I knew to go on without thinking they're superstars, were Free. To me they were a great band. They were far ahead of any other band I know. I think they're the only English band that people should feel they're lucky to have.

Rod Stewart

Ronnie Lane left the Faces in 1973. My first thought was to ask Andy Fraser, who had been the bass player with Free, a band I respected and listened to a lot while we were on tour. Andy wasn't interested, so we then approached Tetsu Yamauchi, who had replaced Andy in Free and was a sweet Japanese guy who barely spoke English. Tetsu appeared to be going through some emotional difficulties at the time, but because he didn't speak English we never really found out what those emotional difficulties were.

Paul Rodgers

To compare Bad Company with Free is difficult, because Free was at an end, and we're at a beginning. I don't know exactly where it's going to go, but I like where it's going. I've realised that I need to be part of a group where everyone in it is equal, and we're all sparking each other off. I`m very happy with this group because everyone is very relaxed.

Andy Fraser

The Faces asked me to join, and I knew I couldn't handle the Faces and their drink. Because we'd toured with them, and it was like: 'well why don't you come and have a quick drink?', and you'd be in there and three bottles of whiskey later 'man, where are you going?', and it was like 'I'm off to bed, okay?'. I was just like nah, I can't handle all of that.'

Paul Kossoff

I'd spent four, maybe five years, being one fourth of a whole personality, which was Free, and when the band broke up, I was on my own. I didn't know what to do.

Mick Ralphs

I had written a lot of songs, some Ian Hunter could sing, but most he felt he couldn't do them justice. After meeting Paul Rodgers at a show, he said that he could sing them. That was really how Bad Company started.

Mick Ralphs

Paul and myself met on a Mott the Hoople tour, he was supporting with a band called Peace and I'd known him from Free. We decided we'd do some writing together, not actually start a band, just as a side project. I used to go down to Paul's house in Guildford and we'd sit around and write songs and come up with ideas.

He was gonna do some of the songs that I couldn't do with Mott the Hoople because he liked them and we were gonna make a record and then Simon Kirke came to Paul's house one day out of nowhere and said what are we doing and I just said 'kicking some ideas around, possibly gonna make an album', and he said 'well, do you mind if I sit in?'

So, I said to Paul, 'all we need now is a bass player and we've got a band!' So, it evolved very naturally, we didn't plan it. It was all kind of accidental I suppose – lucky really.

The first album, we'd written pretty much all of it, because I'd been working with Paul on songs I'd had from the Mott days like 'Can't Get Enough', 'Ready For Love', 'Moving On', and we'd written some stuff together and whilst we were looking for a bass player we rehearsed the songs on a daily basis trying out different bass players. When we came to record them we'd been playing them daily for about four or five months. So, we knew them pretty well inside out and we worked out the arrangement, so it was a very quick recording process. We'd done all the hard work before we went to record them.

Ron Nevison

November 1973, Headley Grange, Hampshire, UK

Led Zeppelin had been renting this house called Headley Grange in Hampshire that they had done previous work in, including *Houses of the Holy*, with the Rolling Stones truck. Now, I am not sure why I was called, but I got the call to go down to Headley Grange. Ultimately what happened was something came up with the band that forced them to put off the recording for a month or six weeks. Because the 'Paul Rodgers band' had just signed with Peter Grant – Zeppelin's manager – he said, 'Why don't you guys go in? I've got the truck, I've got Nevison.' So that's how the Bad Company album happened. So, I went down to Headley Grange to record that. We recorded that in like, two weeks, and then took it back to Olympic Studios to mix it and put some stuff on it.

Mick Ralphs

Well, I used to keep a notebook when we were in the studio where I'd write the tracks and running order. So we had a list of potential bass players who were coming down to audition, and at the time we were at Headley Grange, which is in the countryside in Hampshire and there was a station about a mile away so every day the office would phone up and tell us who was coming down to audition to try out for the bass job. So, Paul and I would go up to the station and pick the poor chap up before he tried out a few songs, but most of them didn't make the gig, not because of their playing but because of other reasons.

Well, one bloke (it says in the notebook) was called 'foaming at the mouth'. Another was called 'bald station'. We went up to the station to pick this chap up and Paul suddenly said, 'Drive on, I've seen him'. And I said, 'Why?' He said, 'He's bald!' And I said, 'Well, he's seen me now, it's too late.' So, we had to go back to the house and spend the whole afternoon going through it knowing that he would end up in the book as not getting the job because he was 'bald at the station'.

Another bloke we tried was a guy called Alan Spanner, he was a really good bass player, he used to be with The Grease Band, but he turned up late and I put in the book that he didn't get the job because he was too good. We wanted someone who was the same character, we've all got a good sense of humour.

Well, we were desperate in the end. We'd tried all these people, and someone said why don't you try Boz [Burrell]? We'd heard of Boz's reputation as being a bit of a lad who liked to drink and things, so we said we've got nothing to lose so let's give it a go. We were in London this time, we arranged to meet Boz at this rehearsal room. Boz arrives half drunk and Paul says what do you wanna do and he said he wanted to go to the pub! So, we thought okay, and all went to the pub and got pissed and came back and played a load of rubbish! We all thought it was great at the time and the next day Paul says 'what do you think?' And I said, 'I dunno, but you offered him the job'. He said, 'did I?' I said 'yeah you did', and he said 'shit!'

So that's how we got Boz! It was hilarious.

Po Powell

1973, Horselunges Manor, East Sussex, UK

I'd worked with Led Zeppelin in 1973 doing *Houses of the Holy* and I became good friends with Peter Grant. He really looked after me, he was fantastic, actually. He took a shine to me and consequently I got a lot of work for his artists at Swan

Song. One day I was down at his house, Horselunges Manor, and he said 'we've put a new band together called Bad Company and we need an album cover.' Peter was so powerful – he didn't particularly want me to meet the band and said 'just come up with some ideas and... also I need a logo for the name Bad Company'.

The brief he gave me was 'think of Bad Company / Good Company like these are bad guys but really they're good guys – renegade cowboy image.' Robin Hood figures in a sense, which kind of suited them, actually.

We didn't want to do anything too obvious and I wasn't interested in having a picture of the band. We thought more about the genre of black and white detective films and forensics and discovering who Bad Company were. The obvious thing was finger prints and palm prints. Also, Bad Company was such a long graphic title to write out that it never looked very comfortable to me as a title for a band. So I suggested we reduce it to 'Bad Co' and we did this graphic, working with George Hardy the illustrator, and photographed some finger prints and created this swirl behind the cut-out of the wording 'Bad Company'. I showed it to Peter and he loved it. And then I went to meet the band and they loved it too. I think what they liked about it, and what Atlantic Records liked about it, was the fact that it had an atmosphere of mystery. Bad Co – you weren't sure what was going on and it was like a detective story or mystery novel.

Of course the music on the first album was just unbelievable. I remember when Peter Grant played me the white vinyl album and you immediately knew it was a hit. Paul and Mick Ralphs had the songs and the first tracks just blew your socks off.

The Free Story

This Free greatest hits double album first appeared across Europe and North America before Island released the UK version in late December 1973, with a cover photo of a guitar neck with a cigarette attached. The UK version was numbered, had a different cover image and early copies included an illustrated booklet featuring a history of the band written by *Sounds* editor Billy Walker. The 20-track album which would go on to peak at No.2 on the chart featured songs from *Tons of Sobs*, *Fire and Water*, *Highway*, *Free Live!* and *Heartbreaker* as well as the single 'My Brother Jake', 'Lady' from Rodgers' post-Free group, Peace and 'Just for the Box' by Kossoff, Kirke, Tetsu and Rabbit.

I went with four older mates from Farnborough. To get us in the mood for the gig we drank cider and vodka on the train there. Paul Rodgers chatted with the audience, introducing Boz Burrell as a jazz bassist, both gigs were very friendly.

I then later saw them in London at the Rainbow with my cousin John, who was a biker. I was 14 and still at school. We shared a bottle of Olde English Cider outside the venue. He dropped me off at my gran's in Wandsworth after the amazing gig. I remember 'Cant Get Enough', 'Bad Company' and the brilliant 'Stealer' being the stand-out tracks.

My kids are late twenties now, into live music and have loads of Free on their playlists. I still listen to Free on vinyl. They had so much soul in their blues. A major influence in my teenage years. I took up bass at school because of Andy Fraser.

Jon Kirkman

13 April 1974, Liverpool Boxing Stadium, UK

I always thought that Bad Company played their second gig at the Liverpool Boxing Stadium. It was an old boxing ring. A complete dump. But you don't think that at the time. It had a capacity of about 1,800 to 2,000 and I paid about £1.50 or £2 and the gig was great. Like a lot of people there, I'd been a big fan of Free. Of course at the time there hadn't been a Bad Company album and they must have been short of material. I was still quite surprised that they did some Free songs – definitely 'The Stealer' at the end. I thought, 'OK.' I'd thought they maybe wanted to draw a line under that. Great gig though and the place went nuts for them.

Paul Senior

14 April 1974, Hard Rock, Manchester, UK

Saw Bad Company on their first tour at Manchester Hard Rock where they included 'Easy on my Soul' and 'The Stealer.' I also saw the Andy Fraser band at Sheffield City Hall.

Got a job in 1974 as a DJ in a local pub and Thursday night was rock night and guess what? Played Free, Bad Company, Mott the Hoople, Led Zeppelin, Deep Purple, Wishbone Ash et al to death. Great nights.

Saw Bad Company again – early the following year I think it was – at the Great British Music festival at Olympia with Nazareth and Be-Bop Deluxe, when the dry ice machine went out of control! Then travelled down from Scotland from my job in Aberdeen to see them in London – Burnin' Sky tour at Earl's Court. Didn't see them again until the Rough Diamonds tour but then continued buying all the Paul Rodgers solo stuff (*Cut Loose*), both Firm albums and then the Law CD. In the 90s I loved the *Muddy Water Blues* CD he did and then saw him at the Kentish Town Forum in London. My wife brought me a copy of the *Bad Company Anthology* (double CD) back from New York around 2000 before Paul commenced touring solo during 2000-2006, when we would follow him around the country at various gigs.

Tape boxes from Bad Company sessions engineered by Richard Digby Smith, April 1974

David Roberts

18 May 1974, The Valley, Charlton Athletic FC, London, UK

Bad Company were on a terrific bill, with The Who headlining, presented as 'The Summer of '74'. That hot Saturday in May there was a raucous, almost violent atmosphere stoked by the inability of the organisers to control the size of the enormous crowd attending, many without tickets. Some rock fans had seemingly left behind the 'love and peace' vibe prevelant at these huge festival gatherings and adopted an almost football hooligan-like persona.

While I'd paid my £2.50 primarily to see The Who, I recall being very impressed by the two bands that all the 80,000 there had never seen before. Montrose, featuring Sammy Hagar were good and loud and Bad Company delivered a thumping set even though it took me a while to realise that the straw-hatted guitar-toting figure stage centre was indeed Paul Rodgers. Boz Burrell was noted as being on particularly good form playing through the monster PA system. Not bad, I remember thinking, for an outfit who hadn't even released their first album.

Andrew Wilkinson

My first exposure to Free was through 'All Right Now'. Hearing that song on the radio, buying the *Fire and Water* album, discovering the album version was better than the single. It would have been around 1974 when I was 18. I lived (and still do) in Rossendale which is in east Lancashire, between Bury and Burnley. At that time every town had at least one record store, and I bought records from Ames Record Bar in Rawtenstall. Like most independent shops, it is long gone.

A guitar sound, which I later learned was a Les Paul and a Marshall stack, made the hairs on the back of my neck stand up. Sometimes powerful, sometimes melodic, coupled with heartfelt singing convinced me I had to learn to play the guitar. And I have never stopped since then.

'All Right Now' continues to be a challenge to play, but it still means a lot to me. Does any song have a better chorus?

A couple of years after discovering Free and following the death of Paul Kossoff, I remember his father David (who was often on TV in those days) speaking about his loss. We knew his potential as a musician, but not as a person.

Mick Austin

June 1974, Granby Hall, Leicester, UK

Talk of Paul Rodgers and Simon Kirke forming another band sounded interesting, but having seen them trying to do anything other than Free appeared to end in maybe one album before vanishing back into the realm of dreams. Then, after a few months, I happened to hear on the car radio 'Can't Get Enough' and I knew straight away this was Bad Company. It had all the traits of Free but was more in a rock vein.

I saw Bad Company at the Granby Hall in Leicester when they first began to tour, they were excellent and it was obvious to any Free fan that the old magic was still there but it was never a reincarnation of Free. They were polished, had great songs and even Mick Ralphs appeared to be tearing huge pages from the Kossoff book of guitar playing. The dynamics were still there but it wasn't Free. The chemistry had changed and it made all the difference.

Bad Company's history wasn't curtailed in the same manner as Free. They were all experienced musicians and understood the business, whereas Free were young and it was all new to them. Bad Company ran a natural life expectancy. My friend, Max Norman, produced their *Rough Diamonds* album, by which time rock n' roll bands had become a little sanitised. But the birth of heavy metal, in my opinion, had a lot to thank the original Free concept for and many, many people still don't understand that equation. The likes of AC/DC and so many other metal bands used the volume and dynamics that Free brought to the public's attention so long ago, but while these bands use the idea, they have smoothed off the rough edges to the point of all pretty much sounding like 'heavy metal' – while Free used harmonies, acoustics, almost folk in places. Free was unique and although many have tried they have never managed to recreate what we heard all those years ago. And I, and everyone else that witnessed those early years, feel so privileged that *we were there*!

Paul Kossoff

I didn't start all the drug stuff when I was with Free – that came afterwards. I just came to a standstill and got swept up by something else. I went through just about everything in the last couple of years, and ended up mainlining for a short period, which I stopped because that was it, the end.

I've been asking myself a long time, Why? I think it's something to do with my make-up as a person for a start-off. Suddenly I wasn't travelling about. Suddenly I wasn't playing. All the natural highs that I was used to had somehow disappeared, and I was almost led by hand into it. Once into drugs you get into fairly morbid trains of thought – morbid interest in death and dead people, stuff like that. It's quite horrific at times. Also the feeling of being in slight danger was like a romance. It's very strange…

I started to identify with Hendrix for instance. I spent more time listening and dreaming than playing.

It was an escape from playing as well, cause that's a big responsibility in itself. You have to prove yourself. I didn't want to pick up a guitar. I felt wrong with it for a long time. It was very heavy on the head. I got it well out of proportion.

Mick Ralphs

When I sit down and write a rock 'n' roll song, I pick up an open-tuned guitar because I find it keeps me down to about three or four chords. And to me, the best rock 'n' roll songs have got three or four chords in them and no more.

With 'Can't Get Enough' I'd written it in an open G-tuning like Keith Richards uses, but when I played the song to Paul, he said 'well I love the song, but can you change the key?' So, we fiddled around on the guitar and eventually he wanted to sing in the key of C, so I thought 'how the hell do you do that?' because it's a lot higher. So I strung a guitar up to open C, hoping that the strings wouldn't break because it was so tight. Anyway I learnt that I had to use thinner strings to avoid the breakage but it had a unique sound that you can't get on a regular guitar. So, I was lumbered with playing it in open C on stage.

It does have that unique sound though, and a lot of people would say come and jam with us and we'll do 'Can't Get Enough', and it'll be hard to explain to them that I can't play it in regular tuning because it won't sound the same. I like open tuning for writing songs because it gives you a different perspective on the guitar. I get fed up with regular tuning so I'll try something different, and an idea might pop out from it.

Brian May

Bad Company — a bolt from the blue! We - boys of Queen - grew up on Free, of course, led by the wonderful soulful vocals of Paul Rodgers. The *Fire and Water* album was one of our Bibles. When Free broke up, we felt a sense of loss. But it's clear as day in my memory - while Queen were on tour in the States, we heard rumours of Paul and magnificent drummer Simon Kirke forming a new band with Mott veteran/creative guitarist Mick Ralphs. It already had to be great! We then heard Led Zep's Peter Grant had signed them up — and then suddenly the *Bad Company*. album appeared at No. 1 in the US charts, and 'Can't Get Enough' was all over rock radio. We felt joy and pride. The album was great, of course, and is still well up in the playlist.

Years later I had the privilege of touring with Paul as our singer, and one of my greatest joys was performing some of those wonderful songs from the Free/Bad Company catalogue with 'The Man.'

Bad Company

The first album released on Led Zeppelin's Swan Song Records label was the debut from Bad Company. Already touring the songs, the much anticipated album, simply titled *Bad Co*, was released on 26 June 1974. The four-piece consisting of Paul Rodgers, Simon Kirke, original Mott the Hoople guitarist Mick Ralphs and bass player Boz Burrell had been recorded late 1973 at Headley Grange.

The writing credits are shared equally between Mick Ralphs and Paul Rodgers. Ralphs penned three songs on the album - 'Can't Get Enough', 'Movin' On' and the Mott the Hoople cover 'Ready For Love' from their 1972 *All The Young Dudes* album, along with co-writes with Rodgers' 'Don't Let Me Down' and 'Seagull'.

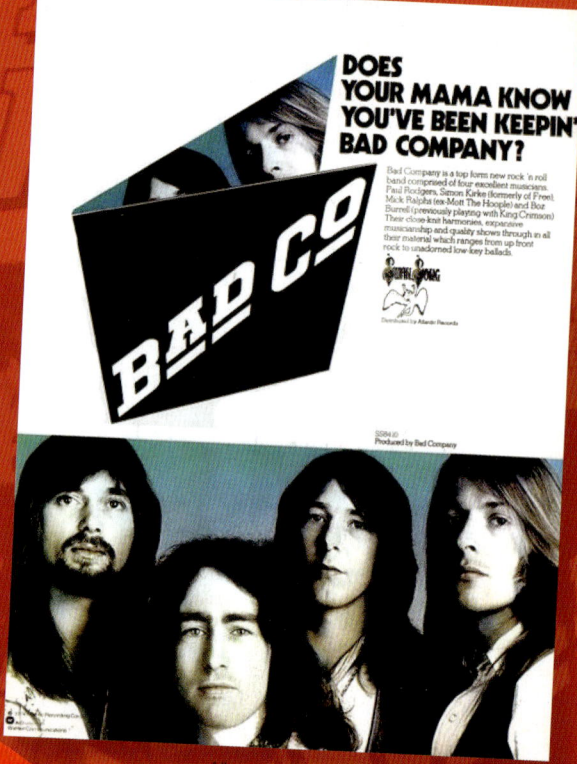

Album artwork photography by Ian T Cossar

Bad Co

Almost immediately, the band experienced critical acclaim and commercial success as their debut album rocketed to No.1 on the US *Billboard* album chart and No.3 in the UK. In the 46 years since its release the album has been certified five times platinum.

Rolling Stone magazine was prompted to report that 'Rodgers' voice is Bad Company's virtuoso instrument; he's one of the most impressive rock singers of the decade.'

Swan Song
BAD COMPANY
SIDE ONE
SS 8410
1. CAN'T GET ENOUGH (4:10) Ralphs
2. ROCK STEADY (3:46) Rodgers
3. READY FOR LOVE (5:00) Ralphs
4. DON'T LET ME DOWN (4:18) Rodgers-Ralphs
(ST-SS-743137)
℗ 1974 SWAN SONG INC.
MANUFACTURED AND DISTRIBUTED BY WEA MUSIC OF CANADA, LTD.

Paul Rodgers　　Mick Ralphs

Luke Morley (Thunder)

It was interesting to see what they would do after Free. The first Bad Company album leans a bit more to R&B and soul in the old-fashioned sense. There's something so measured and mature about that album. With Free there was the element of a youthful unfinished, unvarnished thing going on and Bad Company was very slick. Very good but in a different kind of way for me. And I loved Mick Ralphs as a guitarist.

Chuck Childs

28 July 1974, Auditorium Theater, Chicago, Illinois, USA

I'm from Tinley Park, Illinois. The reason I became a Free fan, was pretty simple. It's all about the music. As a Bad Company fan, I could not get enough of Paul's talented voice and great music, and really wanted more. I was pleasantly surprised that Paul had done this before with Free, another talented group of musicians. Simon [Kirke] was in both bands. Favourite songs include 'Love You So', 'Be my Friend', 'Mr Big', 'Fire and Water' and 'Wishing Well'. I've followed Paul's career ever since. I still can't get enough! Loved the Free Spirit tribute concert on YouTube. In my Rock and Roll Hall of Fame!

I went to my first Bad Company concert at about 17 or 18 years. It was their first US tour, and I had a ticket for the Chicago show. Great show!

Strangely enough, I heard about a party on the south side at Joe Jammer's house the day after the concert which Bad Company were invited to attend, which they did. I just missed the band, except for Boz Burrell. Boz was playing a piano in the house, so I got to meet Boz. Boz was a bit buzzed, and I caught a large glass object that was about to fall off the wall unit piano. I also met Maggie Bell, the backup singer from the Bad Company concert. She gave me a big kiss! Joe Jammer played in Maggie Bell's band for the show, and knew many A-list bands. I went on to attend almost all the other Bad Company concerts in Chicago during the 70s, missing just one due to business. After the Bad Company split, that's when I discovered Free. Wow!

Now, I try to catch Paul's shows whenever I can. He's still amazing!

Can't Get Enough

As the first track on the first Bad Company album, 'Can't Get Enough' introduced the supergroup to the world, with the sound of drummer Simon Kirke counting in and blasting two beats to start things off.

The song became the band's first single release on 12 August and quickly established itself as an essential and immovable presence on radio, and not just rock radio stations, for the remaining months of 1974.

Bad Company's power rock classic would also become their most successful hit single. The *Billboard* chart peak of No.5 was bettered by a *Cashbox* No.1. In the UK the single climbed to a more modest No. 15 but with the *Bad Company* album flying off the shelves of record stores worldwide, the band were hot property.

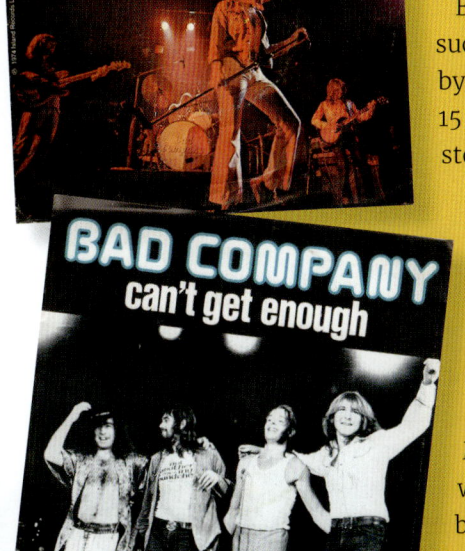

Simon Kirke

'Cant Get Enough?': We were scattered all over this country house [Headley Grange] and I believe it was one of the first songs that we did. I was in the basement, Boz was in the boiler room, Mick Ralphs and Paul Rodgers were up in the main living room where the guitar amps were. So, in order to get their attention, because we couldn't see each other, I did the count: '1, 2... 1, 2, 3...' and then I did this 'guh-brah' to get everyone's attention. And that's how we kicked it off. It was born out of necessity.

Mick Ralphs

For the dual guitar thing on 'Can't Get Enough', I did the original demo when I was in Mott and lived in a flat in Shepherd's Bush, London. I worked on the two parts and recorded on a little revox thing as you did in those days. I remember when we came to do it, Paul said you've got to put that bit in - its part of the song. So, we did it, but Paul wanted to play the harmony, so I remember having to show him the harmony line and when we did the first album, we actually did the whole thing in one take live. He played the harmony part and I played the basic one, originally, I'd done them both, so we did it live instead of doing them one at a time and we just took it. It wasn't perfect but it captured the moment.

Joe Perry

When I first heard Bad Company, it was the song 'Can't Get Enough.' You didn't hear really good rock songs on the radio in the Top 10, but that was one of the exceptions. In the manner that Bad Company put their songs together, with that element of R&B and soul, they distilled the best of what rock 'n' roll is about. For me, the simplest stuff hits you the hardest and Bad Company had that simplicity that really worked for them. That kind of music sounds great in a club or a stadium because it's reduced to its essence.

As a guitar player, Mick Ralphs was an inspiration to me. He had that sense of melody in his playing that's really important. His playing is just right for a band like Bad Company. It's not about being fast or the notes you play, a lot of it's about the notes you don't play. Mick's solos are part of the hooks of the songs as much as Paul's singing. Bad Company's stuff sticks to your ribs; you hum along to not just the song but the solos in the way that you don't do with a lot of guitar players. The band all had one vision and it worked together.

When I was thinking about a singer for the Joe Perry Project, I picked Ralph Morman because of the similarities with his voice and Paul Rodgers. I've always said my favourite singer besides Steven (Tyler) was Paul Rodgers. Paul has a way of singing that is so intimate; almost like he's talking to you.

One of my favourite Bad Company records is 'Burnin' Sky,' that one's really atmospheric. I love that one and 'Master of Ceremony.' To me it sounds like something they just laid down and it just kind of poured out. Bad Company was great in the '70s and they still are. I got to tour with them a few years ago in England, and it was a dream come true to hear those songs every night. There's nothing better than playing with one of your favourite bands on the road. I saw them a couple of times in the '70s and their sound filled the hall because of the way the songs were written and performed. That's hard to do. *Interview with Goldmine Magazine*

Marvin Beasley

My first exposure to Paul Rodgers was like a lot of people with Free's 'All Right Now'. I ultimately got the *Best of Free* album, and the song 'Fire and Water' was a new fave!

Now, going into 1974, this song called 'Can't Get Enough' is getting airplay. 'Hey... that's Paul Rodgers singing! How cool is that?' I find out the new group is called Bad Company.

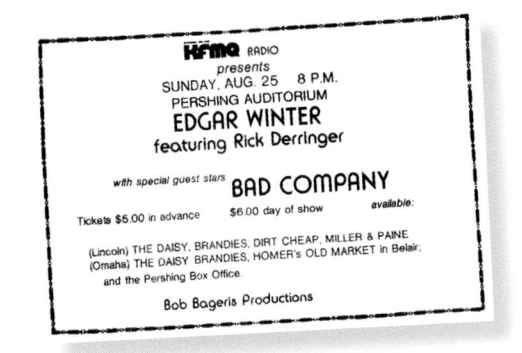

Soon there after I see that Bad Company will be appearing on *Don Kirshner's Rock Concert*. I had my portable cassette recorder propped up to the TV and recorded the show. Awesome performance, and still a favorite to this day .

This was my first exposure to the songs that appeared on the first *Bad Company* album, and to me, the live versions were much heavier than the studio offerings.

I'm really partial to the Kirshner version of the songs, as I listened to them endlessly before I got the studio album.

Then '*Straight Shooter* was special - it was an innocent, fun time for me. 'Good Lovin' Gone Bad' is probably my favorite Paul vocal because it is just so powerful.

Chris Charlesworth

10 August 1974, *Melody Maker*

Bad Company's formation has been a shot in the arm for Paul Rodgers – and he's raving over the band's tour of the States as MM's Chris Charlesworth discovered in New York.

Chris Charlesworth (front with cigarette) and staff on the roof at Melody Maker's office, London

The change in Paul Rodgers was noticeable after just a couple of minutes talking on the phone.

Gone was the brooding young man of a year ago with a chip on his shoulder and little to say. In his place was a man spiced with energy, willing to chat for hours about Bad Company's short existence.

The new band has obviously given Paul a massive shot of adrenalin. The last time we spoke, about the time of the last break-up of Free, he had little to say for himself.

He was obviously depressed at the perpetual bickering surrounding his last band, and had no great hopes about his immediate future to reveal.

It was different on the phone from Chicago. 'It's been really amazing, honest,' he said when I inquired how Bad Company's debut tour of the States, now three weeks old, had been going. 'Everybody says that about their US tour, I know, but it's been real good as far as we are concerned.

'We're only the supporting act on the show which isn't the best spot to be in, but we're making out as best we can. Actually last night we topped the bill at Cleveland, Ohio, for the first time. It was only like a club which held 1,200 people but they crammed 1,500 people in and we had a ball. We did about four encores and it was the best gig so far.

'Most of the places we get between 40 and 45 minutes to play which means we can't really get off as there isn't time. We do most of the tracks from the album if there's time but we have to keep the show up instead of slowing down for a song like 'Seagull'. There isn't time for the quieter stuff, so we have to blast out to make any impression.

'We've done some gigs with Black Oak Arkansas. Their singer is good, with a lot of charisma, but I don't think their music is all that hot. We've played with Edgar Winter, who has a good band, and also done some dates with Peter Frampton.'

Bad Company will be in the States until September 10, a long tour by any standards. 'It's like an apprenticeship for us,' said Paul, 'We are working just about every night and the constant touring is helping a lot.

'When you play night after night you have to relax on stage sometimes and that's good for the band. You can't stay on edge all the time or you'd go crazy.

'I think the music is starting to flow better now and obviously playing this much is tightening us up no end. We have about another 40 gigs to do.'

Already Bad Company's album is moving up the charts here and stands a good chance of hitting the 30 within a couple of weeks. 'A lot of people in the audience have been asking for songs like 'Rock Steady' and 'Can't Get Enough' and that's very pleasing for a new act like us,' said Paul.

'People in the audience seem to recognise us from our old bands, but they ain't yelling for Free numbers or anything like that. And, of course, there are some places where no-one has a clue who we are. We could be a brand new act with brand new musicians as far as some audiences are concerned.

'Those audiences who do know us seem far more concerned with what we are doing now than with our pasts. They're not interested in our old groups. When we hit a new town we usually go over to see the DJs at the FM stations and they are the only ones who are interested in our pasts.

'America is a question of working hard and covering as many places as we can. We can't come over as a super-group here, we have to start from scratch again and this gives the people a chance to discover us for themselves.

'At some shows, people are still moving around and looking for their seats when we are playing and it's up to us to create some kind of atmosphere. That kind of thing toughens you up a lot.

'We could headline a show in England on our reputations but over here it's a different story entirely. You have to work real hard to make a name for yourselves and we're determined to work our asses off. We love to work anyway, and it's a question of the more gigs the better.'

The band are constantly writing new material and already their set features songs written on the plane ride over from England and others put together in hotel rooms. 'We're doing some completely new stuff here that we haven't played before,' said Paul.

'Obviously we can't get as many songs in as we would like, but we're capable of putting on a two hour show now if we could. We like writing on the move, in planes and in hotels, and the new stuff is bits of everything, piano numbers and folksy type songs.'

When the band gets back to Britain in September they'll be taking a couple of weeks break, and then heading into the studio to make their second album. 'We will have more than enough material to record,' said Paul. 'It'll just be a question of putting down the stuff that we feel is most representative of the band.

'After that we'll be doing a British tour in November, much more extensive than the first one.'

Donald J Cable

1 September 1974, Memorial Stadium, Austin, Texas, USA

Saw Bad Company at ZZ Top's first annual BBQ and barn dance. It turned out to be the only one! Also appearing were Joe Cocker and Santana and the whole thing was billed as Rockin' Good News and ZZ Top's Rompin' Stompin' BBQ and Barn Dance.

Five High School friends went in a 55 Ford truck with a camper on it. We all stayed at Hippie Hollow on Lake Travis the night before.

When we got inside the stadium, they wouldn't let us take in our cooler. And there was nothing to eat or drink! I lost track of my friends so I worked my way to the front. The stage was so high I missed Bad Company. The sound just blew right over my head. At one point the crowd went wild and someone in the crowd told me there were five guitar players up there. Found out later that most of the noise was for Jimmy Page, who guested.

It was so hot that day and I managed eventually to get away from the stage to wander in and out of the stadium. After the show we all met up at the truck and spent the night at a gas station. Next morning we iced down the cooler and enjoyed that case of cold beers all the way back to Arlington. Great weekend. Great time. Great way to start off my senior year of high school.

Vinny Holland

4 September 1974, Wollman Skating Rink, Central Park, New York City, USA

I saw Bad Company in Central Park, NY. It was outdoors and the weather was fine. I forget who I went with but I took the bus and subway down from Yonkers, where I grew up.

I didn't have a close position but did get a few nice shots. I was 19 and just starting my photography hobby, which would later become my career.

It was an awesome concert on its own merits but became a bigger event when Jimmy Page came out to jam for the encore. Bad Company had recently been signed by Led Zeppelin's new label.

'My favourite shots from that day back in 1974 in Central Park' - Vinny Holland

Chris Charlesworth

4 September 1974, Wollman Skating Rink, Central Park, New York City, USA

Chris Charlesworth's Melody Maker review of the Central Park gig incorporates an insightful and perfectly-timed interview with Paul Rodgers, as Bad Company top the US album chart three weeks later.

'MOOOOOVIN' ONNNN.' Paul Rodgers stabs forward towards the microphone to deliver the lines, pirouetting as he reaches the front of the stage and grabbing the stand like a weightlifter grabs his barbells. His left leg is a full three feet in front of his right, stretching the white leather pants to their fullest and his long black hair swishes about in the cool New York breeze.

Boz Burrell, in black leather, weaves round and drops to his knees to deliver his lines from the fretless bass guitar, rising and dropping in time with Simon

Kirke's drumbeat. Mick Ralphs, in a mock tigerskin top, just stands and slashes away at the Gibson.

'This,' says Bob Fripp, who isn't one to exaggerate, 'is the best rock 'n' roll I've heard in ages.'

Three gentlemen from Grand Funk watch in awe. And Jimmy Page, always quiet, taps a foot while big Peter Grant's face beams. Grant sure knows how to pick 'em, but Bad Company were a winner before they ever reached the drawing board.

I couldn't count the number of people who've said that Bad Company are due to be the next gigantic rock attraction from England: it's like placing a bet in a one-horse race.

At the time of writing, Bad Company's first album is high up in the charts and still rising. The folk from Swan Song hope it'll reach number one; if it does it will be the first time any group has reached the top spot with their first album since The Beatles. Bad Company is an explosive combination topped off with one of the best rock voices ever to come out of England. At last, it seems, Paul Rodgers is due for the recognition he deserves.

His voice is throaty enough to carry the meatiest rock numbers, yet sufficiently flexible to take on more mellow material. He swaggers with all the arrogant pose of Daltrey or Plant, pushing his chest forward and twitching his hips like a stallion, having mastered the art of the dominant male strut in his days with Free.

Paul Rodgers is exactly the right size for a rock singer: too big and you end up being a freak show like John Baldry, too fat and you resort to flashy clothes like Elton John. He's smallish and skinny, with not an ounce of extra flesh on him. He has a cheeky expression, a mischievous manner. He drinks plenty of brandy, smokes strong cigarettes.

He enjoys being bawdy, and would pitch into a fight without hesitation. Anti-establishment, he doesn't suffer fools at all.

All these qualities, peripheral to the music though they may be, greatly help.

Rodgers, born in Middlesbrough, still retains a faint north-eastern brogue. When he was 13 he first heard The Beatles so he persuaded his father to buy him a guitar, possession of which entitled him to a place in a group formed by a school classmate, Mick Moody, who is now with Snafu.

'I was in the band just because I was the only other kid in the class with a guitar. No other reason,' Paul explained in his New York hotel. 'We kept it up and Mick and I actually played together for a long time.

'We auditioned for drummers and the one we got had 'The Titans' written on his kit, so that's what we called ourselves. I think it must have been the group he was in before.

'Then we got a singer and guitar player called Colin Bradley, who was a lot more experienced than us, and that was my first band. I was actually playing bass. We earned ten quid a night and that was big time in those days.'

During this time Paul had two jobs — as a messenger boy for a local newspaper and as an assistant in a wallpaper shop. He didn't keep either very long.

The Titans, meanwhile, changed their name to The Road Runners, dropped Bradley, and ultimately decided to travel to London. In London they re-christened themselves the Wild Flowers and lived in poverty in a West Hampstead flat.

In 1967 the Wild Flowers broke up and Paul joined a London-based blues band, the Brown Sugar, where he met Paul Kossoff, future guitarist with Free.

'We were playing at the Fickle Pickle in Finsbury Park when he came up and had a blow with us. I stayed with him and the rest is pretty much history by now.'

Kossoff was actually playing in a band called Black Cat Bones, whose drummer was Simon Kirke. Mike Vernon introduced Andy Fraser to Kossoff and Alexis Korner christened them Free after their first rehearsal together at the Nag's Head in Battersea.

Korner, in fact, acted as a father figure to Free before they signed with Chris Blackwell to Island Records and put out their first album, *Tons Of Sobs*.

'The obvious highlight was 'All Right Now', but I think that shook us up a bit. It gave us more success than any of us could handle, even though we'd built up a big following in England before it came out. We had a great thing going up in the North, but the press seemed to ignore us.

'Then, all of a sudden, this record went bang! And we were all knocked for six. It even freaked the record company out 'cos they didn't know how to handle it. Suddenly we were on the front page of all the newspapers, but when the follow-up single didn't happen, it brought us down badly.

'My formula is to do exactly what I want to do regardless of whether or not it's successful, and this gives me the satisfaction of knowing that it was my work and no-one else's. With Bad Company everybody is doing what they want to do and enjoying it and that's coming over to the audience. It's obvious through the music.'

Paul's first venture on leaving Free behind was Peace, who toured Britain once with Mott the Hoople but never recorded an album. 'Yeah, I was about to change the world with Peace,' grinned Paul.

It was Paul's decision to pack up Peace, a decision that coincided with his growing friendship with Mick Ralphs.

Ralphs quit Mott but not before he settled his outstanding commitments with the band and helped them find a replacement. Simon Kirke was a natural choice for the drum-seat, but Boz was more difficult to find. Eighteen bass players were auditioned before they found him.

With Free, Paul had been managed by Island, but he decided the new group needed new management. He contacted Peter Grant - Led Zeppelin's manager - himself.

'I phoned a few people up and talked to them, but I thought to myself first, 'who is the best manager of the lot?' and decided on Peter Grant. He was very enthusiastic and we feel very privileged to be under his wing. He helped us find a bass player, actually, in the sense that he found us a place to rehearse and audition people.'

The current US tour, says Paul, has done wonders for the band. On many occasions they've had to open a show while the audiences are still filing into their seats, and even then they've managed to get an ovation of some kind. 'They've been lighting matches at the end of our set and that's really great for an opening band, so I'm told.

'We're into putting ourselves over exactly as we are. We're a very uncompromising band and we're all heading in exactly the same direction.

'We don't compromise to fashions and glitter and dressing up and all that which is happening now in England. In my opinion that style of band brings the whole tone of music down.

'It's always dangerous to slag off the BBC but I do feel they're partly to blame. They should have more programmes dealing with albums and playing good album tracks rather than all the same singles by all the same artists all the time, or golden oldies.

'When they start going back all the time it gives the impression that nothing is happening and that's really unhealthy.

'Over here in America it's just not like that. The reason why groups from England come over to America is not just the bread — it's the fact that you are able to do anything you want and get away with it.

'But in England you have to conform to some image to a certain extent if you want to get anywhere. We didn't because we're very uncompromising, but that's really why young bands can't get off the ground.

'And some of the kids in England seem to think that the more glitter you wear the better you are, and that's just not true. As far as I'm concerned you can go on wearing what you like, bathing suits even, and you'll do o.k., if you sound good.'

Bad Company will soon be in the studio at work on their second album.

'We're just bursting to record that album,' says Paul. 'We've been trying a few new songs on this tour just to break them in. I feel that when a song is new it sounds new. If we play them first on tour the songs will be fluid and loose rather than tight.

'What I like best is a tight rhythm section and a fluid guitar and vocals, and that doesn't come unless you play the song and know it well before you get into the studio.'

As far as Paul is concerned, Bad Company is IT — the big one he's been looking out for since he left Middlesbrough.

'I started to feel that way with Free at one stage till it all went a bit sour, but I never felt as positive as I do with Bad Company. It's a sense of belonging that we all have and it just feels good to play together. Hard to explain, really.

'Some nights we can be really serious and other nights really humorous. If an audience is serious to the point where we can't get through to them, we start getting really ridiculous.

'One night on this tour we couldn't move the audience, so Simon got off his drums and started to sing and I got on drums and we jammed like that. It broke the ice and then we could get down to playing properly.'

Back on stage in Central Park, Foghat's people are looking a little worried as Bad Company's set reaches the hour mark.

Obviously they'll do an encore — actually it was 'The Stealer' — but none of the crowd were prepared for Jimmy Page to go up and join them.

Dapper Bob Fripp, still standing at the side of the stage, beamed at the sight. He isn't one to lightly pay compliment. 'Yes, definitely the best rock 'n' roll I've heard in ages,' he repeated as Page tore into a solo, playing faster than Ralph's previous break.

In the caravan backstage, a TV crew were setting up their apparatus to make a film of Bad Company for a news programme. That's another compliment.

Barry Morris

18 September 1974, The Rainbow Theatre, Finsbury Park, North London, UK

I hadn't seen Paul Rodgers for a few years because of Free splitting, Bad Company were starting to ride high and they were playing at the Rainbow Theatre in North London. I used to earn a bit of extra money there working on security. I was put by the stage and told to stop people climbing across the orchestra pit and getting onto the stage.

As soon as Bad Company started I couldn't stop myself and jumped on stage doing my air guitar thing, I got hauled off by security and fired on the spot.

I've followed Paul Rodgers all my life, I reckon I've seen him around 50 times, I've never ever seen him give a bad performance, he's a big hero of mine.

Bad Company played the Rainbow three times during 1974 (11 April, 18 September and 18/19 December). The last of the four appearances saw them joined on stage by Swan Song record label mates Jimmy Page and John Paul Jones.

Chris Charlesworth

September 1974, Clearwell Castle, Gloucestershire, UK

Mick Ralphs, clad in blue jeans, tee-shirts with Texas written on the front and dirty white fur-lined coat, hovers around a frying pan in the Baronial kitchen giving maximum attention to preparing a late breakfast of bacon and eggs. 'Paul [Rodgers] likes beans,' he says. 'We had a long discussion the other night on the merits of beans on toast for breakfast. And I love a strong cup of tea. Can't do without it.'

It was the tenth day of Bad Company's residence in this 17th century castle in the Forest of Dean. The previous day Paul Rodgers, Simon Kirke and Boz Burrell, the other three-quarters of Bad Company, packed their bags and left Mick to fend for himself. Rodgers and Boz made for London while Kirke decided to spend a few days with his mum in Bristol.

It has been ten days of fruitful activity for the group.

They've cut 13 tracks as possibles for the next album and rehearsed a two-hour set for their upcoming British tour. Using Ronnie Lane's mobile studio, they cut the tracks in two rooms of the castle while the engineers sat in the truck parked outside the front door.

Closed circuit television kept the musicians in touch with the control booth, and a plentiful supply of mead served at the weekly Clearwater banquets oiled their throats and kept spirits high.

This retreat is much in demand with rock musicians. Deep Purple pioneered the Castle last year, Hawkwind have been in and out, and Peter Frampton is set for a three-week stay next month.

Though the groups use private rooms within the building, the public areas are thronged with tourists and on Saturday night a medieval banquet takes place in the main hall, complete with serving wenches, minstrels, a court jester and page boys.

'It was very odd,' says Mick. 'There we were down stairs playing rock 'n' roll and each time we wanted to listen to a playback we had to pass all these people at the banquet.

'We had to walk through the dining hall to get to the mobile parked outside. Dunno what they must have thought about us.'

Bad Company's first album was recorded in similar circumstances in Hampshire at a country house with a mobile unit. The band feel that this method re-creates the atmosphere of being on the road all living together, and as they regard themselves as essentially a live unit, this is reflected in the records.

A tour of the grounds revealed an ancient device for crushing apples to brew cider, a penny farthing bicycle and a souped-up Ford Mustang, the property of Mr. Ralphs, who is very familiar with the local countryside, having been brought up in Hereford.

Mick wanted to catch the nearest bank before it closed, so we rumbled off in the Mustang surprising more than a few local villagers with both the noise and elaborate paintwork. Coleford, the nearest town to Clearwell, turned out to be the venue of an historic early Mott the Hoople gig which Mick recalled as we cruised the country lanes.

'I remember Verden Allen, who used to be our organist, getting into a fight with a bunch of local yobs and Ian Hunter crashing down into the audience and hitting them with the mic stand. I was terrified. We escaped in a borrowed Austin van which we used at the time.

'We spent all our early days playing around towns like this. They're beautiful to come back to after a tour of America.'

Monmouth was a few miles to the east, so we drove over to allow Mick to call in at the Rockfield studios, on the outskirts of the town. A few old friends were greeted before we set off once again for the return to Clearwell Castle.

'Loads of musicians come from around this area, including myself,' said Mick. 'And the focal point for everyone is Rockfield. We wanted a steel guitar the other night for recording and one of our roadies found one at Rockfield. I think it belonged to Dave Edmunds. I like to call in now and again for old times' sake.'

Back at the castle a coach party had arrived and three elderly women stood in the drive as Mick roared through in the Mustang. The remaining roadies had almost finished packing away the cables some of which were strewn across the lawn at the front of the building.

As the elderly tourists mused around the collection of antiques, Mick took a last look at the recording room before setting off to London. Once again the Castle was restored to peace and rock-free solitude as its original owner intended several hundred years ago.

David Tangye 1974

I remember Bad Company left a bass drum skin at Clearwell Castle with the band name on it. They were in there before us. I was there when I worked with Necromandus, who were managed by Tony Iommi at the time. I wished I'd picked that drum skin up! Also, there was a story going around that Peter Grant had threatened the road crew, if they went on strike and, as such, they would face dire consequences. He wasn't a guy to be messed with either! *David Tangye was the former Personal Assistant to Ozzy Osbourne*

Gary Rossington

(Lynyrd Skynyrd)

To me, Bad Company is one of the best bands ever. As for what makes Bad Company so special, it comes down to the whole energy within the band. They were just so good and they have so many classic songs, from 'Can't Get Enough' to 'Shooting Star' to 'Seagull.'

The members of Skynyrd – me, Ronnie (Van Zant) and Allen Collins – visited the studio when Bad Company was recording 'Shooting Star' and it made us cry. They explained that the lyrics were kind of about Paul Kossoff who was the lead guitarist in Free. It was a really touching song. We were there when Mick Ralphs played the guitar solo on that song and we were cheering him on. Then afterwards, we went outside to Paul's car and there were a bunch of original Ray Charles albums in his trunk. We spoke about how Ray Charles was such a big influence on both him and Ronnie (Van Zant).

We liked the band so much that we named a boat that Ronnie and I owned 'Bad Company' because that was a cool name for people fishing for bass, plus it was a nod to a great band that we loved. In fact, we played a few shows with Bad Company in the '70s. At the time, we were having a lot of fun together after the shows, too. Those were crazy times. We were fans of each other and cheered each other on.

Peter Smith

30 November 1974, City Hall, Newcastle-upon-Tyne, UK

Bad Company returned to Newcastle City Hall eight months after their triumphant debut. In the months between, my mate John and I had seen them at The Who's Charlton concert where they performed a strong set. In between the two gigs Bad Company had released their first album, with the hit single 'Can't Get Enough' and classics such as 'Ready for Love', 'Bad Company' and 'Movin' On', all of which featured in the set back then. Surprisingly, later concert favourite, the beautiful 'Seagull', does not seem to feature in setlists of the time. 'Ready For Love' was what I enjoyed hearing most. I first heard it on the John Peel show as a Mott the Hoople track, and it stuck in my mind from that time.

Support for the tour was Duster Bennett who was a one-man-band who played a bass drum with his foot, a harmonica on a rack around his neck and a 1952 Les Paul Goldtop guitar which had apparently been given to him by Peter Green. He is best known for his first album *Smiling Like I'm Happy*.

A recording of this Newcastle concert exists which suggests that the setlist was: 'Little Miss Fortune', 'Rock Steady', 'Ready For Love', 'Don't Let Me Down', 'Easy On My Soul', 'Bad Company', 'Deal with the Preacher', 'Movin' On', 'Can't Get Enough', 'The Stealer' and 'Rock Me Baby'.

My memories are of another great gig by a band who were at the top of their game.

Chris Charlesworth

7 December 1974, City Hall, Newcastle-upon-Tyne, UK

Reporting for Melody Maker, Chris Charlesworth takes in the second of two Newcastle gigs

Bad Company were big before they were born. Any band that included Paul Rodgers in its ranks and a bassist with the talents of Boz Burrell just couldn't fail, so Bad Company shook the US during the summer and are now back to shake England and Scotland on their second ever UK tour.

They opened at Ipswich last Thursday, and followed that up with a couple of shows at Newcastle City Hall on Friday and Saturday. I caught the Saturday night's show but, curiously enough, didn't enjoy that as much as a euphoric night in New York's Central Park this summer when the BC's potential was so fully realised. Perhaps it was because Jimmy Page joined them on this occasion that the Newcastle concert didn't gel quite so much for me.

A girl on my right thought they were wonderful and a guy on my left thought they weren't a patch on Free. 'It's *Fire and Water* over and over again,' he muttered as Bad Company went through their paces. He was in a minority as the audience greeted Rodgers and his band like old friends – as indeed they are. Paul hails from Middlesbrough and the North East has always made him specially welcome.

It took the band about half a set to move into the top gear they are capable of and it wasn't until Rodgers streamed into 'Can't Get Enough' that things really cooked. That number, and the two encores 'Movin' On' and 'Stealer' were absolute gems, displaying just how good Bad Company can be as a tight, funky unit.

Perhaps the shaky start was due to this being only their third gig on the tour, or perhaps it was because the PA system didn't seem to be working as effectively as it might have done. There were many times when Paul's vocals were lost in the mix, and, of course, Rodgers' singing is really the high point of the band. There are few British rock singers who give off half as much feeling as he does.

The band played three new songs which will doubtless be on their next album. The most impressive was 'Shooting Star', a song about an aspiring rock singer which is bound to become a BC standard. Mick Ralphs' song 'Good Loving Gone Bad' was an up-tempo rocker, while 'The Preacher', the third new piece, is a grinding jerker in the old Free tradition.

The rest of the material came from their first album, and Rodgers switches from guitar to piano throughout. At one point the rest of the band left him on stage alone with an acoustic 12-string to play 'Seagull', not previously aired live. It breaks up the show nicely.

But for my money, Rodgers is at his best without an instrument other than the microphone. He can deliver a song better without frills, stomping and strutting like a proud and arrogant peacock. It's these qualities that have always singled him out from the rank and file.

While Simon Kirke is a competent, hard drummer, the blast from the rhythm comes from Boz whose bass playing reminds me of the relaxed funk of a black soul player. He squats over his gigantic fretless instrument like a man sorely in need of a visit to the restroom, swooping and diving down to ripple out a run that underlines the drive of Rodgers and Mick Ralphs. It seems incomprehensible that Bob Fripp, master of technique, should have produced a bassist with such feeling.

Two encores later the crowd were still yelling for more. They didn't get it, but they couldn't complain. The latter half of the show made up for the shaky beginning and I think that'll have disappeared by now anyway.

1975

Simon Kirke

The main difference musically between Free and Bad Company? I think there was a maturity between the four of us that we didn't have in Free. Boz was coming from more of a jazz background, Mick was a much more rock 'n' roll guitarist - much more loose and cheerful. Ironically, we were a lot more free in Bad Company because we were not bogged down with drinking and drugs. Unfortunately that would come several years later...

Po Powell

1975, Horselunges Manor, East Sussex, UK

Peter Grant called me again for the *Straight Shooter* album cover. By this time I'd developed a good relationship with the band. I'd been on tour with them, photographed them, hung out with them. I really enjoyed their company. It was all about having a laugh. The relationship between Paul and Boz hadn't got uncomfortable at that point. We'd go to the gig, go to a club, have a few drinks, pull a few birds and then go back to the hotel. There was a lot of laughter and a lot of fun.

I remember thinking that Peter Grant's interpretation of Good Company / Bad Company was really good. They were great company to hang out with. They all had a great sense of humour and Paul Rodgers is smart; he's a really sharp guy.

The album cover was two large tumbling big red dice. I did a drawing of the thing and showed it to Peter then the band and that was fine. Then we shot the band at a craps table in a casino in South Kensington and we used that for all the advertising.

Again – I didn't want to go for the obvious and nor did the band. 'Straight Shooter' and you immediately think cowboy images and I just didn't want to go down that route. Already bands like Crosby, Stills, Nash & Young were already adopting that cowboy boot wearing gunslinger kind of image. And I didn't want Bad Company to disappear into that whole cowboy Southern rock thing. There were a myriad of bands doing that.

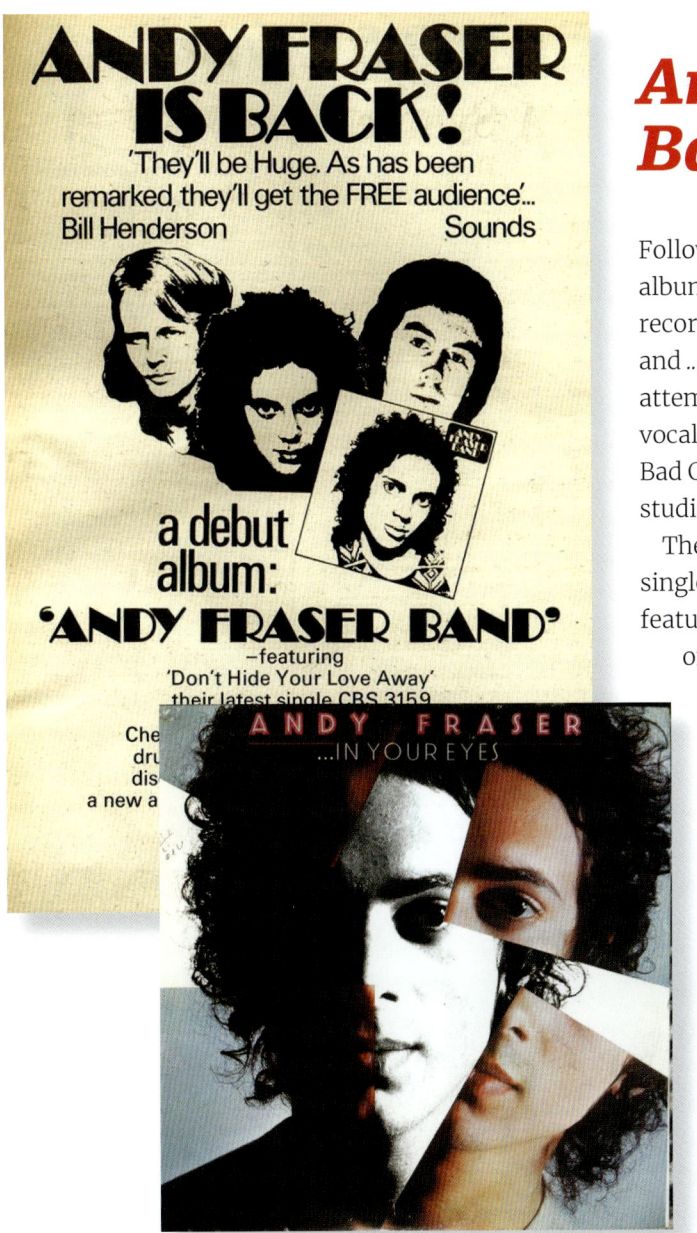

Andy Fraser Band

Following the demise of Sharks, after two albums were released in 1973, Andy Fraser recorded two albums in 1975, *Andy Fraser Band* and *...In Your Eyes*. The 'band' album was an attempt to push himself forward more as a vocalist and with a distinct lack of guitar. Just as Bad Company had done, Andy used the mobile studio arrangement provided by Ronnie Lane.

The nine-track album, which included the single release 'Don't Hide Your Love Away' featured Kim Turner on drums and Nick Judd on keyboards.

'I try to get a very basic root for every song. Two or three words should sum up every song and that should always finish it off. That's what it's all about. You will note that this applies with particular force to 'All Right Now''.

Peter Smith

After leaving Free, Andy Fraser formed Sharks along with vocalist Snips [real name Steve Parsons] and guitarist Chris Spedding. He wasn't with Sharks long.

I saw Sharks in concert when they played Sunderland Locarno, but it was after Fraser had left the band. Sharks were a great live band, and Snips is a very under-rated singer. Snips and Chris re-emerged as King Mob, who looked great, but were short-lived.

Andy next formed the Andy Fraser Band, a trio with Kim Turner and Nick Judd. I saw the band once at a gig in Sunderland Locarno; Andy took the front man role, but the lack of a guitarist seemed strange and didn't work for me. The gig was poorly attended and I never saw the band again, although I do recall them playing Newcastle City Hall around the same time.

Paul Kossoff

I sat pretty low for a couple of years, it came to a point where I had to do something, and I wasn't too confident about it. I was staying with my manager at the time, and he also handled John Martyn, and John asked me if I'd like to do a few songs with him at the end of each of his sets on his tour. I said yes, but I was frightened of getting back up there; it turned out to be exactly the tonic I needed at that time.

Peter Smith

I saw Paul Kossoff play at Sunderland Locarno a couple of times. I think that one of these gigs was billed as The Paul Kossoff Band, and the other as the more familiar name of Back Street Crawler. The gigs I saw in 1974 and 1975 featured local singer Terry Wilson-Slesser from Beckett. Although it was great to see Kossoff in action again, and some of the old guitar magic was still there, it was also clear that his health was not good.

Joe Frisco

26 May, The Spectrum, Philadelphia, Pennsylvania, USA

Bad Company and Foghat was my first concert as a youngster in the 1970s. They played at what now is no longer around, The Spectrum in Philadelphia. It was when smoking was permitted and everyone had lighters for the encore. Think it was the *Straight Shooter* tour, and a time that will never be forgotten.

Bad Company's Artillery Is Heavy Metal

By HUGH CUTLER

Straight Shooter

Hot on the heels of its successful predecessor, *Straight Shooter* confirmed Bad Company's reputation as FM radio favourites. The band's second album contained two power rock break-out singles: 'Good Lovin' Gone Bad' and 'Feel Like Makin' Love'. The 2 April release was also notable for the enduring Paul Rodgers-penned 'Shooting Star' and the first two Bad Company tracks written by Simon Kirke: 'Weep No More' and 'Anna'.

Although the album's popularity was shared equally in the UK and US, peaking at No.3 on both sides of the Atlantic, the singles fared better in the US where the band toured.

Mick Ralphs

Straight Shooter is definitely my favourite album. Big, roaring songs, again all done more or less live. We'd just come off the road and we were still on fire.

Paul Rodgers

'Shooting Star' is the first song that I've written that has a definite story (of a boy who rockets to rock stardom and who eventually dies a rock star death with a bottle of whisky and box of pills by his bedside). It just came to me one night, so I started singing it. I sang the first half and I thought to myself, 'Well it's very weird to include The Beatles in lyrics.' The first line is 'Johnny was a schoolboy when he heard his first Beatles song'. I thought about it, thinking everybody's heard of The Beatles, and has been affected by The Beatles, so I left the line in and just continued with the song.

Side Two

Deal with the Preacher
Wild Fire Woman
Anna
Call on Me

Recorded on Ronnie Lane's Mobile at Clearwell Castle Gloucestershire England September 1974

Mixed at Air Studios London
Cut at The Mastering Lab Los Angeles
Recorded and Mixed by RON NEVISON

Strings on Weep No More by Jimmy Horowitz
Sleeve by Hipgnosis
Special Thanks to Peter Grant
Produced by Bad Company

Paul Kossoff

After Free split up, I never really met anybody that I played with that I got off with, you know what I mean, where something happened, but I remember playing with Terry [Slesser] and him telling me about this bass player and drummer. They were friends of John Bundrick from Texas, and I got to know them through him.

They've been doing sessions for Island for some time and I approached them, asked them if they'd be interested in doing a tour and maybe an album. But as it's turned out we've just stuck together. I wanted a good, hard, tight rhythm section which I found in Terry and Tony, that's Terry Wilson and Tony Braunagel who are Texans, and are very soul-orientated but with a great deal of experience with blues, which is what I play – whether it be traditional or modern.

I remember having played with them in a basement in London, and it was really good, you know, sparks flew, and I remembered it so when it came time to time to think about getting a band together, I called them up and asked them if they fancied doing it. They said yeah, you know, they had been listeners to Free and myself for a long time, and they were really into the idea of doing it. It was all fairly quick; we rehearsed a total of maybe two months, went on a short tour of England, then went in the studio and made the album over a two-month period.

Chris Spencer

15 June 1975, Fairfield Halls, Croydon, UK

I saw Back Street Crawler at Croydon Fairfield Halls, which was recorded for the live album and turned out to be my last ever Kossoff gig. The venue was near my cousin's house. He had bought the tickets - it was my 16th birthday, so I was very pleased that I got served at the bar!

Koss had shorter hair and looked a little overweight. I thought the band was brilliant but my cousin later said Free were miles better live.

We later booked tickets to Guildford Free Arts Festival in 1976. We heard Koss had died on a plane flying to New York. In his memory, I got a Kossoff tattoo 'R.I.P.' that week.

The only free member I didn't see was Andy Fraser, which is a shame. Great live gigs and happy days.

The Band Plays On

Signed to Atlantic Records by Ahmet Ertegun, the Anglo-American line-up comprised: Paul Kossoff (guitar), Mike Montgomery (keyboards), Tony Braunagel (drums), Terry Wilson (bass) and Terry Slesser (vocals). The band completed a nine-date UK tour in May and June 1975, then finished their debut album, *The Band Plays On*, which was released 1 September 1975, on the back of a massive publicity campaign. An extensive tour was announced to coincide with this release, but Kossoff was taken ill with a stomach ulcer and the tour was cancelled. Whilst at the clinic, Kossoff's condition worsened and he was taken to a hospital where he went into cardiac arrest and actually 'died' for 35 minutes.

After a month of recovery, Kossoff made an appearance on the UK TV Show *The Old Grey Whistle Test* in October 1975 and four new dates - Liverpool, Glasgow, Newcastle and London - were arranged for November.

Mike Green

I'd just finished touring with Grimms and I was at home in Hull when I got a phone call offering me a job with Koss. It involved looking after him on a day to day basis and tour managing his band, Back Street Crawler, when they were

ROCK 'N' ROLL FANTASY

1976

Run with the Pack

Released on 21 February, Bad Company's third studio album *Run with the Pack* had been recorded in France during September 1975, this time utilising the Rolling Stones' Mobile Truck. Engineered by Ron Nevison, the record was then mixed in Los Angeles by Eddie Kramer.

On this occasion, the cover was designed by Kosh, the former art director for Apple Records and designer on Abbey Road and for many of The Beatles' solo projects.

Run with the Pack became another huge hit album, rising to No.4 UK and No.5 US, racking up more than four million sales to date.

While the album songwriting credits were again shared equally between Paul Rodgers and Mick Ralphs, it is the band's cover of a Jerry Leiber, Mike Stoller, Doc Pomus composition that became the hit single: 'Young Blood' hit No. 20 on the *Billboard* Hot 100.

FM rock radio sees to it that *Run with the Pack* gets plenty of airplay with 'Silver, Blue & Gold', 'Live for the Music' and the title track on heavy rotation.

'Bad Company could well have taken an easy way out – they're that successful now – but instead they have risen to the occasion. For Rodgers, Ralphs, Kirke and Burrell, *Run with the Pack* should be a standard to match for some time to come.' says *Rolling Stone* magazine

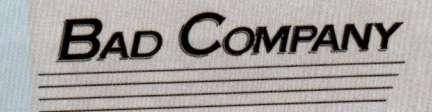

Joe Elliott (Def Leppard)

Bad Company was just a phenomenal outfit. They were tight. They were succinct. There wasn't much fat on them. Bad Company was blues influenced but they weren't a blues band in the sense of B.B. King or Joe Bonamassa. They were playing classic rock music with their feet firmly planted in the blues.

As a kid growing up, when you get over the initial hurt of two of your favorite bands splitting up — Free and Mott the Hoople — but elements of those two bands join forces and create a new group called Bad Company, then you've got the best of both worlds. There was this Zeppelin connection to them so you knew this was something special.

Their first album is genius — 'Can't Get Enough' became a huge hit and helped them crack the States. But for me, my favorite Bad Company album by a country mile is *Run with the Pack*. It was the first album by Bad Company that I bought. Mick Ralphs is such an understated guitarist. Back in the '70s, the licks he played on 'Good Lovin' Gone Bad' and so many others was incredible. Simon Kirke is the drummer who proves the point that you only need four drums. His drumming on things like 'Run with the Pack,' 'Silver, Blue and Gold' and 'Sweet Lil' Sister' is just superb. And no doubt about it, Paul Rodgers is the best white rock blues singer of all time. There's nobody that can touch him. You can hear Aretha Franklin and Otis Redding, all that classic R&B, soul and Stax in Paul's singing. Even though I don't sound like Paul Rodgers, he's one of the reasons I became a singer. I have massive admiration for him and I'm in awe of the way he's kept his voice; the guy still sounds like he did when he was 18!

Jim Meyer

I was 15 and had just entered high school. I was trying to fit in and a kid who was my brother's age (two years older) had me back to his house after school. He played *Run with the Pack* and I was forever a Bad Company fan. I went and bought the older stuff but this is still my favourite. It just takes me back.

Back Street Crawler tour

Prior to a US tour at the start of 1976, Mike Montgomery was replaced by ex-Free keyboard player John 'Rabbit' Bundrick. However, once again, Kossoff's ill health meant too many shows were cancelled or postponed. Recording of the follow-up album *2nd Street* took place whilst the band were in Los Angeles, but much of the guitar playing was the work of 'Snuffy' Walden. A few gigs in February 1976 also featured Walden, with Kossoff standing in as the MC.

Tony Merger

February 1976, New Jersey, USA

I saw Back Street Crawler in New Jersey in February 1976. They played two shows and I went to both and I got to meet Koss after the second show. He was very quiet but liked that I had a copy of *The Free Story* LP with me, that he signed. I told him I'd followed his career, and I thought he was a great guitar player. He was very grateful, and allowed me to take a picture. Something I'll never forget. He was one of my idols. Sadly, he died three weeks later. I did not pick up my guitar for a month. He was a great guitarist, and is missed.

Paul Kossoff

I think my sound, especially my vibrato, has taken a long time to sound mature, and it's taken a long time to reach the speed of vibrato that I now have. I trill with my first, middle, and ring fingers and bend chiefly with my small finger. I'll use my index finger when I'm using vibrato. I like to move people; I don't like to show off. I like to make sounds as I remember sounds that move me. My style is very primitive but at the same time it has developed in its own sense. I do my best to express myself and move people at the same time.

Richard Digby Smith

March 1976, Atlantic recording studios, Broadway, NYC, and Los Angeles, California, USA

In 1976 I recorded an album with Paul Kossoff's band Back Street Crawler with sessions in L.A. and New York. This was to be that band's second album, entitled *2nd Street*.

Paul was in a pretty bad way. John Glover, the band's manager, had put me and Paul in the same New York hotel room; John's logic being that if anyone could keep an eye on Paul it would be me! But I was in no position to mentor and one evening Paul went off out into the Manhattan nightlife, returning in the wee hours with an entourage of adoring hangers-on. I was abruptly awoken and snapped at Paul to get rid of these people and get some sleep, as we were due in the studio the next morning, early. And not just any old studio.

Most of the New York sessions were at Atlantic's famous recording studios on Broadway.

Back in Los Angeles there were only a few guitar overdubs left to complete the recordings before the tapes were to be shipped back to London for the producer Glyn Johns to mix. I was left alone in the studio with Paul on the last night and we worked into the early hours nailing the last bits of guitar. Paul with one headphone on, one off, listening to me sat at the piano, shouting out the chord changes as they arrived. It was painful and slow. Paul was very stoned and could hardly stand. It was almost too much to take, watching and listening to the sluggish inept fingering on the frets, struggling to make the changes. Note by agonising note, we completed the task, unplugged his guitar, switched off the amp and put the tapes away. I said goodbye to the assistant engineer, who had fallen asleep many hours earlier! This was to be the last time. The last session. The last overdub. The last notes.

Paul, John, Glover and Rabbit all flew back to London. I arrived back at my Hollywood apartment in the early hours of Saturday morning. Later that day the phone rang. It was Rabbit. Had I heard the news? Kossoff was dead. He had died on the plane.

What a sorrowful end. So sad for his family. So young. So gifted.

Andy Fraser

Koss lost confidence, when he was spoken about in terms of Hendrix or Clapton he was all feel, when he played those solos he cried every single note. If you were on stage you could actually hear him singing out of tune, his guitar did the singing. When it came to chords, that was really a big problem for him. Their first idea, before I came along, was to perform a Rod Stewart kind of thing, and I came in and said change gear, we're gonna do some songs. I think that was hardest on Koss, and when me and Paul started going in different directions, Koss was stuck in the middle with nowhere to go, and we were his only support. When that was no longer the case, he was unsupported and he didn't feel worthy of the Hendrix compliments. Once the drugs had sort of got a hold of him, he would rather be seen on stage as not playing well because he's drugged up out of his mind, rather than not being very good which is what he feared was the truth. It's a very mixed up kind of mind-bender, but I think that's what happened.

Paul Kossoff (1950-1976)

Paul Kossoff died on a flight from Los Angeles to New York on 19 March 1976 from a pulmonary embolism after a blood clot in his leg moved to his lung, while touring America with Back Street Crawler.

His body was returned to England and cremated at Golders Green Crematorium in North West London. His epitaph in the Summerhouse there reads: 'All Right Now'.

In the wake of his death, a 16-track career retrospective titled *Koss* was issued in 1977. Subsequently, several British Kossoff releases were issued in the 80s. The late 90s saw a renewed interest in Kossoff and another career retrospective was issued, 1997's 14-track *Blue Blue Soul*, as well as five-disc Free box set *Songs of Yesterday*.

David Kossoff

You rest in a peaceful place, my son.
In a summerhouse, near quiet pools,
with shady trees, and roses.
It's not quite you, but neither would
most other last resting places be.
Not much to see; an oaken strip
with carved lettering picked out in black and gold. Most elegant.
Not much to read; your name, your
opening and closing dates, and the
title of your million-seller,
'All Right Now'.

Extract from 'Words for Paul' from David Kossoff's 'You Have a Minute, Lord?'

Derek Carter

I didn't attend Paul Kossoff's funeral in 1976. I was unfortunately away on tour at the time working with Babe Ruth as a roadie. Paul and I had met a few times when we both lived in the Notting Hill area, during 1974/75, but he was never the man I knew. Those were the last times I saw Paul alive. The drugs had taken their toll and it was heartbreaking to see my friend reduced to such a level, he was basically apathetic, the spark was gone. However, on rare moments, his warm loving self showed through.

I later laid flowers for him where his ashes lay close to those of my parents' at Golders Green Crematorium. RIP Paul.

Laurence Tressler

In March 1976 I was on my way to school and passed the local newsagent. Once a week I used to call in to pick up the *New Musical Express*, which was by then an essential read for me. I bought a copy and gazed at the front page to see if any bands were announcing tours and there was the headline – 'Kossoff Dead', with the added details that on a flight from Los Angeles to New York City on 19 March 1976, Paul Kossoff had died from a pulmonary embolism at the age of only 25.

Sadly, the legendary guitarist from Free had died before I had properly learned to appreciate him. It was my love of Bad Company that prompted me to eventually explore the Free catalogue. But I always felt that it happened too late.

Neil Watson

A really strong memory: it was 1976. I was stacking shelves in Tesco and listening to BBC Radio 1 at lunchtime as I usually did. Alexis Korner was on, talking about Paul Kossoff, who I believe had just died. He talked so lovingly about Paul and Free who he'd helped to mentor, back in the very early days of their career.

Jane Fascione

To me Paul Kossoff was one of the best guitarists. I became a fan of Free through my older brother who introduced me to loads of different bands. I never got to see Free live unfortunately. My brother is 10 years older than me and was always playing rock music and that's how I got interested, around the age of 12. I'm 55 now and totally obsessed with music!

I remember watching a documentary by David Kossoff about his son Paul and I was very moved by it even at such a young age. I've also recently read some poetry by David Kossoff and the poem he wrote about his son made me cry. I work as a respite carer and read the book whilst visiting one of our Jewish clients. He asked me if I would read some poetry to him and it, coincidentally, was the David Kossoff book. The book was called *'You have a Minute, Lord?'* I just remember feeling really moved by it. I think I would have been moved whoever it was, a father's son dying so tragically, but the fact it was Paul moved me to tears.

Russell Elliott

I first heard them when 'All Right Now' came out. Bought *Free Live* a few years later. Always been a massive fan and love their music - favourites are the first three, in particular, *Tons of Sobs* and *Fire and Water*.

I got to know someone whose son ran away from home around the same time and crashed with Simon Kirke for a short time. Later, I had the chance to ask him about this and it was interesting to hear how they took care of him (he was about 15).

I was very friendly with Mitt's Mother, Pam as she was my Art and English teacher at school in the early to mid-seventies and she and I talked a lot about music. She was in her mid-50s by then and I was in my mid-teens. I guess that she saw something of Mitt in me as I was a bit lost at the time. I remember her telling me about how she got to know the band quite well and, in particular, Simon Kirke.

I recall bumping into her at school and asking her if she had heard about Paul Kossoff dying. She was visibly upset and shaken to hear the awful news of his passing.

Pol Morgan

My mum died when I was five and I went to live with my aunt and uncle and my cousin Ramie who was ten years older and played guitar. He taught me that Koss was the greatest guitarist ever to live and the best guitar was the 59 Standard, like Paul's blonde one. I still only play blonde Les Paul. I used to live in LA and knew Les Paul's guitar tech, who gave me Les's cell number. But I never called it… too shy!

Anyway I first listened to *Tons of Sobs* at that age and was hooked. I loved Koss's look - I am a little guy too. He was my hero then but now all these years later, he's *still* my Hero, a great player and a great man. RIP Koss.

Kevin Gorman

I was playing over a refuse commercial waste tip in Poyle near Slough, Berkshire, as a 13-year-old in 1976 and came across a box of dumped records half buried in the mud and dug it up. There were about 20 *Free Live!* albums in it.

I took them home and played a copy, it blew me away. The only track I recognised was 'All Right Now'. That's all, I loved it. Loved the band ever since and they are still my favourite to this day.

I run a fan page now on Facebook. I have become friends with the band's children too over the years. I was invited to the Andy Fraser memorial in the States but I had just come out of Wexham Park Hospital after a stroke. It was while bored there in hospital I started the fan page and have over 1000 members, specialising in photos of the band. Paul sent me a well wishes note while I was in hospital and signed the band's artwork.

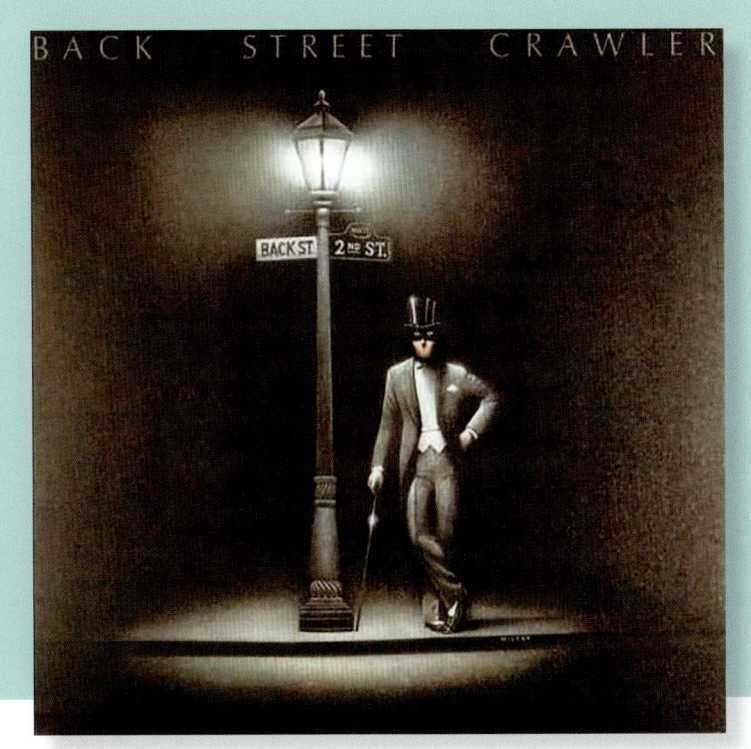

2nd Street

Generally accepted as a better crafted album than its predecessor, and dedicated to Paul Kossoff, Back Street Crawler's *2nd Street* was released in April 1976. It's another classic blues rock 'n' roll album and is the second of four by a band that still managed to keep a devoted fan base after the death of Paul Kossoff, changing management and their name to Crawler.

Scott Norris

2 April 1976, Coliseum, Charlotte, North Carolina, USA

I finally got to see Bad Company live in 1976. But my story begins many years earlier. I remember hearing a song on the radio with a really good groove called 'All Right Now' in 1970 when I was 12-years-old. I never thought much about who the singer was, until four years later, when a band called Bad Company released their first album. I remember listening to 'Can't Get Enough', 'Bad Company', 'Movin' On', and 'Rock Steady' on our local FM station, and thinking, 'this guy sounds like that 'All Right Now' dude. In those days, I was regularly reading a rock magazine called *Circus*, and there was an article about the newly formed band, Bad Company, mentioning that the singer, Paul Rodgers, had been the lead vocalist for Free. As I read a little further, it mentioned that Simon Kirke was the drummer for Free before he and Paul Rodgers teamed up to form Bad Company, who were signed to Led Zeppelin's Swan Song record label. I've been a fan of the band for 46 years, and to this day, their sound is just as fresh and relevant today, as it was when it was released.

At the time of the story, I was living in a small town, Kings Mountain, NC, which is about a half hour drive from Charlotte. The radio station in those days was WROQ 'The Rock' in Charlotte. The closest record store was Ja-Jo's Records in nearby Gastonia. That's where I bought all my albums (no singles).

During my senior year in high school, I saw Bad Company with Kansas in Charlotte on April 2, 1976 in support of *Run with the Pack*, which they had released a month or so earlier.

Vinnie Evanko

5 April 1976, Madison Square Garden, New York City, USA

Madison Square Garden was my first Bad Company gig but I'd earlier discovered them simply from the radio at home in Stamford, Connecticut, when the debut album came out. I heard 'Can't Get Enough' and I was hooked. I bought that album and it quickly became my favourite. I was just getting into good music and discovering FM radio so I was kind of a blank slate but quickly discovered my musical identity.

As for video, of course I saw the *Don Kirschner's Rock Concert* footage but I also remember another TV appearance which I believe was on ABC's *In Concert*. It looked like maybe a promotional video but they played all my favourite tracks off the debut album.

I never met the band, but my first concert was 1976 on the *Run with the Pack* tour at New York's Madison Square Garden, with Kansas as the opening act. This was a terrific show and my absolute favourite part was Simon Kirke's short drum solo - and note that I am not always a fan of drum solos. With all the lights down except the light on Simon, suddenly the lights burst on and Mick Ralphs is ripping through the opening riff of 'Rock Steady'. It was a goosebumps moment, forever etched in my memory.

A side note, and a sad note for me, was coming home and having my mom washing my concert shirt. After one wash just about all the design was gone.

Jumping ahead 33 years to the last time I saw Bad Company live... This time it was at Chastain Park in Atlanta, Georgia, with the Doobie Brothers opening. On this occasion, instead of going to the show with my teenage buddies I went with my 19-year-old son. I think he loved the show as much as I did. We both bought t-shirts and this time I bought a baseball cap too, which I figured would last longer than the t-shirt. It's been eleven years and my Bad Company concert shirt is still holding out and I just wore it a couple of days ago. I still wear the cap too.

Bad Company, Paul Rodgers, Free and a couple of Paul Kossoff's Back Street Crawler albums, are a huge part of my life and all still in regular listening rotation.

Janowsky

I saw Bad Company at Madison Square Garden on the *Straight Shooter* and *Run with the Pack* tours. Incredible shows. Many years later I was lucky enough to interview Simon Kirke with my co-host Paul Curcio for 90.3 FM Kingsborough Community College radio station. He couldn't have been more interesting or nicer. He played a couple of songs for us on acoustic guitar. After that he arranged for two guest passes to see him perform at Joe's Pub in NYC the next night. He gave us a table right near the stage and spoke to my wife and I after the show. I will never forget it!

Marshall I. Schwartzman

5 April 1976, Madison Square Garden, New York City, USA

I was living at the time in northern New Jersey, just outside Manhattan in a town called Fort Lee. I was a Bad Company fan from the very first album, but it wasn't until 1976 - when I was just 13-years-old, that I finally got to see them at Madison Square Garden. My friend Doug and I had nosebleed seats in the upper deck to the right of the stage. It was my first real concert. I distinctly remember they opened with 'Live For the Music,' and when they came on stage, it was like the gods had descended from Olympus.

My recollection of the rest of the concert is rather hazy for reasons you might guess, but if memory serves me correctly, they also played 'The Stealer' (the only Free song they performed that night), an extended version of 'Movin' On' with a jam in the middle, and a rousing rendition of the song 'Bad Company' with Paul Rodgers front-and-center on a black electric piano that he kicked over at the end. Still gives me chills to think about it.

Simon Kirke

So many happy memories. First show headlining at Madison Square Garden.... Also, receiving our platinum album backstage in a Boston arena. Final gig of the tour; we had no idea how well the album was doing - it was kind of kept a secret from us - and Peter Grant presented us with four platinum albums. Yeah that was special.

could have been made so much more of... if you know what I mean. It was a big thing for us, to headline two days at Olympia, but people didn't seem to see it that way.

'Maybe people over in England think that we're pulling a hype by saying we're big in America but we're not. I go back to England and see headlines in papers that, say, Queen are slaying America but when I get here I find they're playing to only 4,000 people. I mean... I don't want to brag, but you understand what I'm getting at, don't you?'

All too right, Mick, but remember you spread yourselves between US and England evenly from the start instead of working in England primarily first. 'Well we did do England first and then went to the States but it wasn't as if we had some master plan to concentrate on America. We want to be accepted everywhere and especially in England, our homeland. Our records have been accepted in England and I'm sure we've got a lot of good fans over there, but I'm saying that there isn't the wave of excitement about the band that there is in America.

'Maybe it's just the volume of this country, maybe it's because we play those huge gigs every night, while in England that's a once a year thing. I know we're influenced by American writers. Our music comes out of blues and soul and we tend to write in that style. American audiences get more into the feel of music and if a band puts feeling over they get off on it.

'In England it seems as if we have to valiantly defend what we do, just because we're not technical like Yes or Genesis. People say the songs we write are ordinary and the lyrics don't say anything new and yet we've got... well, all this going for us in the States. What we're doing is us, it's not contrived in any way and it's full of feeling.

'Look at the Stones. Now they're accepted, nobody knocks them, but if you analyse them, all they're doing is Chuck Berry stuff with up-to-date lyrics, really. Yet people criticise us for those reasons.

'Maybe we're just going through a stage. It's just that in America we feel confident, but in England and Europe it's still as if we're having to prove ourselves all the time. It would be great to be able to go to England and do a tour that receives the kind of feeling that we get on these American dates. We've done 47 gigs so far on this tour, and they've all been different yet all been good in their own way.

'We've made a big impression in a short time and I want that to get back to England.'

Ralphs accepts that Bad Company have varied their set to fend off accusations that they're merely a boogie band, but this has become a natural progression with their having three albums to draw from. 'Yes, we've expanded the initial ideas and we're showing people that we're not just a chord-bashing rock 'n' roll band. We're capable of more musical things but sometimes we don't get credit for our subtlety.

'I don't want to keep sounding egotistical, but we believe in this band, every one of us, and it's all we'll ever want to do. It's not like a stepping stone for something else... I can honestly say that none of us will ever want to get involved with any other group situation.'

Ralphs credits Peter Grant, too, with helping the band along its way. 'He has a lot of respect and the fact that he was interested in us made a lot of people sit up and take notice, but if we hadn't come up with the goods it wouldn't have happened.

'We were the first act to be signed to Swan Song, but when we first got involved with Peter we didn't even know he was planning to start a label with Zeppelin. It's a label that always puts the artist first... there's none of this business about having to get an album finished by a certain time. If the album isn't ready, it's not rushed.

'Every musician that has been involved with record companies is subject to so much obligation because they make you feel honoured to be on their label, especially the big corporations where if you don't sell enough records, you might be dropped the following year. After a while it's not like music any more, it's just like putting out a product that sells. All the people on Swan Song have become a very close little family now. I'm sure that all the people in Zeppelin sat down and discussed Bad Company before they signed us and if any one of them hadn't liked us then we wouldn't have been on the label.

'Last night Robert (Plant) said he was dying to get up there and play, but even if he hadn't done that, he was still proud to be involved with the band. We always want to be Bad Company in our own right and have nothing to do with Led Zeppelin apart from being on their label and having the same manager. Now there's a friendly spirit of competition between us because we respect Zep an incredible amount and they respect us too.'

The occasional Bad Co/Zep jams are never planned and always occur after Bad Company have proved themselves, never before. 'Jimmy is one of the few guitarists I can play with on stage. He's a fellow lead guitarist and one who isn't into a big ego trip. I've played with other guitarists who are always trying to outdo you, trying to play faster and that's such a lot of bulls –. But Jimmy isn't like that, he's tried to make the song happen rather than himself.'

Later the same evening, back in the Rainbow, Boz seemed to sum up the feeling of the weekend, and of the band: 'We're bloody proud of this band,' he said, slurring a little over a vast quantity of drink. 'We know what we've done and we're proud of everything that's happened. Just tell everybody that back home.'

SUMMER RECORDING SESSIONS

Château d'Hérouville, France

The 'Honky Château' an hour or so's drive from Paris, immortalised by Elton John when he recorded there and named his fifth studio album after the place, is the new recording location for Bad Company.

Following in the tradition of Headley Grange and Clearwell Castle, the Chateau gave the band the preferred freedom they needed to record almost 'live' and the results will surface on their fourth album, *Burnin' Sky*, released early in 1977.

MICHAEL NEWMAN

I grew up in the Northwest Suburbs of Chicago. Elk Grove Village to be specific, which borders O'Hare Airport. That's where Wayne and Garth (*Wayne's World* movie) laid on their AMC Pacer while a jet flew over their heads coming in for a landing. It was the fall of 1976 and we were back in school when I first saw and heard Bad Company. I was at my friend's house when I was in 8th grade. His older sister who was in high school had a great record collection. She had all of the Bad Company albums to date. I opened up *Run with the Pack* because it was so cool with that silver cover with the wolves on it. That's when my rock 'n' roll world changed forever! Inside the jacket of *Run with the Pack*, in the motel room where they were lounging, *Bugs Bunny* is on the TV in the background leaning up against a wall eating a carrot. Seeing those four stellar cool dudes with *Bugs Bunny* on the TV while 'Simple Man' just rolled on his turntable. It was an experience I'll never forget. It turned me on to one of the greatest rock 'n' roll bands of all time.

I have seen them everywhere and have everything the four of them recorded together. Six studio albums on 8-track, cassette and vinyl. They now need to be immortalised in that now hyper-political hall that they call the Rock and Roll Hall of Fame, *NOW*!

1977

Burnin' Sky

The fourth studio album by Bad Company was released on March 3, 1977. *Burnin' Sky* was recorded in France at Château d'Hérouville in July and August 1976 with engineer Chris Kimsey assisting. The release date was delayed until March 1977 so as not to compete with the band's then-current album *Run with the Pack*.

Paul Rodgers

The chorus to 'Burnin' Sky' just popped into my head one day. I was in a hotel in Paris the day before we were due to go into the sessions and I needed to write some songs. We had been on the road pretty heavily and we were pretty burned. I worked out some verse chords but we had no lyrics at all. We counted it off and hit the button. We went into it, (singing) 'The sky is burning' and I wrote the lyrics on the spot. It was one take and I made the lyrics up as I went along.'
Interview with Classic Rock Revisited January 12, 2001

Jan Ramsey

20 August 1977, Roanoke Civic Center, Virginia, USA

I saw Bad Company on August 20, 1977 at the Roanoke Civic Center in Roanoke, Virginia just a few weeks before my 16th birthday. I had become a fan of the band in 1974 when a friend of mine, who worked at a local record store, gave me a promotional copy of Bad Company's debut album.

My mom drove two of my high school friends and me to the concert, one and a half hours away. We got a room at the Holiday Inn across the street from the Roanoke Civic Center, and my mom stayed at the hotel while the three of us went to the concert. I do remember the four of us going to a restaurant before the show and how sombre the staff were. These older folks were mourning the death of Elvis Presley who had died the week before. Elvis was scheduled to perform at the Civic Center in just a few days, August 24, I believe.

The Bad Company concert marked the first time I'd ever been on the front row of what was then known as 'festival seating' concerts. I would estimate the crowd at the show was around 5,000 people. I was able to sneak a small camera inside the venue and took a few photos. I honestly cannot remember how I was able to sneak my camera inside the venue! It was not difficult at all to take the photos during the concert. I had no idea at the time that I was standing in front of rock royalty, ex-members of Free, Mott the Hoople and King Crimson, all on the same stage! Nor did I realise I was really listening to the blues, the roots of all the music I listened to then and continue to listen to now. I just remember Paul Rodgers being such an elegant singer on stage, and I was madly in love with his British accent! He was mesmerising.

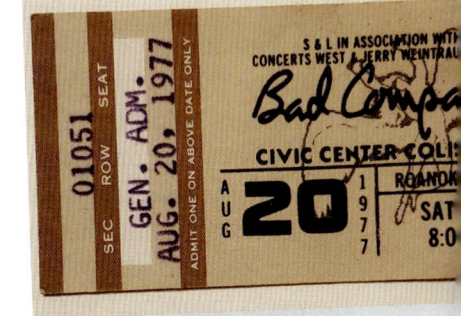

A year or two after seeing Bad Company in concert, I became a fan of Free when I discovered a copy of the *Heartbreaker* album at a record convention and began adding Free albums to my ever-growing album collection!

ROCK 'N' ROLL FANTASY

I'd been in America and I'd seen some posters in the southern States for whiskey. Might have been Jack Daniels or something like that. What they'd done is they'd cut out the bottle of whiskey and stuck it against white. I thought it was a really interesting idea. We created something that was like that. We then did a shot in the Mojave desert outside LA at some run-down old gas station – something that would just give an atmosphere. A sophisticated woman and intimating some kind of relationship with the car wash guy. The cover is a take on Americana.

At the time, Bad Company were becoming huge in America. Around that time they were based in Palm Springs, where I stayed with them for about three weeks and then flew with them in their private jet photographing everything that they did on tour. I remember Paul Rodgers had his trainer with him and he was very much into taekwondo or jiu jitsu or something like that. We were traveling all over the south west states to places like Tuscon and El Paso and I wanted to create this image to reflect how they were almost bigger in America than they were in the UK. It needed to be an image that would have the Americans accept them. It's a narrative album cover.

What's the relationship between the sophisticated woman and the car wash guy? *Desolation Angels* is in the outback – it's desolate and wild. And on the single bag you have an American phone box with a highway in the background at dusk and stuff like that.

All the imagery that went with it was all about bits and pieces of Americana and the band conquering America. It looked really good and different and it stood out in record stores. One of my favourites I did for them. I've still got all the cut-outs from the album cover in a box in the archives: Different size woman cut-outs and different sizes of the guy and the gas station.

Boz Burrell

August – September 1978, Ridge Farm Studios, Surrey, UK

We ended up shaking. Our bottle had gone and we were killing ourselves, so we knocked it on the head. We couldn't have carried on working forever at that pace. But we took some time off and then did the new album down on a farm. We turned an old barn into a studio. It was right under the flight path from Gatwick, and we had to do each take before another plane came over. *Interview with Melody Maker*

Simon Kirke

In 1978 we were very much our own band and were unaffected by popular trends at the time. Punk was in full swing, but that didn't really affect us. If anything it spurred us on to greater efforts - perhaps bands of our stature were getting a little bit too complacent. And punk certainly gave us a kick in the rear.

David Royle

My first introduction to the music? I heard Bad Company on *The Friday Rock Show*, in the Seventies, I couldn't afford the albums, so bought the singles at the time. It wasn't until later I bought the albums.

Tommy Vance
(Radio Broadcaster)

Paul Rodgers is the definitive, the *I emphasise and underline*, definitive blues rock singer. He has the most wonderful most expressive voice, which he knows how to use.

1979

Paul Rodgers

There was a book written by Jack Kerouac, *Desolation Angels*, and I felt that the title of the book summed up perfectly the mood of the band at that time. In my view, while we were Bad Company, rock 'n' roll wall to wall, we still had a message of love to deliver.

Desolation Angels

Desolation Angels, the fifth studio album by Bad Company, was released on 17 March 1979. Recorded at Ridge Farm Studios in Surrey, England in late summer 1978. The 10-track release included another US Top 20 hit single, 'Rock 'n' Roll Fantasy', which climbed to No.13 on the *Billboard* Hot 100. The album returned the band to the higher echelons of the charts, reaching US No.3 and UK No.10, and has sold more than three million copies to date.

The album's title was almost used 10 years earlier to name the second album by Free, which in the end was called simply Free.

Paul Rodgers

From a personal standpoint, listening to the re-release, I think 'Rock & Roll Fantasy' stands out because it very much reflected what we were doing at the time, living and breathing our rock 'n' roll dream of international success and acceptance.

Simon Kirke

Aside from drumming? Well, in Free I played a bit of guitar on a couple of tracks, co-wrote 'Bad Company' with Paul Rodgers as well as several other songs, wrote 'Love You So' for Free, and played electric piano on 'Rhythm Machine' for Bad Company's *Desolation Angels*. Check it out... it's really rather good!

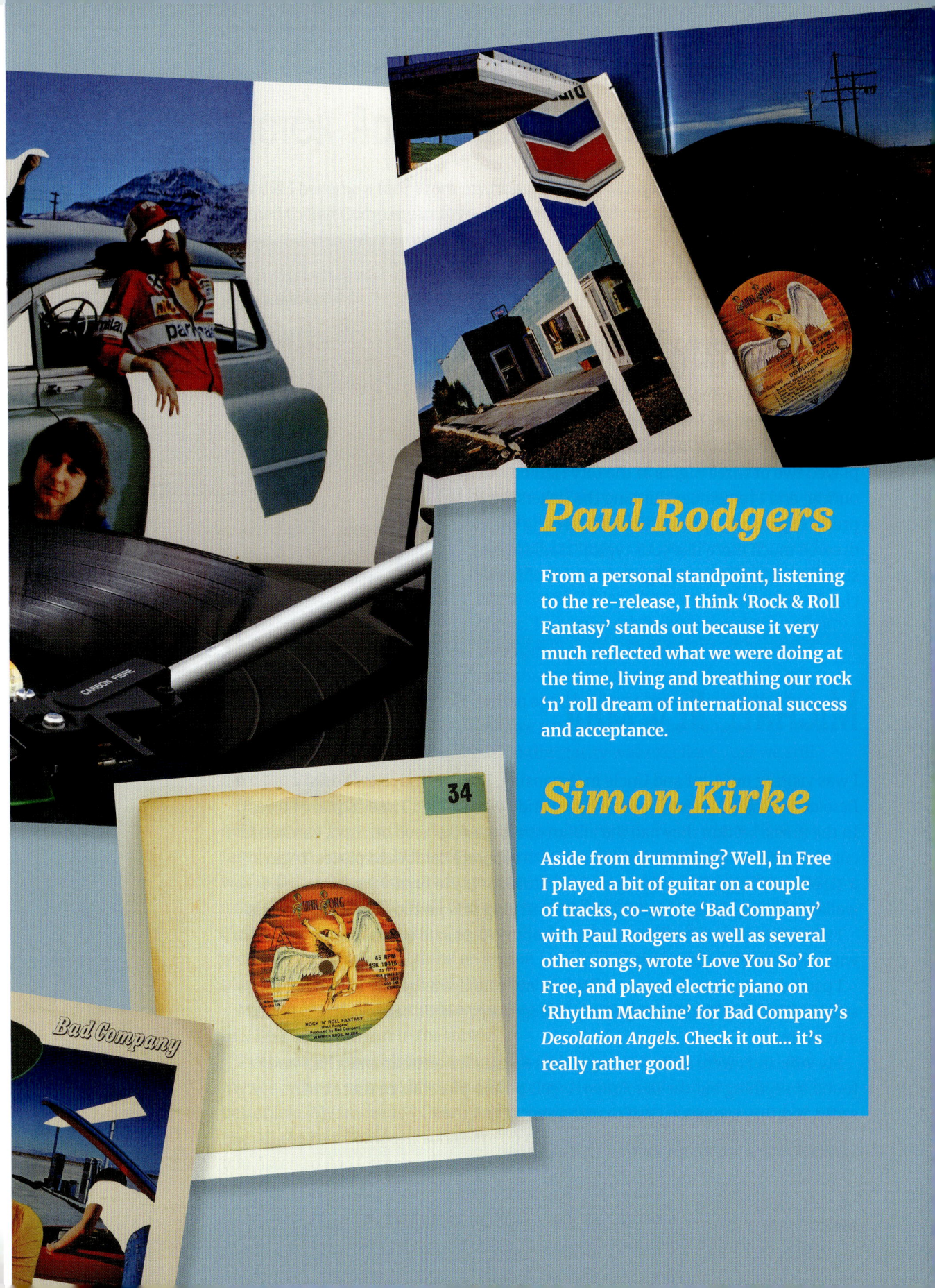

Po Powell

Paul Rodgers was definitely the leader of the band. He asserted himself as the up front figure. I got on with him famously. He was married to a Japanese woman and so was I. He lived not far from me. He lived in Kingston and I lived in Chelsea. We used to meet regularly for dinner on Saturday nights, often at his house. He played me music and we'd go up to his recording studio in the roof.

There was a synergy, together for years and years. So, it wasn't just me as an artist designing an album cover. We had a relationship on a personal level. Paul also had a side to him when he'd had a few drinks that was difficult. It's fairly well documented that he once knocked me out! It was after a gig in Ludwigshafen, Germany when I was banging my hand on the table while music was playing. He said: 'Stop doing that – it's irritating me.' and I carried on and ended up flying half way across the room! I was drunk - it didn't affect me in the slightest and actually I went to my hotel room that night and trashed the fucking room! Absolutely destroyed it! I left early the next morning and caught a flight from Frankfurt to London, but a week later I got a call from Peter Grant to go down and see him and Clive Coulson. I was given the third degree. Peter was a very intimidating man. 'What do you think you were doing? We've got a bill for £2,000!' After I explained that Paul had chinned me and that I was pissed-off, and everyone else trashed their hotel rooms and I thought it was my turn now, Peter Grant gave me the classic line: 'I'm going to ask you one question and you answer me truthfully: Did you enjoy it – trashing that hotel room?' And I said – 'I fucking loved it – I've been dying to do that all my life.' He said, 'Good - We'll pay!'

Scott Chachere

6 May 1979, LSU Assembly Center, Baton Rouge, Louisiana, USA

I was 19-years-old and a Sophomore at LSU, living in Baton Rouge when I first heard Bad Company. I used to make my own mix tapes from the radio in high school and when 'Rock Steady' came on it immediately drew me in. I've been a fan ever since.

Found a ticket stub that tells me I saw them in May 1979 - I remember leaving the restroom at that gig and immediately the lights went down quickly and their show began with 'Burnin' Sky'. Great concert experience.

I related to their music because they could rock it or smooth it down. Mick Ralphs' guitar sound was great and Paul of course is an excellent frontman and vocalist. A good friend of mine sat on the side of the stage and became friends with Mick Ralphs' guitar tech Gary Gilmore. He was able to chat with Mick and allowed to strap on his Telecaster and have an equipment talk.

James Dunlap

13 May 1979, Riverfront Coliseum, Cincinnati, Ohio, USA

Mother's Day, Sunday, May 13, 1979, Cincinnati. *High Times* magazine had an event in Dayton, Ohio, 'The Mother's Day Smoke In'. We rolled up there for a day of supporting the cannabis cause, with a dose or two of micro-dot in between to boot, then headed back home to the Bad Company show that night. It's the only time I literally passed out, more like fainted, at a concert. We were on the floor and between the day party and the night, I was tore up! Side note: I really wasn't sick or too high, musta just had a lack of oxygen to the brain, go figure. I was 15 years old...

Photos taken by Lyndy Lambert from shows in Philly and Atlanta during her time spent on the road with Bad Company. Lyndy also had the band stand in a trash can backstage at a show in Norfolk.

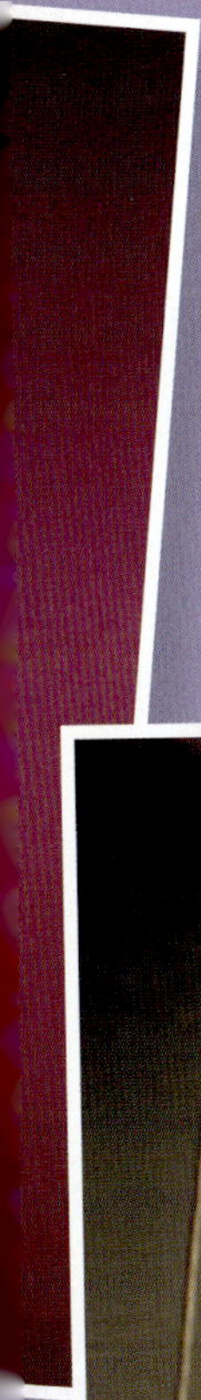

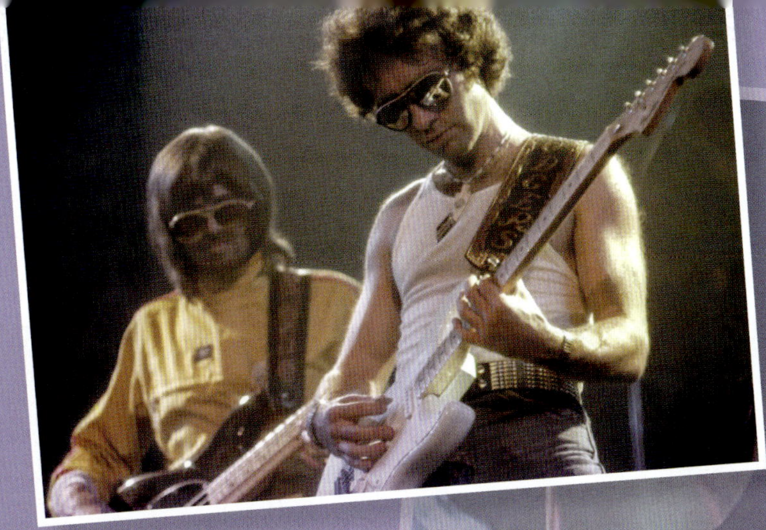

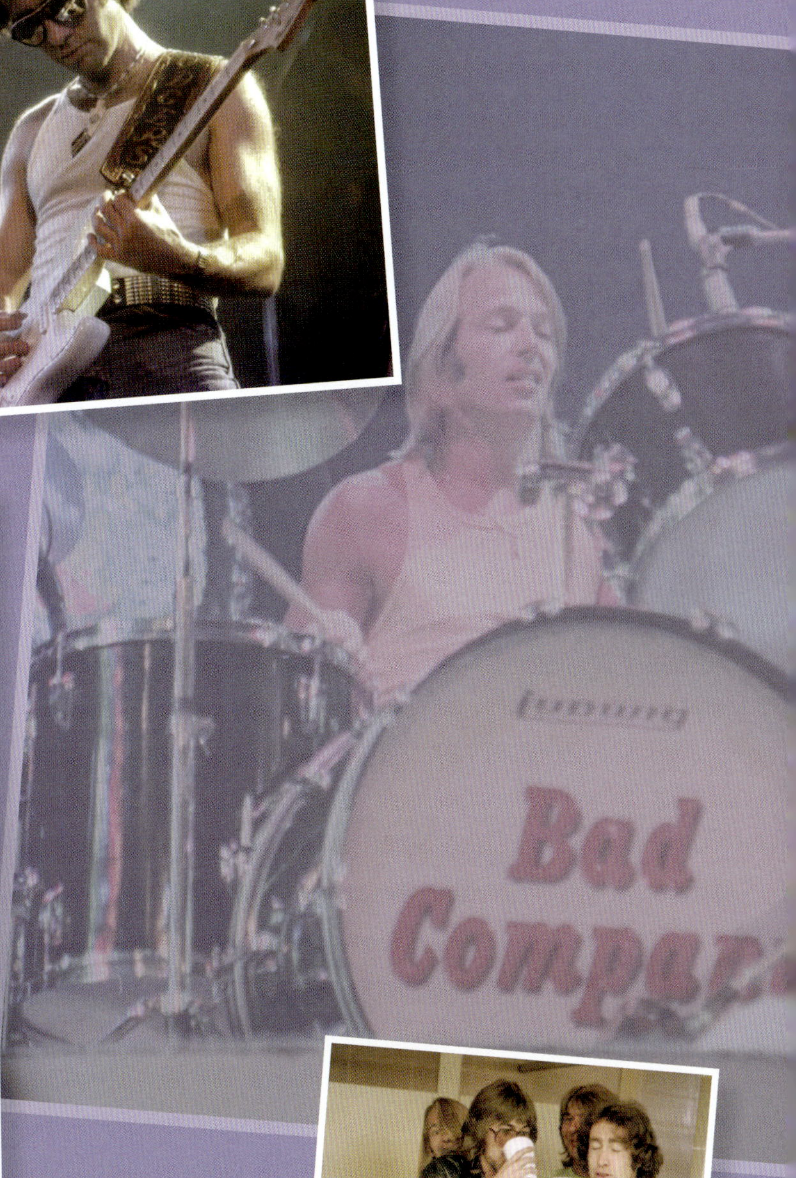
Bad

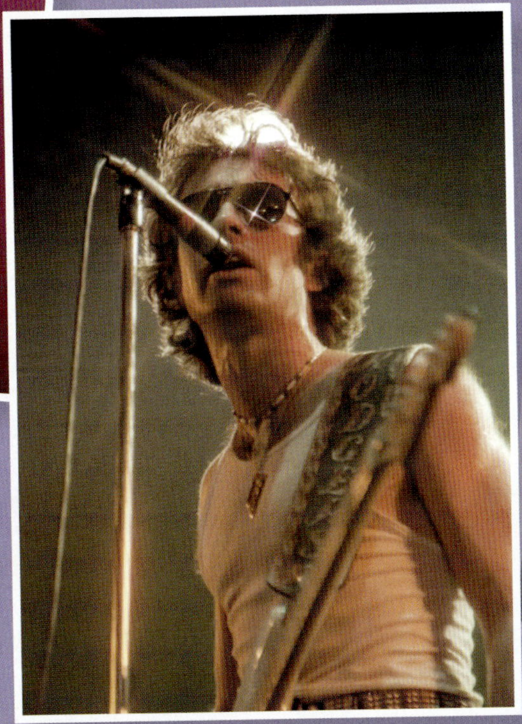

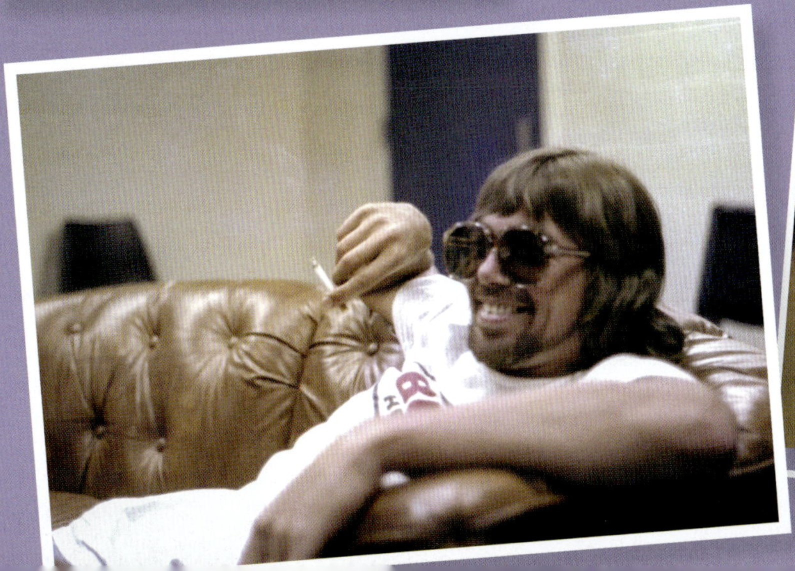

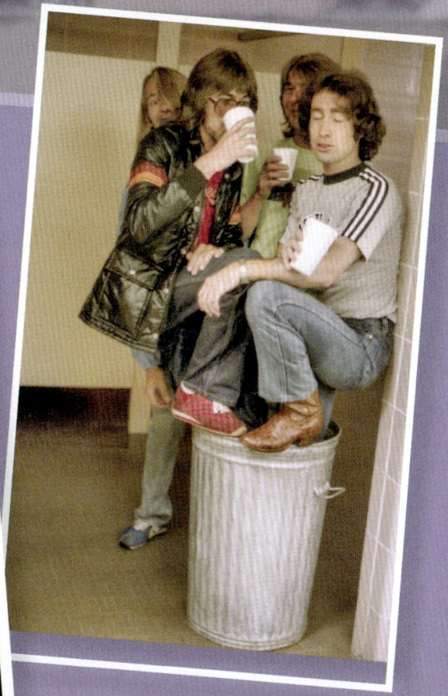

Lyndy Lambert on the Rock 'n' Roll Fantasy tour

July 4 July, Hollywood Sportatorium, Florida, USA

I lived in Miami, where I was attending law school. I loved rock concerts and went to as many as I could. Back then, I knew a lady, Elise, who owned a record store with a BASS ticket outlet (a precursor to Ticketmaster). She would print out several concert tickets when they first went on sale and offer some to me. I usually got front row seats, and the ticket prices back then were $5 – $15 each, affordable to a student. I got two tickets for Bad Company and gave one to my friend, Janet.

A few days before the show, I was at the Yes concert, where I met a professional rock concert photographer. I was a budding photographer and he offered to get me backstage at the concert. He asked me to meet him early, outside the backstage area, and he would get me a pass and show me how to take concert photos.

The venue, the Sportatorium, was situated on the edge of the Everglades. It was built as a sports

Lyndy Lambert joined Bad Company on tour in 1979

arena to host truck pulls, rodeos, and wrestling. They started bringing in big rock artists in 1971 because there were no other arena-sized venues in South Florida. It had a capacity of 15,500, far bigger than any other venue in South Florida at that time. It soon became a rock mecca, hosting many of the biggest touring bands like Pink Floyd, Fleetwood Mac, Lynyrd Skynyrd and Led Zeppelin. But it was a dump. The acoustics were terrible. The crowds were stoned, rowdy, and badly behaved. They were so awful that Bruce Springsteen vowed in 1981 never to play there again.

The Sporto was situated on the intersection of two country roads, two lanes each. On concert nights, traffic backed up for miles. There was only one shabby motel nearby, so most bands stayed in fancy hotels on the beach, at least 20 miles away. To avoid the notorious traffic jams, the bands arrived early for soundcheck and did not leave until after the show. While the fans were hoping for a second encore, the bands would already be loaded in their limos, heading towards their hotels, to beat the traffic and the chaos in the parking lot.

I got to the Sportatorium early, maybe 4 pm. I was able to park next to the backstage area, backing into the spot for easy departure. Few people were around. We did not have cell phones back then, so I had to make myself noticeable for the photographer whenever he showed up. I was fairly noticeable anyway – 5"10" tall with long, platinum blonde hair, and a Florida tan. So, I sat on the hood of my car, wearing a pink one-piece bathing suit and white shorts.

I was brushing my hair when a limo drove past me and pulled into the backstage entrance. A few minutes later, a man jogged out and introduced himself to me as the band's manager. He said Mick wanted to meet me. Frankly, although I liked their music when I heard it on the radio, I was not very familiar with Bad Company at the time. I did not know their names, so I replied, 'who is Mick?' He identified Mick as the lead guitarist. I figured this was a better chance of getting a backstage pass than waiting for a photographer who might never show up, so I followed the manager into the venue.

He bought me into a room where I waited to meet the guitarist. Mick Ralphs came in a few minutes later and we chatted for a while. He was very nice and arranged for me to get an all access pass. He invited me to the band's party after the show, and gave me the name of the hotel and party room number. I had my camera with me and asked if it was okay to shoot some pictures during the show. Mick kindly arranged for me to sit on the stage. A roadie placed a folding chair on the stage for me off to the side, near where Mick played. Needless to say, I did not use my front row seat, but Janet was there.

The show was amazing. I had never seen Bad Company live before. All of their songs were simple, and mostly about love. I preferred complicated, progressive rock acts like Yes, Moody Blues, and Supertramp. But Bad Company blew me away with their energy and talent. Mick Ralphs' power chords fired up the sold-out crowd. And when Paul Rodgers sang, it was heavenly. Rod Stewart once famously said that Paul Rodgers had the best voice in rock 'n' roll, and I wholeheartedly agree. Bad Company epitomised the word 'tight' when applied to a rock band.

One of the many photos taken by Lyndy Lambert on the 79 tour.

They played all of their hits that night, and I realised that I knew the words to most of them. The light show was powerful. Luckily, I had a good camera and plenty of film, so I got some nice photos from a side angle. At some point I remember standing up to dance because it was hard to stay seated. I was in heaven. It was the ultimate rock 'n' roll fantasy for me.

After the encore, Mick briefly talked to me before being whisked away in the limo. I promised him I would drive to the hotel and meet him at the party. I found Janet and we drove separately to the hotel. If I recall correctly, the band was staying at the Diplomat Hotel on Hollywood Beach. Janet and I entered the afterparty room at the hotel and were dismayed to see a few dozen groupies there. We thought about leaving, but there were a few chairs in the back, so we cowered there. About 15 minutes later, the band entered the room and the girls went wild. The bassist, Boz Burrell, walked right through the girls and sat on the floor next to me. Paul Rodgers followed close behind and sat on the floor next to Janet. Boz started chatting with me. I looked over at Mick and he looked a little disappointed. But he and Simon Kirke, the drummer, were quickly engulfed in girls. To cut a long story short, we had a great time and Boz invited me to go on tour with Bad Company!

As the band had the next day off, Janet and I hung out in the pool area and the beach by the hotel with them all day. I took photos of the band while they were swimming in the ocean. Although I was in law school, it was summer break and I did not have a job, so I was free.

6 July 1979, Lakeland Civic Center, Lakeland, Florida, USA

I do not recall whether we drove to the gig the next day in the limos or took their private airplane, but I can tell from my photos that I watched the Lakeland show from the stage. I also took some photos of the band backstage before the show. We returned to the Diplomat Hotel after the Lakeland show, and we hung out at the beach the next day, before flying to Atlanta.

During one of the nights in South Florida, Boz and I, along with a road manager, went to a bar in Ft. Lauderdale that had a live band. Boz got rather drunk and decided to get up and play bass with the band. It didn't go very well, but everyone in the bar was thrilled to have Bad Company's bassist play for them. Bad Co was at the height of their popularity then, so having a famous musician jam with a local band was a fantasy come true.

8 July 1979, Omni Coliseum, Atlanta, Georgia, USA

The next day, we flew to Atlanta in Bad Company's private airplane. It was exciting for me to be on tour with a band of their calibre. Flying in a private airplane was a unique experience for me, a student with little income. I was the only woman on the flight besides the flight attendant. I got a nice photo of Mick, sitting across the aisle from me. We took limos to the Peachtree Plaza Hotel, the tallest building south of New York at the time, with 73 floors. We stayed there for a few nights. I remember waking up one morning in the fog, and our room was above the cloud level.

On stage at the Omni Coliseum that night, Boz was planning to wear his usual yellow, one-piece Simpson car racing suit with fire retardant properties. He was nervous about members of the audience throwing firecrackers or cherry bombs on the stage. Boz explained to me that a member of their crew, a lighting technician, was permanently blinded when someone threw a firecracker on his console. Consequently, they were all very concerned about safety during their concerts. At one show I attended, maybe in Florida, some yahoo in the upper seats set off a firecracker. The band immediately stopped playing and walked off the stage. The house lights went up, and someone got on the PA system stating that the band would return. But if there were any other explosions, the show would end immediately. The idiot was removed from the venue, and they finished the show.

I had taken so many photos of Boz in his race suit already, so I asked him to wear something different in Atlanta. He brought out his beautiful white suit for me, and played the show wearing that. He looked great, and my photos of him in Atlanta were the best I took of him on that tour. Their manager arranged for me to stand in the pit with security so I could take photos from in front of the stage. I got some great photos that night.

I was impressed by how professional Bad Company were during that tour. Before their shows, they drank very little and maybe just took a few hits from a joint to calm jitters. I even rolled a few joints for them. After each show, they had a meeting in their limo to discuss how they performed. They admitted when they made mistakes, determined they would improve the next show. Obviously, I kept quiet during these meetings, but it was fun to listen in.

22 July 1979, Spectrum Arena, Philadelphia, PA, USA

After the Atlanta show, I had to return to Miami. But I did catch up with them all again in Philadelphia. I brought a lot of film with me to this show, and I stood in the pit the entire time. I took some great photos that evening, and Paul, Boz, and Mick hammed it up for me. The concert was outstanding. They seemed to get better with each gig.

Boz Burrell in his white suit

1981

Spring 1981, Ridge Farm Studios, Surrey, UK

The band reconvened at the rural base they used for the recording of *Desolation Angels* to work on a new Bad Company album. These sessions would prove to be the last the original line-up made for a studio album. The result would be *Rough Diamonds*, released in 1982.

1982

Po Powell

Another one of my favourites was the last cover we did for Bad Company, which was *Rough Diamonds*. The reason I like that is because it was a time when the whole business of packaging and changing things like that was happening. And I liked the idea of this jagged-edged cover.

I went to Vegas to shoot the inside pictures of the two showgirls. Peter Grant was not in great shape at the time and was almost a recluse at Horselunges Manor and I remember thinking that it wasn't really the time to be spending money on extravagant packaging. The band were falling apart too. I did the job and it was all fine but it wasn't the band's finest record. But I loved that cover.

Rough Diamonds

The last Bad Company album to feature the original line-up of Paul Rodgers, Mick Ralphs, Boz Burrell and Simon Kirke was released in August 1982. Recorded in acrimonious circumstances at times, the ten tracks reflected a general lack of spark created by almost all the band's output up to this point. *Rough Diamonds* still received a healthy amount of airtime on US rock radio but there were no Top 40 singles and a lack of enthusiasm for the album that translated into less than stellar sales.

Rough Diamonds hit a high of No.15 in the UK album chart and No.26 in the US.

Julie Scott

1982, St. Edmunds School, Canterbury, UK

In 1982 I attended David Kossoff's tour, Late Great Paul at St. Edmunds School in Canterbury. He had established the Paul Kossoff Foundation to present the realities of drug addiction. He talked openly and frankly about his beloved son's life and death accompanied by photographic slides of his early life and his time with Free. I found this incredibly moving and tragic. Speaking to David after the show it became clear that this genuine, lovely man was still devastated over the death of his precious son.

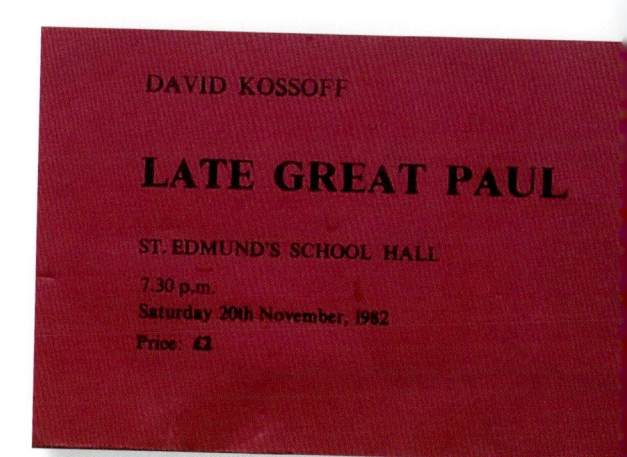

1983

JULIAN MENDELSOHN

1983, Kingston upon Thames, South West London, UK

So privileged to work with Paul Rodgers on a few occasions. I am a massive Free and Bad Company fan so to work with him was amazing. Certainly one of the, if not the, best vocalists I worked with. He was a one-take wonder! Also such a great feel on drums, guitar, keys and bass. Nothing complicated but great timing. I did two albums with him, I really enjoyed doing *Cut Loose* with him. We recorded it as his house in Kingston in London. It was just him playing all the instruments. Of course it was also a great privilege doing the Firm with him and Jimmy Page. Jimmy - another amazing genius! *Julian Mendelsohn: Engineer on Paul Rodgers' debut solo album Cut Loose*

Cut Loose

Paul Rodgers released his debut solo album *Cut Loose* on Atlantic Records during October 1983. For this 10-track album Paul wrote, produced, sang, and played all the instruments - guitar, keyboards, bass guitar, and drums, during recordings at his home studio, Sundown, in Kingston-upon-Thames.

He and Led Zeppelin's Jimmy Page later re-recorded the track 'Live in Peace' for The Firm's 1986 album *Mean Business*. *Cut Loose's* 'Superstar Woman' was originally an unreleased Bad Company song and was re-recorded for this album.

Jimmy Page and Paul: 'As good an amalgamation as I've done' – Paul Rodgers. Michael Brito / Alamy Stock Photo

Peter Smith

7 December 1984, Middlesbrough Town Hall, UK

Paul Rodgers joined forces with Jimmy Page to form The Firm, a British rock supergroup that also comprised Manfred Mann's Earth Band and Uriah Heep drummer Chris Slade and bass player Tony Franklin. The band played two UK gigs in 1984, one in London at Hammersmith Odeon, and another at Middlesbrough Town Hall. This was a big deal at the time, with two rock superstars coming back to the North East. In Paul Rodgers' case, this was also a homecoming show, as he was born in Middlesbrough.

The tickets went on sale from the Town Hall on a weekday, and I was at work at the time. My mate Dave was on night shift that week and was able to go down to Middlesbrough and buy the tickets for us. We were really excited about the gig and full of anticipation. We were hoping for one or two Free, Bad Company or Zeppelin songs, but that wasn't to be. The set consisted of the new Firm album and some songs from Jimmy and Paul's solo work. I remember Paul Rodgers seated at a grand piano for 'Live in Peace' from his earlier solo album. Jimmy Page played songs from the *Death Wish II* soundtrack, which featured his trademark playing of the guitar with a violin bow while beneath the Zeppelin laser pyramid. They also played a great version of the Righteous Brothers' 'You've Lost That Lovin' Feelin'.

It was a very enjoyable show, but I think we were expecting something more.

While I don't have a record of the set list for the Middlesbrough show, I would imagine this set list from their Hammersmith Odeon gig would be similar: 'Closer', 'City Sirens', 'Make or Break,' 'The Morning After', 'Together,' 'Cadillac,' 'Prelude,' 'Money Can't Buy,' 'Radioactive,' 'Live In Peace', 'Midnight Moonlight', 'You've Lost That Lovin' Feelin',' 'The Chase.' 'Someone To Love,' 'Full Circle', 'Boogie Mama, 'and 'Everybody Needs Somebody.'

1985

The Firm

The eponymously titled first album by The Firm was released on 11 February 1985. Paul Rodgers, Jimmy Page, Tony Franklin and Chris Slade had recorded the album in 1984 at Jimmy's Sol Studios in Cookham, on the banks of the River Thames. The successful union of the former Bad Company frontman and Led Zeppelin's guitarist saw the album peak at No.15 on the UK album chart and No.17 on the *Billboard* 200 in the US.

In an interview with Entertainment Tonight, Paul and Jimmy explained the background to this new project, the conflict of personalities and their initial decision not to play Free or Led Zeppelin numbers on the already sold-out tour.

Paul Rodgers
Conflict? Yeah, I think with a couple of egos like us you could get a clash of character, I suppose. But we were probably aware of that initially so we went into it slowly and carefully to see what kind of music we would come up with and how it would come out.

Jimmy Page

It would be stupid of us, having not been on the road for so long, to come back and just establish yourself as a nostalgia entity, neither of us could have done that really.

Paul Rodgers

Well I don't think we've 100% discounted any of that [old Free and Led Zeppelin] stuff, but we just tend to avoid it, basically.

Jimmy Page

Once you got into a tour, I think there were more pressures off the road with all the sort of business aspects than the music. If it was just down to playing the music, then it would be utopian, you know?

Paul Rodgers

Yeah, and I think the pressure starts to get overbearing when it's not happening on stage, you know, or when you don't feel happy with what's happening on stage. The way things are with us you look forward to the gigs.

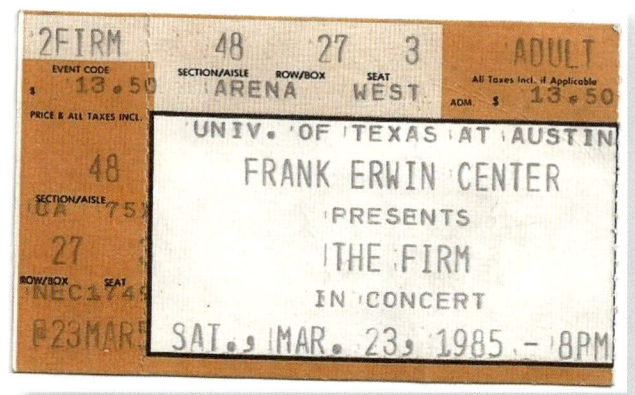

Eoghan Lyng

Paul's work with Jimmy Page remains some of the fieriest of the guitarist's post Zeppelin's career. The Firm's seminal single 'All The King's Horses' remains one of the innovative examples of 80s synth rock. It was in Cork, Ireland's musical hall of rebellious fire, that I bought much of The Firm's output. Right from the get go: these guys meant business!

    Hearing it among a collection of makeshift vinyl, the song sounded as startling in 2014 when I bought it, as it must have done thirty years earlier. After Robert Plant, Rodgers is the singer who found most vitality in Page's work.

Ken Weiss

I spent a good deal of my life in the music business. Paul Rodgers? I'm not sure if we ever met as we traveled in quite different circles. Free and Bad Company aside (I did see Free once or twice), I recall seeing Paul in L.A. with that ragtag outfit The Firm. That was fun if loose. I have always thought Paul Rodgers was as good a singer in music as any, some would suggest the best. I'm not sure who would be better but few sound like him – right up there with Jagger and Plant as stand alone guys.

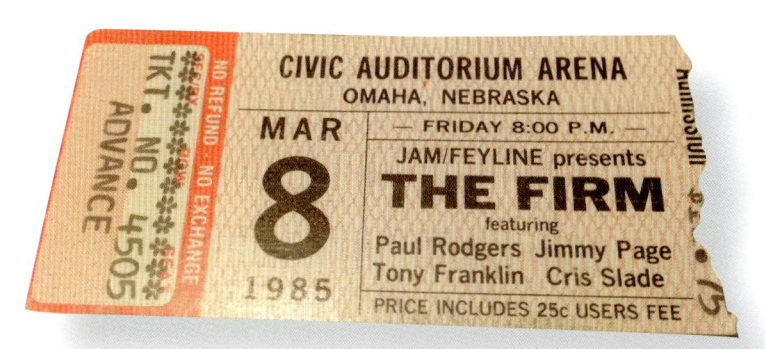

Ken Weiss is Entrepreneur in Residence, as Professor of the Practice, at the University of North Carolina

Lonnie Edelman

11 May 1985, The Spectrum, Philadelphia, USA

I was always a fan, from being just a kid during the Free days, and of course Bad Company, which was just plain badass cool music. I grew up with the radio on more than TV - my parents loved music. My first Bad Company album came from a record store in our local mall (we had one of the earliest-built indoor malls in the country) called Music Scene. It was the quintessential 70s hippie-run music store.

Being a rock fan and narrowly missing a chance to see Led Zeppelin, I was thrilled to hear The Firm - the best of all worlds. I ended up buying both albums and I really wish there had been more, I appreciated the talent and musicianship from the whole band. My favorite song is 'Live in Peace'.

The Firm toured in 1985, and my friends and I bought tickets to see them at The Spectrum in Philadelphia. I was 20 and still living with my parents at the time in a little town called Northampton, 65 miles north of Philadelphia. The show was absolutely perfect. I knew sitting there I was watching masters of their trade, and wondered if such perfection could carry on as long as I was alive. I hoped it could.

A funny thing occurred at that show, and while it's not Paul-centred, it's still cool, at least to me. In the middle of the show the band stopped playing and the lights went dark. Needless to say it got quiet. In the pitch black down on the stage I saw- I know I saw - Page pull out a violin bow. I screamed at the top of my lungs: 'He's got the bow!' People around me looked at me as if I was from Mars. It *was* very quiet and I know to this day much of that venue heard me. Just then a note struck out, the lights lit, and Page pointed the bow at the ceiling where the sound seemed to bounce back from, a la the bit from 'The Song Remains the Same'. The place went nuts. I mean no disrespect to Paul or anyone else with this story. I feel fortunate I was there. I can say I saw them.

Free, Bad Company, and The Firm have been a very, very big part of the soundtrack of my life. One of the earliest vinyl purchases I made as a teen was Bad Company, and they have always been at the top of my playlists and included in my personal tapes and CDs that were my most often played.

Thank you for putting yourself out there, Paul. You did good! You were a huge part of that magical time in the 70s and early 80s when the music was absolutely amazing.

What a magical time.

Yoshi Hoshina

Fourteen years after seeing Free perform in Japan when he was a 17-year-old, rock critic Yoshi Hoshina visited Paul Rodgers in the UK.

At Paul's London home I remember a photo taken in 1985 after a magazine interview with Paul about The Firm's first album.

After the Japanese magazine *Pop Gear* interview, he entertained me with nice food and wine. Also he showed me his private 2nd floor studio. The studio was not big but there was an analogue tape machine and many guitars.

I spent a really great time there and it felt like a dream because he is my favourite singer.

Larry Turner

1985, Chandler, Arizona, USA

A few months after I saw Free in 1973, Led Zeppelin rolled through Albuquerque on their Houses of The Holy tour and I was there. It was a great year to be a 16-year-old. Always loved Zeppelin, but my memory of that show was it was way too loud and Jimmy Page was too intoxicated but, hey, I can say that I got to see Led Zeppelin.

As for The Firm, I was naturally drawn to this supergroup with my favourite vocalist and one of my fave guitarists. I saw them in 1985 in Chandler, Arizona when I was 28 years old. Interestingly, my memories aren't near as vivid as the Free show 12 years earlier. I do remember the songs were very faithful to the studio versions on their two albums and that Paul Rodgers had aged a bit (so had I) but his voice was better than ever...simply phenomenal!

The only reason I wouldn't put this show on my top 25 list, though, is that the songs (other than 'Radioactive' and 'Satisfaction Guaranteed' and maybe a couple others) weren't nearly as strong as the Free and Zeppelin catalogues. Very enjoyable show, though.

10 From 6

Ten songs from six studio albums is the reasoning behind the title of Bad Company's first greatest hits compilation. Released in December 1985, it will go on to sell in sufficient quantities (more than three million to date) to rank as the band's fourth best-selling album.

ROCK 'N' ROLL FANTASY

1986

Mean Business

The Firm's second and final album, *Mean Business*, was released on 3 February 1986. It reached No.22 and No.46 respectively in UK and US charts.

When released as a single 'All the King's Horses' spent four weeks at No. 1 on the *Billboard* Album Rock Tracks.

One of the album's tracks, 'Live in Peace', was first recorded on Paul Rodgers' first solo album in 1983, *Cut Loose*.

The album's title was intended to have a double meaning: that the music business is a hard one, and that the band was serious about its music. Page and Rodgers decided to disband The Firm within months of this album's release.

The Firm live on stage. Photos by Lucy Piller

1987

Cory Beaulieu

My story probably isn't the most fascinating by any means, but finding Free has still been life changing for me.

In 1987 I was living in Massachusetts, USA and had just graduated high school. I was just a 17-year-old kid and had been listening to *very* different music at that time.

My then boyfriend introduced me to classic rock, Bad Company and 'Feel Like Makin' Love.' The love for the song lasted, the boyfriend didn't.

I had never actually done any research into Paul Rodgers' musical history so for years I didn't even know he sang 'All Right Now'. One day, when I was really listening closely, it struck me - wait a sec, this is Paul!

Once the door opened I was all over researching Free and devouring the music. It was an entirely new (to me) side to Paul's voice that took my breath away. Hearing Free instantly relaxes me and excites me all at once and it is go-to music for me, especially when I want to be transported to another place. The raw quality in Paul's voice is so achingly beautiful to me that I get emotional just writing about it.

Finding Free so late makes me sad for the years of listening that I missed, but, I have to remember that they came into my life when they were supposed to and I am eternally grateful. Long live Free.

1988

ANTTI KOPONEN

I'm from Finland and my 'fandom' of Paul Kossoff started somewhere in the late 80s when I first heard either 'Wishing Well' or, you guessed it, 'All Right Now'. I was 14 at the time - very intrigued with the sound of that guitar, and I liked the whole band to a certain extent. That was my first impression. The thing was, I had started to play guitar.

I was already listening to Jimi Hendrix, Randy Rhoads and some other guitar players, who were all dead by then. I wasn't really that interested if guitarists I liked were legendary or anything. It was more about the way they sounded. So, for me it wasn't even about the playing technique at first, but whoever had a personal, original sound.

Paul Kossoff had that sound! He had that warm touch, singing (and somewhat stinging) tone. His playing was slow and emotional, he wasn't a flurry, fast, player, more like he had that depth and soulfulness. A very economical player, he had a sparse use of notes and he focused more on expressing his feelings, which I think he did very well.

His playing is something I could relate to, even back then, without having such ability or style myself. Later on when I learned to play properly, or at least more frequently, I sometimes tried to go for that feeling in my own songs, concentrating more on the depth of notes that I played. I have never really been a fast or tricky player.

Some people have linked the playing of Brian Robertson (Thin Lizzy, Wild Horses and Motörhead) with Koss. I kinda get it. Where Robertson was/is maybe more technical, he also had the blues in his chops. The fact that so many blues guitarists have used Gibson Les Paul is, perhaps, another link.

Kossoff´s own influences like Jimi Hendrix and Eric Clapton, were more technical. Like Clapton, Paul was not a big songwriter in the early days. Both were very good at expressing themselves through the songs written by other people.

My personal favourites from Kossoff are not really the most famous hits by Free, but those more obscure numbers, like the stuff on *Tons of Sobs* and *Heartbreaker* where he had more freedom. And songs like 'Tuesday Morning', 'Time Away' and 'Molten Gold' are fine examples of his inspired improvising on the *Back Street Crawler* solo album.

Whatever flaws Paul Kossoff had in him, he still had a lot of soul in his playing, even on the very last album that he was involved in before his death. The *Second Street* album is one of my favourites from anything that Koss did.

There are hiccups for sure, but songs like 'Leaves In The Wind' still gives me chills. Maybe he knew that he was living on borrowed time and tried to pour as much of his inner feelings that he could cram into a song. I think he succeeded in that. With my own band, Serpent Warning, I don't really play like Koss at all and never have tried, since the style of our band and Free, are vastly different, but I have tried to bring as much emotion to my own playing as I can express.

1989

Lia Zsanna H. Sirkó

It was 30 years ago when I heard Free songs for the first time, sung by my father when I was around 11-12 years old. He was a singer in a tribute band but they played Free songs as well.

Since childhood: still loving Free. I listen to their music almost every day. One of the best bands ever.

1990

Tony Scott

Having worked in the business for many years, including the nationally syndicated show *Rockline*, 95-5 KLOS in Los Angeles, and Westwood One Radio Networks where I still host *The Classic Rock Night Show*, I have had numerous interviews with Paul Rodgers and once did *Rock and Roll Fantasy Camp* with Simon Kirke.

   I vividly remember one of my most enjoyable interviews that I have hosted through the years.

   This particular interview took place at the Westwood One studios near L.A. back in the early 90s. I do believe it was my first time meeting Paul and having an opportunity to sit face to face with him, and it was a live interview.

   Having been a child from a foreign service family, we lived all over the world and by the time it was close for me to graduate high school my family was living in Taiwan and I was beginning my radio career at the American Forces Network Taiwan, discovering rock 'n' roll. This was 1975 and Bad Company had definitely arrived and was all over the airwaves of AFNT and I was crazy about this band, so to be sitting face to face with *the* Paul Rodgers for the first time was thrilling and I gushed a bit.

We talked of so many things during his interview, earliest days, even bands before Free and moved into Bad Company. I brought up 'Seagull' and talked of my years on Taiwan and how that particular song brought back such memories for me. Teenage years on the island, starting radio and discovering Bad Company, sitting on the beach hearing that song and watching seagulls. And Paul said to me, 'So that one eh, Tony - good memories?'

Well, Paul gestured toward a guitar leaning up against the studio wall, it was a guitar that the morning show had a little fun with every once in a while and Paul says: 'Pass me that guitar if you wouldn't mind'.

As I remember it, we went to commercial break and Paul did a quick tune-up on the guitar and when we came out of the break he began to strum and sing 'Seagull'.

I remember people who worked in the building gathering at the studio window watching in awe as Paul played and sang right there for all of us, and live across the country. It was radio at its best. Unrehearsed, spontaneous, jaw dropping perfection and for the listeners especially, something they talked about for a long time.

I interviewed Paul several times and got to know Cynthia, his wife, pretty well too.

The picture accompanying this story was taken from our one on one at SIR studios in Hollywood as Paul prepared for a tour. That interview is on YouTube as 'Tony Scott interviews Paul Rodgers' and I will also always remember the time I had Paul and Cynthia as guests on *Rockline* and Steven Tyler surprised all of us with a live call from Maui.

 Great times. Unforgettable times. Paul remains one of my absolute favourite interviews... any of them. He is the warmest, most humble and easy to talk to person in the biz.

included David Gilmour and Bryan Adams. We loved one of Bryan's songs, so we asked him to come in and play on it. 'Nature of the Beast' it was.

Howard Albert

Much respect for both Free and Bad Company.

In the early 90s we were hot, doing roughy 10 albums a year all for different major labels. When we were producing *The Law* album with Paul Rodgers and Kenney Jones I can't exactly remember how it came about but we were doing a lot of work for Atlantic. Especially with Ahmet Ertegun, Jerry Wexler, Arif Mardin and Tom Dowd. I believe Ahmet had the idea to put sort of a super group together. I believe the Memphis Horns and Joe Lala were in the studio but most of the rest of them, musicians like Dave Gilmour, Bryan Adams and Chris Rea, added their parts separately. Kenney and Paul probably stayed local at the Newport Hotel or the Thunderbird. Both on Miami Beach. What do I think about Paul as a vocalist? One of the best of all time.

Paul Rodgers

The Law: That was a serious attempt to get back on the road. I really wanted to. It was time for me to do it again. I feel very strongly that the record company didn't get behind what we were trying to do for one reason or another.

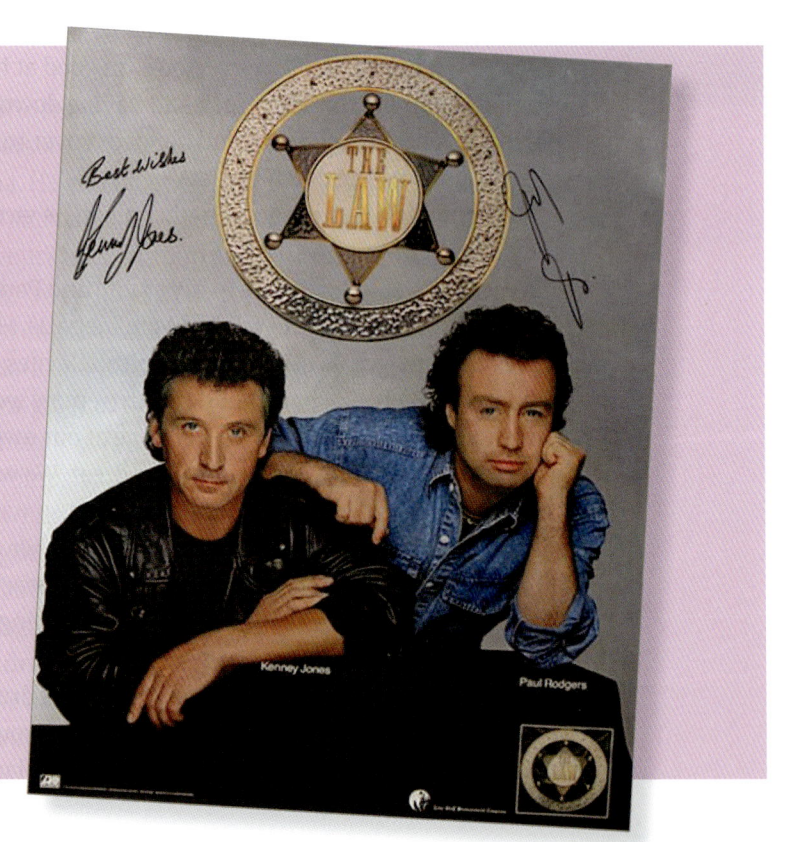

Jon Kirkman

My mate John Young played keyboards in The Law. They only played one gig. Supporting ZZ Top at Milton Keynes Bowl. There were all sorts of plans made but in the end it just never happened. Which was a shame because *The Law* album was a good album. I think they, like a lot of the 70s rock bands, found it difficult in the late 80s and early 90s to get tour dates. The Seattle sound was happening and I think The Law got the Milton Keynes dates because they were under the same management as ZZ Top.

John Young

6 July 1991, Milton Keynes Bowl, Buckinghamshire, UK

I was drafted into The Law after the record was made by one of the guitarists, Jim Barber. We only ever played the one show although I think a lot more shows were in the planning stage.

Obviously the management only dealt with Kenney Jones and Paul Rodgers and as such we just planned for the one show at Milton Keynes Bowl.

We rehearsed at Kenney's house and then drove up to Milton Keynes the day before.

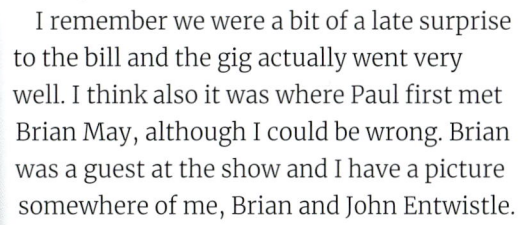

I remember we were a bit of a late surprise to the bill and the gig actually went very well. I think also it was where Paul first met Brian May, although I could be wrong. Brian was a guest at the show and I have a picture somewhere of me, Brian and John Entwistle.

The star of the show that day was Bryan Adams - 45 minutes of hits - and ZZ Top, who headlined the gig but had all sorts of problems on stage.

All in all a good day but it never went any further. That said I carried on recording with Paul for about 12 months after the show at his home studio.

I always remember having a cup of tea with him early one morning (about 1am). He asked me why people didn't buy his demo's as he was trying to sell songs to other artists. My reply was: 'You should stop singing them!' I doubt anyone could sing them better!

Pertti Pulkkanen

Here is my story about becoming a fan of Free in Finland.

It all happened in July 1991 because that was the time when I found the *Fire and Water* album in the library. A few months later I also found *Highway* in the same place and liked it almost as much. I became a fan of Free independently because classic rock has always been my favourite kind of music. And I guess I became hooked on Free when I heard the riff of 'All Right Now' on the radio.

I had known their music was great for a few years before that but it wasn't that easy to find their records. 'All Right Now' and 'Wishing Well' were the first two tracks, which I became familiar with. The former has maybe the best riff in the history of rock and the latter has since become perhaps the most important rock song in my life. *Heartbreaker* was the first Free album which I actually bought, in the late summer of 1993. Since then I have bought all their vinyl albums and remastered CD versions with bonus tracks, which were released in 2002. I have also found a few singles with picture sleeves. I have been lucky to find early vinyl versions of all Free's albums except *Tons of Sobs*, which is a re-release from a couple of years ago.

Because I was born in late 1973, I hadn't been able to catch Free in concert. Five live tracks from Manchester in July 1970, *Beat Club* performances ('Free Me', 'Fire and Water' and 'Mr Big') and 'Be My Friend', 'Mr Big' and 'All Right Now' from Isle of Wight festival in 1970 are perhaps the best live performances from Free, which I have witnessed from the *Free Forever* DVD.

Free has become the most important British rock group in my life. There are so many great songs in their repertoire. The music of Free is full of emotion and rare soulfulness, even seriousness in a positive way. It's easy to identify with some of the lyrics. The voice of Paul Rodgers and guitar playing of Paul Kossoff are unique. To name some favourite tracks from Free I'd like to mention: 'Worry,' 'I'm a Mover' and 'Moonshine' from *Tons of Sobs*, 'I'll Be Creepin',' 'Songs of Yesterday' and 'Free Me' from *Free*, 'Fire and Water,' 'Oh I Wept' and 'Heavy Load' from *Fire and Water*, 'Be My Friend', 'Love You So' and 'Bodie' from *Highway*, 'Get Where I Belong' as a studio track from *Free Live!* 'My Brother Jake' as a track released first as a single, 'Sail On,' 'Magic Ship' and 'Goodbye' from *Free at Last* and 'Wishing Well', 'Come Together in the Morning' and 'Seven Angels' from *Heartbreaker*.

From Free's discography there is a song for almost every kind of mood. I will remain a fan of Free's music and their music makes the world a little bit better place to be.

1992

Devin Morris

I'm from Jackson, Michigan. Throughout high school, I was a fan of country music, strictly Randy Travis, Keith Whitley and Garth Brooks.

I distinctly remember the very moment my taste in music changed forever. It was the summer of 1992 and compact discs had just started to be sold. A friend had put on Bad Company's *10 from 6* and I heard the most incredible thing: 'Feel like Makin' Love.'

That's all it took. I was a fan but not a fan in the sense I am today. I never explored Paul's career past wearing out my *10 from 6* cassette tape in my car. From there I began to explore 1970s hard rock and left country music. Years later I would find *Merchants of Cool* DVD. I honestly had no idea of the name 'Paul Rodgers.' I figured there was no way a singer from the 1970s could still sound good. After all, most artists from that classic rock era had either passed away or were still performing but couldn't come close to the magic of what they once had. That DVD changed my perspective on music. Paul sounded better and looked more amazing than I could possibly imagine. I still watch that DVD and I've never stopped being a full time fan. In 2010 I contacted Lucy Piller through email. I'd seen a photograph on the fan website of her and Paul together and asked if there was any way to meet Paul. I didn't really expect even a reply. To my surprise she was able to put me in contact with Paul's road manager and he was able to arrange a meeting with Paul in Columbus, Ohio.

To this day I can't believe that happened and how gracious Lucy was and still is.

I love being a part of a family of fans that love Paul. We truly have something rich and beautiful to listen to. 'The Voice' brings peace and joy to my soul.

ROCK 'N' ROLL FANTASY

1993

Neil Waite

January 1993, Court Moor School, Fleet, Hampshire, UK

It was a satisfaction tinted with sorrow to know that I had seen three of the four members of Free perform live, knowing I'd never get to see my ultimate guitar hero, Paul Kossoff. But in 1993 I met his father, David Kossoff.

It started when I read a Free article in the music press explaining how actor/author David Kossoff had toured schools in the late 70s and 80s, delivering a one-man stage performance about the death of his son and its effect on the family. Being a teacher, I began to wonder if he would be prepared to come out of retirement and give one last performance at my school. It was certainly worth pursuing. I composed a letter and sent it to David Clayton, who ran the 'Free Appreciation Society'. David Clayton assured me he would pass it on to Mr Kossoff. He was true to his word.

Photo Fleet News

The night David rang me was a good few weeks after I sent the letter and it was the last thing on my mind when he phoned me.

'Ah, hello, is that Neil Waite?'

'Yes, it is.'

'Hello, my name's David Kossoff and I'm ringing about your letter.'

As soon as I realised who it was, I felt ridiculously nervous. My voice went shaky and I started to feel hot. I was talking to the father of the great Paul Kossoff! Assuming he was ringing to say he didn't perform *Late Great Paul* anymore, I was surprised when he announced he would be happy to perform one last show at my school. All he asked in return was a donation to the

Paul Kossoff Foundation, which he set up in order to raise awareness about substance abuse. Over the next two weeks I spoke to David three more times over the phone as we organised the event. He sent me instructions on how the performance would run, with a list of requirements as well as a template poster for me to adapt in order to promote the event. The Headmaster was happy with the arrangements and willingly made a donation of £275 to the foundation. It was decided that the performance would be delivered to all our year 11 students.

As a teacher of 30-plus years I've been nervous about many school events and presentations, but never as much as I was on the day of the *Late Great Paul*

DAVID KOSSOFF FRSA Hon D Litt

Sept 30
92

Dear Mr Waite

The video is a sort of 'softer' version of my performance 'Late Great Paul,' which is done to 14–18s in every kind of school. There is no fee. A donation to the fund of £250 is asked. My own expenses too. It requires the good lights/sound etc of a professional stage performance. It lasts 1¼ hour. It is in no way a 'talk' or lecture. I do it less these days but you are not far. Feel free to telephone.

David Kossoff

---

event. Taken off timetable for the day, I paced back and forth in reception, waiting for him to arrive, feeling excited but anxious. I'm not sure how I expected him to turn up but was genuinely impressed by his arrival in an old brown Ford Cortina. Following introductions, we started setting the stage up, with David very clear about what he wanted and very fussy about exactly how it should look. I was given instructions to go to the Art department and fetch two easels to support a large black and white print of Paul, which was split into two halves, as if it was shattered. When I returned with two slightly different-sized easels, I was told, in no uncertain terms, they had to be identical or the two halves wouldn't match. He was completely right, but I felt berated. It soon became apparent though that this was because he was a perfectionist and wanted things to be right. From then on, his demeanour changed, and he was more relaxed and friendly. Lunch was in the Head's office, with a buffet laid on, which he was very appreciative of. The hour we had over lunch was a wonderful opportunity to talk to David about Paul and find out more about my guitar hero. I was uncertain that he would want to talk about him to me before the performance. Initially, this was the case, but when he realised I was a huge fan, the floodgates opened. I was fascinated to hear him talk about Paul, from childhood through to his days with Free and beyond. He spoke about his son with a huge amount of love and affection, especially when recounting the way Paul learnt to play guitar by watching others. His tone turned sombre as he spoke of Paul's drug addiction and subsequent death in 1976.

After lunch David and I went back to the hall for some final checks, 160 year-11s filing in quietly and nervously. David sat on the stage, as still as a statue. After everyone was seated, he remained where he was, staring straight ahead. It started to feel a little uncomfortable. Maybe that was the idea. Standing up slowly, he walked to a lectern. As he started to speak, there was an audible disturbance at the back of the hall. A group of boys found the situation amusing and decided to make their feelings known. My heart sank and my mind raced as I quickly thought about how to deal with the situation. David stopped immediately and looked up slowly from his script. He leaned sideways as if looking around an imaginary pillar and stared at the group of boys. I'll never forget that moment. The boys stopped instantly, as if under a spell, and nervously looked at the floor. For the rest of the performance you could have heard a pin drop. David Kossoff had the whole room captivated. He had us in the palm of his hand as he took us through Paul's life, from happy-go-lucky childhood through to his tragic death. The anti-drugs message was clear and powerful. At the end of the show there was a long gap before the applause started. It was an incredible performance, one I'll never forget.

After the show, I helped David load his old Ford. He spoke warmly to me and thanked me for contacting him. I asked if he'd ever perform the *Late Great Paul* again, but he replied that, at 75, he was 'too old for this game'. After shaking hands and saying goodbye, I stood and watched as he drove away.

As we go through our lives, we surf between golden moments that punctuate our time on this earth. The day I got to have lunch with David Kossoff and chat to him about his son, my guitar hero Paul Kossoff, was one such moment.

Tammy Wright

I became a Bad Company fan at a super young age. I am now 33 and I still love to listen to them! My Aunt Janet had their tapes back then as it was the early 90s and I would often stay at my grandparents. She would play them on her radio all of the time and I thought they had the best music that I had heard in my entire life. To this day - their music never gets old and has lived on through generations of rockers!

Muddy Water Blues: A Tribute to Muddy Waters

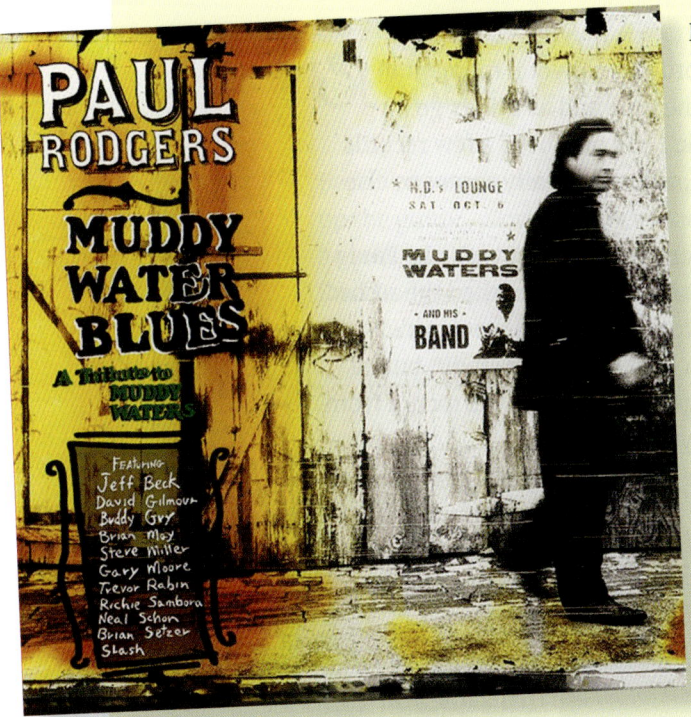

Released in July 1993, *Muddy Water Blues: A Tribute to Muddy Waters* became the second solo album by Paul Rodgers. Although attributed solely to Rodgers, and the only original composition on the album is the Paul-penned title track 'Muddy Water Blues', the 15 tracks featured numerous legendary guitar players, including Jeff Beck, Buddy Guy, David Gilmour, Gary Moore, Brian May, Slash, Trevor Rabin, Steve Miller, Neal Schon, Brian Setzer, Richie Sambora, along with Jason Bonham on drums, Ian Hatton on rhythm guitar and Pino Palladino on bass.

The first pressings of the album also came with a bonus disc which featured Paul revisiting some old Free and Bad Company tunes. 'All Right Now', 'Wishing Well' and 'Fire and Water' from Free and 'Feel Like Makin' Love', 'Can't Get Enough' and the track 'Bad Company' from *Bad Company*.

The release was a bigger success in Britain than America, The album entered the UK album chart at its peak position, No.9, with the title track hitting No.45 on the singles chart.

Steve Newton

14 May 1993, Pacific Coliseum, Vancouver, Canada

The first time I saw Paul Rodgers perform live was back in the 70s, when Bad Company played the Pacific Coliseum on the *Run with the Pack* tour. I didn't see him again until 14 May 1993 but let me tell you - the guy is still one of the finest crooners the blues-rock world has ever seen.

Sticking with the basic guitar/bass/drums line-up he's favoured since the early days of Free, Rodgers devoted most of his set to tunes from his new Muddy Waters tribute album, *Muddy Water Blues*. With former Journey man Neil Schon providing the hot guitar licks, the band worked through old standards like Sonny Boy Williamson's 'Good Morning Little School Girl' and Willie Dixon's 'I'm Your Hoochie Coochie Man', but got the biggest rise from the crowd during Hendrix's 'Purple Haze' and 'Little Wing'. The latter tune was a particularly fine showcase for Rodgers' soulful pipes, and the former afforded Schon a good opportunity to practice his excellent rock-star grimaces.

Although former Little Feat drummer Richie Hayward had been advertised on the bill, other musical commitments required that he be replaced at the last minute by Deen Castronovo, who - along with newly recruited bassist Todd Jensen - pulled the gig off admirably. After about an hour, Rodgers announced that he only had time for one more song, so the band tore into 'The Hunter'.

At this point it became very difficult for yours truly to scribble legible notes, since the table I was seated at reached onto the Commodore's sprung dance floor and the vibrations had my Bic rattling out some weird type of Braille. Nobody said rock journalism would be an easy ride.

When Rodgers encored with 'All Right Now', he proved once and for all that he's the world's best guy at going 'Whoa-yeaah!' The 1970 Free classic even got two rowdies so excited they had to fight about who liked it best.

After the band closed with another Hendrix gem, 'Stone Free', there was little to complain about other than the shortness of the set. Mind you, I had been spoiled silly after seeing Blues Traveler go at it for three hours at the Commodore the night before.

The Hendrix set

Five covers by Paul Rodgers of Jimi Hendrix songs recorded in a live performance at Bayfront Park in Miami, Florida on 4 July 1993 form *The Hendrix Set*, which was released on 2 November. The EP features Neal Schon of Journey on guitar, who also jointly produced the record with Paul.

Norman Hunt

1993 Riverfest Amphitheater, Little Rock, Arkansas, USA

I saw Paul as a solo act opening for Lynyrd Skynyrd. I have to say though, he was really kinda the bright spot of the show that night. In fact I wished he'd played a longer set. He really only played about 45 minutes. He was between bands at the time. And it was about 104 degrees that day when he took the stage.

Eddie Shook

1993 Riverfest Amphitheater, Little Rock, Arkansas, USA

He literally blew the crowd away and by the time Lynyrd Skynyrd came onstage the crowd were already satiated – pretty incredible stuff. Even members of Skynyrd were side stage trying to see what all the excitement was all about.

Whoever booked Rodgers and band as an opener obviously had not done their research on the legendary vocalist / performer.

Shane Knebel

7 August 1993, Pinewood Bowl, Lincoln, Nebraska, USA

I was pretty young when I heard the song 'Bad Company' for the first time. Their music has stuck with me through all the years. Not sure exactly how old I was first hearing the song, but I was probably around 23 or 25 when I saw Bad Company live. That would have been at the Pinewood Bowl in Lincoln, Nebraska.

They were there with Molly Hatchet and Lynyrd Skynyrd. Soooo many bikers, but an awesome show. I remember vividly that it looked like a mini Sturgis! A lot of bikers, but everyone was cool and was there to see some all time classic rock.

Bad Company never fully gets the respect that they should. Still to this date, one of the best concerts I have ever seen.

1994

Paul Rodgers

It broke my heart when Paul Kossoff died. Had it been otherwise we would have definitely worked together now. We would have grown up and matured and come back, most certainly. But with his demise it was obvious there was no way we would get Free back again. It's a funny thing, looking back 20 years, but seeing it in hindsight we were a band of emotions always running high, a very intense band. But the very good side was that we left that very powerful legacy to which people are still attracted.

As a solo artist it's working well for me because it gives me the freedom to do whatever I want – soul, blues, rock 'n' roll. When we started this tour to support the blues album, it was two hours of pure blues, nothing else. But people kept coming up and said, 'Very nice, but why don't you do 'All Right Now'. I gradually started to work them into the set, now we do the whole range – and I'm very proud of what I've done.

Neil Waite

26 June 1994, Wembley Arena, London, UK

I felt deprived that I was born too late to have seen Free play live, but a desire to see as many of the surviving members perform as possible developed into a mission. A trip to The Forum, Kentish Town, London, to see Paul perform in 1994 went some way to satisfying this desire.

Making our way to the front of the stage with my wife, Alison, and best mate, Ian, we were treated to a set of Free and Bad Company classics as well as his latest *Muddy Water Blues* songs. The highlight of the evening was when he announced a special guest. I knew Brian May had guested on the tour, but I was thrilled when Simon Kirke was invited onto the stage for a couple of Free numbers. He'd lost that 70s face contortion but not the ability to play drums with energy and passion. It was an amazing night.

A few months later I noticed an advert in the music press for an event, entitled, 'Gibson's night of 100 Guitars', to be held at Wembley Arena on 26 June 1994. The name Paul Rodgers initially caught my eye, but scanning down the long list of performers I was delighted to see another name, Andy Fraser!

With Alison and Ian, we drove to London on a hot Sunday evening. The show kicked off with an interesting array of bands, including Skin, Terrovision, Thunder, Albert Lee, and Robert Palmer.

We had to wait a good hour before Paul Rodgers took to the stage, but it was worth the wait. He opened with 'Muddy Water Blues' before going straight into 'Feel Like Makin' Love.' The excitement of seeing Paul Rodgers was mixed with a feeling of anxiety – where was Andy Fraser? It was the legendary bass player I had really come to see. Perhaps he was unwell. But Paul finally invited his former bassist onto the stage for a blistering rendition of 'Little Bit of Love', followed by 'Mr Big', with its extraordinary bass solo. And Fraser didn't disappoint, rocking back and forth just like his performance on my worn-out VHS tape. A last song, 'All Right Now', then Fraser left the stage. Both Brian May and Slash were also on stage, but I didn't notice them due to my complete focus on two ex-Free legends. It was another exciting night and I came away satisfied that I'd now seen 75% of a band I loved so much.

1995

Billy Sloan

Somebody once said ... you should never meet your heroes. I don't subscribe to that. If given the opportunity, you should *always* meet your heroes. They are seldom disappointing.

I first met Paul Rodgers in the mid-1990s during an album promo tour in which he visited Glasgow. I interviewed him in my role as music correspondent for Scottish Television.

When he walked into the studios I said: 'I can't sing ... but if I could, I wish I could sing like you.'

I just kinda blurted it out. Couldn't help myself.

He just laughed. We did the interview in a boiler room in the bowels of the STV studios in Cowcaddens, Glasgow. It was all air conditioning ducts and silver clad pipes, but it looked very sci-fi and was a great location for a filmed interview.

We really got on well because he realised I was a *huge* admirer. So as you can imagine, for that one time 16-year-old fan, it was a total thrill.

I interviewed him another couple of times over the years for my newspaper column and again we hit it off. Last time I saw Paul face-to-face was at the Nelson Mandela 90th Birthday Tribute concert at Hyde Park on 27 June 2008.

He was performing with Queen in a line-up which also included The Who, Simple Minds, Annie Lennox and the late Amy Winehouse.

Again I told him I wish I could sing like him ... and again he laughed. Lovely man.

Billy Sloan with Paul Rodgers, Glasgow, Scotland 1995

Lucy Piller

I do remember in the 90s many fans dressed like Paul, wanted to have the same look as him, even his crew started to look like them. I even wanted to look like him - and that's no joke. Girls were wearing many of the same styles he wore on stage. It was very interesting to say the least.

Ennio Di Pede
3 June 1995, Lulu's, Kitchener, Canada

Just couldn't be believed! Paul Rodgers playing two Saturdays in a row after his last show here in Toronto in 1993. His first show was at Lulu's, a very cool club in Kitchener, one and a half hours west of Toronto. My wife and I, with two other friends were gonna meet Lucy Piller there. As we were standing in line she came over, informing us that she had been inside and had a nice chat with Paul, also saying that he was in really good form and looked great.

After a couple of opening bands he appeared with a big introduction from a local FM DJ. It was hard to believe how different Paul looked from '93: much thinner and looking great with Levi's jeans, white T-shirt and a very nice multicolored waistcoat, but I think his shorter hair is what made him look really young. They started off with 'Louisiana Blues'. The mix was fantastic and the other three members behind him sounded great, especially Geoff Whitehorn, playing very tasteful guitar with a beautiful tone. A very energetic 'Feel Like Makin' Love' was next, then a quick band introduction followed by 'Little Bit of Love' with the same great intro he did the year before at Woodstock. 'That's a Free song', said Paul, 'So is this next one'. As Geoff played the first two chords I knew immediately it was 'Be My Friend', a total surprise! After Paul's first verse, there was no way I could stop my eyes from filling with tears. Singing mostly with his eyes closed, with all the emotions in this world, the timing here was unbelievable, but even more was the *feel*. I've always known that Paul is the best there is, but with this killer version he is even a couple of steps above that. I never dreamt that I would ever hear this song live, let alone this great.

'Overloaded' was next up, a new funky tune, with Paul on guitar and also on the following 'Muddy Water Blues'. Then they did 'I'm Ready' and 'Rollin' Stone' with very good guitar from Geoff and amazing ad-libs from Paul. 'Standing Around Crying' followed and at the end of the song Paul shouted: 'That's the blues, a lot a fun!' When Geoff played 'Mr. Big' it was pretty close to the original but he added his own touch to the latter part of the solo, and the bass by Jaz was much faster than Andy's, even Paul seemed surprised - different, but not bad!

Then Paul shouts: 'Here is a song you might remember, I hope we do!' And it's 'Fire and Water' Paul looked our way as they started to play 'The Hunter' – 'Oh Yeah! This one's for Lucy too'. A very nice touch by Paul.

How did they end it? 'We gonna love and leave you with this one' and straight into 'Can't Get Enough'. After a lot of noise, they come back with 'Bad Company', with a very slow start. 'That's why they call me'... Then 'BANG!' – a big explosion that surprised the crowd – sparks all over the stage and everyone going crazy, with Paul loving every minute of it. The very familiar drum opening of 'All Right Now' with Geoff's guitar on top sounded very close to the original. Even the solo was really close to Koss. Another goodbye and then back after a while with 'Little Wing', nice version, but after having heard the Miami take? No comparison. Not so with 'Wishing Well', Paul screaming this one out like only he knows how.

A superb concert that will be remembered for a long, long time. Lucy, Alan and I went to see if we could meet the band after the show.

I must admit I was getting a little nervous. Suddenly Paul came out from this room straight toward us, he got just a few feet away but was grabbed and kissed by this lady in front of me. After a few seconds I shook his hand and gave him a photo, he took a look, asked where it was taken, I told him at the Phoenix show two years earlier. I guess he didn't understand that I wanted him to have it. He signed it and gave it back to me – bonus! I also had a bunch of albums with me: *The Law, Muddy Water Blues, Cut Loose, Highway* and *Free* – the last two with Simon Kirke's autograph already on them. I gave them to him and he was so nice to sign them all for me, I thanked him, shook his hand again and said I was gonna be at the RPM show the following week. I spotted Geoff on the other side and asked for his autograph, he asked for my name and signed it at the back of *Cut Loose*, not many people around us, we'd just met but started chatting like old pals, he was really nice and funny as well. We chatted a bit about guitars and working with Paul and he rightly said: 'He is the best in the business, there just isn't anybody better'.

We all left with such big smiles that lasted for days.

The following Saturday the three of us met at around 5pm at RPM and could hear Paul doing the sound check, so we walked right in and stayed to the left of the stage. He was playing a new song that he was calling 'Have Mercy'(now called 'Chasing Shadows'). After a few more songs all was done. Paul came over with a kiss for Lucy and a handshake for us.

As we were chatting, Geoff came over and joined us, I was pretty surprised that he even remembered my name. Paul had a big laugh when I told him that he was getting even better as he got older. Alan talked to him for quite a while about motorcycles: Paul had a Harley.

We took a few pictures and left. I'm not going to talk much about the show. It was very good, but I liked Lulu's better, Paul sounded great (as usual) but looked a little tired at times: I believe he played four gigs that week.

I saw Paul for a few seconds after the show but Geoff came over to us, I showed him the photos from the Lulu's show and he signed one – 'Cheers Ennio, Geoff Whitehorn '95'. Can't really say enough about this guy and how nice he is. It was wonderful meeting Paul and the boys, I guess deep down he knows what he means to us, that little time spent together was so precious to me, a great privilege.

Paul Rodgers on stage June 10 1995. Photos by Ennio Di Pede

1996

Christine Killen

6 May 1996, The City Hall, Newcastle, Tyneside, UK

Free at the City Hall, Newcastle was the first time I saw Paul Rodgers, but one concert I will never forget was a solo appearance. I remember it well. Me and my husband were in the 2nd row from the front. When Paul encouraged everyone to come to the front of the stage I was there in a flash. My husband has never seen me move so fast. As I had a great spot, I was in line when Paul came along the row and touched everyone's hand. I was on cloud nine and looked back at my husband who was laughing but had his head in his hands. I would like to say that I never washed my hand for a week but that would not be true.

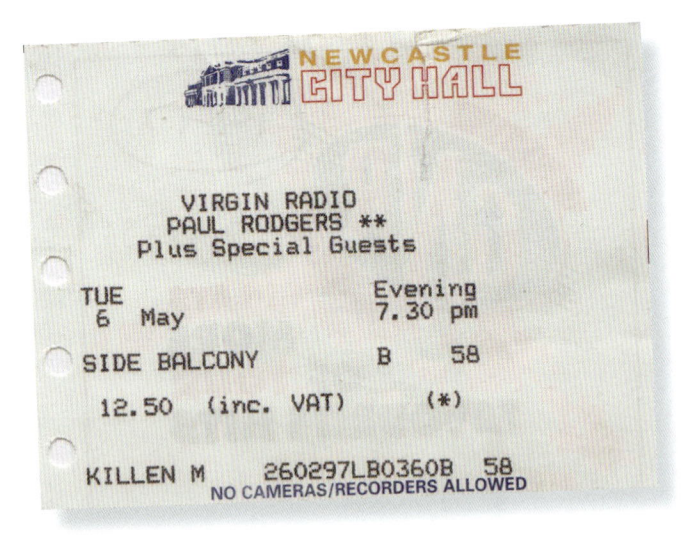

Another memorable moment, one that I will never forget.

Simon Kirke

How did I get involved with the Rock and Roll Fantasy Camp? After my first tour with Ringo in 1996, the promoter David Fishof asked if I would like to be a counselor at his Rock and Roll Fantasy Camp, which he had just started. It caters to people from all walks of life who are interested in furthering their knowledge of their particular instrument of choice. At any given camp there are about 10 counselors, mostly from well known bands. They hang with us for four days, and we teach them, and on the final day there is a gathering of the bands and prizes are given out and so on. We've had a lot of celebs through our doors, as you can see on the website. I did eight camps and got a lot out of it. Just giving something back, I guess.

1997

Paul McCaskell

20 February 1997, Cambridge Corn Exchange, Cambridge, UK

I've seen Paul quite a few times but one gig that stands out was Cambridge 1997 at the Corn Exchange.

In between songs, he said 'Right, what's next?' I was near the front so I shouted out 'Rollin' Stone'! and he pointed at me and said, 'Yeah, that's the one!' Later, he sang the opening line to 'Come Save Me (Julianne)' acapella and then stopped and said, 'We're not playing that rubbish!'

A great night: Steve Lukather and Jason Bonham played their part too. Bliss!

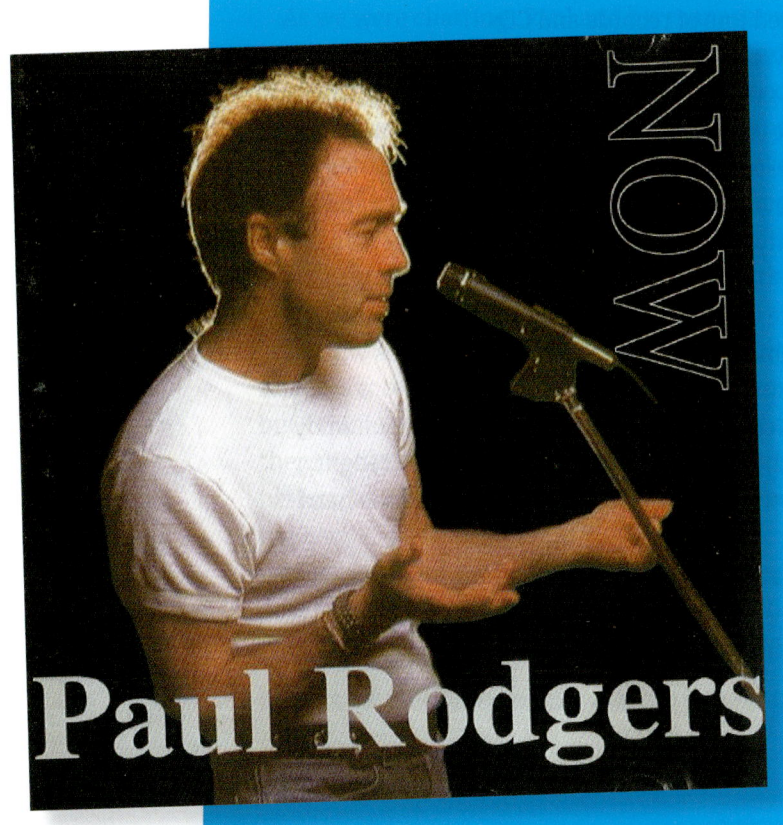

Now

Paul Rodgers' third solo album, *Now*, was released in the spring of 1997 and peaked at No.30 on the UK chart. The recordings feature a British band consisting of Jaz Lochrie on bass, Jimmy Copley on drums and Geoff Whitehorn on guitar. The quartet continued to tour around the world in support of the album.

was in the front row for that show. Steve Miller's camera crew was rude and would not move the big camera from my view of Paul, so I went to the meet and greet gate, and asked to speak with someone from Paul's management team. I do not remember whom I spoke to, but was promised meet and greet tickets for the next time Paul was in town. I gave my address and phone number, and promptly began receiving items in the mail from Swan Song, a *Muddy Water Blues* poster was one, a CD with the new acoustic version of 'Feel Like Makin' Love', as well as several t-shirts and hats.

When he came to Virginia Beach, I received confirmation that my meet and greet passes would be there, as they were. Paul signed my Muddy Waters poster and I was on top of the world. He made me feel special in so many ways. I met him a few more times at meet and greets, he always made sure that I was able to come back to see him.

I have not seen Paul Rodgers perform live in close to 20 years, and I would give anything just to see him one more time.

1998

Paul Rodgers, Mick Ralphs, Boz Burrell and Simon Kirke re-united the original Bad Company line-up to tour and record. Paul and Simon continued until 2002, Mick until 2000 and Boz ended his career with the band in 1999. In 2008, Paul, Mick and Simon once again reformed Bad Company.

1999

Susie Kaplar

January 1999, Club Caprice, Redondo or Manhattan Beach, California, USA

I have been a fan of Bad Company since 1975. One of the songs they put out in 1975, 'Movin' On' was on the charts when we moved from Illinois to California.

In 1999 I won a pair of tickets to see Paul Rodgers at a small venue. I was quite excited! My husband Phil and I drove about 80 miles, taking my Bad Company albums with me, just in case I could get them signed.

The concert was awesome, but the best part was that someone threw a piece of currency (don't recall if it was a $20, $50 or higher) and Paul asked the guy 'what do he want to?' and the guy replied, 'Seagull'. Paul commented that he hadn't brought along an acoustic guitar with him, but he played it solo on his electric guitar. It was so beautiful that I almost cried.

After the concert was over, somehow we started to talk to his girlfriend, who was from Canada. I was trying to meet him and take a photo and get my albums signed. The girlfriend said he was just too tired, but she offered to take my albums to the hotel room to see if he would sign them. I also told her the story about him playing 'Seagull' and how much I enjoyed it.

When she returned, she told me that she told him my story of him playing 'Seagull'. She pointed out that not only did he sign my album, but he drew a couple of seagulls inside the album cover.

I will never forget that experience.

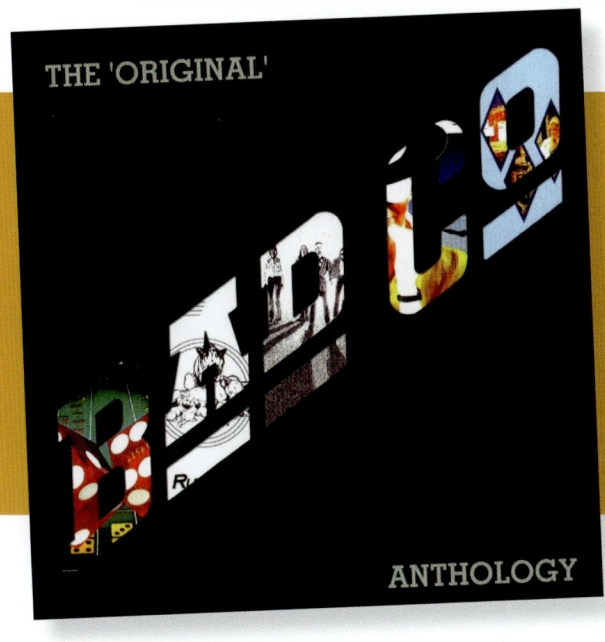

The 'Original' Bad Co. Anthology

The title says it all. The original line-up's greatest tracks, augmented by some new material, was released on 23 March 1999.

Marvin Beasley

1999, Lawrence Joel Coliseum, Winston Salem, North Carolina, USA

In 1999, at the beginning of the reunion tour of Bad Company with the original four members, I was given the opportunity to introduce the band in North Carolina. It was an awesome experience.

I ran into Paul Rodgers backstage in the greenroom area. He was sitting alone, just relaxing. I walked over and introduced myself and as we talked a pro photographer I'd met earlier saw us and I waved him over. He took a shot and Paul said, 'Let's get another!' I could not tell you what we talked about. I was too busy absorbing the fact of who was right in front of me!

Being onstage with the band as they broke into 'Can't Get Enough' and introducing the band was unbelievable.

How I came to be able to introduce the band was a little unusual, but I was very fortunate. I worked for a local TV station in the area, and one of the advertising sales girls came up with a contest involving the Greensboro Music Academy. I was in the control room when the commercial for the contest aired. I couldn't believe what I was hearing and seeing. The Greensboro Music Academy was having a contest, with auditions to introduce Bad Company at the Lawrence Joel Coliseum.

This was great. But as most things like this work, employees of the station aren't eligible. Good for me, then, that this contest was not for station promotion. I called the Academy to find out if anyone could audition. Yes!

When I got to the audition, one other person showed up. The rest is history!

What can be said about Paul Rodgers? A *huge* influence musically, and a great soul.

Laura Roland

Clio Amphitheater, Clio, Michigan, USA

I have listened to Paul Rodgers since the 70s and Bad Company were a part of my life. I lost my best friend and sister to cancer. We would listen to the song, 'Seagull', and others. Paul's music made a difference in my life and the lives of others. My story is from the late 1990s early 2000's.

I met the band, in Michigan, in a small venue at the Clio Amphitheater. I was living in Swartz Creek, Michigan, at the time. Me, and a handful of others, were able to go back stage where a pizza was being delivered to the band and the pizza delivery guys told 'em we, the fans, were outside hoping and waiting to see them. Sure enough, they came out and met us! I asked Paul Rodgers if he would sign the back pocket of my Levi jeans? He laughed, and said, 'She wants me to sign, her bum'. And he did!

I kept the jeans and have a picture somewhere but I'm sad to say that I lost them in a storage unit. It was a terrible story. I lost my sister to cancer and had stored her things and a few of mine in a storage unit because I also went through a tumultuous divorce, and I was one day late on paying the storage unit. The girl did not like me or care for me, for some reason, she sold my things. When I called the next day to pay on it, it was too late. The girl laughed at me and said: '...oh well'.

I lost not only those jeans, but recordings of my sister's voice and a few other gems that I was hanging onto for her daughter, my niece. I know that they are only 'things' but I treasured those 'things.'

Paul Rodgers (Bad Company) and his/their songs, made an impression on and in my life, then and now. His music will last in my heart forever and remind me of those that I love and have lost, good times and bad. Meeting Paul Rodgers was always a dream of mine and it came true! I wish I still had those jeans and his autograph. They were a size 12 and I'm not that size anymore, but I still got it going on!

I haven't been the same person since losing my sister, back in 2013. But thank you for letting me tell my story.

I just want to say, 'thank you Paul Rodgers, for all the great memories.

Michael Hoff

21 July 1999, Rock and Roll Hall of Fame, Cleveland, Ohio, USA

One of my favourite memories of Paul Rodgers was when he was with Bad Company. Myself and my good friend Greg were heading up to Rome, New York from St. Louis, Missouri to attend Woodstock '99 and we had mapped out our adventure well in advance because we were driving.

We had planned on staying the night in Cleveland, Ohio to visit the Rock and Roll Hall of Fame. So after we checked into our hotel and ate some dinner we headed over to the Rock and Roll Hall of Fame as planned. But as soon as we got there we noticed a sign on the door that stated the Rock and Roll Hall of Fame was closed for a private event. We were totally bummed out until we saw a security guard nearby and we asked him what was going. He told us that the closure was due to a sponsored event by the radio station 100.7 WMMS. We told him that we were from St. Louis and we were heading to Woodstock '99 and that we had planned this trip, which included a visit to the Hall of Fame. Well, he says: 'St. Louis?' and we said 'yes sir' and he says 'all right' and gave us wristbands and let us inside.

We had no idea that the original Bad Company was there and was going to perform an acoustic set. This was an unimaginable bonus as we got to see them perform an eight-song unplugged set that was unbelievable and has to be one of the best highlights of my life.

After their set, we got to walk around the museum and see all the great memorabilia they had to offer. What a great night and experience we had. One I will never forget.

2000

Paul Rodgers

Cavern Club, Liverpool, UK

One of the biggest thrills of my career was being invited to play in Liverpool at the Cavern. Standing there on that legendary stage – and it's not even as big as a modern day drum-riser! – was an incredible feeling because it was from there that those four guys went out and changed the world. They literally did. Being there, in that same space as them, actually sent shivers down my spine. At the end of 'Rock and Roll Fantasy' I did a little Beatles medley, because to me the Beatles are part of my rock 'n' roll fantasy—as well as blues and soul and a lot of other things, you know—and it took the roof off the place. So that's something that's stayed in the set too.

Ray Johnson

8 June 2000, The Cavern, Liverpool, UK

I'd been a huge fan of Free and Bad Company and Paul Rodgers right throughout his career and my late brother-in-law, Ronnie Hobson, was actually a roadie for Free. The Cavern gig came about like this. Paul hadn't performed for a while and he'd got a little band together with some of his old pals doing a small tour. We managed to get in touch with his agent and then his manager – we were told that the date was free and a fee needed to be met and we just said to one another 'Let's get him!' The kudos of getting Paul Rodgers in the Cavern was the thing. Then Paul was told about our approach and said, 'Why not? I'd love to do the Cavern!' The gig was on.

There was absolutely a feeling that – having had Paul McCartney play a gig at the Cavern at the end of the previous year that people like Paul Rodgers would want to do the same thing. McCartney provided the springboard for a whole lot of big names wanting to do it.

The day before the show his manager and one of his crew arrived in Liverpool to come and check out the venue. If my memory serves me, we had to bring in a separate mixing desk to suit all the special technical requirements. And his manager said, 'we have a very strict no smoking policy. So from eight o'clock this evening make sure nobody smokes in this room. And we need some stewards tomorrow night to make sure nobody smokes because if anyone does Paul will not perform. If he comes to the venue and gets the slightest whiff of tobacco or smoke, he will not sing. '

We complied and it worked. Everyone coming into the show was asked nicely. Everybody stuck to it.

Paul turned up and we'd arranged to have a brick made for him to be added to the Cavern Wall of Fame, which he was delighted with.

Basically, on the day, I was looking after him and his band - ginseng, the right wines, towels all that sort of thing.

The show itself was just great. Paul Rodgers and just three musicians and Paul on guitar and keyboards on a couple of numbers playing all the Free and Bad Company hits plus a couple of songs from his new solo album. There had been a scramble for tickets because the gig was announced at very short notice. There were 300 in the Cavern but the demand was amazing. He commented that it was such a great night playing in such a small place and glad after a period away that the fans in Liverpool still remembered him. His repartee and sense of humour with the audience was amazing but he's a Geordie lad so similar to a scouser. They say never meet the people you worship, because sometimes it backfires on you, but he was so down to earth and a great guy.

ROCK 'N' ROLL FANTASY

Paul is presented with his brick for the Wall of Fame in Mathew Street by Ray Johnson. Photo: Courtesy The Cavern Club

After the gig I asked him what had he got planned the day after. And he said they had a free day and added: 'we're all big Beatles fans and the guys were asking how you get to see all those big Beatles' sights in Liverpool?' So I replied: 'It just so happens I'm a Beatles guide as well as working at the Cavern. If you want I can take you on the Magical Mystery Tour and show you all these places.' And that's exactly what we did. We went on his tour bus and had a great time. Funny really – I performed for them for a couple of hours, if you see what I mean, and they just listened to me when we went on the tour.

Electric

Released in June 2000, *Electric* is the fourth solo album by Paul Rodgers. Paul had returned to his native North East to record it a year earlier at Lartington Hall Studios, near Barnard Castle, County Durham.

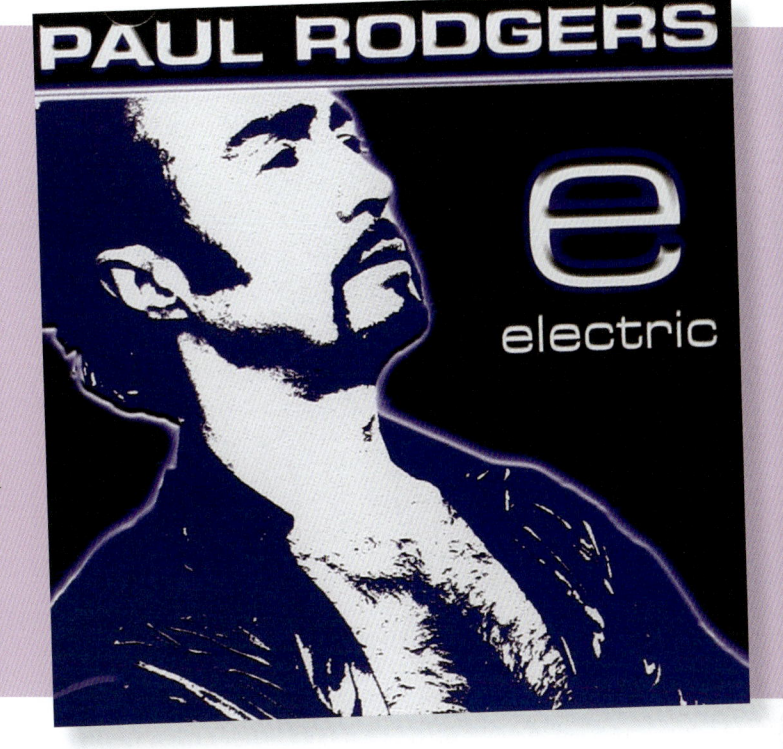

2001

Andrew G. Dick

16 February 2001, Barrowland Ballroom, Glasgow, UK

I was a big fan of Free since the early 1990s in my teens, as a few mates at school were into them. They had a pure rock sound that was being rebuilt by the grunge and alternative scene at that time. Free fitted into that. They were similar to the Black Crowes who I was also into at the time. It was when I started subscribing to the new *Classic Rock* magazine in 1999 that I got properly into Free.

   I saw Paul Rodgers at a solo concert – the support was Asia – way back in 2001 at the Barrowland Ballroom in Glasgow. It was a great gig and one I remember very clearly. Paul mostly played Free songs and Simon Kirke was on drums. I was right down at the barrier. Boy what a voice! As good as on all those albums. Yet to see Paul again, but sure I will.

Jon Kirkman

25 April 2001, Hammersmith Odeon, London, UK

I was working with Asia at the time, when Paul Rodgers was playing the Hammersmith Odeon with Asia as support and Paul was introduced by David Kossoff (Paul Kossoff's father) on stage.

It turned out David Kossoff was staying in the same hotel, the Columbia, as me and I had a chat with him. He was a lovely man and he said something that actually quite shocked me that day. He said: 'You do know John, that Paul has been dead now longer than he's been alive.' Very sad.

Paula Terry

2001, B.B. King Blues Club, New York City, USA

My father introduced me to Bad Company. He used to play them all the time. I heard them when I was 4 years old. And now 40 some odd years later they are my all time favourite band. 'Til the day I die'!

I have seen Bad Company and Paul Rodgers over 50 times. My first time was in 2001 when I won tickets to see Paul at B.B.King's club in New York City. I was actually introduced to Paul: Such a cool experience. I was literally tearing up and my knees were shaking. I was able to grab a picture of him but I chopped off the top of his head!

That was the first of three really fond memories for different reasons in 2001, 2006 and 2018...

Scott Greenhalgh

21 June 2001, Lakewood Amphitheater, Atlanta, Georgia, USA

Bad Company albums were blaring through the speakers all the time in the Greenhalgh household: I was born a fan. I was the child reading the liner notes and discovering the family tree. First discovery? Free. I started with a *Best of* but I soon had every album in my possession. Free is one of my all time favourite bands, to put it mildly.

But my exposure to the music live? That began on 21 June 2001, at the Lakewood Amphitheater in Atlanta. I was going to see Bad Company for the first time with Paul Rodgers.

I'm on cloud nine. Then I walk in to find Bad Company are on before Styx. What? What kind of world do we live in where Styx can follow Bad Company? I love Tommy Shaw but *come on*! The concert was great. Shorter than I would have liked but great. I had no interest in seeing Styx live. My parents had tortured me with that years before when Dennis DeYoung was still at the helm. I was going to meet my idol Paul Rodgers. I was at the show with my old time best friend Sterling. I pointed out people were just walking to and from backstage as they like. Hmm easy, back we go. I turn to Sterling and say, 'look like you're supposed to be here'. I don't say that to be cocky. It's just funny shit you think works when you're young. The first thing I remember is the other guitarist of Styx walks over and says hello. I said hello back and kept walking. Sterling's pissing himself laughing and then I see one of my all time favourite drummers, Simon Kirke. He was flipping through the Free book *Heavy Load* while chatting with this lady but unfortunately I didn't get to speak to him.

Looking round for Paul, I parked myself on a picnic table next to the tour buses, practically waiting to be thrown out, when here he comes running to the bus. I yell: 'Paul!' He turns and walks over. I asked if I could shake his hand and without hesitation he greeted me. The first thing I said was 'I've got everything you've done since *Tons of Sobs*.' He says, 'how do you know that? You're too young...' I replied, 'I was raised right.' He took the time to talk to me for a few minutes and no sooner had he taken off for the bus than a security guard comes over asking for my pass. I told him, 'I don't have one' and I got thrown out – but with a huge smile on my face.

Since that first show, I've seen Bad Company live on multiple occasions, Rodgers solo, and live with Queen. It's hard to pick favourites but the latest Free Spirit tour would take some fucking beating. Simply amazing getting to see songs live by 'the man'. I'd never thought I'd see likes of 'The Stealer' and 'Woman' live. I can die a happy man.

2002

Laurence Tressler

26 July 2002, House of Blues, Disneyland, Orlando, Florida, USA

The year was 2002. My wife Clare had decided that for our holiday that year, we would take our three young girls, Elizabeth, Victoria and Sarah on a trip to Disneyland, Orlando, Florida and take in the usual parks, MGM studios, Animal Kingdom, Epcot etc. The girls loved it, of course, and frankly, so did I, even the Mickey Mouse stuff. Then one day, as a break from the exciting but constantly wearing and tiring days in the parks, we ended up in Downtown Disney, which, for those who don't know, is a sort of retail, restaurant, recreational development, with a heavy Disney imagineered feel about it.

Laurence Tressler takes a break at Disneyland

A club bar bearing the name House of Blues caught my eye. It was an artificial but very authentically created building – deliberately tatty, a recreation of a bar of the type one would expect to find, off the beaten track, in the blues lands of the Deep South, a shack with tin signs next to a big water tower. We wandered up the artificially battered looking uneven wooden steps, entered the intimidating darkened building and into the bar.

I happened to gaze at the walls and my eyes were drawn to the up and coming gigs poster. I couldn't believe it. Bad Company? Really? I loved the band. My mate Woodsie played the first *Bad Company* album non-stop at school, but I now had them all. They hadn't toured the UK for years as far as I was aware. I'd seen them at Birmingham Odeon in March 1979 but that was well over 20 years ago. I think they'd toured the USA a number of times since, but appearances in the UK, as far as I was aware, were very few and far between.

I quickly checked the date and it was the night before we were due to head home after our holiday. My wife said the kids would need a good night's sleep before a long journey home and then added that she wanted the same, so if I wanted to try and get a ticket she was OK with it. I thought great, then realised of course that the chances of getting a ticket, less than a week before the gig, were probably about zero.

I asked behind the bar and couldn't believe it - no problem, I had a ticket. It all seemed too easy. I turned up on the night via a bus, with the timings for the return journey in my head. Way too easy.

The hall was relatively small, intimate I suppose, and comfortably filled, all standing, but not absolutely packed. I bought a pint of the usual lager and stood mid stage about twenty feet back. A great position and a great view. Way, way too easy.

I started to talk to a few people around me and most were, perhaps surprisingly, female. A loud female voice behind me then announced, 'Hey girls we've got Hugh Grant over here'. I was then surrounded by a group of American girls all pulling at my hair and asking me to speak and getting all excited every time I opened my mouth. It all seemed a bit bizarre. Was it the effect of drink or some other recreational stimulant that the group had shared? As far as I was concerned, I looked nothing like Hugh Grant nor sounded like him – but that's not how it appeared to them. They were clearly fascinated by my British accent and were linking arms with me or throwing their arms round me.

The small detail that I have so far failed to mention is that each of these girls was clearly paired up from a group of athletic baseball physiqued American guys. Now this caused me a degree of concern, as I wasn't sure, after two or three Budweisers, how understanding these guys were going to be, bearing in mind their ladies seemed obsessed with and were wrapping themselves around this single, ordinary, English guy. I didn't think my wife would be terribly impressed either, but what could I do?

Then the lights dimmed, the crowd cheered, four silhouetted figures walked on to the darkened stage and I still couldn't really believe it was happening. I heard, 'One, two, a one, two, three' then two strikes from the drumsticks to lead into a huge guitar chord. The unmistakable intro to 'Can't Get Enough'.

I can't remember the full set list or song order, but I do know that they played 'Feel Like Makin' Love', 'Rock Steady', 'Ready for Love', 'Shooting Star', 'Rock 'n' Roll Fantasy', 'Run With the Pack' and 'Bad Company'. I discovered Free comparatively late in life and only as a result of the Bad Company connection. But of course, with Simon Kirke there on stage, playing drums, Paul was able to say, 'Here's one from way back when we were Free' and launched into 'All Right Now'.

They were superb. A great sounding band, providing a fine canvas of sound on which to lay the amazing singing voice of Paul Rodgers. Range, raunch, power, pitch, feeling, tone, emotion – his voice had them all. For the life of me, I cannot remember who played guitar and bass, but I don't think Mick Ralphs featured.

Then, as is so often the case with a great gig, it was all over too soon and I said goodnight and goodbye before I got further accosted or even beaten up. I had about twenty minutes to waste before the bus arrived and wandered into the against the stage right in front of my rock hero. I was able to get his autograph that night and I remember driving home so excited thinking that nothing could ever top this.

Hold that thought! A couple years later I'm about to get married and as I'm going over music for the reception I'm not really having much of a choice and then the big day arrived. Debbie and I were married on 8 May, 2004 and when they called for the bride and groom's first dance, I was expecting K-Ci & JoJo and 'All My Life'. But instead my wife looked up at me and what do I hear? 'Nights Like This' from Paul Rodgers' solo album *Now*, then fading at the end into 'Feel Like Makin' Love'. Now that just topped it all.

Then, first concert my wife went to was Paul Rodgers and Queen in Philadelphia and when we returned home from the concert Debbie came out of our office and said how do you feel like Pittsburgh? I said, 'I'm a Steelers fan, what do you mean?' She says: 'I got us front row seats for Paul Rodgers and Queen in a few days, again! I've also seen Bad Company with Lynyrd Skynyrd, Bad Company with Ted Nugent, Bad Company with Joe Walsh ... I try to see Paul Rodgers anytime he comes around local.

Your No.1 fan in Delaware would like to say - 'Thank You Paul Rodgers' for always being there through the good times and the bad.

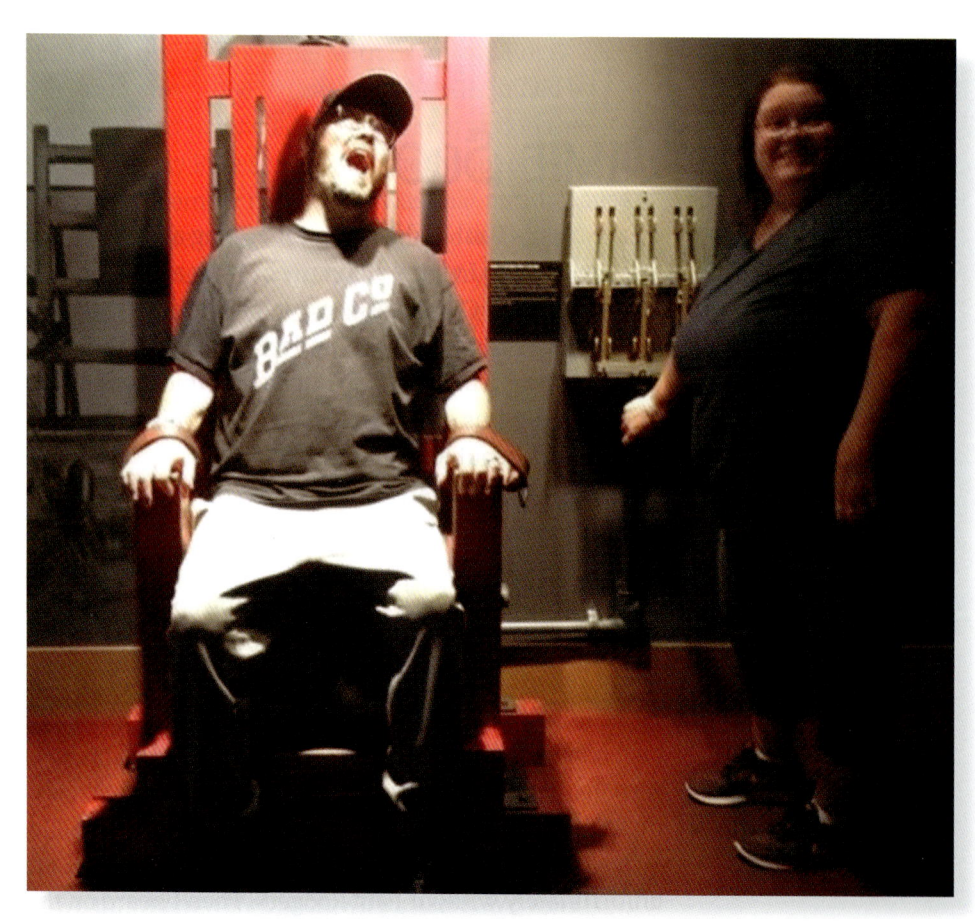

Bad Company: 'Til the day he dies! Jamie Scott and wife Debbie celebrating their 15-year anniversary in Vegas

Andrew Adams

Paul Rodgers' voice captured my initial interest in Free but Paul Kossoff helped that interest grow. In 2004, a year before Paul Kossoff's father David passed away, I bought the bust David had made of his son. Although I've met Paul Rodgers, Simon Kirke and Andy Fraser the nearest I got to Kossoff was speaking to his father and brother on the phone.

David Kossoff tried to ring me to say that the delivery of the bust would be delayed because of Christmas. I'd just walked in the house after finishing work and my wife Julie said to me, 'David Kossoff is on the phone for you'.

I remember saying to her, 'Fuck off! It's Leon pissing about! My mate Leon has a reputation of doing prank calls. She handed me the phone with a knowing smile.

As soon as he spoke, I recognised the voice and I didn't swear... Then Simon Kossoff called me after Christmas to inform me that the bust was on its way. That was a coincidence, as Leon and his wife were visiting us that day. When the phone rang, I said: 'It better not be Kossoff nagging me'. My wife and guests were fair sniggering in the background.

I first got to appreciate Free when I was about seven-years-old. I'm the youngest of five children and my two eldest brothers loved the *Fire and Water* album. I wished I had seen Free but was too young. I'm jealous of all the people that have but we live with missed opportunities. Paul Kossoff is amazing to watch. The way he gets those notes and of course the silent scream. As Paul Rodgers once said, 'Kossoff played every note as if his life depended on it'.

You only have to listen to the live version of 'Moonshine' to appreciate how emotional and delicate he could make the guitar sound. I have of course visited Paul Kossoff's wooden plaque at Golders Green cemetery and have the bust and a painting by my brother Nigel to remember him by. As long as I can listen to the great music and watch the films, I'm happy.

Reminders of Paul Kossoff: The bust Andrew Adams purchased from Paul's father David and an oil painting by Andrew's older brother, Nigel Adams (now Vincent Banksy)

2005

Paul Rodgers

We did a TV show together [with Queen] and they didn't have a singer. Brian [May] came to me and said if you sing 'We Will Rock You' for us, we'll be your backing band for 'All Right Now.' That sounded like a pretty good deal, to have Queen as your backing band! So we played together and the chemistry was so good we decided to do a European tour. That tour turned into four years!

This is two forces joining together – no one is trying to take Freddie's place, no one ever could. I accept that, he was a great singer, great performer and great songwriter, and I wouldn't attempt to impersonate him.

Queen really do play my songs exceptionally well. 'Feel Like Makin' Love' went to a new level when we played it, which I never thought it could. I enjoy singing 'The Show Must Go On', because that was virgin territory for me – Queen never played that live themselves. I really like 'I Want To Break Free', too. It's a complete challenge to interpret that song in a different way! I look at that song in a way that an older Freddie might sing it.

Martin Skala

28 March 2005 Brixton Academy, London, UK

The first gig of the tour, many potential issues. Stupid fan club ticket lottery in which I didn't win but yet somehow ended up with two tickets, a 20-hour bus drive from Prague to London, very cheap accommodation with a very suspicious large black sack as a dustbin. But all the hassle was worth it. After the longest intro ever – the whole 23 minutes of 'Track 13' from the *Made In Heaven* album followed by Eminem's surprising but powerful 'Lose Yourself' – Paul sang the famous line from 'Reachin' Out', gave us a nervous smile, down went the black curtain and Queen were back in full glory.

I remember two funny moments. Brian saying 'I can do what I want, right?' before the acoustic set, the guy next to me shouted ''39!', Brian replied 'are you sure?' and played this long forgotten Queen song that wasn't on the setlist at all (but stayed there for the rest of the tour). Half an hour later Roger leaned to his son who was watching the show from near the speakers: 'Wish me luck!' He started drumming 'I'm In Love With My Car' but after a few seconds clearly got lost and couldn't remember how to continue and Spike had to count and help him get out of the intro...

Antonio Pellegrini

5 April 2005, Assago Forum, Milan, Italy

The first time I attended a Paul Rodgers concert was in April 2005 at the Assago Forum in Milan during the first tour of Queen + Paul Rodgers.

The Forum is full of people, I'm sitting in the second ring, top right. I see the stage well, but as the musicians are far away, they are a bit small in my eyes. Fortunately, the acoustics from where I sit are very good. After the short introduction of 'Reachin' Out', sung by Paul, it's time for Brian May's guitar, which comes on stage with a very powerful sound. The curtain suddenly falls on Queen's 'Tie Your Mother Down'. Paul wears a tight t-shirt, has short hair and a goatee on his chin – his look is very different from the 70's look – and he immediately arouses the enthusiasm of the audience by twirling the microphone pole.

And then it's the turn of a Bad Company song, 'Can't Get Enough', with a really dragging rendition. Brian May and Roger Taylor are very effective playing this rock song. Paul then has fun accompanying Queen's rockabilly 'Crazy Little Thing Called Love' with an acoustic guitar.

After the fast songs of the first part of the concert, Paul moves on the catwalk that leads from the centre of the stage among the audience, to perform 'Seagull' on his own, voice and guitar. Towards the middle of the song, Taylor walks down the catwalk, to accompany him playing congas.

And after a while the first song by Free arrives, 'A Little Bit Of Love', which is kept on the set list only for the first dates of the tour. Again, Queen, and Brian May in particular, manage to do justice to the song, enhancing its rhythmic blues rock cadence.

After a couple of Queen classics the set list comes to another Bad Company song, 'Feel Like Makin' Love'. The acoustic guitar of the guitarist who supports Brian May in the tour kicks off the piece in a delicate and almost country rock way, and then it turns on in the refrain, with May's intense rhythms and Paul's high notes.

The Queen song that Paul really enhances, in my opinion, is 'I Want It All': beautiful, very powerful and played in a masterful way.

The last piece of Rodgers' career to be performed tonight is the classic 'All Right Now'. This was the first Free song I heard when I was a teenager in the 90s and still today the album *Fire And Water* is one of my favourites.

We get to the end of the concert with the classics 'We Will Rock You' and 'We Are The Champions', and suddenly a really exciting day ends.

I lived this evening in an incredulous, surprised and very excited way.

Martin Skala

17 March 2005, Arena, Leipzig, Germany

I didn't enjoyed this concert much. I had the flu and the girl next to me was screaming the whole time. There was just one thing that could save the day and that was meeting the band.

We were waiting at the gate near the backstage door but the limousine drivers clearly had no intentions to stop there. One option was to block the gate but I think we all understand why this idea was quickly abandoned. The second plan sounded better - to get in our car (an extremely slow Renault Clio) and pursue the band in their limousines in order to find out what hotel they were staying in. Surprisingly enough this did work - although the trip included multiple violations of traffic rules as Brian's Mercedes was speeding and we had no other choice than doing the same. After less than half an hour we found out the name of the hotel and the next morning we returned there

Martin Skala and friends meet Paul Rodgers in Leipzig, Germany

to meet the band before they left for the airport. Those were the good old days when very very few fans were patient enough to wait and the band members even stopped for a quick chat.

Tibor Ipacs

23 April 2005, Papp László Budapest Sportaréna, Budapest, Hungary

I have been listening to Paul Rodgers' music since 1996. I received *Fire and Water* on CD for that Christmas.

Unfortunately he never had a solo concert here in Hungary, but he was the singer of Queen + Paul Rodgers in 2005.

A friend of mine suggested going to the hotel they were supposed to be staying at, and we were lucky. Paul Rodgers came out to go for a walk with his bodyguard and he was kind enough and signed my CD booklet and posed for a photo. When I was about to leave, I did not look around properly (still starstruck!), and Mr. Rodgers grabbed my arm saying: ' Watch out!' – as a car was coming. So, in a way, he was my guardian angel for that moment. Thank you, Paul.

Photos by Tibor's friend György Hoffmann were taken shortly before the near accident, prevented by guardian angel Paul Rodgers

Brian May

Paul has his own style, which we integrated into Queen. But what happened was, there was a meeting point where we wanted to go deeply into his music which we were influenced by in the first place. For me, it was a joy to play 'All Right Now,' 'Can't Get Enough' and all those songs.

Photos by Lucy Piller

Jonnie Hodson

4 May 2005, MEN Arena, Manchester, UK

I was about 12: I saw Paul Rodgers live and it changed my life. I know it's a cliché, but if I hadn't seen that show I wouldn't have formed bands and toured the UK and Europe.

My father told me that Queen were going on tour in the North West of England and I couldn't believe it. We didn't really have the Internet at that point, so the information wasn't as instant as it is now. 'What! Who's singing! Brian and Roger!' 'No, they're teaming up with Paul Rodgers from Free and Bad Company' he informed me. I knew 'All Right Now' and 'Can't Get Enough', but at the time I was a Queen fan, I was going to see Brian and Roger.

Off we went, to the MEN Arena, I couldn't wait to see Queen. The lights drop, 'Lose Yourself' by Eminem comes blasting through the speakers, then a boom. 'Lately I've been hard to reach, I been too long on my own...' And there at the end of the thrust stage, from the darkens, appeared the man who would completely change my life.

I truly transcended to another planet, it was the closest thing I think I'd felt to a religious experience that I could remember. My mother took me to church as a kid, and when everyone was singing I remember thinking that that was what religion was. This topped it. I was gone, totally fixated. I told my Dad that night, 'when I grow up, I'm going to be that guy'. I wonder now if my father knew how serious I was!

The next day I went and bought as much Paul Rodgers music as my pocket money would buy me. Everytime the family would go out I'd stand in my room trying to copy that voice. Free hit me like a tonne of bricks, then came Bad Company. *Muddy Water Blues* took me back further, I went and buried myself in that music. Most of the music I listen to today comes from Paul.

I'd take every opportunity in school to sing on stage, singing in the musicals at the end of the year. When it came to going to college, I wanted to go do music. The head of performing arts told me I wasn't good enough as a singer to do that, but I should do acting instead.

I went to Liverpool Arts College to do an acting course and immediately sought out the other musicians. I dropped out of college to follow music and long story short I formed bands and hit the road. Fifteen years on, Paul Rodgers is my yardstick and the soundtrack to my life. Every time I think I've nailed a show, I listen to Paul Rodgers live and tell myself there's still a long way to go! Going to a Paul Rodgers show is a lesson for a singer.

I'm lucky enough to have met him a couple of times and he's always a true gentleman, with advice, kind words and time to talk. I once heard Paul say Otis Redding taught him to sing, so really Paul Rodgers is my Otis Redding. I'm not only a fan, I'm a student of Paul Rodgers. At some point, I'll have to find a way of thanking him.

Phil Chapman

4th May 2005 MEN Arena, Manchester, UK

I saw Queen + Paul Rodgers on 4 May 2005, at the Manchester Evening News Arena, during the Return of the Champions tour.

I'd seen Queen with Freddie Mercury in the 1970s and 1980s, but had never seen Free, or Bad Company, so I was really looking forward to this gig. The show started with Paul Rodgers singing 'Reaching Out' (from the 1996 Rock Therapy project), before launching into 'Tie Your Mother Down', which got the whole place rocking. Paul Rodgers' voice sounded great and worked really well with Queen's classic 1970s rocker. I was hoping for more of the Paul Rodgers back-

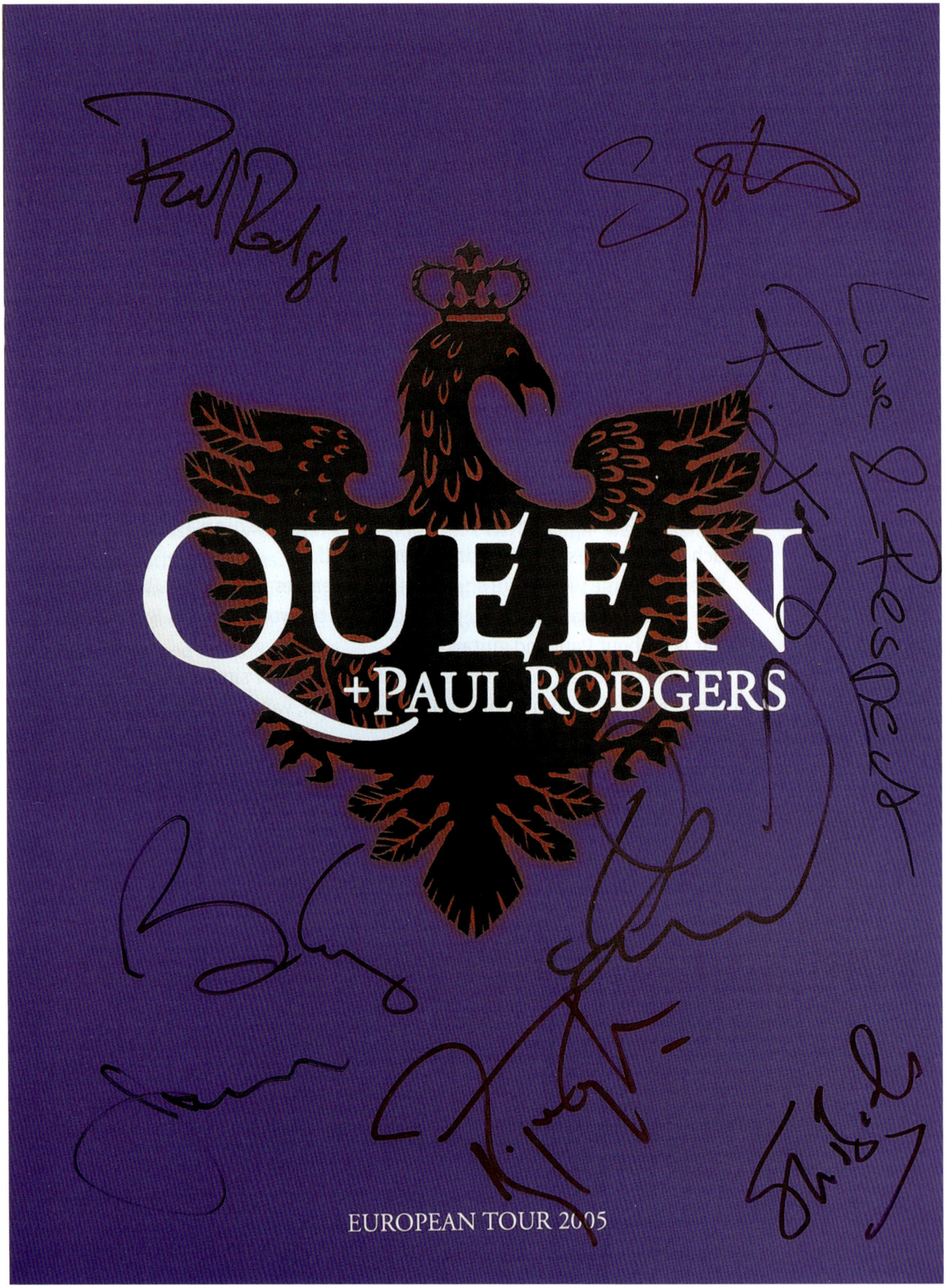
QUEEN
+PAUL RODGERS
EUROPEAN TOUR 2005

2006

Paula Terry

3 and 4 March 2006, The AmericanAirlines Arena Miami and Jacksonville Veterans Memorial Arena, Jacksonville, Florida, USA

My second fond memory was when Paul was playing with Queen. Two of my friends came to Florida to visit and we went to Miami and Jacksonville to see them. My two friends had never seen Paul before but knew how much I loved Bad Company. The special memory? That was when Paul walked out on stage and my friend Dana started to cry because I was so incredibly happy: Seeing my favourite artist with my favourite friends was just amazing. My friends were huge Duran Duran fans and we had seen them 20 times in one year, so I made us T-shirts that said: 'Duranies Gone Bad'!

Paula Terry and her fellow Durannies gone bad

Michael Jentzsch

26 March 2006, Xcel Center, St. Paul, Minnesota, USA

My fondest memories of attending a Paul Rodgers show came during the Return of the Champions concert at the Xcel Center in St. Paul. We were there with our daughter Alyssa and had great seats close to the stage and at the catwalk. At the start of the concert a security guard at the catwalk motioned my daughter to come over and stand right at the barrier. About a third into the concert Paul walked back towards the stage on the catwalk, saw our little girl, did a double take, kneeled down and high-fived her. After that, every time he walked back he would wink or smile at her.

A lot of people came to us after the end of the concert to tell us how cool they thought that was. To this day we still talk about that.

Kathy Rankin

11 April 2006, Rose Garden, Portland, Oregon, USA

Another show I remember well is Queen + Paul Rodgers. I was sitting at the end of the catwalk. So lucky to be that close to see Brian May and Paul Rodgers. I went more to hear Paul Rodgers sing Bad Company tunes. But I love Queen too! He came out and sang and it was beautiful.

Paul was shaking hands at the end of the concert but walked right past me. I figured, oh well. I tried to get his attention. After their encore, he came back toward me and I was surprised that he reached out to me and shook my hand! I wasn't begging! I saw the biggest smile across his face. Happy me! Then he was gone and I was the last person that shook his hand. I will never forget that night!

I left feeling a natural buzz. Nothing describes how music changes how you feel. Wow! It is better than any drug.

Brian May, Roger Taylor and Paul Rodgers photos by Kathy Rankin

Boz Burrell (1946-2006)

Boz Burrell on stage with Paul Rodgers and Mick Ralphs. Photo by Lyndy Lambert

Bad Company's bass player, Boz Burrell, died from a heart attack during his band's rehearsals in Marbella, Spain on 21 September, aged 61. In 1963, Boz was singing with a band called the Tea Time Four, whose line up included Ian McLagan (Small Faces). During his musical career Burrell also worked with King Crimson, Roger Chapman, Alvin Lee and Jon Lord amongst others.

BMI honours 'All Right Now'

On 3 October 2006 the BMI London awards included a Million Air award for three million airplays of 'All Right Now' by Free in the USA. First released on 15 May 1970 'All Right Now' was a No.1 hit in over 20 territories, No.2 on the UK singles chart and No.4 on the US Billboard Hot 100 chart.

After being featured in a Wrigley's chewing gum TV advert in 1991 the song again reached the top 10 on the UK singles chart after being remixed and re-released.

2007

Live in Glasgow

Recordings made in concert on 3 October 2006 at Clyde Auditorium provide the tracks for Paul Rodgers' first live solo album. The 17-track set is dedicated to Paul's first manager in The Road Runners, Joe Bradley, the recently deceased Boz Burrell and Atlantic Records boss Ahmet Ertegün. The album was released on 16 April 2007 and a DVD from the same concert followed a month later.

2008

27 June 2008, Hyde Park, London, UK

The Nelson Mandela 90th Birthday tribute concert closing act was Queen + Paul Rodgers. Brian May, Roger Taylor and Paul Rodgers had previously performed at a 46664 Fancourt in South Africa back in 2005.

The much-anticipated Queen and Paul Rodgers studio album was released on 15 September 2008. Paul, Brian May and Roger Taylor began sessions for what would become *The Cosmos Rocks* at Roger Taylor's Priory studio in late 2006, having completed the American leg of a world tour.

The only studio album by Queen + Paul Rodgers (and Queen's 16th album overall), contained 14 new tracks written by May, Taylor, and Rodgers and was the first studio album of new material from the two remaining members of Queen since 1995's *Made in Heaven*.

The first single, 'Say It's Not True' was released nine months before the album. The second, 'C-lebrity' featured Foo Fighter Taylor Hawkins on backing vocals. *The Cosmos Rocks* peaked at No.5 on the UK chart and became a top 20 chart hit in over 10 other European countries.

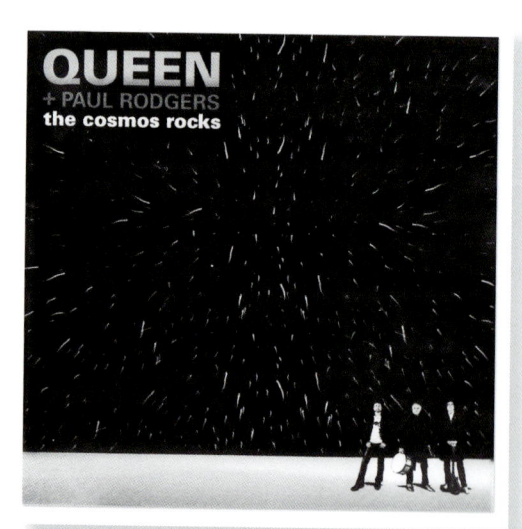

Paul Rodgers

We didn't know what we were going to do or sound like, so we were just playing to see what came up. Some of the songs on the album are very natural and organic, like 'Voodoo', but there are others that are beautifully produced, too.

Martin Skala

28 September 2008, Assago Forum, Milan, Italy

We decided to go and welcome all the members from the band at the VIP airport in Milan but the entrance was closed. About 40 fans were waiting around in hope of getting an autograph but the security was strict and let only taxis in to the area. Yes, you guessed right - we called a taxi and paid five EUR for a 1 km ride, the driver just basically got us through the gate while my friend Alex and me pretended to be English businessmen hurrying to catch a flight. Half an hour later we experienced the most intimate meeting with the band one could imagine - in the VIP lounge. And as always, Paul was the nicest person to talk to but also Brian May and Roger Taylor happily posed for a quick photo.

After the gig my Italian friends invited me out for dinner. The owner of the restaurant was not only a huge Queen fan but also a loyal supporter of one of the Milan football clubs and as a result of certain illegal actions on away matches he had to report himself at the local police station during each home match… one of which sadly took place on the very same day as the concert of Queen + Paul Rodgers so he missed the gig.

Queen + Paul Rodgers captured live by Martin Skala, September 2008 in Belgium, Luxembourg and Milan, Italy

341

Antonio Pellegrini

28 September 2008, Assago Forum, Milan, Italy

This new tour, and the show schedule, were dedicated to the promotion of the newly released *The Cosmos Rocks* album. There were four new tracks played live in Milan, and four tracks from Paul Rodgers' previous career.

    A few hundred Italian fans were crowded outside the Forum waiting to enter in the morning. Later on in the afternoon I headed to Assago.

    In 2005, I was sitting in the second ring and I couldn't see the musicians well as they were a bit far away, so this time I got a ticket for the first ring and I could sit in a very good place, just to the right of the stage. I'm standing in front of the side platform where Paul and Brian May often place themselves during the concert.

    The band was now a bit tighter and the songs were masterfully performed. Paul also managed to give new energy to Queen's songs that were now a bit predictable, like 'Crazy Little Thing Called Love'.

    The first song by Paul in the set was 'Seagull', sung by him alone on acoustic guitar and vocals. Also 'Bad Company' is performed, played by Paul on piano, a song that is accompanied by the whole band. Listening to him live is an exciting experience: you just close your eyes and his voice takes you back to the 70s.

Queen + Paul Rodgers then played 'Feel Like Makin' Love'. In my opinion, this is the song that has matured the most in the band's performance. There was a long introduction where Paul lets himself go with beautiful blues-flavoured vocals.

But the highlight was at the end, with Free's 'All Right Now'. It's clear Paul Rodgers and Queen are not a forced union. Brian May loves this song, and he performs the solo without changing it, but keeping it as faithful as possible to the original by Paul Kossoff.

Assago Forum photos by Antonio Pellegrini

The concert was a triumph, the most beautiful Queen + Paul Rodgers one I've seen. The band was in great shape and the Queen + Paul Rodgers formula worked very well. Although the collaboration ended in 2009, it left a memory that won't easily fade away for the fans that have seen those shows.

Christine Killen

4 November 2008, City Hall, Newcastle-upon-Tyne, Tyneside, UK

The two concerts I saw Paul Rodgers with Queen at were incredible. I know that I am biased but he looked as if he had been with them for years. He was so natural and really enjoying himself. He was pitch and word perfect. If anyone had any doubts about him, then these quickly disappeared. All Queen fans knew nobody would take Freddie's place but this was the next best thing. All Queen and Paul Rodgers fans had an unbelievable night. Paul was magnificent.

2009

Paul Senior

17 June 2009, Hard Rock Live, Hollywood, Florida, USA

My wife, son and I were on holiday in Orlando, Florida. While we were there, I saw in the press that the original Bad Company were playing at Hard Rock in Hollywood, Miami. My wife and son stayed in Orlando and I got a ticket and went to the gig. Luckily I managed to chat to Simon Kirke before the concert. Then I blagged it back stage for a meet and greet and chatted to Paul Rodgers. Mick Ralphs and Simon for what seemed like ages.

   That year was a special one for me. I also saw Mott the Hoople (on three separate nights in September), Bob Dylan, Lynyrd Skynyrd (who my wife had met in a pub before a gig in Sheffield in 1975), AC/DC and Rod Stewart. Finally, we travelled down from Sheffield to London to see Paul Rodgers play a one off gig in November at Hammersmith Apollo.

Tammy Johnstone

27 June 2009, Bethel Woods Center for the Arts, Bethel, New York, USA

We met Paul Rodgers when Bad Company played in Bethel, New York, the old Woodstock site. My husband Gord and I drove from Moncton, NB, Canada.

The Doobie Brothers opened and during intermission we bought beers for some people we just met. They in turn gave us backstage passes because they couldn't stay after the concert. I can't remember the name of the people that gave us the passes but they said they couldn't have met two better people to give them to.

After the amazing concert – the first time members of both bands had actually been on stage together – we went to meet the band backstage. There were a few people in front in the queue and we were the last.

The first thing my husband said was something about soccer to Paul. That's when Paul asked us where we were from, and when we said Canada his band immediately broke into 'O Canada'. The funny thing was that security was trying to take us out, but Paul kept singing!

An amazing memory of my favourite artist.

Billy Sloan

What makes Paul Rodgers' music so special? First and foremost, it's the voice. He is peerless. That old cliché that a performer could sing the telephone directory – and it would still be brilliant – applies to him. He's also a wonderful interpreter of other people's material. Paul brought a real rock edge to Queen's back catalogue. It was always going to be difficult to follow in the footsteps of the legendary Freddie Mercury, but he did a fantastic job.

His vocals on the *Live In Ukraine* album of 2009 cement Queen's legacy. He breathed new life into tracks like 'Tie Your Mother Down', 'Hammer To Fall' and 'We Will Rock You'.

You also feel he means it, 100%. There's nothing fake about Paul Rodgers.

His work with Free got me hooked for life but Bad Company was firm proof lightning CAN strike twice. Songs such as 'Feel Like Makin' Love', 'Rock 'n' Roll Fantasy', 'Shooting Star' and in particular, 'Bad Company' are outstanding.

He also does a brilliant version of 'Let Me Roll It' on the star studded 2014 Paul McCartney tribute album, *The Art of McCartney*.

The sheer passion of his work on albums such as *Muddy Water Blues* (1993) and *The Royal Sessions* (2014) shines through too.

Christopher Russo

4 July 2009, Resorts Casino, Atlantic City, New Jersey, USA

As a 27-year-old I am of a later Bad Company generation, but just as dedicated a fan as earlier generations. I first discovered Bad Company growing up listening to the radio.

My real love for Bad Company began one day while I was in high school. My dad had been cleaning out the garage when he found an old VHS tape he had made of a Bad Company concert from back in the late 1990s. I played the tape in my room and was amazed at how tight the band and the songs sounded. Even the songs I had never heard before hooked me in. While watching this I went to their website and found out they were planning some shows later in the year. Later it was announced that the final show of the tour would be at the Resorts Casino in Atlantic City. I knew I had to go. By this time I had even started buying their CDs and was growing more attached to their music beyond just the hits. They were quickly becoming one of my top favourite bands. The timing was just right. I was itching to see them in action! It all came together perfectly!

Finally saw the show with my dad. What a great night! The band was tight and the songs sounded great. It was a night I didn't want to end. I've since seen them a few more times and they never disappoint. In my opinion they've only gotten better.

I'd say Mick Ralphs is one of the most underrated guitarists and songwriters of rock, Simon Kirke has not only become an even more intense meat and potatoes drummer over the years but has even shown himself to be a gifted musician in his own right, and Paul Rodgers? What can be said that hasn't been said? One of the most soulful and powerful voices in rock, and always a great presence on stage. Not only an outstanding vocalist and frontman but a terrific musician and songwriter. A big compliment I can give him is his ability to change up the style of singing the songs without it changing the essence of the songs we know. If anything he has only improved the songs with how he approaches them live. Not many singers can do that.

How we all miss Boz Burrell: such a gifted bass player in what he brought to the band. But let's give credit to Howard Leese and Todd Ronning for what they contribute in helping keep the band playing for the fans. Bad Company as a band is as strong today as it ever was.

John Wood

November 2009, Hard Rock Cafe, London, UK

My love affair with Bad Company began when I heard 'Can't Get Enough' on the radio. It blew me away. Then I discovered that the band was formed from elements of Free along with Mick Ralphs from Mott the Hoople and Boz Burrell from King Crimson and had signed to Led Zeppelin's Swan Song label.
I managed to see them for the first time supporting The Who at Charlton Athletic Stadium back in the 70s. I was blown away!

But then I left school and went to work and although I bought all the LPs I didn't get to see them.

I was sad to hear of the death of Boz Burrell and then the band splitting up but in November 2009 I got a call from someone at Planet Rock saying that I'd won a competition to go to a special Bad Company intimate gig at the Hard Rock Cafe in London. I did think that I was having my leg pulled but when the passes arrived I knew that this would be special.

And I was right: Paul, Mick and Simon made the announcement that Bad Company would be touring the UK in 2010, and I, along with the other lucky prize winners, was treated to several acoustic numbers played by the band that day. Better still, I was able to get my *Bad Company Anthology* CD case insert signed by the boys.

Then on the 11 April 2010 I saw them perform at Wembley Arena. What a performance. I have been, and will always be, a fan.

2010

Rob Nottingham

4 April 2010, Sheffield City Hall, South Yorkshire, UK

Having been a Paul Rodgers fan since buying 'Little Bit of Love', I saw Bad Company in 2010 at Sheffield City Hall. A good friend managed to get the two tickets, which had a meet and greet attached with a backstage hospitality pass. He didn't tell me about that until we got to the venue and you can imagine my surprise.

Mick Ralphs and Simon Kirke were very friendly and then I got to meet the main man in a separate room, so we waited in the hallway. I had so many questions I wanted to ask but went numb and froze when I met him. Fantastic!

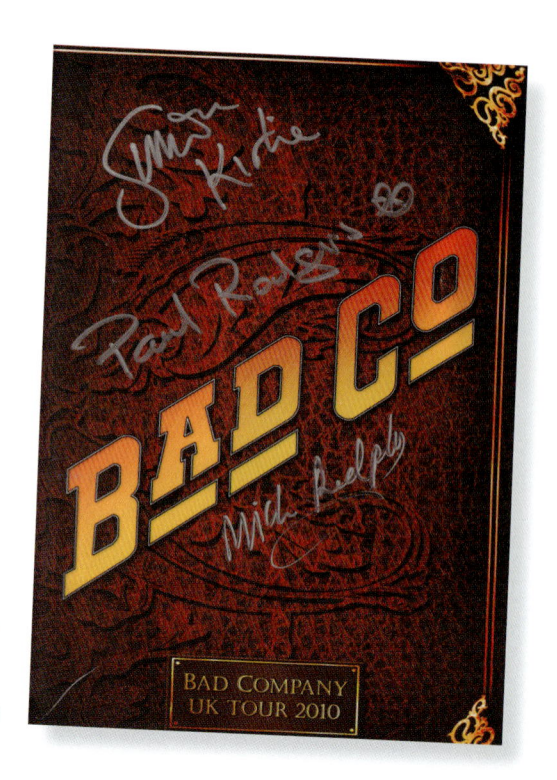

2011

Howard Leese

How long have I been playing with Paul Rodgers? Three years. This will be the fourth summer. It is really a funny story of how I got that gig. I was playing in Seattle with a couple of friends of mine. We were doing a 70s hard rock trio with a singer. We did a lot of Trower, Hendrix and Free, you know the heavy guitar heroes! We did it just for the hell of it. We'd set up three stacks of Marshalls and just go. We had our own little following in Seattle. We were doing it for all the right reasons. We weren't trying to make a record deal. We were just trying to go out and play once in a while and have a good time.

Howard Leese on stage with Paul Rodgers in 2016

We got spotted by Paul's manager. Paul had moved to Canada and was looking for a band in the Northwest. He looked around Vancouver and didn't find anyone he liked so he started sniffing around Seattle. They heard about our thing and they came in to check us out and we were playing 'Fire And Water'. They hired the whole band. My trio is called the Brigade. More than a coincidence? You never know, man.

Free was my favourite band. I always thought what fun it would be to be in a band with that guy. After Ann Wilson where do you go? A fan came up to me the other day and she was going, 'Dude, how did you do that? You were with the best girl singer and now you're with the best guy singer. You can never work with anyone else again! It would be a step down for you!' I thought that was probably right. I have worked with the two best.

Joining Bad Company I had to learn all the stuff. They called me on a Tuesday and said I had a gig in Pine Knob in Detroit on Friday. We never had a real rehearsal. Paul comes to sound check once in a while and we jam but we don't really formally rehearse. He will call and tell us what tunes to learn and we will work on it but it is real, real loose. He'll even call stuff out on stage. He will walk up to me and go, 'I feel like doing a bit of Hendrix. What do you know?' I tell him I know all of it and he will call out what he wants to play and we will just play it. He will even start singing other songs. We will be doing 'Satisfaction Guaranteed' by The Firm and we get to the ending and he will start singing another song. I don't know where it is going to go. It's cool. He changes the set. We never get the set until we are walking up the stairs.

David McLaren

19 April 2011, Clyde Auditorium, Glasgow, UK

In 2007, my wife Lorraine and I made our first trip to the US, staying in New York City. After we booked our trip we noticed that Paul Rodgers was appearing in concert in B.B. King's nightclub. We bought tickets and I emailed his website to say how much we were looking forward to the concert. On the night we had fantastic seats close to the stage. During the show Paul mentioned that he had got married to Cynthia the day before: Clearly a special time for him. He also said he had fans in the

Lorraine McLaren and Paul Rodgers

audience from many parts of the world, including Scotland where I live. I immediately stood up and applauded that he made mention of my country but never thought anything more about it.

Anyway, we spent a fabulous week in NYC and then flew home. A couple of days I happened to check my emails and found a message from Paul's management team inviting us to meet him after the concert! I was totally gutted to have missed this once in a lifetime opportunity to meet Paul.

A year later I happened to come across an email address for a guy called Brad Gregory, who I understand worked as an assistant to Paul. I emailed Brad and explained what happened. He very kindly arranged to send me an autographed message from Paul saying see you one day.

Fast forward to April 2011 and we went to see Paul in Glasgow. We arrived early afternoon and waited for the tour bus to arrive. By chance my wife approached a lady who got off the bus and asked if she had a minute to hear our story about missing the chance to meet Paul in NYC. It transpired the lady was Cynthia, who listened to our story. She arranged to give us better seating tickets closer to the stage and then advised us to stay in our seats after the concert and she would take us to meet Paul backstage. When we met Paul, who had already been briefed by Cynthia, he could not have been nicer.

I took this amazing opportunity to ask him three questions:

Question 1: Who is the most impressive person you have ever met? Answer: Nelson Mandela

Question 2: Was 'My Brother Jake' a real person? Answer: Jake is a fictitious character written by Andy Fraser

Question 3: Have you thought about writing a biography? Answer: He told me that he had been asked many times but he said that he would need to take a year out to properly give it the time it deserves.

Sheila Tarleton

I never saw either Free or Bad Company live. The nearest I got to Paul Rodgers was meeting his son Steve when he was supporting Deborah Bonham's band at a club on the outskirts of Barnsley one Saturday night several years ago. He came on and did his set to less than rapturous applause, although his performance was a good one. In the break before the other band came on I went to the bar at the back and saw him leaning against the wall on his own looking a bit dejected. I went over and told him I enjoyed his set and told him that his reception was probably less about the performance but more to do with the fact that Barnsley FC had taken a drubbing at home that afternoon (losing something like 5-0). That seemed to cheer him up somewhat.

Ben Green

Paul Rodgers flanked by Ben Green and his father Stuart. Right: the 'Seagull' artwork that Ben's parents had made for him on his 21st birthday

I was 14-years-old when I was walking up the stairs at home and overheard my Dad, Stuart, playing his acoustic guitar along to a live DVD. Dad playing his guitar was a regular occurrence in our house, so normally I would have probably walked by without a thought. However, this specific evening, he was playing along to who I now know to be Paul Rodgers. This voice hit me in that moment and I knew I had to listen further. I asked my Dad who this man was and what the song was called. He said, 'this is Paul

Rodgers and I am going to teach you to play guitar right now.' We sat and played along to 'Seagull', an experience neither of us will ever forget. This gave me the confidence to start singing and I now front bands, just like my idol. Me and my Dad also go out and gig together and host open mics where we often play 'Seagull' and recount the story of how my love for Paul Rodgers came about.

Paul Rodgers has given me some incredible memories. From meeting him for the first time at a gig in Chelsea, UK, to shaking his hand at the Royal Albert Hall, to having his song 'Nights Like This' played as me and my wife Laura walked down the aisle after getting married. His voice and music still gives me so much joy and allowed me and my Dad to bond in a way we still hold dear to this day.

Hisako Kuramoto

13 July 2011, The Royal Albert Hall, London, UK

I am a great fan of Paul Rodgers, from the Far East. I have been loving his voice and songs for so long. When Paul first visited Japan for Free concerts, I couldn't go because I was a child. Time passed and I was able to see Bad Company, solo tours and Paul and Queen. But more than anything I desired to meet Paul. Then my lifelong dream came true. I was able to travel to England and meet Paul and his lovely wife Cynthia. I made a costume that looked like Paul's costume and joined his UK tour four times and met him. I was a happy woman!

Paul's wife Cynthia with Hisako

I love Paul's songs because the words are simple and universal. Since I am Japanese and English is not my native language, I can understand easily. When the heavy tune and Paul's gorgeous deep voice overlap, I feel amazed!

Therese Lentz

30 July 2011, LC Pavilion, Columbus, Ohio, USA

Being in high school and college in the mid 70s into the 80s, Bad Company was obviously huge during that time. My husband and I graduated from high school together and share a love of Paul Rodgers and Bad Company.

When we heard that Paul Rodgers was playing at a local outdoor venue we actually had a family wedding to attend that day but planned to leave the reception a bit early and head to the concert. We changed clothes in the car and arrived just before Paul came on. As soon as the first note was played it was a crazy-fun time with everyone singing and dancing and we were up close in the pit area near the stage.

Therese Lentz with friends at LC Pavilion, Columbus

Paul sounded just as great as he always had and it literally transported me right back to being in high school again - seriously - just like a dream come true.

We danced and sang throughout the entire concert and I decided right there and then that I would try to see Paul perform every single year, if at all possible. And I have managed to do just that. From our home in Westerville, Ohio, we have travelled all around the state: Cleveland area, Blossom Music Center, Cincinnati, Columbus again, Louisville, for the Bourbon and Music Fest, Indiana and last year he returned to Columbus. The last few years, we have been joined by another couple that are great friends and have chased my dream. We have never, ever been disappointed by Paul's shows (only that he couldn't play longer!) and I look forward to planning the next Bad Company/Paul Rodgers concert every year.

He is quite simply the best voice and performer out there and always the high point of my summer.

Barbara Senior

3 December 2011, The Venue, Chichester, UK

It was in late 2011 when we travelled from our home in Doncaster to a small Paul Rodgers gig in Chichester. Paul did about three charity concerts at his own expense down there for Deborah Bonham, and on this occasion there were some fabulous auction items, one of which I'd got my eye on. Actually, I had my eye on all of them really! But one I particularly wanted was the lyrics to 'All Right Now' which Paul had written out and signed. I went to bid and my husband Paul, who's a typical Yorkshireman, kept pulling my arm down and telling me not to. So, I missed out on that.

After the gig, I was talking to Paul's wife Cynthia and telling her how I'd missed out but that actually my ultimate dream would be to have the first verse of 'Shooting Star' because its my favourite track. And I told her if Paul would do that I'd donate to the Willows charity gladly.

Anyway, they went back to Canada and a few weeks later – it was something like three days before Christmas – what comes in the post? The handwritten lyrics to 'Shooting Star' with 'Love Paul' on the bottom. I'd forgotten about it to be perfectly honest. But when I opened the package I was dancing round the room!

Now, those lyrics are my prize possession. Paul and Cynthia went all the way back to Canada and didn't forget and did it for me. I thought that was wonderful of them. They are just such kind people.

Barbara Senior and her prized possession, photographed by her husband and equally loyal Paul Rodgers fan, Paul Senior

2012

Dagmara Szymanska

My first memory of Paul Rodgers? I was listening to the radio station Antyradio. Janusz 'Kosa' Kosinski, the radio DJ, played not obvious rock music. One of

This Czech tour date was special for Polish fans – the closest opportunity to see Queen + Paul Rodgers. Fans here are: Lukasz Betram, Dagmara Szymanska, Przemek Kacprzak, Bogdan Grzech and Dominika Dmowska, Kinga Pawelec.

the songs was 'Come Together In The Morning.' The melody and vocals charmed me. I didn't know much about Free but he also played other Free and Bad Company songs on the show. That was 2004. Then I heard Paul Rodgers had joined my beloved band. Yes, I'm a

Queenmaniac! I work in a Polish fan club for the band. I've been to four Queen + Paul Rodgers concerts and managed to get an email to Paul's assistant. I was organising the Queen fan conventions in Poland and I asked for something for a charity auction. To my surprise a parcel came from Canada, with a personal letter from Paul's wife. I have it today.

In 2008, we were very sad when the concert in Gdansk Shipyard, Poland was cancelled. So me and some of my friends were very happy to go to a gig in Poland in 2012. I was able to meet Paul in person in Poland. It was an amazing meeting. He's a warm, kind man. It will always stay in my heart. I have pictures from meetings and concerts. And for several years I have been running a fan page on Facebook about Paul for Polish fans. And so my love for Queen connected me with him.

Another special memory is the performance of the song 'Seagull' by one of the best vocalists in Poland - Krzysztof Cugowski from Budka Suflera. The discovery that Paul is valued by the greats: that is nice.

I still hope that Paul will come back to Poland. That will be will be an opportunity to meet again and shake hands.

Pat Anderson

28 March 2012, D&R Theatre, Aberdeen, Washington, USA

I have been in radio broadcasting for 30 years. I grew up hearing Bad Company on the radio and had the pleasure of programming those songs on the airwaves in my professional career. I've had the opportunity to interview Paul Rodgers several times over the years on KDUX radio, and it is through that privilege I discovered the music of Free. Sure, I always knew the great song 'All Right Now' but it was through my conversations with Paul that I came to love and appreciate Free and relay that to my listeners. Paul is an incredible ambassador for that music and the love he has for his former bandmates was very apparent.

We were fortunate to have Paul play a solo show in Aberdeen, at the D&R Theatre, where he helped us raise over $4,000 for the PAWS Animal Shelter. We'll always be appreciative. It's goodwill such as this that continues to create fans as well.

Jennifer Krannacker

2 May 2012, SunFest Festival Grounds, West Palm Beach, Florida, USA

My husband John's tat!

The first time I saw Paul live was an amazing experience. A very magical time as I was four months pregnant.

Paul was amazing, singing beyond perfection. We were up front and close to the stage and from that day, I was hooked. My husband, John, who's been a fan his whole life was ecstatic knowing we share the same love.

I've now seen Paul and Bad Company numerous times and the best moment was meeting the band and the people associated with Paul, his wife Cynthia, his personal assistant Brenda Murti and everyone at Willows animal sanctuary. We are true fans and collect Paul Rodgers, Free and Bad Company memorabilia and are Willow's patrons.

The best is yet to come, as my daughter Giana is now as much of a fan as we are. She's looking forward to meeting Paul and she's only seven! Must have been from that time in my stomach. Just part of my rock 'n' rolll fantasy!

2014

Chris Robertson

Paul Rodgers is hands-down the greatest rock 'n' roll singer that's ever lived. One of [drummer] John Fred's favourite songs is 'Fire and Water'. And I was like, 'I want to see if I can even sing it!' You gotta be slightly crazy to attempt singing a Paul Rodgers song, but I think we did a cool version. It's acoustic, but still kinda heavy. *Black Stone Cherry's version of 'Fire and Water' appeared on the Classic Rock cover mount CD Black Stone Cherry – Hits, Rarities & Live.*

Justin Arbgast

16 July 2014, PNC Music Pavilion, Charlotte, North Carolina, USA

A day to remember was the show I attended which marked the 40th anniversary of Bad Company in 2014. I'm only 27-years-old, and I became a fan way back before that show when I was about 10, when my Dad, Perry Arbgast, played me the Bad Company *Merchants of Cool* DVD. I was blown away. From Paul Rodgers singing to his stage presence - I loved it all. After that it didn't take long for me to know every Bad Company song. I mean every song! I was completely hooked. The only thing I hadn't done was see them live. I remember watching TV and this commercial came on, it was Bad Company coming to my town, Raleigh at the Walnut Creek Amphitheater. I was so excited. I ran outside to tell my dad. He couldn't believe it. So my dad told me that he had a friend that could get us good seats for the concert. But when it was the day of the concert my Dad's friend couldn't get the tickets. We were so upset.

So my dad went to the venue box office, while I waited at home. I just didn't want to get disappointed again but when he came back he had a big smile on his face. Two seats in the 4th row in the middle! I was speechless.

One of the best days of my life. We got there really early. There were no other cars in the parking lot so we didn't even have to pay for parking. Even better still, while we were waiting outside we could hear Bad Company doing a sound check.

Arriving in our seats, I couldn't believe how close we were to the stage. I remember when I first saw Paul Rodgers at the concert. The whole band came out except Paul. And then I saw Paul in the back on the right jumping up and down like he was getting ready for a boxing match. When the concert was over my dad and I went to the parking lot to my car and we noticed I had a flat tyre, but it it didn't bother us! We were so jazzed about the show we didn't care. So we just sat in the parking lot listening to Bad Company tunes until all of the other cars left. And then we changed the tyre. So we were the first ones there and the last ones to leave. And since that show in 2009 I've seen Paul Rodgers eight more times, either with Paul Rodgers' solo band or Bad Company. And the really special show from all of them was the 40th anniversary concert in 2014 at the PNC Music Pavilion in Charlotte.

Once again, my Dad and I had really good seats, but what made this show so memorable was what happened after it. Browsing the merchandise stand like we always did, we came across this lovely lady. So we got a signed Bad Company LP. And then it dawned on me: This is Cynthia, Paul Rodgers' wife. I had a tattoo on my forearm that has Paul Rodgers' heart and peace symbol, so I showed it to her. Cynthia took a step back and said 'I designed that', so I just had to have my picture taken with her. We got talking and as we were about to leave my Dad said: 'Nice meeting you.' And Cynthia said: 'don't you want to meet Paul?'

We just couldn't believe it! So Cynthia took us backstage to meet Paul. He was just standing there like he was waiting for us. So I showed him the tattoo and I just remember him saying: 'Wow! Did you show this to Cynthia.' So me and my dad had a photo taken with Paul. And then we met Simon Kirke! I had to pinch myself. I couldn't believe this was happening. A special, special night.

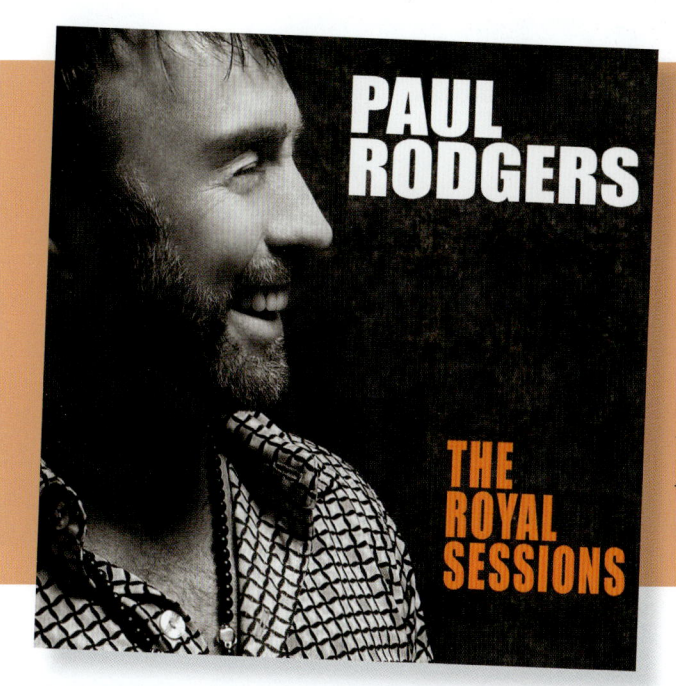

The Royal Sessions

Released on 4 February 2014, *The Royal Sessions* was a Paul Rodgers solo project where he selected and sang blues, R&B and soul classics that inspired him when he was a teenager. Recorded at Royal Studios in Memphis, Tennessee, Paul donated all the album's proceeds to the Stax Music Academy's after school music programme.

Paul Rodgers

One of the things *The Royal Sessions* has done is recharge my love for music. I don't want to over-emphasise singing. It's about the musicians. I always feel part of the band. I'm listening to everything everybody's playing and I'm responding and I expect them to do the same. For instance, on 'Walk On By', when Leroy Hodges slides that bass note just before I sing the hook, he was anticipating me, the emotion, the pain, the girl walking away. *Interview with Mojo magazine*

2015

Lyndy Lambert

February 2015, Rock Legends Cruise III, Independence of the Seas, somewhere on the Caribbean Sea

This was my first Rock Legends Cruise, and I have been on many since. On February 19, 2015, we set sail from Fort Lauderdale, Florida on Royal Caribbean's Independence of the Seas. The ship spent a day at Nassau, Bahamas, but bands continued to play when we were at port. Along with Paul Rodgers, who was one of the headliners, we were treated to the Doobie Brothers, 38 Special, Alice Cooper, Blue Oyster Cult, Ten Years After, The Outlaws, and many more excellent musicians. Paul's son, Steve Rodgers, opened for Paul as a solo artist during one of the two gigs Paul and his band played on the ship.

Simon Kirke and Paul Rodgers live on the Rock Legends Cruise III. Photos by Lyndy Lambert

I saw both of Paul's shows. I also attended Sal Cirrincione's interview with Paul and Alice Cooper on Saturday morning. The interview was dominated by Cooper, who has hosted his own radio show for many years. Alice Cooper is quite entertaining and an excellent raconteur. Poor Paul barely got a word in edgewise. Additionally, Paul, like many other artists, had a photo op for his fans. I attended that as well, with the hope of mentioning to Paul that I had been on tour with Bad Company in 1979. I was wearing the gold necklace that Boz Burrell had given me commemorating that tour. When it was my turn, the handlers rushed me through so quickly I did not have a chance to say anything. I only managed to flash the necklace at Paul and he looked at it quizzically. He seemed to have a flash of recognition before I was whisked away.

Anyway, the concerts were the primary reason for the cruise, and Paul and his band were terrific, as usual. I had waited in line before both shows so I could be right up front. I always prefer to be as close to the stage as possible, even though the sound is often too loud and distorted next to the stage. Watching and photographing the band interact with each other and with the audience is the highlight of every concert for me. I blame Bad Company for my proximity preference. When I was invited on tour with them in 1979, they let me either sit on the side of the stage, or arranged for me to be in the pit, so I could get the best photos of them. Bad Company spoiled me, in a very good way.

Paul and his band played several Bad Company hits, including my favourites, the eponymous song 'Bad Company', 'Rock 'n' Roll Fantasy', and 'Feel Like Makin' Love'. They rocked a few blues covers, like 'Born Under a Bad Sign', and some Free songs. They ended their set with a powerful rendition of the Free song, 'All Right Now'. As usual, there was no encore, because the crew had to quickly set up the stage for the next band.

I was looking forward to seeing Paul on the latest Rock Legends Cruise, in February 2020, but he cancelled a few months before and was replaced by Nancy Wilson of Heart. Wilson did a nice job, but she was no substitute for the remarkable voice of Paul Rodgers.

Andy Fraser (1952-2015)

Andy Fraser died age 62 on 16 March 2015 at his home in California of a heart attack caused by atherosclerosis.

Fraser produced and co-wrote 'All Right Now' with Paul Rodgers, and also co-wrote many other songs for Free including the hit singles 'My Brother Jake' and 'The Stealer'. He also saw success with his song 'Every Kinda People', which Robert Palmer recorded in 1978 for his *Double Fun* album.

WENN Rights Ltd / Alamy Stock Photo

Luke Morley (Thunder)

In 2015 I did some gigs with Simon Kirke, and on a very long bus ride across Sweden we talked about Free. Simon had his little baby acoustic guitar with him and he played a few Free songs. I wanted to know how they developed this impeccable economy in their music. He said: 'We just played' – so you have to believe it's instinctive.

Those gigs with Simon came about when a friend of mine, Spike, who was very friendly with Frankie Miller, put together a band playing Frankie stuff for an album playing undiscovered songs that Frankie's missus had collected together. He sent me two tracks he wanted me to play on, and the rhythm section on both of those was Fraser and Kirke. It was great. It was like being lead guitar in Free for five seconds! Then, a couple of years on from that Spike asked me if I wanted to do some gigs with that material along with Simon and Andy. I said I'm in.

Two weeks later I got another call from Spike who said: "You'll never guess what's happened – Andy Fraser's died".

Well I said it was Simon's call whether we did the tour and eventually he said yes and we went ahead with it. But the set list changed from all Frankie Miller songs to Frankie songs and some Free songs as a tribute to Andy Fraser.

Simon is a very cool guy and I thoroughly enjoyed playing with him. He's also a good piano player and very tasteful.

Alan Levendon

I've always been a Free fan, I saw them at the 1970 Isle of Wight Festival. In 2015 I returned to the Island with my wife for a walking holiday coinciding with my birthday on 16 March. We visited East Afton Downs, on the 17th and sat on the hill overlooking the festival site. I pointed out where the stage and the fenced off area had been. Got back to the hotel that evening, turned on the radio and heard Andy Fraser had died the day before.

Thomas Crockett

Andy Fraser was such an incredible person - not just a musician. I am nobody famous, just a huge Free fan and musician who was immensely inspired by Paul Kossoff. Andy Fraser was actually my first MySpace friend. I figured what the heck: I saw he was there so I contacted him and he was awesome and honest and real. I know this is not that uncommon nowadays, many people contact famous people and have conversations and friendships, as have I through the music biz. But I was blown away when Andy was so cool and personable.

2016

Jakob Hallett

First heard Free in Argyll and Bute, Scotland, where I still live today. I was about 15 and it was an unforgettable experience. I was in that kind of metal/hard rock phase at that age, and I was really into Zeppelin and Sabbath and other guys like that. Anyway, I was hunting through my Dad's LPs and came across this really eerie looking cover with what appeared to be Mickey Mouse laying in a glass coffin! I later found out it was called *Tons of Sobs* (what a great Nietzschean title, so nihilistic! I loved that). So, I put this record on the turntable, and I can distinctly remember my jaw dropping when 'Worry' came on, I had mistakenly thought with the album starting with 'Over the Green Hills' that the album was going to be a prog-folk record!

   I was in love with that record for months, and played nothing else. But it wasn't until I found my Dad's copy of *Fire and Water* and heard Andy's bass solo on Mr. Big for the first time that I thought, 'yeah, these guys really are geniuses.' And to think Andy was only 17 at the time of that recording, just spine-tingling stuff. I am still impressed with how quickly they went from playing straight 12-bar blues, to complex melodic ballads and harmonic acoustic numbers. Just incredible.

   Free just seemed to take all their musical influences and blew them out of the water with their own unique approach. I actually put them up there with The Beatles. People like to laugh at me for that, but Free were four super-talented guys who not only existed at the same time, but they luckily found each other, and together made some beautiful memories for all of us to enjoy forevermore. Since discovering Free, I haven't even wanted to listen to Zeppelin!

Red Rocks Amphitheatre

Eric Blaylock

15 May 2016, Red Rocks Amphitheatre, Denver, Colorado, USA

After a long wait I got to see Bad Company for the second time. On this occasion it was at Red Rocks in May of 2016. I went by myself because I had just moved to Colorado and didn't have friends to go with me, but I wasn't going to miss making Bad Company my first Red Rocks experience! I got the ticket online and Joe Walsh warmed them up. The show had as much energy as the first and was awesome.

Lucy Piller

28th May 2016, MidFlorida Amphitheatre, Tampa, Florida, USA

There is no way I can say which gig was the best I had ever seen. I have seen Paul so many times, and *every* time I say 'wow', that was the best. But a few years ago when I saw Bad Company in Florida, I do recall Paul's voice was so spot on and he had so much power, I did say to myself while watching it, Lucy this is outstanding, this is the one, it's the finest Paul show I have ever seen him perform at. It was 28 May 2016 at the MidFlorida Amphitheatre. It was actually on my birthday and Bad Company performed 'Lucy in the Sky with Diamonds' for the first time, especially for me. While he sang the song he was looking down to me to make sure I was there.

Bad Company West Palm Beach, Florida.
Photos by Lyndy Lambert

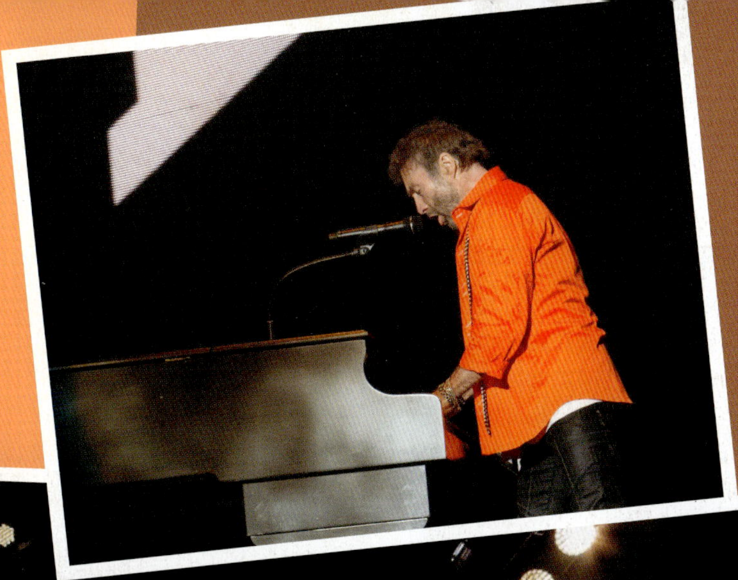

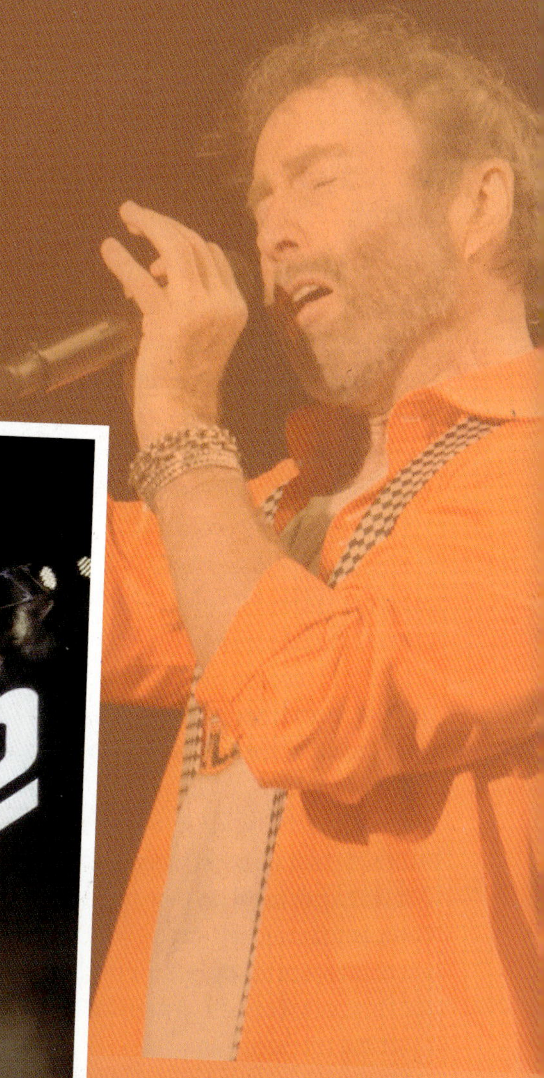

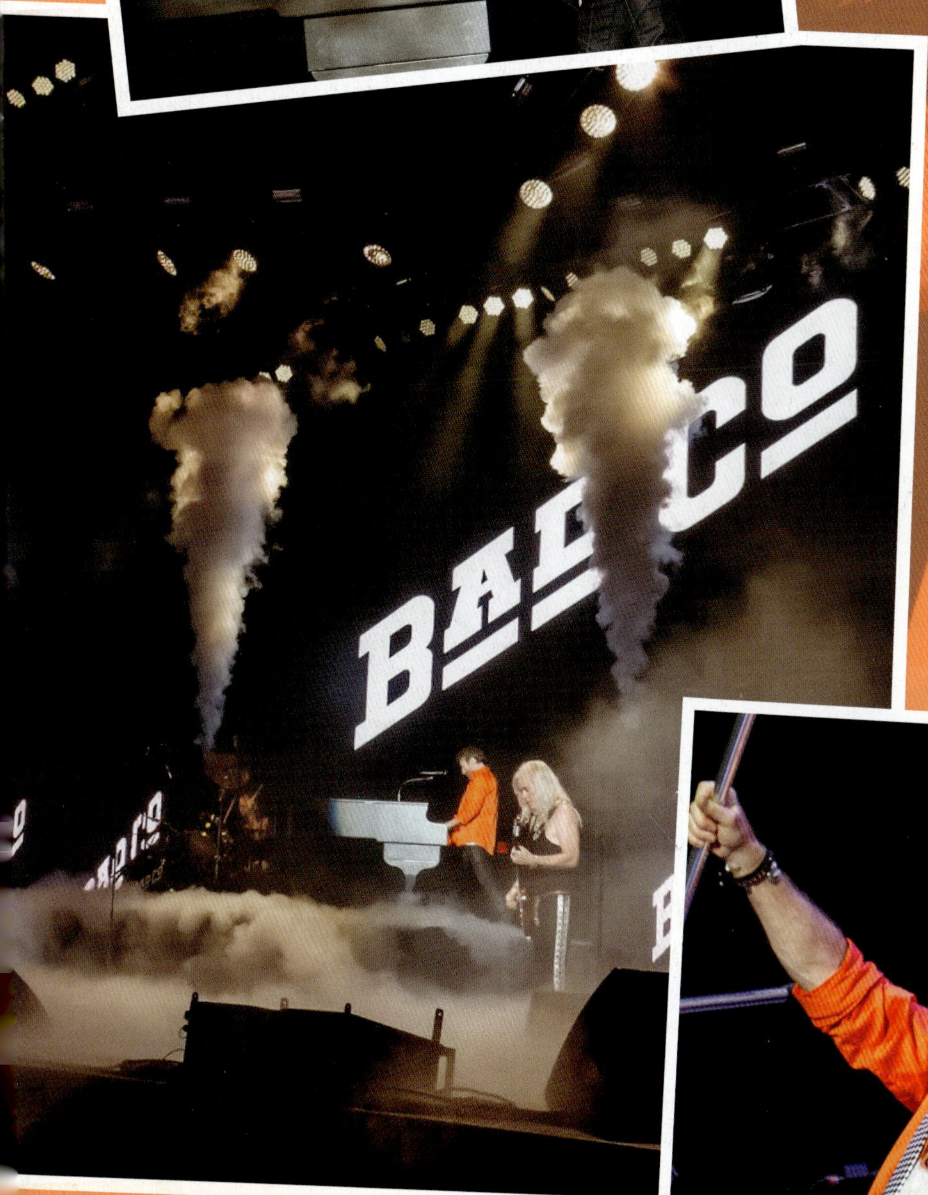

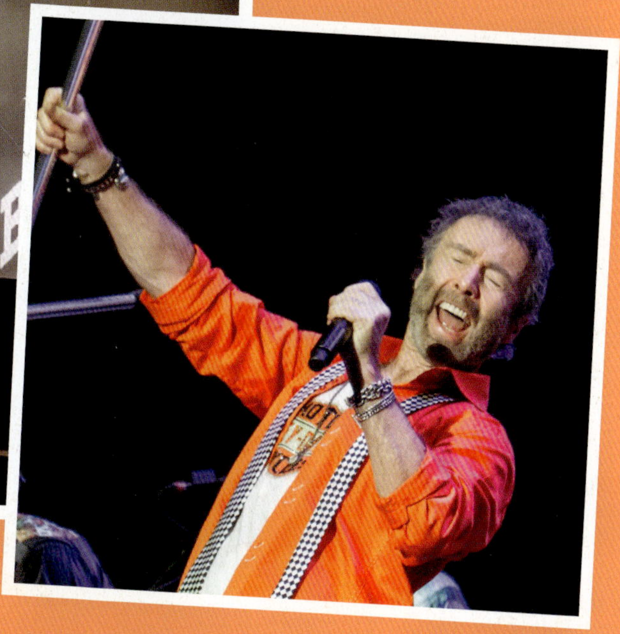

Lyndy Lambert

29 May 2016, Perfect Vodka Amphitheatre, West Palm Beach, Florida, USA

When I learned that two of my perennially favorite artists, Bad Company and Joe Walsh, had teamed up for a tour, I immediately purchased a single VIP seat for their concert. I scored Row E, but when I was being led to my seat by an usher, I was delighted to find it was an unobstructed front row seat, off to the side. The venue is usually known around South Florida as the Cruzan Amphitheatre, but Perfect Vodka had purchased naming rights before this show. It is a huge outdoor venue, with a capacity of 20,000. Less than half of the seats are covered, and the rest are on the lawn.

I arrived early to avoid traffic, and met my friends there for a tailgate party, with champagne, shrimp, caviar, and fruit. Doors opened at 7 pm, and I managed to get my small camera through security, which is sometimes difficult there. Bad Company opened at 7:45 pm, and we settled in for an amazing concert.

Paul Rodgers and Simon Kirke were the only original Bad Company members at this gig. Boz Burrell had passed away many years before, and I heard that Mick Ralphs had some health issues. They were sorely missed, but their replacements were excellent.

The legendary Rich Robinson, founder and lead guitarist for The Black Crowes, filled in for Mick. The band was rounded out with bassist Todd Ronning, and Howard Leese, Paul's regular guitarist when he plays solo.

It was a hot night, in more ways than just Florida's summer temperature. Bad Company started out strong with 'Live for the Music', followed by 'Gone, Gone, Gone', which was written by Boz for the *Desolation Angels* album. 'Gone, Gone, Gone' was the first song Boz had written for Bad Company, and he was very proud of it. It was a touching tribute to him.

Then they played my favourite, 'Feel Like Makin' Love'. Every time I hear Paul sing this song live, I, and every other woman at the show, wishes that Paul was singing that song to us privately. It starts softly, then gradually builds up to a climax, when Paul sings, at the top of his marvellous voice, 'I want to give you the sun, I want to give you the moon, and all the stars above, cause I feel like makin' love.' I still get strong, emotional and physical reactions to Paul's powerful rendition of this song.

Bad Company played a cracking version of 'Lucy in the Sky with Diamonds' then crowd pleasers 'Shooting Star' and 'Rock 'n' Roll Fantasy', among others. We were all dancing in the aisles, on the number nine cloud, by then. They completed their set with the song 'Bad Company' as the encore. If there is a more perfect rock song for an encore, I am not aware of it. They played for a little less than an hour, and every song was bursting with energy. They were a hard act for Joe Walsh to follow, but Walsh was up for the task. What an amazing combination of artists. I left hoping they'd do another dual headliner someday soon.

Joe Walsh

I've known Paul and Simon for years and as a matter of fact, we've been thrown out of some of the finest hotels in the world! I respect them both as musicians and consider them dear friends.

Cory Beaulieu

9 June 2016, The Xfinity Center, Mansfield, MA, USA

I didn't get to attend a Bad Company show until 2016. I went with a friend who, after knowing each other for 20 years, we suddenly realized we had music in common. Don't ask why it took so long, but I credit Bad Company with cementing my connection to this friend because she understood my love and now we are concert queens together!

Anyway, at the show we didn't have the greatest seats so after the opener- Joe Walsh! - she scored box seats from a group of guys who only came to see Joe. Still wrapping my head around that one. That was my very first show.

It's definitely hard to put my feelings about Paul's voice into perspective. I believe it was a benefit to me to discover Free after Bad Company because I got to appreciate the work Paul has put into developing and refining his voice over all of these years. I find his hard work so inspiring. In a difficult business he has stayed focused on his gift and honed it and I admire that kind of dedication. I've never felt like I had a passion about anything until hearing Free.

The way Paul's voice shreds in songs like 'Songs of Yesterday' and 'Oh I Wept' just stops me in my tracks and forces me to close my eyes, take a deep breath, and just *feel* it. I'm listening to 'Heavy Load' as I type this and I have to keep stopping to absorb the feeling. The music just touches me deep in my soul. I feel a connection to it that makes me feel warm and happy.

Self confessed 'concert queens': Cory Beaulieu (nearest to the camera) with her friend Deb Metcalf

Tim Tirelli

25 October 2016, SSE Hydro, Glasgow, UK

At home in Reggio Emilia, Italy, it is four o'clock in the morning. The alarm clock rings, I get up without too much trouble, I'm excited, I'm going to go to Malpensa to take the plane and fly to Glasgow to see 'my' Bad Company. They called it the UK Swan Song tour 2016. It's all a bit cryptic, will this really be the last tour? Is it a tribute to the Swan Song record label? No matter, I have never seen the band live, I cannot risk it, I have to go. At five o'clock Saura and I climb into the car –I'm really going to Scotland to see the Bad Company!

More than just a concert, I go to see Paul, Simon and Mick – heroes of my adolescence. I try to keep my expectations in check and keep myself calm, but I can feel the butterflies in the stomach, and I am still in Italy!

At 11.30 Scotia time, our plane lands. We make our way to our hotel, take a shower, a couple of hours of sleep and we're back on the road. We have a rendezvous at 6pm at the restaurant La Fiorentina with Billy and Alison Fletcher, two old friends of mine, both fans of rock music and football. I have been in touch with Billy since 1985, the year I started the *Oh Jimmy* fanzine. It's 12 years since I saw the mighty, as I call him, Billy Fletcher.

The Hydro, the place where the concert is held, it is not far away, a short walk and there we are. Everything is orderly, no stress. Saura buys one of the official merchandise t-shirts, I buy the tour programme. An usher takes us to our seats. We are in a great position, 10/12 rows from the stage and there's an audience of about 8,000 inside. Richie Sambora and Orianthi, his partner, are already on stage. The former guitarist of Bon Jovi appears like Sylvester Stallone in the movie *Rocky*. Undershirt vest, cap and that look of a southern Italian.

Fifteen minutes for the gear change and at 9.15 Bad Company walk on stage. It almost seems not true to me… here they are.

Simon Kirke beats four and while the group attacks 'Live for the Music' some smoke jets erupt from the front of the stage. For a moment I stagger, I am at the mercy of a very strong emotion that brings me almost to tears. I came here exactly for this very moment, to feel this flood of feelings. A sensation you only enjoy a few times in life, right when you fall madly in love with someone, or when your football team wins the Champions League after 45 years…

The group is in very good form, the songs that make up the repertoire of Bad Company are not complicated, but either way it takes a certain musical coherence and a high level of passion to make them work well. Paul is a consummate entertainer and sublime rock singer, Simon drives the band with skills and Mick plays the guitar better than I expected.

The audience surprises me. There are no youngsters, only men and women (many women) who were teenagers in the 70s, but they are hot and wild. They can barely stand on their seats.

Saura sets off for the stratosphere when Paul sits at the piano for 'Run With the Pack.' I see her dancing, wiggling, singing and shouting. I look at her: before we met she did not even know who Bad Company were. I get lost observing Mick Ralphs. For some reason I love him so much, perhaps the reason is that as a guitarist I guess I'm a lot like him. Goodness, how I love this man, I think to myself. Even as I finish the thought, Saura whispers in my ear 'I love Mick Ralphs!' I'm lucky to have her by my side.

After some classic Bad Company we get a new song, 'Troubleshooter'. Are they planning a new album, we wonder?

Then they return to the hits with 'Movin' On' and the crowd goes wild. Mick wears a Telecaster in C open tuning. Just moments before the solo I see that he struggles to pull out the slide guitar bottleneck from his shirt pocket.

When the evening comes to an end the right word is triumph.

Maybe I exaggerate in saying that this was the best concert of my life, but I can't help it. Billy, Alison and Saura agree. We bid goodnight to Billy and Alison, and we head to the heart of Glasgow, back to the hotel. I can not sleep now, I have to read the whole tour programme that I bought.

I wake up Wednesday morning in fine form, the awareness of having seen Bad Company fills me with energy. We have breakfast at Costa's, we enjoy the city centre, the town's cathedral and the university. Later we meet up with Billy, head to Ibrox Stadium and watch Rangers play St. Johnstone.

I saw Bad Company, I saw Rangers. I can sleep peaceful.

Gavin Owen

17 October 2016, Motorpoint Arena, Cardiff, UK

I remember mainly going for Richie Sambora as I'm a Bon Jovi fan, but I was familiar with the big Bad Company hits.

I wasn't familiar with support act Jasmine Rodgers before hand but I was pleasantly surprised by her set considering she was opening for two major rock acts. Playing an acoustic set she did a stirling job playing her folk inspired songs and the standout for me was her single 'Icicles'. Richie Sambora and Orianthi played a nice mix of songs from each other's back catalogue and covers including John Lennon's 'Imagine' and a great rendition of Sonny and Cher's 'I Got You Babe', but the best was Richie Sambora doing the title track from his 1991 solo album *Stranger In This Town*.

I thought I'd got my money's worth from that until Bad Company took to the stage and played a brilliant set consisting of the songs I was familiar with and some I wasn't familiar with. Paul Rodgers was in fine voice and sounded just as good as he did on the band's 1970s recordings.

Antonio Pellegrini

29 October 2016, O2 Arena, London, UK

I'm in London for the Bad Company concert: finally I have the chance to attend a show by one of my all-time favourite bands.

On the weekend between 28 and 30 October, the O2 Arena in London hosts the *Blues Fest 2016* and this year the names of the festival are really interesting: in addition to Bad Company, there are Jeff Beck, whom I've already seen in concert in Italy, Van Morrison, Richie Sambora, The Strypes and Mary J. Blige.

An uncomfortable low cost flight from Genoa to London takes me to my destination and, after a tour in the city, I'm ready for my night.

Steve Rodgers, Paul's son, opens the concert: a beautiful voice between soul and blues, that starts to warm the arena up. He plays some of his own songs, accompanying himself with the keyboard, acoustic guitar and electric guitar.

When Rodgers junior leaves the scene, it is the turn of a very well known name. It's Richie Sambora, Bon Jovi's historic guitarist, on stage tonight with Orianthi, also a great guitarist, and Richie's girlfriend, a sexy rocker. Both of them, besides playing their own instrument, are singing tonight, especially Richie. My eyes, however, are not so much for Bon Jovi's guitarist as for his woman, who can pull out an incredible sound out of her six-string guitar. The solos are remarkable, and there's no denying her wild rock charm. On the last track, Steven Van Zandt joins the band.

The evening warms up, emotions rise to the chest, until it's time for the night's headliners: Bad Company.

The survivors of the original Bad Company are three out of four... With Paul, there's still Mick Ralphs on guitar, whom I love, and Simon Kirke on drums. Boz Burrell is unfortunately no longer with us. There's Howard Leese on guitar and Todd Ronning on bass, both from Paul's solo band, now part of Bad Company.

The amps are turned on and the music starts right away, with 'Live for the Music', 'Gone, Gone, Gone' and 'Feel Like Makin' Love'. This crazy start would be enough to justify the trip. The set list is outstanding. In addition to the hits, it includes some lesser-known songs and even an unreleased one.

It's a really addictive show, because of the quality of the songs and the incredible sound performance of the great musicians on stage. The sound is tight and powerful, but at the same time it's never aggressive and is characterised by wonderful blues rock nuances.

The scenography is essential but suitable for the show, and it is mainly composed of lights and projections. During 'Shooting Star' and in other parts of the live show, some touching images of some great musicians no longer with us are projected: from Jimi Hendrix to Paul Kossoff of Free, passing through Freddie Mercury and Janis Joplin.

Mick Ralphs, forced to skip the whole American leg of the tour because of ill health, this evening walks nonchalantly around the stage and often turns towards Simon, as if to confirm their rhythmic understanding: he's magnificently low profile! Simon supports the pieces as always effectively, giving an energetic performance.

The most exciting of all is Paul. Despite being the last date of a two-week English tour, he is in good shape, and he still reaches remarkable peaks with his voice. It is a wonderful, mellow, and extremely bluesy voice, not surprisingly he has been nicknamed 'The Voice'. The limelight during the concert is all for him, and it's all about his charisma and stage presence.

The concert lasts about an hour and a half, but time is running fast and the show ends far too quickly. So my short vacation to London also

Photos by Antonio Pellegrini

came to an end and I travelled back to Italy, hoping to see Paul Rodgers and Bad Company in concert again soon. But this London concert will remain forever among my favourites.

Nic Greenaway

29 October 2016, O2 Arena, London, UK

I saw Bad Company twice. The first time was at Hammersmith Apollo and I think that only my mate Frank and I went up. We had reasonable seats and thoroughly enjoyed the gig, though we were a little disappointed that Mick Ralphs wasn't in the band at that time. They played most of the songs that we could've expected but the highlight was when Mick himself came on playing two or three numbers at the end. I can't remember what they all were but one was 'Can't Get Enough' which finished off the evening really, really well.

The next time I saw Bad Company was at the O2 in London in 2016. This time Howard Leese was on rhythm guitar with Mick on lead - where he should be! I went with a couple of friends who had never seen Free or Bad Company and they were both knocked out by the sheer professionalism of the band. They played all the old favourites and one new number, 'Trouble Shooter' which was a mid-tempo rocker with Paul on acoustic. The whole set was absolutely stunning.

This time, being in the Internet age, I streamed a couple of numbers via Facebook Live, which gained the band a few new fans from amongst my younger friends.

I was incredibly sad a week later to hear that Mick had had a stroke and we could never again see what, to me, is the classic Bad Company line-up. Most importantly, I hope he gets better and is able to enjoy life. He's certainly enriched mine (including a Mott the Hoople gig at the Royal Albert Hall many, many years ago).

Thanks to Mick for the Memories.

Alastair Smith

In 2016 Paul revisited his hometown of Middlesbrough, to record a song with his son, Steve, called 'This Place Called Home' in aid of a local hospice. His mention of the 'Steel River', the River Tees, demonstrated his love of his background in the industrial area where he grew up.

2017

Rob Nottingham

19 May 2017 Sheffield City Hall, Sheffield, UK

After seeing Bad Company at a meet and greet in 2010 and having regretted not having my photo taken with the great man and asking him certain questions, I thought my chance had gone in seeing him again. Then in 2017 I heard he was appearing in Sheffield again on the Free Spirit tour. My friend Rob Fletcher also heard he was touring but as we were unable to get any tickets we decided to catch the train to Sheffield and go and pay on the door if possible.

Having secured our tickets at the box office we watched the concert, and what a great concert it was. Wall to wall classic Free songs. After the gig I was adamant I was going to buy a souvenir T-shirt, CD or programme. Whilst standing in line waiting my turn, I saw a guitar and knew I had to have it. The sale of the guitar was to support Paul's animal sanctuary charity and I bought it for £500.

Going into a couple of pubs after the gig and the train home was a little terrifying because my friend kept telling people all about the guitar! But it was all good in the end and a great 60th birthday present for me that year.

Ken Johnson

19 May 2017, Sheffield City Hall, Sheffield, UK

My school 6th form mate Andy's mum and dad had a caravan at Hornsea on the Yorkshire coast, and we played Free's second album all that holiday in 1970/71. Two girls turned up and came to stay at the van. They were going to see Free at Bridlington and they wanted us to go with them. Andy and I had already been

Ken and Sue Johnson with Paul in Sheffield

Paul clearly enjoyed himself and the guitarist, Pete Bullick, had obviously worked hard to recreate the sound of Koss. He had a Les Paul of course, well he had to! The big, heavy sound from twin humbuckers and solid body, with perpetual sustain, in the hands of a master, is truly awesome art. Why play a hundred stuttering notes when you can make one note cry with emotion. And no one did that better than Kos, but the new boy came very close.

Some months later I went to Redditch for the unveiling of a statue in memory of local boy John Bonham, which had been organised by his sister Deborah. It is a very impressive statue that is a fitting memorial to Bonzo. I was standing next to this big bloke, as Deborah made a short speech. When I turned to look at him I recognised him immediately. He was the guitarist from the band, who had recreated Koss. What are the chances? I wasted no time in telling him how great I thought the gig was, how amazing was his guitar playing and how the band as a whole had really done justice to Free and particularly Koss. He was very gracious and thanked me for my comments.

Of course, the tour is recorded for posterity on a CD/DVD set, but believe me, you really had to be there.

Peter Hennessey

28 May 2017, Royal Albert Hall, London, UK

I'd been hooked on seeing Free live in the 70s. And I was lucky enough to chat to Paul Kossoff's father years after his son died. I remember meeting David Kossoff when he came to talk to the children in the school where I worked. We chatted about Paul over tea in the staff room. He talked very movingly about him.

Then on 28 May 2017 I went to the Royal Albert Hall to see Paul in the Free Spirit concert. It was brilliant; an unforgettable night. It made me happy that I had delayed a major operation so as not to miss the show!

I had the operation two days later and, just like the concert, it was a huge success. Needless to say, my recuperation was greatly assisted by listening to Free!

Julie Scott

28 May 2017, Royal Albert Hall, London, UK

Over the years I have seen Peace (with Paul Kossoff jamming on stage), The Firm, Bad Company, Paul Rodgers and Queen + Paul Rodgers. In May 2017 my daughter, Emily, purchased tickets online to see the Free Spirit tour and we travelled up by coach to the Royal Albert Hall, London. Meeting Lucy Piller for the first time in the bar before the show, and being photographed with other fans was a great start to the evening. Emily quipped that the audience were noticeably older! That said, when Paul Rodgers walked out onto the stage the noise was deafening. The first note of 'Little Bit Of Love' took me back nearly 50 years to my youth. The audience were loud, the atmosphere fantastic and the continuous repertoire of Free's music was awesome. The place absolutely rocked!

Julie Scott and the gang

Free have, and always will be, special to me. From the moment I first heard *Tons Of Sobs*, and with my memories of the shows and all of the music that I, and many other fans, have enjoyed, all I can say is a huge Thank You!

Kelsey Grammar

Actor, writer, producer, director Kelsey Grammar reveals how one Bad Company track has been so important to his family when talking about his life on the iconic BBC radio show Desert Island Discs.

This song is for my children and for my wife. When Faith was born, we asked them to put on a track and as Faith was taking her first breath the next song that came on was this song – Bad Company's 'Shooting Star'. Every one of our kids since has basically been born to this same song.

2018

Paula Terry

13 February 2018, Fort Lauderdale, Florida, USA

The third of my favourite memories is from 2018. After losing my father 11 months prior, we went to see Bad Company in Fort Lauderdale. I took my dad's death very hard - cried and thought of him everyday. That night at the concert Bad Company played 'Young Blood' by The Coasters. Bad Company's version was one of my dad's favourite songs. I started balling such happy tears!

Just hearing Bad Company songs makes me happy. Anyone that knows me knows they are my favourite band, even friends as far back as middle school and high school.

My husband and I just adopted three children. Two of them sing 'Can't Get Enough of Your Love' all the time and it just so happens to be my ringtone for my husband!

Thanks for all the memories Paul, Simon, Mick, and Boz.

Mike Truex

10 August 2018, Rouff Mortgage Music Center, Noblesville, Indiana, USA

I've been a fan since 'All Right Now' and had a front row seat and meet and greet on Paul's 2018 tour with Jeff Beck and Ann Wilson when they played Indianapolis. So when I walked up to Paul to meet him I was worried about what to say, but he stopped me and said 'Wait, you never said your name'. I thought, wow, I didn't but Paul wants to know who I am, didn't see that coming! Then I told him I'm Mike Truex' and I've been a fan since 'All Right Now' and I told him to get The Firm back together - Jimmy wants to tour and a Zeppelin reunion isn't happening! Paul said, 'that's not bad, I'll call Jimmy tomorrow!'

It was a fantastic experience meeting Paul. The Firm's music stills sounds great, 'Radioactive' 'You've Lost That Loving Feeling' cover were two standout songs.

Jimmy D Smith

His voice is like fine wine and has only gotten better over time. My first time hearing him live was on Bad Company's *Desolation Angels* tour and then with The Firm and here recently on tour with Jeff Beck.

Absolutely one of the greatest rock vocalists of our time.

Neal McKeown

17 August 2018, Municipal Auditorium, Nashville, Tennessee, USA

Back in August 2018 I paid for a meet and greet with Paul in Nashville, Tennessee. I had a lotta questions running through my head to ask him but I finally settled on one because I am a huge Lynyrd Skynyrd fan of the original band. And I know how much Free and Bad Company were big influences on the Skynyrd boys.

We were third in a line of over 30 people and I was really nervous and excited about getting to meet a member of rock 'n' roll royalty. When it was our turn to meet Paul we walked up and he turned around, said 'hello', shook our hands and asked me and my girlfriend our names.

Then I asked him: 'Was Bad Company's song 'Simple Man' a nod to Lynyrd Skynyrd's 'Simple Man?' And Paul said, 'No, Mick had already had that song written before we formed Bad Company.' And he went on to add that they, as in Bad Company, were huge fans of Lynyrd Skynyrd. Anyway, Paul just kept on talking and I was really fascinated that he probably thought that I asked a great question, and when it was time to get our photo taken with him he was still talking about Lynyrd Skynyrd. When we walked away Paul grasped my hand and said, 'It was really a pleasure talking to you'.

He could not have been nicer and was really sincere, meeting his fans. An event I will remember for the rest of my life.

Kathy Rankin

29 September 2018, Emerald Queen Events Center, Tacoma, Washington, USA

Recently, at the Emerald Queen in Tacoma, I was so fortunate to get to cover a story about the Paul Rodgers show for my local online publication. I actually got word I was allowed to take photos of that show just a week or so before the concert. So when that email came in and said I was approved, I did the happy dance! For days literally.

Having secured my legit photo pass I took photos for only the first three songs, but when Paul started to play the harmonica during 'Feel Like Makin' Love' I was mesmerised. It was hard to focus or concentrate on the actual photo, but somehow I got a freaking awesome shot of him with the harp. Lucky for me it was the third song and the last song that I was allowed to shoot.

Photos by Kathy Rankin

My heart was pounding the night of the show! I couldn't believe that I was getting to take these pictures, it meant more to me than anything! I am forever grateful that he shared a piece of his life with me that night. So you see, the photos are more than photos. They are the sweet memories of that song 'Feel Like Makin' Love' and the story that I shared with my boyfriend Tom back in 1977 when I was in senior high school. Sadly Tom passed from cancer.

That night my heart was pounding, I could hear it! I left that concert the happiest woman on this planet.

And Paul Rodgers hasn't aged a bit, I thought. He still has it. Aren't we lucky?

2019

Lyndy Lambert

22 February 2019, Hard Rock, Hollywood, Florida, USA

The Seminole Indians own Hard Rock Casinos and venues worldwide. Their flagship venue is located on their tribal lands in Hollywood, Florida. The first Hard Rock Hollywood, built in 2004, had a capacity of 5,500 and attracted many artists. Bad Company played there in August 2008, when they reunited for a single gig to record a live album and DVD aptly named *Hard Rock Live*. It was the first time Paul, Mick, and Simon had played live together since a brief reunion in 1999. I was there with my daughter. They did a wonderful tribute to Boz Burrell, who had tragically died in 2006. When they played Boz's song 'Gone, Gone, Gone', they had a montage of photos of Boz on the Jumbotron behind the stage. It was very touching and I have to admit I cried. I did not know that Boz had died until I did some online research on him shortly before the concert. I wore the necklace he had given me and showed it to some of the folks sitting nearby.

The next time I saw Bad Company at the Hard Rock was in February 2019, but it was at a temporary theatre the Seminoles were using while their grand Guitar Hotel was being built. My daughter came with me to that show, too, and we were 13 rows from the stage. Bad Company was smoking hot, as usual. Paul's voice is as strong now as it was in 1979 when I first met them. Sadly, Mick was not there because of his illness, but Howard Leese did a fine job filling in for him.

The hardest part about going to a Bad Company concert in South Florida is the general reluctance of the fans to get up and dance. It is challenging to sit still during a Bad Company concert, but my daughter and I 'behaved' until they played 'Rock 'n' Roll Fantasy', just before their two encores. Then the band ended with a lovely version of Jimi Hendrix's 'Little Wing.' Howard Leese was magnificent on the guitar solos, and Paul's honey voice was perfect for the vocals. It was a particularly moving experience for me because in 1979 Boz had introduced me to Mitch Mitchell, the drummer for Jimi Hendrix, and we became fast friends.

I am happy to report that my daughter is now a Bad Company fan and we hope to see them in concert again soon.

Paul Rodgers and Simon Kirke on stage at the Hard Rock, Hollywood, Florida. Photos by Lyndy Lambert

Simon Kirke

Well I do have a solo career going on: albeit a humble one. I love playing guitar and piano and telling stories and I plan to pursue it as long as I can. I don't make much money at it but I'm a musician and I love playing music. Simple as that.

I don't get tired of playing drums as long as I get a chance to supplement it with playing other instruments and singing, which happens when I do my solo shows. I've been playing drums now for 55 years and I still get a thrill when a track is soulful, with good lyrics and instrumentation.

I'm actually doing a second album with a band called LoneRider, a British band, and the singer is wonderful, as is the guitar player and bass player. There are several songs on the album that are real classics in my opinion.

Bob Mortimer

Comedian Bob Mortimer chooses 'On My Way' by Free on the BBC's Desert Island Discs and recalls a shared passion for the band with the other half of his double act Jim Moir, AKA Vic Reeves.

I had elder brothers and they all had something that they really loved. One of them was a Mod, one was a rocker and he had his heroes and one of them liked Jimi Hendrix, but I didn't have anyone.

And then, when I was about 13, I went to see this band called Free, who I'd never heard, at Middlesbrough Town Hall, and I just fell in love with them and found my thing. I'd found my heroes, you know? I was stood at the front with my chin on the stage – I was only young – and there was Andy Fraser the bass player right next to me. And I adore their music and always have done. It's interesting because Jim's the same. Jim's favourite band ever was Free and it's funny when we look back because he came from a town near me, Darlington, and there was a lot of events back in our youth that we were both actually at. 'I was at that Free gig. I was at Redcar when they were on.' So we never met, but we were at the same venues.

Colin Bradley and his wife with Paul

Colin Bradley

20 August 2019, Artpark, Lewiston, New York, USA

I see Paul several times a year, usually when he is touring through Ontario, and of course we keep in touch with a phone call every now and then. I last saw him perform in August 2019 with Bad Company in Lewiston, which is just a ten minute drive across the border from where I live in Niagara on the Lake. His son Steve opened the show with just an acoustic guitar and blew the audience away. The subsequent Bad Company performance was possibly the best live show by the band that I have ever seen, and I have seen many over the years. *Colin Bradley was a member of the 1960s group, The Road Runners, with Paul Rodgers*

2020

Simon Kirke

People have named their boats after us, a tag team wrestling duo, jet skis... I was asked to be a witness at a wedding as the couple walked down the aisle to 'Feel Like Makin' Love'! And the only time Bad Company ever missed a gig in our career was when the airport we were flying into, somewhere in Connecticut, was fogged in.

I don't honestly think there was ever a really bad Bad Company gig. In the early days we might've been a little the worse for wear occasionally due to substances. But we always put on a good show. There are some great recordings from the 1976 tour of the US and also with the last line-up recently, which goes to show that age really is just a number with us.

Lucy Piller

Memorabilia? Over the years I just kept everything and still have most of it in boxes, but once I started *ARN Allrightnow.com* in the 90s, then it got more serious. I would buy many items from music shows or rare items and tracks and found it very interesting to find all of Paul's videos from around the world, mostly in NTSE, which today I can't even play without the right video player.

My home to me is the shrine of Paul and his music and my office only has Paul and his bands in it. I have spoken to so many fans from around the world from this one office, with local artists performing in the rocking chair. On top of that I had Bad Company without Paul visit one summer after a show to perform with various local artists of Atlanta, and also had Simon Kirke perform.

Today my husband Robert totally supports me, it was actually his idea to start a website before websites were known. No one had computers back then, so most things were done by mail, then in the late 80s I started ARN, this opened up a new world to me to find fans hidden in every part of the world. My daughter is certainly a fan and has been going to his shows since she was a ten-year-old. She is now 30.

Regarding my friends, All the ARN members are my friends, they come first in my life after my family, they have been so supportive over the years. Many of us meet up before shows, after shows and sometimes they even get a surprise visitor – yes, Paul Rodgers turned up one day at the hotel we were staying at. It was the greatest treat fans could ever have. He stayed with us, listened to fans' stories and just was one of us for the evening. How precious that was.

I counted how many times I saw Free, which is 33, but I have no idea how many times I have seen Paul over the years. I sometimes attended a full tour in the early days of Paul Rodgers solo shows so let's just say I've seen him quite a lot!

When I look around my office and see the different things I picked up over the years, I can't pick something out as any more special than the next thing I might come across. Everything has its own story. But I do have a ring Paul gave me a few years back, which I love to wear as it always makes me feel safe, and of course the amazing Bad Company signed guitar he gave to me as a gift.

My main website is www.allrightnow.com. When Myspace came out I made many sites covering Paul's bands, then I introduced Facebook groups, like Official Paul Rodgers Fans, Bad Company Official Fan Club, Free Fans (ARN) and also have one for Paul's son and daughter plus many more.

Living in the USA now, I have had the opportunity to see Paul many times as he is in Canada, but from here I have travelled from Atlanta to Europe and Aruba to see him play and numerous times to the West Coast.

I totally respect Paul's privacy so do not bother him. He always takes the time to hang out with me backstage before and after most shows. To me he is like a brother, he has always been in my life, and I always look forward to having a chat with him over music, or the world around us or the places he is playing in.

Lucy Piller is the Official Fan Club president

Jon Kirkman

Seeing Paul Rodgers these days – he's singing as well if not better than he did in the 70s. Not a lot of people from that era can do that. He's got more control over his voice now and it's still an amazing instrument. A very special singer. When I saw him with Queen, that was, again, an incredible gig. Paul just sang those songs so well. As a band, if you've got Paul Rodgers singing for you, it's one area you don't have to worry about.

Lucy Piller

What makes Paul Rodgers' music special are his lyrics, his divine melodies, and the soul in his voice. As many have said, he can sing the names out of the telephone book and it would sound amazing, but then who has a telephone book these days!

When Paul sings the soul reaches us in a way no other singer can do. His body projects his music, his hands tell the story, he uses his mic as his partner with every performance. He is so cool on stage, male fans want to be just like him.

Claire Pope

'All Right Now' is my absolute favourite song, always up to dance to that one. I'll also have it played at my funeral! Not yet though!

Luke Morley

Free and Bad Company were massively influential in what we've done in Thunder. Paul Rodgers is Danny's [Bowes] favourite singer along with maybe Stevie Wonder. Any band, any singers around my age – they all cite Free as their influence. If you listen to their records now, they still sound fantastic. It's the antithesis of 80s music to me. Free sounds about as organic as it gets.

Photo by Bradley Gregory

The music of all four members of Free has stayed with me the whole of my life and I have converted many along the way. The best memory is of my son at an early age – he's now 29 and a very accomplished guitarist – would say on a drive, "Dad, put that highway music on' and clench his fist in the air. He meant Free and Bad Company and as I loaded up the six stacker I thought, that's my boy!

Other Free and later associated band gigs I attended included Bad Company in 1974 on their first tour then at the Rainbow Theatre in 1975 with Jimmy Page joining in, Andy Fraser Band about 1976 at The Marquee and Rainbow Theatre in 1977. Alexis Korner was there and I chatted to him in the bar.

I saw Koss with John Martyn in about 1974, Back Street Crawler at the New Victoria in November 1976 and also saw Stray Dog many times, as well as Sharks – although Andy had already left.

I have also seen Paul Rodgers in Melbourne three times – I wish he'd come more often!

Brian O'Neill

30 August 1970, Isle of Wight Festival, UK

We were 16, very innocent lads from Glamorgan, and managed to find a great place to camp near the arena itself. The empty space was a bit puzzling till I looked up from tent pitching to see we were right by the Hell's Angels' marquee!

Free were on during the day on Sunday afternoon. We already knew their stuff courtesy of those Island samplers, so expectation was high. They were incredible and fired the crowd up, with 'All Right Now' and 'Mr Big' barnstormers.

Schoolmates (from left) Ceri Roderick, Brian O'Neill and Mark Kempson unintentionally rock a Pink Floyd look at the time of the 1970 Isle of Wight Festival

It seems strange now, but they always seemed to be a people's band, as much as Hawkwind or the Pink Fairies, with a huge love for Koss even before he died. I guess his vulnerability communicated even at this level.

Even now I can feel the sheer propulsion of the rhythm section, with Koss fleshing the sound and Paul Rodgers the classic frontman. Such a unit; everything where it should be.

I slept 24 hours when we got back. Tired but happy, as they say!

David Clayton
20 October 1997, Ronnie Scott's, Soho, London, UK

Free Appreciation Society /© John Peck

Having seen Paul on two fair sized British tours, a show in France and also one of the huge Skynyrd supports in America it was really nice to see the man move back, albeit briefly, into a smaller and much more intimate venue. Here's what I wrote at the time:

Ronnie Scott's now in its 39th year seats a grand total of 250 people and all six of the 'Paul Rodgers Plays The Blues' shows were, unsurprisingly, sold out. Perhaps another 50 get in unreserved and stand around the cramped bar or at the back of the room. The mix of people is interesting and there are obviously a fair few of the Jazz club members in attendance. Sitting among them are the usual range of Paul's own fans, most astonished to be sitting in a club where anyone from the first row of tables can swing an arm and hit the legs of at least one band member!

The stage itself is small but has size enough to hold the band. Both Jaz and Geoff are as far over as they can be to afford Paul some space but I do notice over the week that Jaz occasionally eyes Paul when he lifts the mic stand in case he needs to shift sharply to avoid any possible flesh to metal contact!

Monday night I find myself sitting right in front of Jaz. The first set begins at 11pm. The band walk on to a rather formal introduction with large smiles and Paul sets them off with his 'mojo' yell signalling the start of 'Louisiana Blues'. He's looking good tonight in black cowboy boots, faded blue jeans and tight white V neck T-shirt.

The sound balance is good but the band seems a little restrained and are obviously trying to keep the volume down a little. Paul is in his element and is in very good voice indeed, the vocals are clear as a bell. I do believe there actually is a little bit of nerves going on up there. They finish and are greeted with warm applause. Paul is broadly grinning now and he explains they are just a little jet lagged but intend getting down to business with some more blues tunes. He quickly introduces 'I'm Ready' and they tear into it. The press release for these shows did tell of a 'mainly acoustic set' but it seems this idea has been abandoned. Can't say I'm disappointed actually. This is looking pretty good.

'Hoochie Coochie Man' follows as Paul leans heavily on the *Muddy Water Blues* album for the bulk of this first set. Good version and I don't think I've heard them do this before. Paul in particular seems to be enjoying this song and he makes use of the silent gaps in the riff with various ad-libs and a few finger snaps. I'm surprised when I suddenly start to wonder whether Paul still plays 'harp' as he did in the early days of Free - that could have been pretty cool in there, Paul!

Both audience and band are warming up a bit now and as Paul picks up the red strat. It's a pretty sure guess that they're about to do 'Muddy Water Blues'.

The set seems to fly past and a fine 'Standing Around Crying' leads into a pretty intense 'Rollin' Stone' where Paul hangs onto the mic stand and pumps it back and forth to the rhythm. Very fine vocal performances here and great guitar from Geoff, with lots of interplay between him and Paul.

'Shadow Of The Sun' is a surprise inclusion as far as I'm concerned but in fact within this club environment it sounds absolutely great. It's amazing how much difference this setting makes and it's quite an eye opener when I have to say this was actually one of the highlights of the opening night!

'Crosscut Saw' makes a live appearance for the first time. It sounds good and Paul mentions at its close that it's 'The dirtiest song I know!' They round off set one with another Albert King tune and Geoff straps on the Les Paul for a blast through 'The Hunter'. Good solid first set and before they leave the stage certain sections of the audience seem rather surprised when Paul says, 'We'll be back in around an hour, stick around.' The arrangement at Ronnie Scott's works thus. John Etheridge plays for an hour, Paul plays for an hour, then John Etheridge plays again and Paul finishes off the evening with a second set that starts at around 1am!

Part two opens with a rather splendid and very gentle 'Good Morning Little School Girl'. Paul likes this a lot and really does extend the end with some rather naughty ad-libs.

I don't recognise the opening to the next number but I'm pretty much gobsmacked when Paul steps up to the mic and begins, 'Well, they call it Stormy Monday...' This is a really nice surprise and that line is greeted with much applause and whistling. I wonder how long it is since Paul did this song on-stage. I know he vaguely remembers this might have been the song that he and Koss first jammed with on that fateful night when the Black Cat Bones guitarist went to check out the singer with Brown Sugar at The Fickle Pickle. That night marked the very beginning of Free. His eyes are closed and the performance is exquisite. This is an area of blues where Paul's voice has absolutely no equal, and he makes it look so damn easy, effortless. I try to freeze the moment in my mind so I can replay it to my heart's content later. This was quite outstanding and I had serious goose-bumps.

The set finishes with 'Fire And Water', which includes Jim's drum solo. At the end the band stand and soak up the adulation, which is well deserved. 'Are we going off?' asks Whitehorn, pointing to the dressing room door. 'Nah' says Paul. He explains that it's been a long day and it's too much effort to go off and come back again, so Jim begins the intro to 'All Right Now' and the audience go pretty much nuts! As the song weaves its way past the guitar solo I watch the crowd engage singing voices. It's quite amazing, even the old jazz guys are singing along!

I speak to Paul briefly after the set and he asks what it was like being in the audience. 'We were all a bit nervous about it actually - playing at lower volume. I don't think we're used to it, you know - being subtle. Was it alright?' Yes Paul, it certainly was...

Karen Alvarez

In 1979, at almost ten-years-old, little did I know that my own 'Rock 'n' Roll Fantasy' was just beginning. I remember hearing the opening of that song by Mick Ralphs in Bad Company, and then came 'The Voice!' The stop-me-in-my-tracks vocals of Paul Rodgers. I couldn't get enough of it: 'Reaching for the sky, churning up the ground'! The song 'Bad Company' itself is like a rolling thunderstorm! Simon Kirke's drumming on 'Moving On' definitely kept me moving and bouncing around. Boz Burrell's bass on 'Ready for Love' and 'Burning Sky', created such a deep groove.

Years later, I saw Paul with Queen and was blown away. How the roof did not come off the arena, I do not know. Months after that, I saw Paul solo and when he came away from the piano after playing 'Silver Blue & Gold', I held up my hands clapping and he came over, took both of my hands in his and gave them a squeeze. I don't remember much after that... except for that I was on Cloud 9!

Karen Alvarez and her son Daniel meet the band backstage, on 28 May 2016, in Tampa, Florida

I met Simon the following year and was in awe of the fact that he'd helped to create all those great tracks. And he was sitting right next to me! He was incredibly nice and very down-to-earth. I took my son with me, who was six at the time and taking drum lessons. Daniel was left speechless meeting Simon and was suddenly shy and unable to play!

Then I met Paul, later that same year. I was incredibly nervous, but he could not have been any nicer, seeing me in all my excitement. I could not believe this was the man - 'The Voice' - and again, he was standing right next to me!

Years later, I was lucky enough to see a show with Paul, Simon and Mick Ralphs together on stage and was blown away with how they fed off each other and played so well. What a thrill that was! Meeting them after the showing was fantastic. Everyone was in good spirits and Mick was quite jovial, fun to chat with. Meeting him, and thanking all three of them for the music, really did complete my own personal 'Rock 'n' Roll Fantasy'.

The Contributors

The publishers of *Rock 'n' Roll Fantasy* wish to point out that this book is in no way meant to be a comprehensive account of the careers of the band members included. The content reflects the contributions from fans, musicians and associates whose memories might not always be 100% accurate when recalling events and dates.

There may also be occasional contradictions and the publishers have tended to take the view that we should amend the stories sent to us as little as possible, to enable the 'voice' of the contributor to be as authentic as possible. That said, in some cases, it has been necessary to shorten or alter some accounts and we hope that contributors will understand and be sympathetic to any changes made to their original text.

We thank all the contributors that contacted us in such overwhelming numbers to tell their stories and would like to record special thanks to the following who were so extraordinarily helpful in the making of this book:

Klemen Breznikar from psychedelicbabymag.com, for various Andy Fraser quotes. Gibson.com, *Mojo* magazine, Greg Brodsky at Best Classic Bands.com, Ground Guitar.com, SongFacts.com, Jimi Hendrix: *Made in England* by Brian Southall and *The Guinness Book of British Hit Singles & Albums*, Sian Llewellyn from Classic Rock, Lyndy Lambert, whose contribution grew from a paragraph or two and a couple of photos to the photo spreads we managed to secure at the eleventh hour.

Richard Digby Smith for allowing us to use the fascinating passages from his book *One Two Three Four*.

Ray Johnson, who drove through pelting rain in the Lake District to find a signal on his phone to talk through his contribution.

Mike Hobbs, who has written (or contributed to) 30 non-fiction books, several on music. His novel, "The Chevalier", about a C18 French transvestite spy, is published by Canelo (all online platforms).

Po Powell, whose forthcoming book *Through The Prism*, published by Thames & Hudson is sure to include more stories about his work with and for Paul Rodgers.

Derek Carter for his contribution and apologies for not having room to mention the excellent bands, Bulldozer and Panache, he played in, apart from here.

Malcolm Colton for the kind use of his Isle of Wight 1969 photos.

David Clayton from the Free Appreciation Society, Dave Jones from The Cavern, Liverpool, Dave Evely and all at Sound Performance, Malcolm Wyatt: writewyattuk.com, Ian Cossar for all the album and singles artwork photography: iantcossarphotographer.wordpress.com

Special thanks also to Lucy Piller who downloaded all her knowledge, photos and memorabilia for us on a kind of *Rock 'n' Roll Fantasy* conveyor belt, Chris Charlesworth for his *Melody Maker* reviews, Patrick Prince and John Curley from *Goldmine* Magazine, Rhino Records, Martin Skala for his photos and his website www.QueenConcerts.com.

And a very special thanks to David Spero for helping make this book happen.